PROGRAM EVALUATION

Methods and Case Studies

Second Edition

PROGRAM EVALUATION

Methods and Case Studies

EMIL J. POSAVAC, *Loyola University of Chicago*

RAYMOND G. CAREY, *Parkside Associates, Inc.*

Prentice-Hall, Inc., Englewood Cliffs, New Jersey 07632

Library of Congress Cataloging in Publication Data

POSAVAC, EMIL J.
  Program evaluation.

  Bibliography: p.
  Includes index.
  1. Evaluation research (Social action programs)—United
States. I. Carey, Raymond G. II. Title.
H62.5.U5P62 1985   361.6′1′072   84-3296
ISBN 0-13-729484-0

Editorial/production supervision and
  interior design: Sylvia Moore
Cover design: Wanda Lubelska
Manufacturing buyer: Ron Chapman

Printed in the United States of America
10   9   8   7   6   5   4   3   2   1

ISBN 0-13-729484-0   01

Prentice-Hall International, Inc., *London*
Prentice-Hall of Australia Pty. Limited, *Sydney*
Editora Prentice-Hall do Brasil, Ltda., *Rio de Janeiro*
Prentice-Hall Canada Inc., *Toronto*
Prentice-Hall of India Private Limited, *New Delhi*
Prentice-Hall of Japan, Inc., *Tokyo*
Prentice-Hall of Southeast Asia Pte. Ltd., *Singapore*
Whitehall Books Limited, *Wellington, New Zealand*

To
Wendy and Steve
Rita, Mike, and Mark

Contents

Acknowledgments

The following organizations and journals are thanked for permission to reprint or adapt material for this text: Institute for Program Evaluation, Inc., Roanoke, Virginia; *Hospital and Community Psychiatry; The American Journal of Public Health; British Journal of Addiction; Evaluation; Behavior Research and Therapy; Journal of Applied Behavior Analysis; Evaluation Quarterly;* Illinois Health Care Research Symposium; American Psychological Association; and Insurance Institute for Highway Safety.

A number of secretaries and assistants have helped us in the preparation of the manuscript. At various times the following people have given much-appreciated help: Carolyn Foraker, Karen Gianfortune, Bernadette Jaroch-Hagerman, and Susan Borkowski Lueger.

The authors are grateful to their respective institutions for encouragement during the writing of this text. The first author's contribution to the first edition was greatly facilitated by a sabbatical leave awarded by Loyola University of Chicago. The second author acknowledges with thanks the explicit support received from Lutheran General Hospital.

The authors also wish to express their appreciation for the helpful comments of the following reviewers: Amado M. Padilla, University of California at Los Angeles; Alan Siman, School of Social Work, San Diego State University; Ross F. Conner, University of California at Irvine; Brian T. Yates, American University; Myron Mast, School of Public Service, Grand Valley State Colleges; Clara Mayo, Boston University; Richard M. Wolf, Teachers College of Columbia University; Robert J. Calsyn, University of Missouri at St. Louis; Francis G. Caro, Institute for Social Welfare

Research of the Community Service Society of New York; and Fred B. Bryant, Loyola University of Chicago.

The first author thanks his wife, Wendy Cook Posavac, for reading and commenting on the manuscript and for providing unfailing encouragement through all stages of this text's preparation. He also thanks his son, Steve, for accepting his father's apparent obsession, in spite of being somewhat surprised by how long it takes to write or revise a book. The second author acknowledges with gratitude the contributions to his personal and professional development made by his parents, Elizabeth Carey and the late Raymond G. Carey.

part I

AN OVERVIEW OF PROGRAM EVALUATION

What do marriage counseling, blood pressure screening, school hot lunch programs, education at Harvard, job training at Leavenworth Prison, and day care for children of working mothers all have in common?

All these activities are human services designed and administered to help people. Of a myriad of services and products available in modern industrial societies, the greater proportion of workers and professionals are involved in meeting human needs for health care, education, training, counseling, emotional support, rehabilitation, and so on. The field of human services includes programs and facilities to help people lead more satisfying, healthier, safer, and more productive lives. Many of these needs have traditionally been met through the extended family or through voluntary charity; however, such needs increasingly are being met through organized, publicly funded efforts. These efforts are often called programs. In the past thirty years, governmental agencies have become more involved in providing or supporting human service programs and organizations. For example, Medicare payments account for between 40 and 45 percent of the revenues of many hospitals (Millenson, 1983).

The evaluation methods presented in this book are equally applicable to the activities of profit-making organizations. Although scientific and engineering problems are important in industrial settings, success in business is often a question of success in managing human resources. Attempts to improve productivity, employee morale, or product quality all depend on good planning techniques, accurate feedback on the impact of the plan adopted, and the desire to utilize that feedback. Furthermore, research on the need for and the effectiveness of a new product requires skills similar to those used by evaluators. In addition, the success of an advertising campaign can be evaluated using procedures very similar to those described in this text. Although this text and the examples it uses reflect the fact that most well-known program evaluations have been in publicly funded organizations, the principles of program evaluation have wide applicability.

The first four chapters of this book provide an orientation to the field and an overview of the methods and goals of program evaluation. In Chapter 1 we describe organizations and the types of programs and services offered. The people responsible for these organizations have many questions about how to plan the programs and judge their effectiveness. The contributions of program evaluation to the various stages of program development and implementation are illustrated.

An overview of the approach evaluators take in preparing to conduct program evaluations is provided in Chapter 2. Often program evaluations succeed or fail due to decisions made during the initial contacts with program managers or sponsors. The principles described apply to all the types of evaluations discussed and illustrated in later chapters.

Because program evaluation is essentially a science of information and its utilization, evaluators must be prepared to assess the quality of the information forming the basis of their work. In Chapter 3 the reader is shown the major ways of gathering information on service programs and how to judge the quality of information obtained. This presentation reflects the need for multiple sources of information in evaluation work; various sources have different strengths and weaknesses. The chapter should expand the reader's appreciation of measurement principles in applied settings.

When research is conducted in organizations serving people's educational, health, employment, emotional, and other needs, special care is exercised to protect the interests of the students, patients, employees, and clients of these organizations. Chapter 4 deals with such ethical issues as well as with the conflicts of interest that can arise when data are collected in organizational settings.

How This Book is Organized

The chapters of this book are arranged in a systematic fashion that reflects the steps followed in conducting a program evaluation. The flow chart that follows provides a preview of what is to come. The reader can keep track of how each chapter fits into the organization of the text and

The organization of this book.

can identify the major aspects of the program evaluator's responsibilities by referring to this figure now and as the course progresses.

We hope this text imparts some of the excitement of participating in the growing, developing field of program evaluation. The field is not fully defined; its techniques are varied; and conducting a program evaluation is challenging. But we believe it will have a positive influence on our society.

1

Program Evaluation and Organizations

Program evaluation is a new and exciting applied social science; people active in the field hold high expectations for its usefulness. Society is in the process of recognizing both the importance of human resources and the importance of providing human services in an efficient manner. To meet these needs, program evaluation attempts to provide information about human services in the same way accountants and auditors provide information about financial resources. The mission of this new social science (called program evaluation, or simply evaluation) is to assist in improving the quality of human services. More specifically, program evaluation is a collection of methods, skills, and sensitivities necessary to determine whether a human service is needed and likely to be used, whether it is sufficiently intense to meet the need identified, whether the service is offered as planned, and whether the human service actually does help people in need. Through these activities evaluators seek ways to improve programs, utilizing concepts from psychology, sociology, administrative and policy sciences, economics, and education. Before discussing specific applications of program evaluation methods, we will describe the field as a whole and illustrate how evaluation and evaluators fit into organizations.

WHY PROGRAM EVALUATION
DEVELOPED

Quality of Service Not Assumed

In recent years the rejection of a particular assumption has made the efforts of many people who teach, counsel, provide medical care, or work with community groups more challenging—but possibly more productive. No longer is it assumed that well-meaning individuals or groups who institute a new health, education, training, rehabilitation, or other service actually help people. Today innovative programs as well as expansions of standard services can seldom be funded without some means of demonstrating that the costs of the service are justified by the improved state of the clientele. Although Congress initiated the requirement that services supported by federal grants be evaluated (see, for example, Neigher et al., 1982), the source of a program's funding has little effect on whether the program must be evaluated: It must.

The increasing use of social science methods to improve the effectiveness of human service programs and institutions made evaluation a "growth industry" during the 1970s (Guttentag, 1976). There were several reasons for this growth. Well-meaning, expensive, and ambitious attempts to overcome the effects of disadvantaged backgrounds during the middle and late 1960s were by and large ineffective; at least the impact of these efforts did not measure up to the optimistic expectations held by many program developers, government officials, as well as the general public. During the 1970s considerable caution was expressed about beginning national programs whose effectiveness had not already been demonstrated. Boruch, Cordray, Pion, and Leviton (1983) show, however, that such warnings were often not heeded.

Besides the need to show that proposed programs will be effective, there are persistent needs to demonstrate that existing programs are worth having and are managed efficiently. Frequently government programs are not explicitly terminated. Instead, new approaches to problems are implemented alongside of old programs. Some have suggested that programs be authorized for a specific length of time—five years, for example. After the specified period of time expires, the program goes out of existence unless its success has been documented and it has been reauthorized (Chelimsky, 1978). Although federal legislation has not been passed requiring this degree of evaluation of federal programs, this idea illustrates a rigorous use of program evaluation methods to guide legislation.

Difficulty in Defining
and Measuring Results

Another reason why the demand for the evaluation of people-oriented services grew is that it is difficult to describe the intended outcomes of human organizations services as compared to those of product-oriented organizations. Whenever the intended outcome is hard to define, assessments of success are very complicated. Industrial firms make things that can be seen, weighed, and counted. Department stores, supermarkets, and bakeries sell merchandise. To evaluate the success of such organizations is easy—at least in theory. To judge success, it is necessary to determine whether the products were in fact made and sold, and whether the amount collected for the products exceeded the cost of making and selling them. In practice, these questions are complex, due to the nature of large businesses; however, the approach to judging the ultimate success of such an organization is easy to define and widely accepted.

The use of human resources is just as important as the use of financial resources; however, society has had a harder time developing appropriate criteria of success. In some human services the nature of the "products" is as difficult to describe as are the methods of assessing their quality. What are the goals of a remedial education program? How do we know that a child has obtained what a program was designed to offer? When is an injured person rehabilitated? What level of rehabilitation should be hoped for? If the state provides hot lunches to a school, but the children throw out the vegetables, is the program a failure? Should we change the menu or teach nutrition to the parents? If, after marriage counseling, a couple gets a divorce, was the counseling inadequate?

Regulation of Human Services

If human services were available only on a fee-for-service basis, evaluating them might be left to free-market forces. The services that were purchased would, by definition, be successful; unwanted services would fail because there would be few, if any, buyers. The free-market approach has not been permitted to govern the field of human services. There are two major reasons why this is so. First, it has been assumed that the public cannot easily differentiate between poor and good human service providers. How many patients, for example, can really tell when a physician is competent? For this reason, physicians and many other service providers are required to obtain a state license before providing services to people. Traditionally, qualifications for offering services were based on training; however, a trend is developing that will require a demonstration of skill before licensing.

A second reason why free-market forces do not control human services is that the recipient usually pays for the service indirectly. Private insurance companies, large charitable organizations, local governments, and, increasingly, the federal and state governments cover the costs of many human services. Once a service program is covered, the intended recipients have little to say about how it is administered or what is provided. However, it is important that insurance and public funds be used wisely and productively. The need to demonstrate the effectiveness of human services is critical.

HOW PROGRAM EVALUATION
IS USED IN ORGANIZATIONS

Types of Organizations
Requiring Evaluations

The preceding paragraphs have been very general, and the reader may have had some difficulty knowing just what sort of programs are being discussed. The following is a brief discussion of the types of human services that can and ought to be evaluated.

Health care. Hospitals, clinics, extended care facilities, nursing homes, mental health centers, and similar organizations sponsor many services for their patients and clients. Such facilities expend much money on services whose effectiveness has never been fully documented. Educational services for patients, some forms of psychotherapy, certain novel medical treatments, recreational programs, and innovative ways of treating medical/behavioral problems are among the types of programs that should be evaluated in some fashion. Common sense and good management practices concur that the effectiveness of such programs should be documented in order to justify the continued expenditure of funds. Peer review and examination of records (such as hospital charts) are among the methods of program evaluation specifically developed within the health care field, although other methods also apply.

Criminal justice. Police departments, court systems, and prisons all sponsor programs to encourage respect for law enforcement, to develop citizen–law enforcement officer rapport, and to intervene in the lives of potential and convicted criminals. They also run many other programs to achieve varied goals. According to the Department of Justice, the federal government alone sponsors programs costing hundreds of millions of dollars to reduce juvenile delinquency. The effectiveness of these and other criminal justice programs is often questioned. Carefully done evaluations can aid both in the selection of new programs and in the improvement of existing programs.

Educational. Schools and colleges should evaluate the effectiveness of their teaching staffs as well as specific programs (such as enrichment and remedial programs). The efectiveness of new curricula should be assessed before their introduction. Evaluation of such a wide variety of educational programs requires many different approaches.

Industry and business. Training programs are widely used in all types of business. The effectiveness of such training programs should be evaluated periodically. Newly designed training programs are especially in need of evaluation. A new company-sponsored safety training program, for example, would be an ideal program to evaluate using cost-benefit techniques, because both the cost of the program and the cost of accidents can be calculated.

Public administration. Local communities support a variety of service programs. Preventive medicine (for example, blood pressure checks), park district programs, and fire safety inspections are among the varied service programs that are sponsored by local communities. These programs need evaluation. Are they reaching the populations for whom they were planned? Are the recommendations of safety inspectors followed? Are people in need of medical care detected?

Various Kinds of Programs

Some human service programs are developed to help individuals with acute but temporary needs; others seek to correct or alleviate longstanding problems; yet others help to prevent future problems or to develop the potential of students, workers, and managers.

Acute needs include the need for health care for injuries and for illnesses, the need for emotional and financial support after accidents or criminal attack, and the need for housing after a home or apartment fire. Such needs are pressing and must be met without delay if lives are to be saved or if worse emotional harm is to be averted. We are all aware of hospital care and emergency rooms, which alleviate physical needs. Acute needs of an emotional nature are sometimes met through community mental health crisis services. Some police departments try to help victims of crimes handle their emotional reactions. The help these programs offer is short term and must be quickly mobilized for maximum effectiveness.

Alcoholism counseling, drug abuse treatment programs, psychotherapy, physical rehabilitation, and training services in correctional facilities seek to help people with longstanding problems. There is a very high failure rate within such programs. Often neither the cause nor the actual nature of the problem is easy to define. Thus, the programs are difficult to design, hard to deliver, and confusing to evaluate. Evaluation of these services has traditionally been minimal. However, because the amount of money and human resources devoted to mental health and criminal justice programs is staggering, evaluation work in these fields is being encouraged, if not required by funding bodies.

Some human services are of a preventive nature. For example, law enforcement agencies suggest ways to make a home or a store less inviting to criminals; health education programs provide nutritional information to enable people to avoid certain health problems; and health screening programs detect illness or weakness that, if unchecked, could lead to serious disorders or even early death.

Educational programs constitute a major part of the human services industry. The products and goals of these programs are difficult to describe fully. Americans sponsor education at a variety of levels and for a variety of purposes from kindergarten through postgraduate work—and in a variety of settings from formal classrooms, to IBM management seminars, to the U.S. Army. People participate in educational programs to gain accreditation or become licensed to practice various occupations or professions, to learn specific skills, for enjoyment, for self-help, to enhance their social standing, and for intellectual and psychological growth. Accounting for the funds spent on education must take into consideration the specific purposes of the program being studied.

Programs developed to reduce the effects of economic disadvantages make up another large area of human services. Welfare, job-training programs, Medicaid, Medicare, and Social Security are large-scale programs; their major function is to help people maintain life despite limited financial resources.

An issue that affects all the programs mentioned above is the growing technological revolution made possible by microelectronics. Wonders are promised by vendors of computers, new diagnostic equipment, communication systems, and so on. However, organizations considering the purchase of such equipment must first determine its value for their work. More than a few desk-top computers have remained unused. Furthermore, some technologically advanced systems have not performed well. Second, such equipment causes changes in work environments that may adversely influence employee morale. Third, organizations are becoming increasingly aware that choices must be made among available technologies, since few organizations can afford everything offered. Evaluators can help supply the information needed to make these choices.

Programs are delivered by a variety of agencies with very different characteristics. Human services can be administered as regional or national projects involving millions or even billions of dollars. At the other extreme, a program can be directed to a small group of people in a given institution over a very short time period.

We have purposely concentrated our discussions throughout this text on evaluations of the smaller programs likely to be encountered by evaluators working for school districts, hospitals, personnel departments, social service agencies, city or state governments, and so on. Although some national programs are described, the focus on smaller programs is useful in an introductory text because most readers are more familiar with local government or organization-level programs than they are with national programs. Johnston (1983) suggests that organization-level, in-house evaluators will carry the major responsibilities for program evaluation during the coming years, while the number of major, national evaluation projects will decrease. We do not intend to imply that the methods used to evaluate national projects are totally different from the methods used by the evaluator in a particular agency. However, it is likely that the complexity of the statistical analyses increases as the scale of the evaluation increases; the more participants providing data, the more complex the analysis can be. Although complex analytical tools are useful, the use of simpler techniques is sufficient for most evaluators and may produce greater utilization by administrators who find statistics to be an incomprehensible—if not intimidating—topic.

Reasons to Evaluate Programs

There are many reasons for conducting program evaluations. Among these reasons are:

- Fulfillment of accreditation requirements
- Accounting for funds
- Answering requests for information
- Making administrative decisions
- Assisting staff in program development
- Learning about unintended effects of programs

The uses of evaluation will be described in more detail in the chapters on methods. At this point we discuss these major reasons only briefly.

First, many facilities are required to evaluate their programs for accreditation purposes. Colleges, hospitals, and mental health centers need accreditation to maintain viable facilities. Although many accreditation evaluations are nonempirical, and an organization may not require a high level of effectiveness to maintain accreditation, the threat of the loss of accreditation serves to maintain a certain quality of service.

Second, the vast majority of grant applications to government and philanthropic agencies require a discussion of the techniques to be used to evaluate the effectiveness of the activities supported by the grant. If a program to teach elderly people about nutrition is supported, the program administrators will be required to gather empirical evidence that the elderly are being reached and that the program has increased their nutritional knowledge and practices. If programs are to be accountable to government or charitable agencies (and, indirectly, to the public), it should be possible to show some results for the expenditure of funds.

A third reason to gather evaluative information is to facilitate the completion of the vast number of surveys government bureaus require for the continuation of funds. If an agency does not keep systematic records, each request for information will require a time-consuming manual search through files. If evaluation purposes are recognized and records are kept up in ways that are easily accessible, the evaluator will be a valuable member of the facility's staff.

Fourth, a variety of administrative decisions can be enhanced by evaluative data. An agency may be requested to expand its programs. However, budgets cannot be stretched to cover all the services that community residents or an enthusiastic staff suggest. Administrators are ultimately responsible for allocating resources. They must face questions such as: If job counseling is begun, what current service is to be eliminated or deemphasized? Is the proposed program suited to the needs of the local community? If evaluation activity has been a routine aspect of the facility, some material will already be at hand to help in the decision. In addition, if the principles of objective evaluation are accepted, it is more likely that an empirical approach to making decisions would be followed. An objective approach to decision making would be an improvement over the typical strategy of selecting programs on the basis of impressionistic and anecdotal evidence, or political pressures.

A fifth purpose of evaluation is to obtain information to improve practices. Without feedback concerning effectiveness, people cannot improve their skills. Providers of human services need information concerning how well they do their work. Also, evaluators can provide feedback on how well human service providers are viewed by those receiving the service. Good interpersonal relations are more important to human service providers than to people whose jobs require only superficial contact with people.

Sixth, a program has various effects on the facility and the community, as well as on the program's participants. Some of these effects are intended, some are unintended. Just as useful medicines can have negative side effects, so too can useful and successful programs. This issue was addressed by Scriven (1967), who coined the term *goal-free evaluation*. Goal-free evaluations seek to learn about all program effects. For example, the introduction of Western, mechanized farming methods in some third-world nations has led to increased unemployment because tractors do the work of many laborers. A focused evaluation that assessed only whether food output increased might overlook this all-important negative, unintended effect.

What Program Evaluation Is Not

In seeking to define an area, it is helpful to describe what it does not include. Program evaluation is not to be confused with basic research or with individual assessment.

Basic research concerns questions of *theoretical* interest, without regard to immediate needs of people or organizations. In contrast, program evaluation tries to help people improve their effectiveness, assist administrators to make program-level decisions, and make it possible for programs to be accountable to the public. If evaluators do not provide information that is relevant to decisions, they are not fulfilling their major purpose.

Furthermore, evaluation, but usually not basic research, is often done under a time pressure and in settings (hospitals, courts, schools, training offices) designed for the delivery of a service, not for research.

If program evaluation is indeed a new social science with unique methods, it will require basic research on new evaluation methods and new procedures to encourage implementation of findings. Individuals creating such advances are essential to the practice of program evaluation; however, they do not fill the role of a program evaluator. Readers who have taken social science courses in which the role of basic research is held up as an ideal may be surprised to find that the place of applications is so central in this text.

The second professional activity often confused with program evaluation is individual assessment. Educational psychologists, personnel workers, counseling psychologists, and others have traditionally provided diagnostic information for human service organizations. These people have served by administering intelligence, aptitude, interest, achievement, personality, and other tests for the purpose of "evaluating" an individual's need for a service or one's qualifications for a job or for advancement. These activities are not part of the program evaluator's role. Some of the material in the following chapters refers to ways of providing information about individuals. However, information describing people will be derived from measures of performance in their jobs or from measures thought to be sensitive to changes caused by a human service program. For example, program evaluators might measure depression to find an effect of counseling or of another service, but not for the purpose of assessing a person's mental state.

Common Types of Evaluations

An evaluation of a program can be conducted from a number of points of view. This text divides evaluations in two ways: (1) according to the type of question asked about the program; and (2) according to the purpose of the evaluation.

The questions asked of programs can be classified into four general types: *need, process, outcome,* and *efficiency.* Each type of question leads to a particular focus and will be involved in our presentation. Process and outcome, however, will be our main consideration in later chapters.

The evaluation of need.   An assessment of need seeks to answer questions such as:

- What is the socioeconomic profile of the community?
- What are the particular needs of this community with respect to the type of program being considered (for example, health, mental health, employment, education, crime prevention)?
- What forms of service are likely to be attractive to this particular community?

The measurement of needs is a prerequisite to effective program planning. Today more evaluators view planning as closely related to evaluation. Planning is, in fact, a form of evaluation—one that occurs before the program is implemented. In the late 1970s the close association of planning and evaluation became evident, and a journal entitled *Evaluation and Program Planning* was founded.

In order to be a good advocate and a good planner, one must have correct information about need. Certain techniques are useful for measuring or estimating need. Although some of these techniques are less quantitative than are other aspects of evaluation, the accumulation and synthesis of information is a necessary aspect of need assessment. This text includes a brief discussion of the evaluation of need. Those readers who become involved in this area will find references to some key works on this subject at the end of Chapter 5.

The evaluation of process.   Once a program has been developed and begun, evaluators will turn to documenting the extent to which the program was implemented *as designed* and is serving the *target* population. One might think of process evaluation as an examination of the effort put into the program. The kinds of questions a process evaluation seeks to answer are:

- Is the program attracting a sufficient number of clients?
- Are clients representative of the target population?
- How much does the staff actually contact the clients?
- Does the workload of the staff match that planned?
- Are there differences among staff members in effort expended?

While the answers to these questions do not indicate whether the program is successful, they are still important; and anyone responsible for directing, funding, or expanding the program wants to hear them. It is conceivable that a good plan has been inadequately implemented or that a successful program is not serving the population it was commissioned and funded to serve. Early warnings about such problems provided by a process evaluation would give the directors an opportunity to redirect the program to give it a chance to be successful.

An extreme illustration of the need to verify the implementation of a program was provided by the finding that a Russian tractor factory was reported to be a model of efficiency when, in fact, construction problems had been so severe that it was not even built. To avoid criticism for failure, those who were responsible for having it built simply faked confirmation of construction and fabricated the production records ("The Potemkin Factory," 1980).

The information necessary for a process evaluation is often available in the agency; however, it is typically not in a usable form. Material describing the clients is on application or intake forms, but it is seldom summarized. Details of services received are part of prose notes made by care givers and added to the files. Retrieving filed information requires a special effort and considerable expense. Process evaluations are best conducted when a system of reporting is designed to facilitate gathering and summarizing useful information. In Chapter 6 we illustrate the use of simple information systems for human service settings. References are provided for descriptions of more ambitious systems.

The evaluation of outcome.   If a study of implementation does show that the program was successfully put into place, an assessment of the outcome achieved by the people in a program may become a major focus of evaluators. For example:

- Do the people who take a speed-reading course read fast?
- Do they read faster than those not taking the course?
- Can evidence be found that taking the course *causes* increased reading speeds?

Although it is reasonable to ask these questions, it will be clear just by the length of our treatment of outcome evaluation that it is difficult to identify the causes of behavioral changes observed in people. For example, many people begin psychotherapy during a life crisis. If several months later they feel better and seem better adjusted, the change may be due to therapy, to the natural resolution of the crisis, to a combination of both, or to something else entirely. If a change in on-the-job requirements is followed by better morale, can we say that the program change caused the better morale, or should we conclude that it was simply the attention of management that led to improved morale? Perhaps a better national economic outlook was the actual cause.

The presentation of methods will range from the very simple through the very complex. There are situations in which a research plan with many technical weaknesses will be quite appropriate for answering the questions facing administrators and public representatives at certain times. Other more demanding questions will require more complicated research plans. In fact, evaluators might work with more complicated research designs than do laboratory research scientists. This is true because laboratory social scientists can control some of the experiences of the people involved in the research. In contrast, evaluators gather data from people participating in actual, ongoing programs. Although these people are very interested in the benefits they can obtain from the program, their interest in the needs of the evaluators is marginal at best. The evaluators will be seen by some as requiring their energy and time without providing any service in return.

When designing and conducting outcome evaluations, evaluators need to define the ways to measure success. The evaluators of the national Head Start preschool program chose improved cognitive skills as the outcome of most interest. They were criticized as having defined the goals too narrowly, because health examinations and improved nutrition were also included in the program (Datta, 1976b). The definitions of successful outcome may well vary if we compare the opinions of various interested groups, such as the agency funding the program, the program staff, and the participants. A job-training program may be funded to provide job skills so that the long-term unemployed may obtain jobs with private companies. The staff, in contrast, may view the training as a reward for participation in local elections. Last, the trainees may view the program as a good, albeit temporary, job. Whose definition of outcome is to be used?

At times the outcome sought by one or more of the groups will be purposely hidden from evaluators. In politically sensitive settings careful evaluators will be in an uncomfortable position if publicly stated goals conflict with privately held goals. Developing methods to measure success is difficult when goals are clear; when they are hidden, evaluators' jobs are all the more difficult. We will discuss ethical concerns that are relevant when evaluators believe a program is using resources for purposes other than those intended. For example, in Dade County, Florida, an investigator charged that some funds for unemployed workers were used to hire relatives of politicians (*Time*, July 24, 1978). If the outcomes of programs are regularly evaluated, such misuse of money should be more readily discovered than in the past.

Another problem centers on the issue of how long after participation the outcome is supposed to be maintained. People leaving a program typically return to the same environment that was at least partially responsible for their problems to begin with. The good intentions of alcoholics may not withstand the social pressures of their peers. Cigarettes are smoked by habit in a number of situations, such as after meals, or when one is worried or bored. Breaking down longstanding habits is very difficult. Although changes may be caused by an intensive program, the changes may only be superficial and dissolve in a matter of months, weeks, or days. If so, was the program a failure? Such questions about outcomes are treated in Chapters 7 through 10.

The evaluation of efficiency. While a program may help the participants, administrators and legislators must also address the issue of cost. Evaluations of efficiency raise the following questions:

- Does the program achieve its success at a reasonable cost?
- Can dollar values be assigned to the outcomes achieved?
- Does the program achieve a better level of success than other programs costing the same or less to administer?

There are often competing suggestions for the best ways to help people in need. Are people who are convicted of a crime in need of psychological counseling for emotional conflicts, moral instruction on values, vocational training for holding a job, or academic instruction to help them complete school? Institutions cannot do everything. Choices must be made among possible services. To make choices, the criteria on which to base the choice must be defined.

Two important criteria used to compare programs are effectiveness and cost. If two programs appear equally effective, then the less expensive program is getting more results per dollar. If the more expensive program is more effective, the problem becomes more difficult. Is the additional improvement worth the additional cost? Another complication is added because most programs seek to cause changes involving more than one characteristic. One program may spur improvement in several areas, and another affect different characteristics. Weighing the relative effectiveness of two such programs is very difficult if the decision maker wishes to be objective. An introduction to cost-benefit and cost-effectiveness analyses is given in Chapter 11.

PURPOSE OF PROGRAM EVALUATION

There really is only one major purpose for program evaluation activities, although this purpose is often broken down into several subpurposes. Human behavior is adaptive only when people obtain feedback from the environment. Our physical existence literally depends on the feedback within our bodies to regulate breathing and heart rate, levels of hormones and chemicals, eating and drinking, and so forth. Social behavior also requires feedback, but such feedback is not as dependable as that of our bodily systems. Delayed feedback, not clearly associated with the behavior causing it, is not very informative. Some writers have said that environmental problems are hard to solve because of the long delay between environmentally destructive policies and the feedback indicating a weakening of natural systems (Meadows and Perelman, 1973). Program evaluation seeks to provide feedback in social systems.

What effect do social interventions such as jail sentences, nutrition counseling, community hotlines, crime prevention measures, or job-

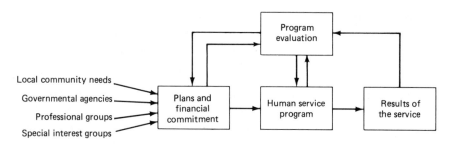

FIGURE 1.1 Schematic diagram of the place of evaluation as a feedback loop for a human service program.

training programs have on the people expected to need these interventions? Figure 1.1 illustrates the place of program evaluation as the feedback loop in human services and delivery activities. Program evaluation can be a powerful tool for improving the effectiveness of organizations (Davis, 1982; Zammuto, 1982). The rational processes of assessing needs, measuring the implementation of programs to meet those needs, evaluating the achievement of carefully formed goals and objectives, and comparing the degree of achievement and the costs involved with those of similar programs serves to improve the use of human and material resources in organizations. Most evaluators subscribe to the idea that providing feedback to organizations will help those organizations meet the needs of their clients and remain effective and vital.

This general feedback principle often furthers two purposes. Evaluations can be done to improve the plans for services or their delivery, to raise the outcomes of programs, or to increase the efficiency of services; such evaluations are called *formative evaluations* (Scriven, 1967), because they are designed to help form the programs themselves. Evaluations may also help us decide whether a program should be started, continued, or chosen from among two or more alternatives; such evaluations are called *summative evaluations* (Scriven, 1967). There is a finality to summative evaluations; once the value of the program is assessed, it is possible that the program might be ended. In actuality, few evaluations really determine whether or not a program will be terminated (Hansen, 1978; Weiss, 1972a). There are many sources of information about programs available to administrators, legislators, and community leaders. Because program evaluations are only one of these sources, evaluators are not surprised when clear evaluation reports are not followed by definitive decisions. Thus, nearly all evaluations are formative, hopefully serving to improve the program evaluated.

Evaluations are also done for less than noble purposes, some of which are discussed in the next chapter.

TRENDS MAKING EVALUATION
NECESSARY

The growing interest in program evaluation is the result of several trends in American society. *Accountability* has become a word often heard in government and human service settings. Accountability refers to the justification of how resources have been used, and to the responsibility for achieving realistic results as an outcome of one's efforts (Scriven, 1981). The call for accountability seems to have resulted from the consumer movement, professionals' own desires to improve services, an awareness of good management practices, a recognition of the limits of society's ability to support human services, and legislation.

The Consumer Movement

In recent years a number of groups have been organized to make the needs of the consumer known to large corporations. This movement has had repercussions in human service fields. The philosophy behind this approach is summarized in the following comment: "The assumption that *operating* a service is equivalent to *rendering* service, and that both are equivalent to rendering *quality* service are no longer being honored as inherently valid" (Speer and Trapp, 1976, p. 217). The right of professionals to make unchallenged judgments has been curtailed. A form of medical care evaluation—malpractice suits and the threat of malpractice suits—has already altered the practice of medicine. No professional is above being held accountable. Government administrators, teachers, nurses, military officers, and even priests are among those whose performance is now being more closely analyzed. Increasingly, respect and acceptance have to be earned by performance, not by certification or status.

Professional Concern

The service providers themselves have often cooperated and provided leadership in the movement toward the evaluation of human services. In the early part of the twentieth century, American medical care received initial evaluation from the medical societies themselves. An outcome evaluation conducted by the American College of Surgeons in the early decades of this century revealed such a poor level of outcome that the reports of this particular evaluation were destroyed (*National Standards for Community Mental Health Centers,* 1977). Medical outcome evaluation on a national scale was not attempted again until the 1970s. The evaluation activity of hospital and medical groups was further encouraged in 1965, when Congress mandated that a form of national health care review be implemented by hospitals participating in Medicare (Egdahl and Gertman, 1976).

Managerial Effectiveness

Good management procedures have become more widely used in human service fields. McConkey (1975), while serving as a statewide United Fund chairperson, was distressed to learn that some organizations requested funds but provided neither a description of their services nor evidence that the services produced positive outcomes. Human service administrators are much more aware of the necessity of effective management than they were in the past. The Crusade of Mercy (United Fund) of Chicago, Illinois, ran full-page ads picturing their "priorities committee." The caption under their picture stated that the "hardest noses of Chicago run the Crusade of Mercy." The caption went on to describe the auditing procedure used and how some agencies are dropped from support.

The reasons for tardy development of careful management procedures in human services may lie in two major areas: (1) the difficulty of specifying what the outcome of an effective human service should be; and (2) the origins of many human services in small charitable settings. Commercial firms can be clearer than can human service agencies about the goals they seek to attain. In addition, commercial managers have not had the "God-will-provide" attitude of the sincere but unsophisticated people who traditionally ran charity services. This is not to say that human service settings do or should act on the same values as business firms. Nevertheless, there is much to be learned from modern management methods.

Program evaluation in human services received impetus from the development of several data-oriented tools for managers. Tools for studying and improving the ways in which organizations function in accomplishing their purposes, such as operations research (Johnson, 1967) and systems analysis (FitzGerald, 1973), have helped evaluators with their work in human service organizations. Program evaluation can help managers learn which programs are successful and which programs are serving target populations. Such information can make some of the administrator's decisions more objective.

Limitations on Resources

The recognition that society cannot fulfill every possible need that people may have requires that priorities be set. Which is more valuable—treatment of alcoholics in the work force, or park programs for potentially delinquent children? Seldom are questions phrased so simply; however, the point to be made is important—devoting resources to one program means that these resources cannot be devoted to another program. Each program has its own supporters and beneficiaries. The conflicting wishes of these groups can make decision makers feel pulled in two, three, or more directions. Programs, of course, can be ranked on the basis of the power of the backers of the various programs. Still, it would be better to use objective information to rank programs on the basis of their potential effectiveness. In this way the resources of society may be expended in a fairer and more useful manner than has traditionally been the case.

Legislative Mandates

The federal government has increasingly insisted on the evaluation of programs. The social programs of the federal government have grown considerably during the 1960s and 1970s. Health, Education, and Welfare (HEW) programs required approximately $2 billion in 1953, which was 3 percent of the federal budget. By 1975 HEW programs made up 14 percent of the federal budget, not counting social security costs (*U.S. News & World Report,* 1975). Social programs have a reputation for costing more than they were expected to cost when initially planned. Medicare and Medicaid, for example, cost $39 billion in 1977 but only $6 billion in 1967 (*Newsweek,* 1977). Important for our purposes was the result of the congressional reaction to rapid cost escalation. Congress sought to contain Medicare costs by monitoring the time required for treatment and by examining the quality of treatment given (Gosfield, 1975).

In addition to monitoring health care, the federal government has sought to limit the expansion of health care facilities. The belief that health care facilities are used whenever they are provided has often been voiced. It seems that more disease conditions "require" hospitalization when more inpatient facilities become available (Ball, 1978). If that is so, then careful planning—taking into consideration existing facilities and community need—must precede hospital expansion. Congress has required more thorough planning through the National Health Planning and Resources Development Act (Public Law 93–641).

The government's role in evaluation is also evident in the requirement that recipients of educational or service grants be directed to evaluate their work. For example, the evaluation requirements in the Elementary and Secondary Education Act of 1965 (McLaughlin, 1974) encouraged the development of educational evaluation. Such requirements are often met with less than adequate research methods. However, we believe that thinking in evaluative terms is a step forward.

Although the federal government alone has the power to require steps to be taken to evaluate programs, other groups are becoming increasingly active. For example, Blue Cross and Blue Shield, administered by people in health care professions, have traditionally paid whatever bills were submitted by hospitals and doctors. Recently these groups have become more strict about what charges will be honored. In 1977 some twenty medical/surgical procedures were listed by Blue Cross as ineffective and not be be paid for, because research has shown that these procedures either provide no relief for patients or have been superseded by better diagnostic procedures (*Blue Shield News,* 1977).

Because of these trends, the field of evaluation is expanding. This text is an introduction to program evaluation for people who are considering entering the field as a career, or who need to understand the methods and concepts of the field.

THE ROLE OF EVALUATORS

Work Settings

Before actually describing the specifics of program evaluation, it would be worthwhile to describe where evaluators work. There are three major work settings for professional evaluators. Some evaluators work for the organization that desires certain programs to be evaluated. Such people are called in-house evaluators. Because of the trends discussed in the previous section, program evaluation is necessary if administrators want their services to survive the competition for funds within their agency or within the city, state, or federal budget.

A second role is employment with governmental or regulatory agencies. The Government Accounting Office, for example, is reponsible to Congress for reports on how legislative programs are working out. The GAO's reports can influence legislation on welfare, health, education, and so forth. Some states have created evaluation units, often in the offices of the state auditor. The act creating the Legislative Auditor in Minnesota states that this official is to

> . . . determine the degree to which the activities and programs entered into or funded by the state are accomplishing their goals and objectives, including the evaluation of goals and objectives, measurement of program results and effectiveness, alternative means of achieving the same results, and efficiency in the allocation of resources ("Spotlight," 1982, p. 2).

Since states have responsibilities in the areas of education, health care, welfare, safety, highways, and so forth, evaluators in state offices will work on a variety of topics.

The third major work setting for evaluators is private research firms. Such firms submit proposals in response to "Requests for proposals" announcing competitions for evaluations of governmental programs. The proposals are judged on the basis of cost and quality of methods proposed for the project. They are evaluated in much the same way as are competitive bids for construction projects; a contract for the project is given to the firm or evaluator group that has submitted the highest quality proposal within the allotted budget. (Some university faculty members conduct evaluations independently; they work in much the same way as evaluators who work with research firms.)

In addition to professional evaluators, many individuals in educational, personnel, training, rehabilitation, management, and corrections roles (among others) perform evaluations as part of their responsibilities. Readers who currently fill or intend to seek positions in such settings will find that the concepts and skills presented in this text are valuable in their work even if they never have a position labeled "evaluator."

Consultants Compared to In-House Evaluators

There are only two general ways an evaluator can relate to the organization needing the evaluation: (1) Evaluators can work for the organization and do a variety of evaluations; or (2) they can come to the organization from a research firm or a university to work on a specific program only. For the purposes of discussion, the terms *in-house evaluator* and *consultant* are used to summarize these two different roles. The particular role filled has implications for the size of the evaluation project attempted and for some of the characteristics of the research itself.

Factors related to competence. In terms of *knowledge about a program,* in-house evaluators have the advantage, since they have better access to program directors and to the organization's administration. A person who is physically present forty hours a week is likely to see the program in action, to know the staff, and to learn about its reputation from other people in the organization. The information gained informally by a secretary in the cafeteria would be unavailable to a consultant not based in the organization. The more that is known about the actual workings of the program, the easier it is to ask the relevant questions in an evaluation.

The *technical expertise* of the evaluator is important. An in-house evaluator often works with a small group of two or three. Some evaluators work alone. However, working alone provides limited opportunities for helpful feedback. In contrast, the consultant may have the resources of a larger organization to draw upon.

A different facet of the question of technical expertise is suggested by the necessity of performing evaluation work in many different areas of an organization. During one period of two years, the authors of this text performed work on psychosomatic illness, stroke disability, a dietary supplement, patient satisfaction, medical education programs, and employee satisfaction, among other topics. It is challenging and stimulating to work in new areas; however, there is also a risk that inexperience in a given area may lead to oversimplifications. By selecting a consultant with experience in a specific program area, an organization may avoid the errors that may occur when an in-house evaluator faces a problem in a new area of the organization.

Personal qualities.   There are personal qualities unrelated to technical competence that are important to evaluators. Evaluators can do more effective work if they are objective, trusted by administrators, and interested in improving the program being evaluated.

In terms of *trust,* in-house evaluators are most likely to have the edge. Being well known and, hopefully, having been found worthy of trust, in-house evaluators usually find program directors and staff more willing to devote time to the evaluation, to admit problems, and to share confidences than they would be with a consultant not previously known.

An in-house evaluator can also be expected to have a *desire to improve the organization* sponsoring the program and paying the evaluator's salary. Although intentions are sometimes misunderstood, it is always in the best interests of evaluators to find ways to improve the organizations in which they work. Consultants might not have the same motivations, being less dependent for continuing support on the organization sponsoring the program.

On the other hand, whether or not one is dependent on the organization for a job may affect one's *objectivity,* which is important if reports are to be credible. The objectivity of in-house evaluators may be questioned because they may know the program designer and the staff delivering the service. It is not easy to criticize the work of a friend. The consultant, on the other hand, is unlikely to have developed personal relationships within the organization and thus may be more objective. An in-house evaluator may also hesitate to report critical findings because future work may be jeopardized. Research in an applied setting depends on the cooperation of many people. If they believe that negative results will come out of the project, the needed cooperation may be hard to obtain.

There is another side to the question, however. Nonobjective evaluators will lose their credibility and, thus, their effectiveness. In the short run it might be quite easy to ignore sensitive issues. The authors prepared a report that showed positive outcomes for the patients in a medical/psychological program (Carey and Posavac, 1977b). If the report had stopped there, it would have been welcomed. However, it went on to show that other patients obtained the same degree of positive benefit at less cost in a different program. This observation was not welcome. It is important to emphasize, though, that this short-term loss should be weighed against the likelihood that willingness to report negative or ambivalent findings will increase one's credibility in the long run.

The purpose of the evaluation required. Earlier in this chapter two purposes of evaluative studies were described—formative and summative. In-house and consultant evaluators can and do perform both types of evaluations. However, there are certain situations that are better served by one or the other type of evaluator. The in-house evaluator is likely to be more effective than a consultant in implementing procedures to follow for formative evaluations. Such evaluators will be available and committed enough to see the project through, and because formative evaluations cannot lead to a traumatic decision to end a program, negative results will not destroy the evaluator's role in the organization. If, in contrast, a summative evaluation is wanted because there is a strong suspicion that a program is failing, an outside evaluator will probably be more helpful than in-house personnel. A school board, knowing that it had to close one of three grade schools because enrollment had dropped, decided to select a consultant with no ties to the school district to recommend which school to close. The consultant performed an evaluation of efficiency for each school and recommended that the least efficient school be closed. Although there were some hard feelings, and a number of verbal attacks were leveled at the consultant and his report, the selection of the school to be closed was made and implemented with fewer difficulties than was the case in neighboring school districts making a similar decision, but relying entirely on local expertise.

Conflicts Between Evaluators and Organizations

Evaluators fill a position between (on one hand) the role of the research social scientist concerned about theory, the design of experiments, and the analysis of data—but for the most part uninvolved in the delivery of human services—and (on the other hand) the role of the practitioner dealing with people in need and seldom interested in or trained in the methods of data collection and analysis. Evaluators are able to read the language and to use the tools of the research social scientist. Research design, validation, reliability, statistical significance, and so forth are familiar to evaluators. In addition, the effective evaluator will be sensitive to the concerns and style of the service delivery staff. Finally, evaluators interact with administrators, who are ultimately responsible for the effectiveness and cost of the program. Because the field is so new and the tasks assigned to the evaluator are so varied, the role of the evaluator is not widely understood.

Participating in such a new field has advantanges and disadvantages. The advantages include the intellectual stimulation provided by exposure to people serving various roles in human service programs and the satisfaction of seeing research methods used in ways that can be of potential benefit. The disadvantages include being viewed as intrusive and unnecessary by some service delivery personnel. As will be seen in the chapters that follow, the most effective evaluators show that they are allies of service providers, while at the same time asking searching questions and requiring documentation of answers.

It is unfortunately true that shortsighted self-interest has opposed objective evaluation. Spinney (Isaacson, 1983) testified to Congress about how military planners ignored the findings of their own research and those of evaluation analysts when ambitious officers wanted pet projects funded. It should also be noted that some political orientations are opposed to government participation in many social services, regardless of the effectiveness of these governmental activities (Levin, 1982; Walsh, 1983). Campbell (1983), one of the early leaders in the evaluation field, has become concerned about the possibility of collecting valid information when people are threatened by an evaluation of their work or ideas. Others expect active, but changed, roles for evaluators in future years (Cronbach, 1980; Johnston, 1983; McClintock, 1983). These observers foresee a growth in the use of information prepared by people working in the organizations sponsoring the program or service. Furthermore, it seems likely that a responsible investment of resources by federal, state, and local governments, as well as by business and charitable organizations, will continue to require careful monitoring as well as evaluations of effectiveness (Rossi, 1983).

It is true that requirements to evaluate programs do not necessarily mean (1) that evaluations are uniformly good (they are not); (2) that evaluations are always utilized (they sometimes are ignored); or (3) that ineffective programs no longer exist (they do). However, many social scientists believe that the widespread requirement for evaluation, if coupled with increased sophistication in evaluation methods, will contribute to the achievement of the desirable goals of improving the effectiveness of social programs and making new programs more sensitive to the needs of the people to be served (Guttentag, 1977; Triandis, 1978; Wertheimer, 1978).

Getting a Job as an Evaluator

As mentioned above, many organizations conduct evaluations but do not call their evaluation activities "program evaluations." Some entry-level jobs go under the names "program analyst" or "planner." A number of graduate students have gotten such positions in city government during some phase of their studies. To get a job in program evaluation, one must sometimes be creative in suggesting how organizations can use an evaluator's skills. For example, one could draw an analogy between an auditor working with financial matters and an evaluator working with people-oriented issues. Just as one wouldn't run a business without adequate monitoring of cash flow, one really shouldn't run an organization without knowing how employees react to company policies and benefits, whether customers like the services, or if managers work better after being trained (Perloff, 1983).

In order to understand the problems of organizations that might hire an evaluator, it is helpful to learn something about the ways individuals in those organizations think. There are professional organizations for people in personnel, marketing, training, and so on; and the journals they publish can usually be found in libraries. Capper (1983) has suggested joining the organizations and meeting people in the businesses that might need evaluation skills. The crucial question is: How will evaluation improve the quality of the work done by the organization? To provide a credible answer, the evaluator must understand the needs of the organization.

People who are serious about getting started as evaluation consultants need brochures describing their services. Drawing up a brochure forces one to be clear about just what services can be offered to a business. Making appointments with directors of personnel, planning, training, and so on can be helpful, because this allows one to be seen. Having potential clients connect a face with a brochure helps develop credibility.

A number of people have suggested that conducting a project for free is a way of becoming known and demonstrating the value of program evaluation. Several students of the first author have been offered jobs after doing a class project for an organization.

Even after getting a job as an evaluator, it is still important to demonstrate that evaluation can help in running an effective program. Some managers will be threatened by the idea of someone collecting data on the effectiveness of their work groups. Still, becoming known in the organization as competent and trustworthy, and developing a broader knowledge of how feedback about effectiveness can help different aspects of the organization, will help keep a steady flow of work for the evaluation office.

Evaluation and Other Activities
of an Organization

Professional interaction among people with similar interests is often beneficial to all concerned. An evaluator working alone will find it hard to grow and to develop professionally. If an organization is too small to employ more than one full-time evaluator, it may be wise to attach evaluation to another function of the organization. Four functions that are sometimes joined with evaluation are research, education, planning, and human resources.

Research.   Some human service organizations routinely sponsor research directly with operating funds or indirectly with grant funds. Evaluation can become one function of the research team. For example, a police department was awarded a grant to study the effect of providing emotional support to the victims of crime. The social scientists responsible for that research would be excellent colleagues of an evaluator. University-affiliated hospitals carry on research. Individuals conducting research into psychiatric problems or emotional issues related to serious illness have interests similar enough to those of evaluators to serve as colleagues.

Education. Some organizations have joined the functions of education and evaluation. There is a longstanding precedent for this marriage in educational psychology. New study materials and curricula are evaluated before being widely used by schools. Universities are combining faculty development and evaluation into one office. Many organizations besides schools sponsor educational programs. For example, industries have safety education programs, apprenticeship programs, job-training programs for minorities, and so on. Sponsoring firms want to know if the programs are achieving their goals.

Planning. Planning is an activity in which evaluators can assist. It is common for service providers to serve as a planning group. This choice is wise; however, many direct-service providers are not data oriented, feel uncomfortable constructing need surveys, and may be unable to analyze the information obtained. Evaluators can help by showing them how effective the plans are likely to be and how consumers evaluate proposed projects or services.

Human resources. Large businesses often have a vice-president of human resources. This office oversees all policies concerning hiring, compensation, and the professional development of employees. Compensation plans, training programs, management effectiveness seminars, and so forth all require evaluation if an organization is to be as effective as possible.

SUMMARY

National trends, such as the consumer movement, professional concern, increased managerial effectiveness, limitations on resources, and specific congressional mandates have converged to create a need for methods to make rational managerial and legislative decisions in human services. The social science methods of program evaluation include planning, program monitoring, outcome assessment, and benefit/cost considerations. Evaluators are quantitative social scientists working to improve the delivery of human services. Their efforts to effect such improvements are on a program level, not on the individual person/client/patient level frequently associated with human service organizations.

STUDY QUESTIONS

1. From newspaper and magazine articles, gather examples of the trend toward increased accountability and examples of the use of program evaluations in the formation of public policy. You might find articles dealing with medical care (malpractice, peer review, costs), education (children reading well or not reading well), program planning (need assessment), relative costs of programs with similar goals, or other issues.

2. What aspects of program evaluation might be used in organizational settings with which you are familiar? Illustrate.

3. List the advantages and disadvantages of making program evaluation a part of American human services delivery systems. Save your list, and when you have finished the text, consider how you might change the list.

4. Some people suggest that while society wants to believe that something is being done about social problems, most people really do not care if the programs actually have an impact on the problems. Consider the question of whether people really want to know if educational, welfare, health, and other services actually work.

FURTHER READING

DEMONE, H. W., AND HARSHBARGER, D. 1973. The planning and administration of human services. In *Developments in human services,* vol. 1, ed. H. C. Schulberg, F. Baker, and S. R. Roen. New York: Behavioral Publications.

WEISS, C. H. 1975. Evaluation research in the political context. In *Handbook of evaluation research,* vol. 1, E. L. Struening and M. Guttentag, chap. 2. Beverly Hills, Calif.: Sage.

2

Planning
an Evaluation

The initiation of a program evaluation may arise in several different ways. The program personnel themselves may initiate the request. The program sponsors (such as the funding agency or the head of the institution in which the program functions) might order an evaluation as a condition for beginning or continuing a program. The evaluation or quality assurance department might sense the opportunity for a productive project and submit a preliminary proposal to either the program sponsors or the program director.

Whatever the source of the proposal, evaluators need to address a number of issues and make certain decisions before the collection of data begins. Before committing their resources, they need to learn about the goals and mechanics of the program, about the people who sponsor the program, about the program personnel, and about groups that may resist the evaluation of the program. After obtaining this information evaluators must then decide whether an evaluation can be done. If the program is planned in a way that permits evaluation, then a decision needs to be made as to whether an evaluation should be done immediately, whether it should be done in the way in which it is proposed, or whether it should be done at all.

In the first part of this chapter, we provide an overview of the order and manner in which the above issues can be approached, identifying the steps to be taken between the time of the initial proposal and the beginning of data collection. The time and effort devoted to each step will vary, depending on the complexity of the program, the relationship of the evaluator to the program sponsors and personnel, and the urgency of time constraints. Some steps, such as selecting or developing measures, are very complex, and Chapter 3 will explain them in detail. In the second part of this chapter, we deal with potential sources of resistance to program evaluation.

SIX STEPS IN PLANNING AN EVALUATION

Step 1: Identify relevant people.

The first thing effective evaluators do is identify relevant people; that is, those who have a serious interest in the program and whose lives may potentially be affected by the evaluation. Relevant people are those who are heavily personally involved in the program, who derive some or all of their income from the program, whose future status or career might be affected by the quality of the program, or who are the clients or potential recipients of the program services. Such groups have been called stakeholders (Bryk, 1983), since they have a stake in the program and its evaluation.

Program personnel should be considered first. They will usually be more personally involved in the program than either the sponsors or the clients. The program director will be the key person to whom evaluators will relate during the entire project. It will help to learn as much about the background, interest, attitudes, and reputation of the program director as possible. In addition, other people involved in the delivery of program services must not be overlooked. It is also important to involve them in the planning stage so that they will assume ownership of the project and provide maximum support during the data collection stage. If possible, evaluators should learn about the relationship between the director and other program personnel, so that they can be dealt with more effectively during the planning meetings to be described below. For example, if the director tends to be a dictatorial person, it will be more difficult for evaluators to draw out the ideas of other personnel and determine when a consensus exists or when a power decision has been made by the director.

Program sponsors should be considered next. At times program personnel are the sponsors. In other cases sponsors will be funding agencies, governmental bodies, or administrators of the institution in which the program exists. Often there will be a single person to whom the evaluators are to relate. The funding agency may delegate one or two representatives to handle the commissioning and supervising of an evaluation project. In an institution such as a hospital, the program sponsor might be the vice-president or administrator to whom the program director reports and who is ultimately responsible for the management of the program. Contact with the program sponsor will be especially important during the initial stages of planning and at the end of the evaluation. At the beginning it is important that the sponsor fully supports the proposed evaluation and that all the program personnel are aware of that support. At the end of the evaluation, it is important that the report be presented to sponsors in such a way that it will be fully utilized in decision making. The presentation of the report and effective utilization of findings will be discussed more fully in Chapters 12 and 13.

Finally, the clients or recipients of the program services need to be identified. The amount and type of contact with the clients will depend on the nature of the program and of the evaluation. For example, if a cancer care unit is to be evaluated, are the program recipients only the cancer patients, or are the relatives of the patients also included? Are all cancer patients included, or only those with an established diagnosis of cancer, or with certain types of cancer?

Step 2: Arrange preliminary meetings.

Before a final decision is made to undertake an evaluation, and before the writing of a detailed proposal, it is advisable to meet with relevant people to gather background information on five questions: (1) Who wants the evaluation? (2) What type of evaluation is desired? (3) Why do they want it? (4) When do they want it? and (5) What resources are available?

Who wants the evaluation?   The ideal situation occurs when both the program sponsor and the program personnel desire to have the program evaluated. In this instance the evaluators will usually be interacting with competent people who are secure in their professional expertise, who are open to suggestions for improvement, and who welcome the opportunity to have documentation for what they feel is a successful program.

If the program sponsors initiate the evaluation proposal—either without the knowledge of, or against the desires of, the program personnel—the evaluators are faced with making the program personnel comfortable with the goals and methodology of the evaluation before data collection begins. If evaluators do not succeed in doing this, they face the possibility of open opposition or a lack of essential cooperation on the part of the program personnel. On the other hand, when the program personnel see the evaluators as "allies" rather than as "the enemy," they are more likely to give the evaluators both much-needed assistance in the difficult job of data collection and valuable insights into the interpretation of the data.

If the program personnel initiate the evaluation proposal—either without the knowledge of, or against the desires of, the program sponsors—the evaluators need to convince the sponsors of the usefulness of the evaluation, or it will be very difficult to have any worthwhile changes effected. Sponsors who do not assume ownership of the evaluation project during the planning stage are inclined to allow the finished reports to lie unused in their offices.

What type of evaluation is desired? Early in the evaluators' meetings with program sponsors and personnel, it will be clear that the term *program evaluation* does not have the same meaning for everyone. More often than not, program personnel will be thinking in terms of a formative evaluation that will help them modify and improve the program. On the other hand, program sponsors may desire a summative evaluation; they may be under pressure to divert resources to another program and must decide whether or not to continue the present program. Finally, some program personnel and sponsors will have little awareness of the whole concept of *program* evaluation and will therefore be expecting *individual* performance appraisal.

The task of evaluators at this point is to clarify the pertinent concepts for those who do not understand them and to help the relevant people decide what type of evaluation best meets their desires, needs, and resources. The choice is seldom between one type of evaluation and another. Often it is possible to incorporate some elements of various types of evaluations into the total scope of the project, depending on the complexity of the program goals and the resources available for the project. For example, in the evaluation of "Sesame Street" conducted by Cook et al. (1975), various types of assessment were included in the overall evaluation. He assessed (1) whether the program reached its target audience; (2) effectiveness by analysis of learning scores; (3) the magnitude of effects relative to the magnitude of the need that gave rise to the problem; (4) the ratio of benefits to cost; (5) the aspects of the complex home viewing situations that led to learning, and the conditions of TV viewing that most promote learning; and (6) the value of program objectives—that is, the importance of stimulating the growth of all social groups of preschool children versus that of narrowing the academic achievement gap between economically advantaged and disadvantaged children.

Why is the evaluation desired? Closely tied to the previous question is the issue of why evaluation is desired. The commissioning of an evaluation is rarely the product of an inquiring scientific spirit. More often it meets the needs of political forces. Evaluation furnishes ammunition for institutional combatants in fluid lines of battle and in transient alliances. Program sponsors often need to satisfy constituents and want to keep politically advantageous programs alive. Effective evaluators will put a high priority on identifying the reasons why the evaluation is desired. Were there some groups in the organization who objected to the evaluation? What were their motives? Is there real commitment among the program personnel and program sponsors to using the results of the evaluation to improve decision making? Ideally, program personnel are seeking answers to pressing questions about the program's future: Should it be continued? Should it be expanded? Should it be modified?

One aspect of the evaluators' role is to help both the sponsors and program personnel arrive at a consensus on the precise decision(s) to be made. For example, in the evaluation of a physical medicine and rehabilitation program (Carey and Posavac, 1978), the decision under consideration was not whether or not the program should be continued, because the program was generally recognized as useful and had abundant referrals both from physicians on the hospital staff and from physicians at other hospitals. However, the program personnel were concerned about patients who were discharged to their homes as apparent successes. They did not really know whether these patients maintained their levels of rehabilitation. After extended discussion it became clear that the primary focus of the evaluation was whether a follow-up program was needed for those patients who were discharged as successfully rehabilitated.

In other instances evaluations are conducted to determine how much of an impact a program has on other areas of the sponsoring institution. In such a case the program personnel are not decision oriented; rather, they seek to assure themselves that no serious side effects arise from the introduction of a new program. For example, the authors evaluated the impact of a physician residency program at a teaching hospital on other areas within the hospital. The study uncovered certain tensions and conflicts that might develop into serious problems unless they were attend to immediately. The evaluators concluded the report with suggested corrective actions to be considered by the medical education committee.

Some evaluations done for public relations or political purposes are acceptable. For example, administrators may be reasonably certain that they have an effective program and may wish to generate greater support for that program. In other words, they desire greater visibility for the program with influential people who can provide increased political or financial support.

Evaluation may also be done solely to fulfill grant requirements. Many grants from governmental and private sources include an evaluation requirement. In this situation the decision to evaluate originates from pressure external to the program itself. For example, all projects for disadvantaged pupils funded under Title I of the Elementary Secondary Education Act are required to be evaluated. The imposition of evaluation requirements is not without merit. When the need to ask evaluative questions is forced on people, they may become more self-critical than they would otherwise have been. There is a need to gather support for a good program and to justify a program to the people who fund it.

However, some reasons for program evaluation are undesirable. For example, an administrator may use program evaluation as a ploy to avoid making a decision. Administrators who are pressured about the viability of a given program can buy time by saying that the program is being evaluated; by giving as little support as possible to the evaluators, they ensure that the evaluation will take a long time to be completed. If there is a need to buy still more time when the evaluation is completed, administrators may appoint a committee to study the evaluation report. Evaluation is also inappropriate when administrators know what decisions they will make but wish to go through the charade of program evaluation to give their decision legitimacy.

When is the evaluation desired? The scope of an evaluation project can be limited by situational factors. If the evaluators are given a deadline, they may be forced to make choices that are not ideal. For example, measures specifically designed for a program may have to be foregone in favor of existing questionnaires or instruments, although these existing instruments may not have the desired reliability, validity, or applicability. The number of respondents or participants in the study may have to be limited, thereby decreasing the probability of detecting the true effect of the program. Adequate control groups may not be immediately available, although they might be available at a later date. Evaluators must decide whether they should proceed under less than ideal circumstances, delay the evaluation, or refuse to do the evaluation in order to avoid the possibility of generating misleading results. For example, Carey and Posavac (1979) were invited to evaluate a new cancer care center five months before it was to be introduced within an acute care hospital. A five-month lead time was not long enough to develop new measures for all the program objectives, nor to collect data from a large sample of cancer patients before the institution of the center. To save time, the evaluators measured patient moods with an existing instrument used in previous research with cancer patients.

Even when there is no deadline, program personnel may be eager for results and push evaluators for an estimated completion date. It is usually better not to commit oneself to a deadline that can be met only if everything occurs on schedule. Murphy's law ("If anything can go wrong, it will") is especially applicable in program evaluation: Data collectors become ill; respondents are unavailable; the mail is slow; computers break down when they are most needed.

When an estimated date for the completion of the report is required, extra time should be allotted. If evaluators finish behind schedule, they are suspected of being disorganized at best, or incompetent at worst. On the other hand, when they finish ahead of schedule, they build a reputation for speed and efficiency. Nevertheless, it is important to remember that evaluators work in settings in which time is important—more important than in the setting in which university-based research is usually conducted.

What resources are available? Besides time, another situational factor that can limit an evaluation is the availability of resources. For example, if in-house evaluators are working within a budget, how much can they spend on a given project? Will they have the assistance of program personnel or volunteers, so that they can hold down the expense of data collection? Will involvement in a new project delay or eliminate another evaluation project of greater importance?

If no formal contract was signed, it is also advisable for outside evaluators to put into writing an exact list of what is covered and not covered in a cost estimate, and specify the time when payment should be made. The agreement should be signed by a responsible officer of the contracting institution or by the program sponsor. Verbal agreements pave the way to hard feelings. This does not imply a lack of good faith on the part of either party. Honest misunderstandings occur because busy people can be distracted and fail to remember the details of an agreement.

Step 3: Assess the evaluability of the program.

The next step is to decide whether an evaluation should be done. This process, referred to as an "evaluability assessment" (Schmidt, Scanlon, and Bell, 1979; Wholey, 1979), is a descriptive and analytic method intended to produce a reasoned basis for proceeding with an evaluation. After meeting with the relevant stakeholders to gather information on program conceptualization, objectives, and resources, a conscious decision should be made either to conduct or not to conduct an evaluation.

A program is not ready to be evaluated until its theoretical basis has been developed, sufficient resources have been allotted, and sponsors are ready to implement it in a substantial fashion. Nor should an evaluation be undertaken when the expectations for the program are implausible, or if it is not feasible to collect the evidence required to demonstrate the effectiveness of the program. For example, before a Hospice Program for terminally ill people can be evaluated, the policy makers must agree on the answers to such questions as: What is the definition of a "terminally ill" patient? Are patients with only certain illnesses to be served? Is care for bereaved relatives to be included in the scope of Hospice services? Nor is a program evaluable if it is not ready to be implemented as planned. If, for example, a school had planned to introduce a computer course for its eighth-grade students involving a full-time instructor and ten computer terminals, it cannot be evaluated if there are only two terminals and a part-time instructor.

Horst and others (1974) discuss some underlying causes of why those in charge of programs and those who evaluate them have not joined their efforts in a manner that more frequently results in program improvements. They suggest three underlying causes, which they say are not the responsibility of the evaluator: (1) a failure to define the problem addressed or the program intervention being made; (2) a lack of clear logic—that is, the connection between the program intervention and the immediate outcome is not understood clearly enough to permit testing; and (3) a lack of management—that is, those in charge of the program lack the authority or ability to follow through on evaluation results. Cronbach (1982) suggests that evaluations should only be done when the evaluation and its recommendations are likely to get a fair hearing.

It is necessary to point out that at times evaluators do not have the freedom to decide not to conduct an evaluation. In-house evaluators may be assigned to conduct an evaluation. Consultants may accept a contract in order to maintain a staff, even if conditions are not perfect for carrying out the best evaluation. The main consideration is to make a conscious decision—not merely to drift into a project just because it is there. Chapter 4 suggests that when faced with an unevaluable program, an evaluator may be able to help program sponsors redefine an evaluation project.

Step 4: Examine the literature.

Evaluators often work on a wide variety of projects. An independent evaluator, for example, may evaluate a school system, then a community program for alcoholics, and then the organizational climate in a bank. Such a researcher must become familiar with an enormous amount of literature. Although this is difficult, some evaluators prefer such work; they enjoy the variety and do not like to restrict their efforts to a single area of interest.

Evaluators who specialize in limited areas have a less formidable task in drawing up a proposal. If they have been exclusively evaluating educational systems, mental health programs, or personnel problems in organizations, they develop an extensive knowledge of evaluation in their specialty. They can also build more easily on their own past research and contribute to the development of theory in that area.

However, when evaluators work in an area that is new for them, it is important to make a careful search of the literature before designing or developing new instruments. Evaluators should learn from the successes and failures of others and get a picture of the methodological, political, and practical difficulties that must be overcome.

Depending on the type of evaluation, computerized search services might be a good place to begin a search. Data on Program Evaluation (DOPE), MED-LINE, Psychological Abstracts Search and Retrieval (PASAR), and Educational Resource Information Center (ERIC) are four such useful systems. A search of professional journals recommended by program personnel is also helpful. After a few useful articles have been identified, the bibliographies of these articles will provide additional references.

While reading the articles, evaluators should keep these key questions in mind: Has any evaluation been done on this type of program? What designs were used? Were new measures developed? How reliable and valid were the measures? What type of statistical analysis was used? Was it appropriate? Is there a consensus among the findings of various studies? If there is conflict, is this due to sampling procedures, design, or interpretation of findings? What issues were not addressed or investigated?

Step 5: Determine the methodology.

After reviewing the literature, the evaluators are ready to make some methodological decisions regarding strategy and design, population and sampling procedures, control or comparison groups, operational measures, data collection, and statistical analysis. Separate chapters are devoted to some of these issues, but it is helpful to examine the main issues now so that the reader can better understand their interrelationships and how they fit into the planning stage of an evaluation.

Strategy and design.   Strategy and design will largely be determined by the type of evaluation needed. Will the project be a need evaluation? A process evaluation? An outcome evaluation? An evaluation of cost effectiveness? Perhaps the project will include more than one kind of evaluation.

Strategy and design will also be influenced by whether the program is already in operation or whether it is still in the planning stage. If a new program is to be initiated, its effectiveness can be evaluated by gathering data on one or more occasions prior to the introduction of the program and comparing these data to information collected after its introduction. If the program can be introduced to some segments of a target population on a staggered basis, this is more desirable than introducing the program to the entire population at the same time. With this strategy evaluators can make multiple comparisons of the same group over time, and between groups.

Population and sampling.   Once the target population (participants, respondents) has been identified, evaluators need to decide whether to include the entire population or to take a sample from that population.

There are at least two arguments for including the entire population. The first is political or psychological—namely, people may be offended if they are not included. For example, the organizational attitudes of nurses at a given hospital could be accurately measured by taking a stratified random sample from the various nursing services. However, experience has shown that the hospital climate survey itself has a more positive impact on nurses' job satisfaction when all nurses are given the opportunity to express their views through the survey.

The second reason for including the entire population is methodological. If a sample is too small, there is a great danger of being unable to detect program effects even when the program is effective (a Type II error). For example, if a random sample of ten program participants is compared to a sample of ten who did not participate in the program, the program would have to have quite sizable effects before the results would be statistically significant. A naive use of statistical significance testing has been responsible for overlooking true program effects in some evaluations (Cohen, 1982).

There are two main arguments for using a random sample of participants rather than the entire population when the populations are large—namely, time and money. Program evaluation must be done within a budget, and usually there are some time restraints. When Andrew Greeley (1972) studied the effects of the Vatican Council on Catholic priests in the United States, he quite properly used a 10 percent stratified random sample of the 55,000 Catholic priests. Diocesan and religious order priests, priests of different age groups, priests from different geographical areas, and priests with different job categories (pastors, associate pastors, and those in special work) were represented in the sample. Greeley was able to get more than an 80 percent return from his sample and had sufficient numbers for studying subsets of the population. Because he chose to work with a sample rather than with the entire population, he kept within his budget and had the project completed in a reasonable time.

Whether one chooses to include the entire population in the evaluation or to do a random sampling, a very important factor must be kept in mind—the probability that some people will drop out of the study. It is important to identify the characteristics of nonparticipants and those who drop out at various points of time. Both the rate of dropouts and the reasons for dropping out have a bearing on the conclusions to be made from the data collected.

If more than 50 percent of the target population or random sample are lost, the extrapolation of the findings to the entire population cannot be done with any confidence. Therefore, with a population of 1,000 respondents, evaluators will generally be able to make more valid interpretations if they take a 10 percent sample and obtain a 75 percent response rate ($N = 75$) than if they try to reach the entire population and obtain only a 30 percent response rate ($N = 300$).

The composition of the participant group will have an effect on subject dropout rates. For example, in a hospital setting it is more difficult to obtain a high percentage of returns from housekeeping personnel than from nursing personnel on a written employee questionnaire. This occurs because many housekeeping personnel have difficulty in reading English. In contacting patients in the aforementioned cancer care center study, it was difficult to obtain an adequate response rate because of the serious physical conditions of the target population. Therefore, the questionnaires had to be as short and simple as possible in order to obtain a response rate of 50 percent or better.

Control and comparison groups. When participants are randomly assigned to a group where they do not receive the services of the program being evaluated, they constitute a true *control group.* When participants in a program are compared to a group not receiving the services of the program but not randomly assigned to a group, we speak of a *comparison group* (or a *nonequivalent control group*). If the goal of the evaluation is to determine whether the program caused a change in the participants, the ideal evaluation involves random assignment of participants to the treatment and control groups. (We will point out in later chapters that establishing causal evidence is often not the objective of program evaluations. See also Cronbach, 1982.)

Random assignment is frequently impossible; however, there may be ways to achieve the equivalent of this, even when the evaluators do not have total control of the situation. For example, in an evaluation of primary nursing in a hospital,[1] the evaluators did not have control over which patients were assigned to the units with primary nursing or to those with team nursing. However, investigation showed that all physicians allowed their patients to be assigned to medical units on the basis of bed availability. This meant that although the evaluators had no control over the assignment of patients, situational factors resulted in random assignment. Demographic records of the patients in each group demonstrated that this system of random assignment resulted in two groups that were reasonably comparable.

One way of strengthening the interpretation of findings when one cannot have true control groups is to have more than one comparison group. For example, this was of great value in the cancer care center evaluation previously mentioned. On some criteria patients in the special cancer unit reported attitudes significantly more favorable than did one comparison group and significantly less favorable than did the other comparison group. On other criteria the patients in the special unit scored higher than both comparison groups. Therefore, with the use of two comparison groups, the evaluators were able to identify the advantages of the program with greater precision.

Nevertheless, one can question whether meaningful evaluation must always be comparative. Are there not some *absolute* standards of performance or quality against which results can be compared? For example, if one is evaluating a newly introduced drive-in banking service and 80 percent of banking customers are pleased, does one need a control or comparison group? It would not seem to be necessary if the program sponsors (the bank) had set an 80 percent satisfaction rate as their goal. Nevertheless, it

[1]Primary nursing refers to a situation in which an individual nurse is assigned to give complete care to a few patients in a unit. It is distinguished from team nursing, in which a group of nurses works under a head nurse to provide care as needed to an entire unit of patients, perhaps alternating their responsibilities from day to day. Primary nurses work more closely with physicians in developing care plans and in discharge planning.

would be of value to know what the level of customer satisfaction had been before the new service was made available.

Selection of measures.   The key idea with respect to measurement is to plan for multiple measures from multiple sources. Obviously, one of the main sources of data in program evaluation is the client. However, clients can provide data in more than one way. Clients can provide self-report measures by responding to direct questions about their perceptions and satisfaction with the program. They can also take tests designed to measure attitudes or moods that might have been affected by the program. Some such tests are described in the next chapter.

The behavior of clients can also be a source of data. For example, satisfaction with a new job-training program might be measured by the percentage of applicants who drop out of the new program as compared to other programs. Or the emotional adjustment of various groups of widows might be measured by the percentage of each group who remarried.

Another important source of data is significant others, that is, those people who are in close contact with the clients—for example, spouses, relatives, or close friends. Under some circumstances their perceptions may have less danger of bias than those of the clients themselves. For example, Ellsworth (1979) developed a multiple-scale measure of the progress of mental health patients to be taken by the spouse or main relative with whom the patient lived after discharge from the hospital.

Finally, program personnel are a source of data. Because program people are often skilled professionals, their perceptions in some ways can have greater validity than the perceptions of either the clients or significant others. On the other hand, they may tend to be biased by their personal involvement in the program.

In addition to collecting data from various sources, evaluators should consider whether multiple measures from each source are necessary or desirable. For example, instead of using an instrument that measures only anxiety, it might be preferable to use an instrument that also provides a measure of depression, fatigue, or confusion (moods sometimes closely associated with anxiety). Or (for example), if evaluators are measuring the effectiveness of a program for the rehabilitation of stroke patients, it might be important to have separate measures for activities of daily living (such as walking, feeding oneself, dressing oneself, and so forth) and for speech skills. Right and left hemiplegics experience qualitatively different damage and can be expected to respond differently to speech therapy than they do to physical therapy. In the evaluation of the rehabilitation program mentioned above, Carey and Posavac (1978) used two scales to measure progress within the hospital and three additional scales to measure progress at home after discharge from the hospital.

Data collection.   Who will handle the day-to-day mechanics of data collection? This will usually involve an on-site coordinator who will keep the program evaluators abreast of the whereabouts of the program clients, personnel, and other sources of data, so that they can be contacted at appropriate times by the evaluation team. This is ordinarily a thankless and tedious task; and the evaluators need a reliable person to handle it.

Data collectors need to be sensitive to the issue of confidentiality. First, confidential information must be kept confidential. If information was obtained with a previous understanding of confidentiality, it should not be released until explicit approval is obtained. Second, the obligation of others to keep information confidential must be respected. Evaluators do not have a right to all information, even when it might have a bearing on the evaluation. Other values may at times conflict with the needs of evaluators. Care must be taken not to ask information from people in a manner they find to be an invasion of privacy.

Choice of statistics.   In any type of evaluation, appropriate statistics that will demonstrate both the level of statistical significance and the magnitude of effects are needed. It is preferable to use statistical procedures that are simple, because the findings will be presented to program sponsors and personnel who often do not have a great deal of mathematical expertise. Nonevaluators should ideally be able to understand and to be convinced by the interpretation of the results; they should not merely be impressed by statistical sophistication. At times multiple-regression analysis and analysis of covariance will be the statistics of choice. However, it is good to keep in mind that nonevaluators will usually be more comfortable with less-complicated statistics. One approach is to use statistical analyses that are as powerful as necessary, but to illustrate the conclusions drawn using percentages or—even better—graphs.

Final report.   Finally, some thought should be given during the planning stage to the format of the final report. Graphs and bar charts are usually preferable to tables of statistics. Where tables of statistics are necessary, they should be kept to a minimum and put in an appendix. It is advisable to rough out a few tables or charts and use some estimated figures to see whether or not the type and amount of data are appropriate for the planned layout. Often a consideration of the style of the report will suggest changes in the plans for data collection and analysis. Chapter 12 is devoted to more complete discussion of evaluation reports.

Step 6: Present a written proposal

After reviewing the literature and thinking through the various methodological considerations outlined in Step 5, the evaluators are ready to prepare a written proposal for presentation to program personnel. The overall purpose is to be certain that the evaluators and program personnel agree on the nature and goals of the program, the type of evaluation desired, the operational measures of the program goals, and the readiness of the program for evaluation. It is psychologically important for the program personnel to fully understand the evaluation process, feel comfortable with it, and (if possible) be enthusiastic about it.

Some issues that were previously discussed during the initial meetings may have to be worked through once again. Program personnel may now see procedural problems that were not at first apparent. It may be necessary to delay the beginning of data collection either because they feel the program is not sufficiently operational to undergo evaluation or because the temporary presence of extraneous factors might interfere with the interpretation of data. For example, if the proposal calls for the collection of data from hospital patients on their reactions to resident physicians who make rounds with attending physicians, it would be advisable to collect this at a time when medical students are not also making rounds with the resident and attending physicians. Otherwise, the patients might confuse the residents with medical students who have not graduated from medical school and are not providing care to patients. The problem can be handled by delaying data collection until the months when the medical students are not present on the floor.

POTENTIAL SOURCES OF RESISTANCE TO PROGRAM EVALUATION

Political and psychological factors can undermine an evaluation project. Some factors are based on genuine concerns, while others are based on misunderstandings of evaluation. Effective evaluators will identify these factors during the planning stage, bring them to the surface promptly, and resolve them gently and directly.

Expectations of a "Slam-Bang" Effect

Program personnel are generally enthusiastic and confident about the potential effects of their program. Because they are enthusiastic and put forth a maximum effort, they expect their new program to have dramatic results—a "slam-bang" effect. They will have a tendency to feel betrayed if evaluators are able to demonstrate only a moderate improvement over the old program. The difficulty can arise when the program that was replaced was already achieving its goals reasonably well, and the new program is expected to improve on the replaced program.

One way to handle the high level of expectation is to help program personnel arrive at some rule of thumb for improvement that can reasonably be expected. For example, if elementary school students are reading at appropriate levels, a new reading program is unlikely to raise their reading levels very much. The sponsors of a new reading program should be satisfied if they raise the reading achievement just a little. Perhaps students will like reading better. Anything beyond that is unrealistic.

There are other reasons why the expected "slam-bang" effect may not occur. Whenever a group of participants is chosen for comparison with a group of participants in a new program, the comparison group will almost always be receiving some kind of service. It is rare that participants in a new program are compared to a group that receives no service at all. When evaluators are comparing two modalities of services, both of which are considered good, it is unlikely that they will find great differences between the treatment group and the comparison group. For example, if a group of psychosomatic patients admitted to a special program in a hospital are compared to psychosomatic patients treated privately by physicians but without the benefit of the special program, both groups should improve—because both groups are receiving professional treatment. Often the value of such a program is better demonstrated by showing that the type of patient treated in the special program is more in need of the services offered and that improvement of equal magnitude is more difficult to attain with severely distressed patients. When this approach is explained to the staff, it may help to lower "slam-bang" expectations.

Self-Styled Experts in Evaluation

Frequently program personnel have had some experience working on a research project. Because of this experience, they may feel attached to a specific evaluation design. For example, they may insist on testing subjects prior to a treatment or new program, while the evaluators feel that a pretest may artificially sensitize the subjects to the treatment to be evaluated.

Self-styled experts may also want to use their own favorite measurement instrument, even when the professional evaluators feel that it will needlessly lengthen a questionnaire they judge to be adequate for measuring the goals of the program. Evaluators are advised to take the time to listen to such suggestions carefully and with an open mind; the ideas may have some merit. If the suggestions seem counterproductive or not feasible, evaluators should be gentle but firm in adhering to the design and measures they feel are appropriate. If evaluators give in to pressure against their better judgment, they will have no one to blame but themselves if the project is poorly executed.

Fear That Evaluations Will Inhibit Innovation

Personnel in human service organizations may worry that evaluation will interfere with innovation by inhibiting them from experimenting with new techniques. In both process and outcome evaluations, the staff may feel that evaluation permits absolutely no variation in the program during the period of data collection. This is partially true insofar as there cannot be major structural changes in the program that would alter the essential goals or nature of the program. However, the need for retaining program identity does not mean that clinicians or program personnel cannot be flexible in the day-to-day operation of the program within broad structural boundaries. Every program will have variability built into it. Evaluation will not limit this. However, it is wise not to attempt to evaluate a program that is just getting started; major changes can occur as staff become clearer about their objectives.

Fear That The Program Will Be Terminated

Although it is seldom true that a negative evaluation will lead to a program's termination, it is possible that an evaluation could result in the curtailment or elimination of a program when results demonstrate that a given approach is not working out as expected. In fact, cost-effectiveness evaluation is specifically concerned with cutting losses in time, effort, and money. However, before sponsors can completely eliminate a program designed to meet a specific problem, they are ordinarily under some pressure to decide what to put in its place. Therefore, it is more likely that an evaluation will result in the reassessment of a program rather than its elimination.

Early in the planning stage, effective evaluators will try to have program personnel view them as valuable and needed associates. Evaluators can often achieve this goal by describing their work in terms of "documenting success." Program sponsors are inclined to demand accountability from program personnel as a condition for funding. Evaluators are there to assist program personnel in fulfilling this obligation to the sponsors.

It is not always possible to dispel the threat of evaluation completely. The reputation of the evaluators for trustworthiness and competence is a valuable asset. One practice that will allay some anxiety is to promise the program personnel that they will see the final draft of a report and be asked for their suggestions and clarifications before it is sent to the sponsors. Nevertheless, evaluators will not be able to eliminate anxiety completely in people who are basically insecure or who have doubts about their own competence. In a good program these persons will be in the minority.

Fear That Information Will Be Abused

In addition to the fear that a program may be terminated, there may exist some concern that information gained about the performance of staff may be abused. Even competent clinicians are rightly concerned about merit reviews, future promotion, and career advancement. Past experience may have taught them to be wary of evaluators who have overstepped the boundaries of program evaluation or who have been careless about maintaining confidences. Once again, being trustworthy is critical in allaying these suspicions. The reputation of evaluators for integrity and for being responsible is the most valuable asset for defusing this suspicion. It is easy to lose trust and hard to regain it once it has been lost. Effective evaluators will not only explicitly try to convey the idea that program evaluation is distinct from individual performance appraisal, but they will carefully avoid speaking or acting in such a way that might even give the appearance that they are engaged in such an activity.

Fear That Qualitative Methods May Be Supplanted

Clinicians, teachers, probation officers, and other service personnel rightly feel that their day-to-day observations are a valuable source of input both for improving the functioning of a program and for evaluating its effect. They may feel that the evaluators' questionnaires, complicated research designs, and statistical techniques are less sensitive than are their own personal observations and evaluations. At times they are right.

However, the point to be made with program personnel is that their input is one very valuable source of evaluation data. Nevertheless, their subjective evaluations can be biased and can be strengthened by both quantitative and qualitative data gathered from other sources. Their subjective observations will be of greatest importance when the data are being interpreted. The ideal is not to eliminate either the quantitative or qualitative approaches but rather to integrate and blend the findings from both methodologies.

Accusations That Evaluation Methods Are Insensitive

Closely allied to the objection that quantitative evaluation methodology devalues subjective observations is the accusation that evaluation designs are insensitive to the intricacies of human services. Program objectives are often varied and complex. Progress is often slow and irregular. For example, a hospital program for psychiatric patients presents a very difficult evaluation project. This is true because it is very difficult to find many persons with exactly the same diagnosis. The severity of the problem often varies widely. Individual goals differ greatly from patient to patient. Behavior considered to be progress for one patient cannot be rated as progress for another. Similar comments could be made about children in educational programs and adults in job-training programs.

There is a good deal of merit in the charge of insensitivity. Evaluators will gain the confidence of managers and staff not only by being aware of this problem but also by articulating this awareness in such a manner that program staff members are reassured that the intricacies of human services have been appropriately addressed. Early in the planning stage, the program personnel can be assured that the evaluation will not begin until they have had the opportunity to carefully review the evaluation proposal and feel comfortable that their concerns in this area have been addressed properly.

Evaluation Drains Program Money

The seven sources of resistance described thus far are focused on various aspects of evaluation but not on the concept of evaluation itself. Two objections to evaluation strike at the very concept of program evaluation. The first objection is that program evaluation drains money that could be spent on direct service. As the statement stands, it is true. However, the main question is whether evaluation can improve service. The alternative to spending money on evaluation is to risk spending money on services that are of doubtful value. Those who present this objection fail to face the reality that the day of accountability has arrived. Today it is hard to find a program funded either by government agencies or by private foundations that does not carry the stipulation that a certain amount of money in the grant be spent on evaluation.

Those who are not convinced by the accountability argument may be convinced by a more pragmatic one: Evaluation research, if done well, may help spread a good idea and may result in attracting more money and resources to a program.

Evaluation Has Little Impact

Some critics of evaluation point out that frequently evaluation has very little impact on programs. There is a good deal of validity to this objection. Evaluators have often been frustrated by seeing their reports set aside and disregarded.

However, evaluators should reflect on the hard reality that evaluation research is not a benign social science activity but rather a political decision-making tool. If relevant, evaluation results will be included among the other factors behind decisions. Because evaluation researchers work in a political context, the results of their work must be timely and relevant to decision making (Cronbach, 1982). Well-designed and carefully executed studies are valuable only when they speak to issues that are important to the organization. When evaluators fail to show how the evaluation is relevant, they have not completed their work.

In spite of the apparent validity of complaints about lack of impact, there is also some evidence that these complaints are overstated. First, evaluation studies have had a cumulative effect in certain areas. For example, the common finding that class size has marginal effects on learning may at first incline one to set aside the factor of class size as being of minimal importance. However, research done on schools in other countries has now shown that the marginal effect of class size holds only within the range of class sizes customarily found in American schools (Berk and Rossi, 1976). Therefore, it sometimes takes time before the significance of evaluation research can be put into perspective.

Second, evaluation research has some long-term value insofar as it challenges conventional wisdom. For example, those who sanctioned and conducted the New Jersey negative income tax experiment boldly tested one of the oldest, most central economic assumptions. Most economists and politicians predicted that even a limited amount of guaranteed income would lead to massive malingering and a loss of motivation to work. The study yielded mixed results, some significantly at odds with expectations. To the extent that the results of the experiment can be generalized to the national low-income population, they indicate that a national program of guaranteed income at the benefit levels considered in this experiment would have only relatively small effects on the labor supply of male family heads (Haveman and Watts, 1976). The potential of evaluation research for challenging conventional wisdom is also illustrated by the Coleman Report (Coleman et al., 1966). This evaluation showed that schools make smaller contributions to the learning of children than does family background.

An unexpected benefit of the apparently limited impact of evaluation on programs has been the shift from summative evaluation to a greater emphasis on formative evaluation. This shift has helped to increase the involvement of evaluators in the planning stages of programs. This new emphasis and orientation of program evaluation is reflected in the subject matter and style of this text. Chapter 5 develops the role of the evaluator in program planning in greater detail.

SUMMARY

Following the six steps in planning an evaluation project serves to get the evaluation off to a good start. Note the steps are suggested to help the evaluator to be responsive to the needs of the people most concerned about the evaluation. Responsive evaluators will have fewer problems with the resistances outlined in the second part of the chapter, compared to evaluators who seem less concerned about stakeholder needs.

STUDY QUESTIONS

1. As an outside consultant you are invited by a large manufacturing plant to evaluate a new training program for managers, called "Management Contact," which you are told applies the principles of transactional analysis to employer-employee relations. Explain the steps you would take and what you would need to know in approaching this job. What would be the major difficulties you would see?

2. You are part of an evaluation team retained by a major university. The chairman of the department of psychology instructs you to evaluate a new section to be established called "Community Psychology." How would you approach this task? What would be the major pitfalls to avoid?

FURTHER READING

RIECKEN, H. W., AND BORUCH, R. F., EDS. 1974. *Social experimentation: A method for planning and evaluating social intervention*, chaps. 6 and 7. New York: Academic Press.

3

Measurement Principles and Tools

The selection of appropriate variables and strategies to measure those variables is of critical importance in designing an evaluation. The authors decided to present this subject here because these principles apply to all the forms of evaluation described in later chapters. The selection of measures is not easy, and a poor choice could reduce an otherwise well-planned evaluation to a futile endeavor. Each approach has advantages and disadvantages; therefore, a measurement approach useful in one evaluation may be inappropriate in another.

SOURCES OF DATA FOR EVALUATIONS

There are six major sources of data relevant to evaluations: (1) the program records; (2) the program participants; (3) the staff delivering the program; (4) family members or other people with significant relationships to the participants; (5) special evaluation teams; and (6) community-level indexes. The characteristics of the program to be evaluated, the questions addressed to the evaluator, and the resources available will determine which sources are used.

The Program Records

A search of the program's records and files, its archives, can provide reliable and inexpensive data for the evaluator. Archival data are most useful when the evaluation includes an examination of client characteristics, types of service provided, workload of the staff members, costs of providing services, or trends across long time intervals. When archival data are objective (for example, number of visits, type of service, or identity of the care giver), the data will be very valid. On the other hand, diagnoses and other subjective entries may not be quite so valid. Furthermore, Krause and Jackson (1983) found that state summary records were quite inaccurate compared to an agency's own records. Two of the most important advantages of archival data are: (1) The measurement process does not affect the program participant; and (2) there can be no participant loss due to refusal or inability to participate. Some aspects of archival searches used as feedback material are discussed at greater length in Chapter 6.

Maintaining confidentiality is a problem that can become acute when using the program's records. Some evaluations using public documents need not be concerned with limiting access to the data. However, many evaluations utilize hospital, personnel, or counselor records that are clearly confidential. Some information in files may even be damaging to a person's social and financial affairs. The inadvertent release of such data might even open evaluators to legal suits. In less sensitive situations evaluators would look unprofessional, and the loss of credibility might result in their being denied access to records the next time it is requested. Evaluators cannot function without access to data.

There are a number of ways in which evaluators can protect the confidentiality of data used in the evaluation. For example, it is not always necessary to identify data by a person's name. At times researchers have used information to identify records that only the clients or patients themselves would recognize. For example, the first name and birthdate of a respondent's mother would provide a code for gathering all of the person's data together without using the person's name. If it might be necessary to contact the respondent in the future, the project director alone should keep a master list of the respondents' names and addresses and the associated code information. Some workers using very sensitive material have stored the names and code information in a different country. Most readers of this text will not be dealing with data that sensitive. For those who find themselves in sensitive positions, more sophisticated methods for guaranteeing confidentiality are discussed by Riecken and Boruch (1974) and by Campbell et al. (1977).

The Program Participants

There are several reasons to look to the program participants for evaluative information. First, the person who actually receives a service is often in an excellent position to evaluate many aspects of the program. The direct contact the clients have with the staff provides them with important knowledge about the program that no one else has. Second, only the clients have access to their own feelings about the program and staff. Third, for many criteria the clients will be the most knowledgeable about their current state, especially at follow-up intervals. Further, they might well be the only available source of information about the use they make of additional follow-up services. A fourth advantage is that the information they provide is often relatively inexpensive to gather. Fifth, self-assessments have been found to be at least as accurate as other assessment approaches for a variety of behavioral and emotional dimensions (Shrauger and Osberg, 1981).

On the other side of the coin, however, certain participants may be too incapacitated to be valid sources of evaluation information. In planning an evaluation of a physical medicine and rehabilitation unit, one will quickly discover that few recent stroke victims can validly describe their own capabilities. Some are unable to talk, others have poor judgment, and others are so crushed emotionally by their impairments that it seems cruel to discuss their problems with them. Certain types of patients seeking psychotherapy cannot provide valid data; however, many others can.

Perhaps participants can provide good data for some aspects of the program but not others. General hospital patients usually know if rooms are clean, whether nurses and resident physicians treat them politely, and how long they have to wait outside the X-ray room. However, they cannot evaluate the choice of medication or the competence of their surgeons.

Evaluators are faced with the task of motivating the program participants to provide personal information about their attitudes and judgments. Participants may refuse to cooperate due to fear of public disclosure of personal information. Routinely, anonymity in the final report is offered. Many people do not understand the social scientist's disinterest in the personal facts about individuals. Nor do they understand the necessity of using overall group averages and proportions in the final report. They are familiar with the case study approach often used in popular newspaper and magazine reports of medical, correctional, counseling, and educational programs. It is not surprising then that some respondents do not believe promises of anonymity. One respondent to a survey administered in a group setting without a way to identify the respondents wrote the following: "I have tried to be honest. I hope I don't lose my job." American society is going through a litigious and suspicious period. Evaluators cannot afford to give respondents cause to question their motives for requesting personal information.

Even when people are not afraid of public disclosure, they must still be motivated to spend time completing the forms and surveys. One approach is to appeal to the person's interest in improving the program being evaluated. Many people are sufficiently altruistic to be willing to share their feelings if they realize that their time can contribute to the improvement of services for others. However, they are not so altruistic that they will spend a long time or struggle with a poorly written survey.

Which program participants are most likely to cooperate? The experience of survey users is that those with the most favorable impressions of a program or facility are the most likely to respond. The 86 percent who responded to a lengthy survey on a chaplaincy internship were independently evaluated by their supervisors as having performed better during the internship year than the 14 percent who did not return the survey (Posavac, 1975).

The Staff

Program staff people are important sources of data for evaluations. Staff members are trained to assess the degree of the participants' impairments and are in a good position to assess improvement. Also, they are the most likely to know how well a program is managed and how well the program runs on a day-to-day basis. On the negative side, staff members can be expected to be biased toward seeing improvement. After committing their efforts to helping people improve their skills or adjustment, it may be hard to accept failure.

Over and above these concerns, the evaluators need to recognize that evaluating a program is in some ways an evaluation of the staff's performance. Few people unhesitatingly welcome an evaluation of the effectiveness of the services they provide. Most people will be concerned about the use to which an evaluation will be put. If they are worried, they will resist the evaluation. Some college professors refuse to permit students conducting course evaluations to enter the classrooms. Some psychotherapists argue that checklists of symptoms and rating forms are blind to the crucial but subtle changes in a client that the therapist alone can sense. Because evaluation is not a developed science with unquestioned techniques (see Cronbach, 1977), it is easy to find weaknesses in the most carefully planned program evaluation. One way to reduce staff resistance is to provide some benefit for the staff as a byproduct of the evaluation of their program. Opportunities for improvement, workshops, and individual guidance, for example, should be tied in with an evaluation, so that it is a learning experience. One must recognize that some evaluations have not been learning experiences. At times evaluators have even neglected to make a presentation to the staff of the program evaluated. Making a presentation to the staff is the least evaluators can do in return for the staff's cooperation.

Significant Others

If a program is designed to change the behavior (counseling and corrective programs) or the health of a person, family members will be affected. They must adjust their own behaviors as patients or clients change. Significant others see the recipients of human services (except for inpatients and prisoners) more frequently than the staff does, and they see the participants in natural settings, not merely in the short-term, artificial setting created by the program. Family members may have biases just as staff members do; however, the direction of these biases may be hard to predict. In a comparison of nurses' ratings with spouses' ratings of the capabilities of stroke patients, we learned that nurses rated the patients as more proficient in performing daily activities (dressing, eating, grooming) than the spouses did. On the other hand, spouses rated the patients as being more proficient in cognitive tasks (speaking, reading, memory) than the nurses did.[1] In any program some family members will report more improvement than actually occurred, while others will report less. Because the focus is on program-level outcomes, not *individual* assessments, these idiosyncratic biases are less important than systematic biases such as those found with the stroke patients.

When requesting information about program participants from significant others, it is necessary to have the participants' permission beforehand. People will vary in their willingness to have spouses or others provide personal information to the evaluation staff. In evaluations of hospitalized psychiatric inpatients, Ellsworth (1979) reports that 21 percent were too incapacitated to give or withhold permission, 19 percent refused to give permission, and 7 percent could not name a significant other to complete the evaluation forms. Therefore, a smaller proportion of the population can be assessed using the ratings of significant others as compared to the proportion who can provide self-ratings. Motivating respondents to cooperate will follow the lines previously mentioned—emphasizing the long-term improvement of the program for others. In seeking permission to contact a patient's or client's significant other, care should be taken that the request does not imply that good treatment in the program is contingent on the person's giving permission for such contact. Further, it is important that permission forms be written at a level that is comprehensible to the program participant. Often these forms are written at a level more suitable for a professional researcher (Gray, Cooke, and Tannenbaum, 1978).

Special Evaluation Teams

A specially trained team knowledgeable in both research techniques and the service skills of the program staff can provide the best evaluation of a program if cost is no object and if the goal is to obtain the least-biased evaluation possible (Endicott and Spitzer, 1975). Certainly, professionals trained in the disciplines most closely related to the type of program being evaluated will be better able to evaluate a program than will evaluators trained primarily in research methods. Also, such appropriately trained but independent evaluators are less likely to "see" improvements than emo-

---

[1]For the interested reader, this finding was explained in the following fashion: Spouses, being familiar with the stroke patient, needed fewer cues for effective communication; like all people, stroke patients tend to perform grooming and self-care types of behaviors at a higher level for strangers than for family members.

tionally involved staff members. However, it is seldom true that money is no object, and usually evaluators would rather produce a useful evaluation with a likelihood of improving the program than the most valid, detailed evaluation theoretically possible. Therefore, data gathered by people who have earned the trust of staff may well lead to evaluations having more potential positive impact on the program and its staff than that obtainable by outside evaluators.

Community Indexes

Some programs are planned to improve community-level variables. Examples of programs designed to influence the community would be a crime-reporting program designed to increase citizen participation in criminal surveillance and to change community-level indexes, such as arrest rates and crime rates; a reading program designed to raise the achievement levels of the children in a school district; and a citizen-developed project to monitor housing code violations that is designed to increase or maintain the quality of the housing in a neighborhood. Jason and Liotta (1982) used number of busy signals, time to answer a telephone call, and seconds on hold as measures of businesses' and community agencies' responsiveness to citizen needs.

The major difficulty with using community-level indexes is that there are many causal links between the program and the hoped-for end result. There are so many variables that may influence arrest rate, quality of housing, or reading level that an effective program may not be detectable. In addition, there are many things that can interfere with the implementation of the program before the community level is reached. An evaluator who uses only community-level indexes in an outcome study may be left quite in the dark about the causes of apparent failure or success.

Which Source Should Be Used?

The choice of sources of data depends on the cost of obtaining data, the type of decision to be made on the basis of the evaluation, the size of the program, and the time available to conduct the evaluation. If a program needs feedback information, it is likely that records, participant attitudes, and family reports may be very helpful. If a decision is planned to expand (or to eliminate) an expensive, controversial program, the judgments and observations of outside experts may be the only source of data that will suffice. Such decisions must be made carefully on the basis of a widely accepted evaluation.

Regardless of the type of program or anticipated decision, evaluators should strive to use multiple measures from more than one source. In choosing multiple measures, it is especially important to select measures that are not likely to share the same biases. For example, a subjective assessment of the success of a program by a client may be mirrored by the subjective feelings of the client's spouse. If, on the other hand, a measure of subjective feelings is used with ratings of ability to function in specific settings or with objective achievement, evaluators are less likely to obtain sets of data with the same biases. When the same implication is drawn from a variety of sources, the evaluation will be treated as having greater credibility.

However, it also is possible that the multiple approaches will not agree. Shipley (1976) conducted an evaluation of a companion program for mentally ill patients. College students served as volunteer companions to discharged psychiatric patients. The volunteers, patients, and hospital staff all subjectively evaluated the program in quite glowing terms. However, more objective measures of the patients' behavior (by staff ratings and by frequency and duration of rehospitalizations) revealed quite *variable* reactions. Some patients apparently benefited, and others did not. His use of multiple measures led Shipley to a conclusion different from those of previous studies using only subjective attitude measures. Sullivan and Snowden (1981) found that staff, clients, standard tests, and agency files did not agree about the problems clients had. Evaluators need to be sensitive to the possibility that their selection of sources of data and of specific measures can lead to misleading conclusions.

The fact that evaluators frequently work with people trained in service delivery techniques, not in research methods, means that evaluators have considerable discretion in choosing the criteria of effectiveness and the analyses of those criteria. Berk (1977), Berk and Rossi (1976), and Zigler and Trickett (1978) go so far as to say that through their choice of variables and methods of analyses, evaluators can determine the results of an evaluation before it is conducted. Thus, to be fair to programs and to the consumers of program evaluations, evaluators must examine their own attitudes as they design an evaluation. Otherwise, their own biases may determine their findings. The following section describes the most important issues to consider when choosing assessment procedures.

PRINCIPLES IN CHOOSING ASSESSMENT PROCEDURES

Evaluators use several criteria in selecting methods of gathering the data required in an evaluation. Keeping these principles in mind while planning a study will save evaluators time and inconvenience later.

Multiple Variables

In the beginning of this chapter, we recommended the use of multiple sources of information. It is also recommended that evaluators use multiple variables from a single source; the elevation of a single variable to be *the* criterion of success will probably corrupt it. A grisly example is the variable "body count" used in daily reports on the Vietnam War. The nature of the war made it hard to claim territorial gains. Thus, dead enemy soldiers were to be counted as a measure of the success of friendly forces. It became apparent that focusing on this variable led to its being inflated by counting every death as that of an enemy, even when those killed were civilians not taking part in the fighting. Barbour and Wolfson (1973) describe the difficulty of defining productivity of police officers. Concentrating on arrests may unintentionally encourage poor practices in gathering evidence necessary for convictions; or police officers may make arrests when the interests of justice would be better served without an arrest, such as in domestic quarrels. Turner (1977) described the effect of a poorly defined criterion for mental health workers who refer clients to other public agencies. The criterion of successful referrals was defined as "90 percent of referred clients actually make contact with the new agency." The evaluator quickly learned that the mental health workers were escorting the individuals to the other agencies. Although the workers were scoring well on the criterion of successful referral—those referred to other agencies did make contact—other aspects of their work were left unfinished.

One way to avoid corrupting the criteria chosen and to avoid distorting the operation of a human service system is to use multiple variables. It is especially important that the variables serve as a check on one another. Thus, *both* arrest rate and conviction rate should be used as the measures of police productivity. Percentage of successful referrals *and* number of clients served should be used as criteria for assessing the work of a mental health worker screening people in need of various services.

Important Variables

Because program evaluation is an applied social science, the variables to be measured must be relevant to the specific informational needs of facility management, community representatives, those responsible for budgets, and others. Thus, in planning an evaluation, evaluators must learn what questions are pressing and are as yet unanswered. The variables to be measured are then chosen on the basis of their importance to the questions facing administrators and program staff.

The time at which a variable is measured may determine whether it provides appropriate information. The impact of educational services can often be assessed at the end of a program. Other human services are provided with the goal of altering the course of a person's life. Thus, the success of a program for juvenile delinquents can be better judged by the degree to which participants stay out of trouble with the law over a period of time. The participant's status at the end of a program is less informative than his or her status three or six months later. Still other programs should be evaluated on the basis of their success over a period of years.

The major way to approach selecting important and relevant variables is through discussions with staff and managers. If there is no decision to be affected by the variable, regardless of its value, or if no program standards mention the variable, then it probably is not important or relevant to the evaluation. If the location of the program participants' homes is not at all important to administrators, evaluators probably will not record it. However, at times evaluators may feel that a variable *should* be important and would be seen as important once summarized. Evaluators should not feel completely limited to recording just the information their clients (program managers and staff) recognize as important. In other chapters we point out specific instances in which information that was not requested came as a surprise to the program staff. Furthermore, unintended negative side effects, which will certainly not be mentioned in program goals, should not be ignored.

Sensitivity to Change

There are two general types of measures of psychological and intellectual variables. One type seeks to assess an individual's general, typical level on some variable, and the other type seeks to assess current mood or achievement. Some writers have called the first type a measure of *trait* (Spielberger, 1972). The other type of measure has been developed to assess effects that trait instruments seek to minimize. Such an instrument is called a measure of *state*. A measure of state seeks to assess the individual's current level on a variable. The extent to which a measure of state is influenced by the individual's typical way of being is defined as a weakness of such a measure.

The distinction between intelligence tests and classroom tests may help to illustrate this point. Before a course few class members are expected to score well on a test covering the course material. However, after the course students are expected to do well if they have mastered the course material. The classroom test should be sensitive to the changes that have occurred in the skills of the students. Fairly stable characteristics of the students (such as intelligence) should not be primary factors leading to differences among the students' classroom test scores. In contrast, stable characteristics are expected to lie behind the differences obtained using standard intelligence tests. Although intelligence is certainly not fixed and does change in response to many environmental influences, the developers of intelligence tests sought to find test items that were minimally influenced by the individual's mood and immediate situation. It is not possible for a test to be completely unaffected by a person's habitual way of acting prior to entering the program; however, when measuring program outcome, the goal is to use instruments least affected by stable prior conditions and thus most likely to detect real changes in participants.

Evaluators usually choose measures of program output that are maximally sensitive to change, because change is what evaluators are trying to detect. This point is especially important in the evaluation of various forms of psychotherapy; therapists, who are so familiar with standardized personality tests, often approach program evaluation in the same manner as they approach individual client assessment. Individual assessment instruments are designed to measure personality and intelligence traits. Tests that show marked sensitivity to situational differences are not desirable for personality and intelligence measurement. In contrast, evaluators want a measurement instrument that is sensitive to respondents' current (hopefully improved) state. Using a trait measure to detect change puts the program at a considerable disadvantage by needlessly raising the probability of overlooking the change that did in fact occur.

A final point about sensitivity to change was alluded to in the previous chapter—very good performance is hard to improve. Just as it is harder to go from an *A* to a perfect paper than it is to go from a *C* to a *C+*, it is hard to improve a program participant's condition or level of satisfaction if the program is already fairly effective and well received.

Criteria of success in such a setting cannot change much. Evaluations dependent on detecting such small changes will usually conclude that the innovative program is no better than the old one, even when the innovative program is indeed better. There are statistical approaches to dealing with such situations; however, they are beyond the scope of this text.

Valid Measures

In an evaluation the instruments must validly measure the behaviors the program is designed to change. These behaviors may be the ultimate criteria behaviors (such as long life, better adjustment, employment) or more immediate behaviors that are believed to be useful in achieving the planned long-term outcomes (such as higher quality work and improved leadership practices).

In order to assure themselves of the validity of chosen measures, evaluators should share the measures with the program staff. If staff members have not approved the measures, they may later disown a negative evaluation as being based on invalid tools. Implementation of suggestions for program change may be strongly resisted if staff members did not share in the choice of instruments. However, evaluators must not depend totally on the staff members to suggest the measures, because program staff members are often inexperienced in social science methodology.

In general, any measurement tool will be more likely to have acceptable validity if the tool focuses on objective behavior rather than on undefined or vague terms. Objective behaviors (such as "late to work less than one day out of the week" or "speaks in groups") are more likely to be measured validly than less precise phrases (such as "is punctual" or "is assertive"), regardless of what specific measurement approach is chosen. Mager (1972) presents an informal but thorough discussion of the usefulness of behavioral criteria rather than personality trait words in specifying the achievement of a goal.

Some variables may appear to be valid when in fact they are very misleading. Campbell (1969) presented several measures of the frequencies of types of crime in Chicago plotted over time. In 1957 a liberal, highly regarded person was installed as chief of police. The year after his term began, official statistics on the number of thefts under $50 increased dramatically. Did the new chief cause a crime wave? Not likely. Instead, his reforms led to a more thorough reporting of crime and perhaps some reclassification of crimes. A check on the interpretation that the chief caused a crime wave was provided by the homicide rate. Homicides seldom go unreported and cannot be reclassified into a different crime category. When frequency of homicides was plotted over time, there was no noticeable change after the chief began. A very similar increase in crime statistics in Chicago occurred in the early months of 1983, when reporting standards were again improved ("Good news," 1983). Evaluators try to select and interpret variables carefully in order to avoid a misleading conclusion based on a poor choice of performance criteria.

Reliable Measures

Social behaviors cannot be measured perfectly, because such measurements are affected by the respondent's mood, attitude, and understanding of directions—things that are extraneous to the behavior of interest. The degree to which people who are theoretically equivalent on a social variable such as depression actually score the same on a test is the test's reliability. In somewhat oversimplified terms, a reliable test will yield much the same values if administered twice within a short period of time. Reliability, like validity, is higher if the scores are minimally influenced by the passing mood of the person completing the instrument, whether that person is a program participant, staff member, or evaluator.

Variables referring to objective information and behavior are likely to be more reliable than subjective ratings or opinions. This does not mean to imply that ratings should never be used. We simply want to stress that it is harder to judge whether people are, for example, ambitious, than to record whether they have found jobs or have been promoted at work. Subjective ratings are usually less reliable being influenced not only by the behavior of the person being rated but also by the person doing the ratings.

Evaluators must appreciate the differences between the use of measures to estimate the general level of a *group* on some variable and their use to assess an *individual* on the variable. The greater the number of individuals whose responses are combined to estimate the level of the group, the more stable the estimate. Thus, surveys, and other forms of measurement that would be rejected as insufficiently reliable to assess the views or behaviors of individuals may be very useful as measures of a group's views or behaviors. The following paragraphs illustrate the importance of the difference between estimating an individual's score and a group's score.

By using the standard deviation of a test and its reliability, it is possible to calculate a range of values that is likely to include the individual's true score. For example, assume that a person scored 105 on an IQ test with a standard deviation of 15 and a reliability of .95. The true scores of 68 percent of the people getting 105 will be between $105 \pm 15 \sqrt{1 - .95}$, or between 101.6 and 108.4. The standard deviation times the square root of 1 minus the reliability is called the *standard error of estimate* and is applied when an *individual's* score is the question of interest (see Brown, 1976).

On the other hand, when a *group's* mean score is to be estimated, the *standard error of the mean* is the statistic to be used, instead of the standard deviation as in the calculation given above. If a group of 100 people scored an average of 105 on the IQ test, the standard error of the mean is $15/\sqrt{100}$, or 1.5. We can conclude that 68 percent of such *groups* have true mean scores of between $105 \pm 15 \sqrt{1 - .95}$, or between 104.7 and 105.3. Compare this range with the range calculated in the previous paragraph. Even a measure with a reliability of only .40 would yield a sufficiently precise group estimate, although a test with such a low reliability would be inappropriate for use with individuals.[2]

There are a variety of reliability indexes that are reported in test manuals. Some are very relevant to evaluation work, and others are not useful for evaluators. The classic *test-retest* approach to reliability is not as important to evaluation as it is to the area of psychological assessment. The reason for this was alluded to in the section on sensitivity to change. Tests that are developed to be stable over time measure well-entrenched, habitual behaviors and are precisely the sort of tests evaluators do not want. Evaluators require measures of behaviors that are subject to change.

Split-half reliability, which is found by correlating the scores respondents earned on the odd-numbered test items with the scores earned on the even-numbered test items, is quite important to evaluators. Split-half reliability gauges the extent to which a psychological measure is homogeneous, that is, sensitive to one concept or characteristic rather than to a mixture of things. If a reading program is to be evaluated, the instrument to measure reading achievement should not include items requiring broad general knowledge or quantitative skills.

Evaluators must also look for *interrater reliability,* that is, agreement be-

---

[2]Readers wishing more details on these points should examine an introductory statistics text, such as McCall (1975), and a testing text, such as Brown (1976).

tween independent raters. Often the criteria of success of a program include ratings made by professionals or relatives. An instrument that yields similar ratings when used by different observers is usually better than one that yields quite different values. Obviously, if the observers view the rated individuals in very different situations—at home versus in school—low interrater reliability may tell us more about the differences in situations than about the reliabilities of the ratings.

Nonreactive Measures

The mere act of requesting information from people or observing people can influence the behavior being studied. Measurement instruments will create questions that some people have never considered before. Raising the issue may make people more aware of things they previously ignored. The test itself will bore some respondents, offend some, and please others. The greater the behavioral change created by the measurement instrument, the greater its *reactivity*. Measuring the effect of human services is not at all similar to making physical measurements of inanimate objects.

Usually evaluators do not want to select measurement procedures that influence the people studied. If the instruments have an impact, the evaluation loses some of its usefulness, because the outcomes may be different once the instruments are no longer used. Completely nonreactive measurement is an ideal seldom actually achieved. An extended discussion of reactivity has been prepared by Webb et al. (1981).

At times a tool becomes part of the program not only because it provides data but also because it influences those concerned to follow correct procedures; or it raises questions that need to be answered if the program is to be a success. Figure 7.3 is an example of an evaluation tool designed to cause staff members to do certain things that were previously overlooked. If the staff members serving alcoholics responsibly complete the form, they will not only provide evaluation data for the state board but will also be fulfilling crucial steps in the ideal treatment of alcoholics.

Cost-Effective Measures

In planning a program evaluation, the cost of the test materials and the costs of gathering data must not be forgotten. It is necessary to select instruments that will measure the required variables within acceptable cost limits. Several principles are usually true. First, time and money invested in making test materials attractive and easy to use will be repaid in higher response rates. Second, money spent on published forms will be small relative to the costs of the evaluation staff in collecting and analyzing the data. Third, because interviews cost far more than do other measurement approaches, they are not used unless the potential respondents are unable to use written material, need prompting or encouragement to respond, will not respond to written surveys, or may be expected to be defensive or misleading in answering written surveys. Interviews are also useful because the interviewer can rephrase questions or select new questions depending on the respondents' answers; however, this flexibility raises the cost of the evaluation.

Fourth, the effect of the instruments on participant loss must be considered. No participant would be lost to the research in a study of the program's records. Many participants, on the other hand, will be lost if a lengthy survey is mailed to people after they have left the program. Thus, an instrument that is itself inexpensive may not be cost effective (1) if evaluators must spend a considerable amount of time following up on many tardy respondents; or (2) if so few respond that the results are not representative of any group.

TYPES OF MEASURES

Evaluators employ several general types of measures. The major distinction among the approaches is the degree to which they depend on self-reported impressions versus objective observations. The principles just introduced will be used to describe the strengths and weaknesses of the approaches presented.

Written Surveys Completed
by Program Participants

Probably the most widely used technique for evaluating programs is the written survey. The survey technique provides the most information per dollar or hour investment by the evaluation staff. Surveys are not expensive to reproduce or to buy. If they are complex and especially constructed for a particular evaluation, their cost will be higher. (Guidelines for writing survey items will be discussed later in this chapter.)

Surveys vary greatly in their reliability and validity because the topics they cover are so different. A survey asking former clients to give a global, subjective evaluation of their experience in therapy will not be highly reliable; responses will vary with the moods of the people responding or with the particular aspect of the service they think about. Similarly, students' evaluations of teachers may be influenced by whether a difficult assignment is due soon or whether test results have just been returned. On the other hand, a survey may yield quite reliable judgments if it focuses on current behavior, such as jobs held, further treatment sought, source of referral, and so on. Many of these same remarks apply to the validity of surveys as well. The more objective the material evaluators request, the more likely that responses will be valid estimates of the issue in question.

The loss of participants to the evaluation may be large if the samples are mobile, if the survey is long, or if the participants feel ambivalent toward the program. Evaluators must be prepared to follow up a mailed survey with reminder letters or phone calls to those who do not return the survey within two weeks (Anderson and Berdie, 1975). If only a minority of the sample returns a survey, the responses of the whole sample cannot be estimated. Certainly, receiving returns from fewer than 50 percent of the sample makes the survey useless for many purposes—but not for all purposes, as will be mentioned later.

Regardless of how the survey is to be used, those who do not respond will still be different from those who return the survey. In one study the 66 percent who returned a survey about their experience in outpatient counseling participated in an average of 20.2 counseling sessions, and those who did not respond participated in an average of only 9.5 sessions (Posavac and Hartung, 1977). Experienced survey users expect to find such differences and recognize the limitations these differences impose on the certainty with which conclusions may be drawn.

Ratings of the Program
Participants by Others

Ratings by people important in the program participants' lives can be used as measures of program success. As with surveys, ratings made by significant others may be very reliable if they focus on relatively objective behavior, such as absenteeism, participation in discussions, or physical health. On the other hand, they may be unreliable if they focus on undefined and vague variables, such as adjustment or success in the program. Our experience with forms mailed to spouses indicates that the return rate for forms mailed to significant others is similar to that of mailed self-report surveys.

The cost of ratings may be high if professional staff members are expected to perform numerous or detailed ratings. If ratings are done by nonprofessionals and are kept brief, the cost may be acceptably low. Who is expected to do the ratings will be related to how complete the data will be. Members of the evaluation team will probably complete nearly all the ratings planned; however, significant others may resent the intrusion of the team, and professional staff members may feel that the ratings are an oversimplification of their professional judgment. The best that evaluators can do is to keep the rating form easy to use and to stress that the focus of the study is to obtain documentation of program effectiveness—not information on personal affairs. If people are willing to take a long-range view, they will see that they have an ultimate self-interest in improving program effectiveness.

Interviews

Gathering evaluative information by personal interview is useful when evaluators need to develop an understanding of the program, when they want to obtain information from people with unique information, or when they are not at all sure what is most important to interviewees (Guba and Lincoln, 1981). Since interviewing is an expensive way to gather data, it is not done unless it is necessary. Interviewing is not simply shooting the breeze with program clients or staff. It is a difficult job that requires considerable preparation. The interviewer seeks to find a convenient time to talk with the potential respondent. Good interviewers are thoroughly familiar with the questions to be used in the interview sessions. Effective interviewers dress and act in ways that put the interviewee at ease and encourage comments and elaboration. The value-neutral reactions shown by television and radio reporters during extended interviews done to allow the newsmaker to give his or her side of a story can serve as a model for beginning interviewers. One technique used to verify that one understands an answer is to rephrase it in one's own words. Often asking for correction or affirmation while rephrasing an answer will help clarify the interviewee's own thoughts and lead to further elaboration.

The single most crucial error in planning interviews is to prepare questions that can be answered with a "Yes/No" or other dichotomous answer. Patton (1980) presented a dialogue between a parent and a teenager which illustrated how dichotomous questions can defeat attempts at communication. The parent asked a number of questions about the movie the teenager had gone to see but learned almost nothing about the teenager's evening. Instead of asking "Did you like it?" the parent could have asked "What did you like about it?" Patton points out that while in everyday conversation we often elaborate on the answers we give to dichotomous questions, in the interview setting people are more likely to answer the question just as it was asked. When preparing interview questions, always ask yourself: If the interviewee answers this question in a literal fashion, will I learn what I want to know?

An alternative to interviewing a participant face to face is a telephone interview. The cost of a telephone interview is much lower, and research indicates that the material obtained is of nearly equal validity (*ISR Newsletter*, 1978). A letter received before the telephone call explaining the need for the study and requesting cooperation may improve a respondent's receptivity.

Behavioral Observations

Probably the method with the most potential for providing valid information is the behavioral observation approach. The ultimate outcome of any program is expected to be behavioral change. Examples include better ways of handling anger, better performance on the job, or ability to write a theme. The goals of a program are often difficult to translate into behavioral terms, and people are usually unavailable for observations. However, when the behaviors are public, observations may be feasible. Actual seat belt usage was measured by observers at stop signs and stop lights in an evaluation of a television advertising campaign to increase the proportion of passenger-car users who use their seat belts (Robertson et al., 1974). Actual observation of the behavior expected to be changed produces an evaluation of high credibility.

Achievement Tests

In conducting evaluations of educational programs, measuring cognitive and intellectual achievement will frequently be the method of choice. Evaluators of educational programs have a valuable resource in achievement tests. Achievement tests with high reliability are well developed and are widely accepted in educational settings (Anastasi, 1982). There is some concern about whether standard achievement tests validly measure the goals of some educational programs; however, these criticisms are mild compared to debate about measures of emotional state (Waskow and Perloff, 1975). When educational programs are assigned goals that include the development of both academic and social skills (see, for example, Datta, 1976b), evaluations of the outcome of educational programs cannot depend solely on achievement test scores.

STANDARD VERSUS
SPECIALLY CONSTRUCTED
INSTRUMENTS

Evaluators must decide whether to search for a standard instrument to measure the achievement of program goals or whether to prepare an instrument especially for a given evaluation. This choice is of most relevance to evaluators working in the areas of mental health and education, where many standard measures are available. Evaluators in criminal justice, administrative services, or industrial settings may have less opportunity to use published measures.

Published Measures

Standard, published measures can be easily obtained, have probably been prepared more thoroughly than an individual evaluator can afford to do, and have been administered widely enough to have obtained norms. If evaluators have access to norms, the material gathered from program participants will be much more easily understood. This is especially true when similar groups of people not receiving the program are unavailable.

Waskow and Perloff (1975) prepared a description of the best set of change measures for use in mental health settings. For the most part these are published, validated measures specifically developed to measure change brought about by psychotherapy. In order to illustrate several types of measures, a few are discussed below.

Personal adjustment and role skills scales (PARS). Ellsworth (1975) has developed a set of scales that can be used to evaluate the outcome of mental health care. PARS was developed for use by a person who lives in the client's family. A spouse would be the most knowledgeable rater, but an adult son or daughter or a parent would certainly be quite acceptable. Pretreatment and posttreatment forms for both males and females are available. Ellsworth has recently developed a children's form of the PARS. A sample of items from the PARS is given in Figure 3.1. The items are oriented towards behaviors, not diagnoses.

One unique feature of the PARS is the development of change norms. Ellsworth has obtained PARS ratings of inpatients and outpatients at the beginning and ninety days after the end of psychotherapy. For people with a specific pretherapy PARS rating, the change norms indicate how much change can be expected on the average. Using change norms, an evaluator can determine the extent of improvement without testing comparison groups. In essence, the norms provide information about a comparison group for users without access to people not in the program. The change norms also permit the comparison of types of treatment, therapists, or facilities, using the degree of improvement achieved by the clients receiving different forms of treatment.

Global level-of-functioning scales. A general rating scale for assessing degree of overall psychological health is useful for mental health program evaluation. An unnamed measure of function has been recommended by Carter and Newman (1976) for routine use in counseling or mental health centers. The scale provides nine levels of function, as shown in Figure 3.2. Instructions for using the scale are given by Carter and Newman (1976). The advantage of this simple nine-level scale is that once a clinician is familiar with the scale, it can be completed very quickly. Such a single-rating measure would not be sufficiently reliable for use as an individual assessment tool; however, for a program evaluation in which the ratings of many clients made by many clinicians are to be averaged, the instrument is quite adequate.

Although the scale in Figure 3.2 was prepared for a mental health setting, the principles used in constructing this scale apply to many other settings as well. The crucial characteristic is the development of behaviorally defined levels of function. For example, in a vocational setting a useful rating might concern how much supervision a trainee requires. A level of 1 might indicate that the trainee needs constant supervision with continuous

INSTRUCTIONS:

A. Please describe the person's community adjustment <u>during the past month</u> by answering each question below.

B. Please answer <u>every</u> question even though you might feel unsure of your answer.

C. Mark your answer to each question by making an X in the box under your answer choice, like this:

| X |

	Answer choices			
<u>DURING LAST MONTH</u>, <u>HAS SHE</u> . . .	1 Rarely	2 Some- times	3 Usually	4 Always
1 . . . Shown consideration for you. <u>Mark one answer</u> <u>for each question</u>	☐	☐	☐	☐
2 . . . Shown interest in what you say (mark one answer)	☐	☐	☐	☐
3 . . . Been able to talk it through when angry	☐	☐	☐	☐
4 . . . Shown affection toward you	☐	☐	☐	☐
5 . . . Gotten along with family members	☐	☐	☐	☐

	Answer choices			
<u>DURING LAST MONTH</u>, <u>HAS SHE</u> . . .	1 Almost Never	2 Some- times	3 Often	4 Almost Always
6 . . . Acted restless and tense	☐	☐	☐	☐
7 . . . Said things looked discouraging or hopeless	☐	☐	☐	☐
8 . . . Had difficulty falling or remaining asleep	☐	☐	☐	☐
9 . . . Been nervous	☐	☐	☐	☐
10 . . . Talked about being afraid	☐	☐	☐	☐

FIGURE 3.1 Selected items from the Personal Adjustment and Role Skills Scale, Female Pretreatment Form. (Reproduced by permission of Institute for Program Evaluation, Inc. Copyright 1974 by IPEV, Inc.)

oral instructions to complete the job. The highest rating might be given when the trainee can complete the job independently and can even handle major problems without assistance.

Preparing Special Measures

The major disadvantages of published measures are easy to imagine. The program being studied may have goals and purposes not related to any currently published material. For example, there are relatively few special hospital units specifically for nonterminal cancer patients. When the authors were asked to design materials to measure patient reaction to such a new unit, we found little in the literature to help. Once the evaluators have decided that no existing measure is appropriate, a new instrument must be prepared. However, evaluators must be realistic about how much time they can afford to put into the construction of new instruments. The time pressure of work in service settings precludes the routine development of innovative research instruments.

The format of a survey.   The format of a survey will be an important factor in gaining the cooperation of respondents, analyzing the data, and interpreting the results. If the survey is to be self-administered, the layout must be attractive, uncluttered, and easy to use. A structured answer format is preferable to an open-ended question approach. If a structured survey format is adopted, the survey might still be cluttered if the questions each have different response alternatives. For example, mixing "Yes" and "No" questions, "Agree-Neutral-Disagree" attitude statements, and "Frequently-Seldom-Never" reports of past behavior will make the survey harder to complete. The greater the proportion of questions that can be answered in the same answer format, the better. Figure 3.3 contains an example of a specially prepared survey that violates good practices. The respondents must repeatedly figure out what type of answer is required of them. People inexperienced in preparing surveys often construct surveys that are difficult to use. Figure 3.4, in contrast, would be easy to complete. The degree of difficulty experienced in completing a survey will affect the proportion of respondents who will complete it. Not only does a standard response format encourage a greater response rate, but it also increases the ease with which the results can be presented and interpreted; since the results can be summarized on one table, comparisons can easily be made among survey items. The use of an unnecessary variety of response formats can cause as much confusion for readers of a report as it does for respondents to a survey.

When an evaluator seeks the actual words of program participants, and when the range of possible reactions are not known, surveys using open-ended questions are often useful. Patton (1980) used both a structured answer format survey and open-ended questions in evaluating an ed-

I. Overview of Scale

The scale is used to describe a client's overall ability to function autonomously in the community. A scale rating is assigned *at the time of every clinical encounter* by balancing the relative contributions of four criteria as they affect a person's overall ability to function autonomously:

1. Personal self-care
2. Social functioning in ordinary social unit and in the general community
3. Vocational and/or educational productivity
4. Evidence of emotional stability and stress tolerance

Dysfunctioning in any one or more of the four areas could affect a person's overall ability to function autonomously.

II. Some Details Describing the Four Criteria

The criteria should always be translated to fit the age bracket and circumstances of the individual. Special notes are indicated below where such considerations may be necessary.

1. Personal Self-Care (for children, adjust to age level)
   a. Personal maintenance of washing, dressing, eating, elimination chores
   b. Ability to recognize and avoid common dangers
   c. Taking responsibility for own maintenance, e.g., caring for own room, personal belongings, daily schedule, personal finances, selecting own clothing and accessories

2. Social Functioning (adjust by age, living conditions, and possibly by community)
   a. *Familiar*—the degree to which those familiar with the person, particularly those in the ordinary social unit (family, roommate, boarding house residents) can tolerate and interact with the person, i.e., jointly socialize and/or participate in recreational activities with the person
   b. *Impersonal*—the degree to which relative strangers can interact with the person and vice versa, e.g., store clerks, policemen, or others encountered in ordinary vocational or recreational activities

3. Vocational and/or Educational Functioning
   a. *Working Adults*
      (1) The ability to support one's self and one's dependents
      (2) The ability to meet the demands and pressures of one's chosen (or present) vocation, be it lawyer or janitor
   b. *Homemakers and/or Parents and/or Elderly Persons*
      (1) The ability to organize and/or monitor the daily routines of the household, e.g., meals, child care, washing, etc.
      (2) The ability to organize, maintain and/or monitor family budgeting, shopping, social and/or recreational activities
   c. *Children*
      (1) Should be considered by general age categories of 0–5, 6–11, 12–14, 15–18
      (2) Play and social activities such that constructive and productive social learning can occur
      (3) Educational activities and performance such as would be expected of that age

FIGURE 3.2 A global rating scale of psychological functioning developed by the Central Montgomery Mental Health and Mental Retardation Center, Norristown, Pennsylvania. (Reproduced from Carter and Newman, 1976.)

4. Evidence of Emotional Stability and Stress Tolerance
   a. The degree to which the symptom(s) reflects personality disorganization of such degree that the symptoms and the accompanying disorganization cause discomfort to whomever the person ordinarily interacts with.
   b. The degree to which the person can tolerate the amount of expected daily variation in *present* social, vocational and/or educational realms.

III. Definition of the Nine Scale Levels of Functioning

With regard to the balance of the four criteria (personal self-care, social, vocational/educational, and emotional symptoms/stress tolerance), the person's ability to function autonomously in the community is at Level X, where X can assume one of the following nine (9) levels:

LEVEL 1: Dysfunctional in all four areas and is almost totally dependent upon others to provide a supportive protective environment.

LEVEL 2: Not working; ordinary social unit cannot or will not tolerate the person; can perform minimal self-care functions but cannot assume most responsibilities or tolerate social encounters beyond restrictive settings (e.g., in group, play, or occupational therapy).

LEVEL 3: Not working; probably living in ordinary social unit but not without considerable strain on the person and/or on others in the household. Symptoms are such that movement in the community should be restricted or supervised.

LEVEL 4: Probably not working, although may be capable of working in a very protective setting; able to live in ordinary social unit and contribute to the daily routine of the household; can assume responsibility for all personal self-care matters; stressful social encounters ought to be avoided or carefully supervised.

LEVEL 5: Emotional stability and stress tolerance are sufficiently low that successful functioning in the social and/or vocational/educational realms is marginal. The person is barely able to hold on to either job or social unit, or both, without direct therapeutic intervention and a diminution of conflicts in either or both realms.

LEVEL 6: The person's vocational and/or social areas of functioning are stabilized, but only because of direct therapeutic intervention. Symptom presence and severity are probably sufficient to be both noticeable and somewhat disconcerting to the client and/or to those around the client in daily contact.

LEVEL 7: The person is functioning and coping well socially and vocationally (educationally); however, symptom reoccurrences are sufficiently frequent to necessitate some sort of regular therapeutic intervention.

LEVEL 8: Functioning well in all areas with little evidence of distress present. However, a history of symptom reoccurrence suggests periodic correspondence with the Center; e.g., a client may receive a medication check from a family physician, who then contacts the Center monthly, or the client returns for bi-monthly social activities.

LEVEL 9: The person is functioning well in all areas and no contact with the MH/MR services is recommended.

NOTE: Levels 5 through 8 describe persons who are usually functioning satisfactorily in the community, but for whom problems in one or more of the criteria areas force some degree of dependency on a form of therapeutic intervention.

```
┌─────────────────────────────────────────────────────────────────────┐
│ High School Evaluation Form                                         │
│                                                                     │
│ 1.    How do you like attending your high school? (Circle one.)     │
│                                                                     │
│ Very Much      Much        OK          Little       Not at all      │
│     1           2           3            4              5            │
│                                                                     │
│ 2.    How would you describe your teachers? (Check one)             │
│                                                                     │
│       ____ 1. Mostly excellent      ____ 4. Mostly marginal         │
│       ____ 2. Mostly good           ____ 5. Mostly Poor             │
│       ____ 3. Half good/half marginal                              │
│                                                                     │
│ 3. To what extent would you agree with the following statement: The physical │
│    facilities of my high school (classrooms, halls, gym, lunchroom, etc.) are │
│    good.                                                            │
│                                                                     │
│    Strongly      Disagree    Neutral      Agree      Strongly       │
│    disagree                                          agree          │
│                                                                     │
│ 4. Are your teachers good teachers and willing to talk with students after │
│    regular classes?    Yes _____    No _____                     │
│                                                                     │
│ 5. What is the place of interscholastic team competition in your school? │
│                                                                     │
│    _____ Not at all important                                     │
│    _____ Very important                                           │
│    _____ Not sure                                                 │
└─────────────────────────────────────────────────────────────────────┘
```

FIGURE 3.3 Example of survey items violating many of the principles of easy-to-use, self-administered surveys.

ucational setting. The actual words of the respondents were presented in a way that made it impossible to ignore the unavoidably dry statistical summary of the closed-ended survey questions. At other times evaluators use open-ended questions because they do not know what specific questions to ask. Requesting personal reactions or suggestions for change are two instances in which evaluators do not want to restrict respondents' answers in any way. It is time consuming to categorize and summarize free-form answers. Potential users of open-ended questions should consult materials on qualitative methods (Guba and Lincoln, 1981; Patton, 1980) for detailed directions on analyzing these answers.

Preparing survey items. There are a number of useful guidelines for preparing survey items. The most important principle is to remember who is going to respond to the items. A statement that is clear to an evaluator may not be clear to someone reading it from a very different vantage point. Questions that have the best chance of being understood will be written clearly, simply, and briefly. Such statements cannot be prepared in one sit-

After leaving the hospital, some coronary patients have questions about their physical condition, recovery, recommended changes in diet, exercise, and/or smoking habits.

Please indicate if you feel you would like *more information* on any of the following topics. Circle your answers.

How much additional information do you want about these topics?	Does not apply	None	A little more	Some more	Much more
1. Cholestrol restrictions	DNA	N	L	S	M
2. Salt restrictions	DNA	N	L	S	M
3. Recommended weight loss	DNA	N	L	S	M
4. My medications	DNA	N	L	S	M
5. Restrictions on alcohol use	DNA	N	L	S	M
6. Sexual activity	DNA	N	L	S	M
7. Smoking	DNA	N	L	S	M
8. A good exercise program	DNA	N	L	S	M
9. Excessive emotional stress	DNA	N	L	S	M
10. Handling stress	DNA	N	L	S	M
11. Understanding of my heart attack	DNA	N	L	S	M
12. Anxiety	DNA	N	L	S	M
13. Depression	DNA	N	L	S	M
14. Other _____ (Please specify)			L	S	M

A coronary patient faces many potential problems during the period of convalescence. Which issues did you encounter and how difficult was your adjustment? Circle your answers.

How much difficulty did (or do) you experience over these potential problems?	Does not apply	None	Little	Some	Much
1. Going back to work	DNA	N	L	S	M
2. Sexual activity	DNA	N	L	S	M
3. Smoking	DNA	N	L	S	M
4. Diet	DNA	N	L	S	M
5. Anxiety	DNA	N	L	S	M
6. Depression	DNA	N	L	S	M
7. Activity restrictions	DNA	N	L	S	M
8. Understanding my doctor	DNA	N	L	S	M
9. My spouse's reaction to my health	DNA	N	L	S	M
10. My family's reaction to my health	DNA	N	L	S	M
11. Other _____ (Please specify)			L	S	M

FIGURE 3.4 A section of a self-administered needs-assessment survey that is easy to use because standard alternatives are provided for each item.

ting. On the contrary, they must be written, scrutinized, criticized, rewritten, pretested, and rewritten. Items written one week will not seem as acceptable the following week. If the first draft cannot be improved, evaluators have not learned to criticize their own work.

There are several characteristics of clear survey items. The items should avoid negatives. Negatively worded sentences take more effort to read and are misunderstood more frequently than positively worded sentences. Double negatives are especially difficult to read. Well-written items use short, common words rather than less common or longer words. Good survey items focus on one issue. An item such as "My physical therapist was polite and competent" combines two issues. In this case it is possible to interpret an affirmative answer but not possible to interpret a negative answer. What should the director of the unit do if many people answer negatively—have a workshop on charm or on the latest physical therapy practices? Finally, we urge that survey items be grammatically correct.

Several practices can help to detect survey items that need improving. First, the sentence should be read aloud. Often awkward phrasing is more obvious when read aloud than when simply silently reviewed. Second, someone on the program staff should read the draft items. Third, evaluators should think critically of how to interpret each possible answer to the item. As mentioned above, sometimes one answer can be interpreted but another cannot. Fourth, if ambiguities remain, they will probably be detected if the revised draft is administered as an interview with several people from the population to be sampled.

SUMMARY

The most important concept in this chapter concerns the use of multiple measures from multiple sources. The use of multiple sources of information is one of the basic characteristics of valid and useful evaluations. When choosing measures of variables, evaluators should use the criteria of a good measurement instrument to evaluate the specific instruments selected. Is something *important* being measured? Is the measure *sensitive to change,* even small changes? Does the measure seem *valid, reliable,* and *cost effective*? Is *reactivity* to the instrument a problem?

STUDY QUESTIONS

1. The following questions violate some of the characteristics of well-phrased survey items. Improve the wording or the structured options of these questions.
    a. Would you like to continue receiving counseling at the ABC Mental Health Center? _____ Yes _____ No

    b.   Is the warmth of the staff an important reason for your continued participation in the XYZ Center? _____ Yes _____ No

    c.   Please rate the quality of the care you received in the recovery room after your recent surgery.

        _____ Excellent _____ Good _____ Fair _____ Poor

    d.   Police officers do not really care about the feelings of the victims of a crime.

        _____ Strongly Agree _____ Agree _____ Disagree _____ Strongly Disagree

    e.   The times that services are available during the day should be extended because people are waiting too long for appointments. _____ Yes _____ No

2.   Rewrite the items in Figure 3.3 so that they have a common response format.

3.   In planning an evaluation of the ALPHA County Community Mental Health Center, the Freudian counselors insist that the Rorschach Inkblot Test be administered at one-month intervals to current clients. What would your reaction be to this proposal?

4.   When an evaluation of clinical services was planned, the evaluator introduced the level-of-functioning scale given in Figure 3.2. Some clinicians resisted this suggestion by saying that the scale merely refers to coping behaviors, *not* to intrapsychic growth. What would you respond?

5.   Suppose someone looks up the reliability of an assessment scale and correctly reports that it is .76. The conclusion is then drawn that because .76 is too low for reliable individual psychological assessment, the scale should not be used for program evaluation purposes. Does this conclusion logically follow? How can an evaluator answer this objection?

FURTHER READING

NUNNALLY, J. C., AND DURHAM, R. L. 1975. Validity, reliability, and special problems of measurement in evaluation research. In *Handbook of evaluation research*, vol. 1., ed. E. L. Struening and M. Guttentag, chap. 10. Beverly Hills, Calif.: Sage.

NUNNALLY, J. C., AND WILSON, W. H. 1975. Method and theory for developing measures in evaluation research. In *Handbook of evaluation research*, vol. 1, ed. E. L. Struening and M. Guttentag, chap. 9. Beverly Hills, Calif.: Sage.

SUDMAN, S., AND BRADBURN, N. M. 1982. *Asking questions*. San Francisco: Jossey-Bass.

WEISS, C. H. 1975. Interviewing in evaluation research. In *Handbook of evaluation research*, vol. 1., ed. E. L. Struening and M. Guttentag, chap. 11. Beverly Hills, Calif.: Sage.

The single best source of measures useful in educational settings is

BUROS, O. K. 1978. *Eighth mental measurements yearbook*. Lincoln, Neb.: University of Nebraska Press.

There are many sources of variables and scales for someone who is developing an evaluation plan for a mental health facility. A few of the best are:

CARTER, D. E., AND NEWMAN, F. L. 1976. *A client-oriented system of mental health service delivery and program management: A workbook and guide.* Rockville, Md.: National Institute of Mental Health. DHEW Pub. No. (ADM) 76–307. U.S. Government Printing Office Stock No. 017-024-00523-1.

HAGEDORN, H. J.; BECK, K. J.; NEUBERT, S. F.; AND WERLIN, S. H. 1976. *A working manual of simple program evaluation techniques for community mental health centers.* Rockville, Md.: National Institute of Mental Health. DHEW Pub. No. (ADM) 76–404. U.S. Government Printing Office Stock No. 017-024-00539-8.

HARGREAVES, W. A.; ATTKISSON, C. C.; AND SORENSEN, J. D., EDS. 1977. *Resource materials for community mental health program evaluation.* 2nd ed. Rockville, Md.: National Institute of Mental Health. DHEW Pub. No. (ADM) 77–328. U.S. Government Printing Office Stock No. 017-024-00554-1.

WASKOW, I. E., AND PERLOFF, M. B., EDS. 1975. *Psychotherapy change measures.* Rockville, Md.: National Institute of Mental Health. DHEW Pub. No. (ADM) 74–120. U.S. Government Printing Office Stock No. 1724-00397.

Sources for measures of attitudes on a variety of topics include the following collections.

ROBINSON, J. P.; ATHANASIOU, R.; AND HEAD, K. B. 1969. *Measures of occupational attitudes and occupational characteristics.* Ann Arbor, Mich.: Institute for Social Research.

ROBINSON, J. P.; RUSK, J. G.; AND HEAD, K. B. 1968. *Measures of political attitudes.* Ann Arbor, Mich.: Institute for Social Research.

ROBINSON, J. P., AND SHAVER, P. R. 1973. *Measures of social psychological attitudes.* Ann Arbor, Mich.: Institute for Social Research.

4

Ethical Standards
of Conducting
Program Evaluations

Evaluators often find themselves in ethical conflicts seldom experienced by social scientists engaged in basic research. Illustrative dilemmas are provided in two hypothetical situations. Although these scenarios are hypothetical, experienced evaluators will be able to identify with the problems described in the following paragraphs.

A project that cannot be done well. Evelyn Marshall works for a social science research firm, Evaluation, Inc. Her firm is interested in getting a contract to evaluate an early parole program instituted by a state legislature. The question to be answered is whether early parole leads to more or less lawful behavior after release from prison, as compared to the behavior of prisoners paroled after serving the normal time. Marshall realizes that the legislature really wants an evaluation that will examine whether the program is causally related to a lowered arrest rate after release, and that the evaluation is needed within one year. However, she also learns that the parole board will not randomly assign prisoners to receive early parole and that there are legal reasons why random assignment may be impossible. Under these constraints Marshall knows twelve months is not a sufficiently long time to test the effectiveness of the program. Should she and her firm conduct the evaluation even though they cannot do what the legislators want?

Advocacy versus evaluation. Morris Franklin has completed an evaluation of Central Community Mental Health Center's outreach program for high school students whose poor school performance is thought to be related to drug abuse. As typically occurs, Franklin found (a) evidence supporting the program's effectiveness (students, parents, and school administrators like the program); (b) evidence that doesn't support the program (grades of the participants did not improve); and (c) some ambivalent evidence that could be interpreted as favorable or unfavorable depending on one's point of view (program students hold more part-time jobs than those not in the program). Franklin's report was received well by his supervisor. Meetings were scheduled to address the participants' grades and the other problems that were uncovered. Evaluator Franklin felt that he had done a good job. Later that month, however, Franklin's supervisor asked him to write a proposal to the school board supporting an extension of the program to other high schools. When the negative findings were mentioned, his supervisor told him to ignore the negative findings and "to be upbeat." Would it be unethical to write the proposal and not mention the known weaknesses of the program that the evaluation detected?

STANDARDS FOR THE PRACTICE OF EVALUATION

The need for ethical standards in research and in program evaluation has been felt by a number of organizations and individuals. Professional organizations have developed extensive statements of what it means to provide service and to conduct research in an ethical manner (e.g., Ethical principles, 1981). The American Psychological Association (1982) devoted a considerable amount of time and resources to a detailed study of ethical and unethical research practices. This project resulted in a ten-point statement of ethical principles accompanied by a lengthy commentary describing the meaning of the principles, illustrating violations of the principles, and showing how responsible investigators protect the rights of research subjects.

This text interprets ethical standards for evaluators in a fashion that is even broader than that adopted by the American Psychological Association. Since the findings of a program evaluation may be applied in an organization, there are many more chances for the evaluator to violate ethical principles than there are for the basic researcher to do so. In recent years two statements describing principles evaluators should follow have been published. One set of principles was prepared by the Evaluation Research Society (Rossi, 1982), and one was drawn up by a committee sponsored by professional organizations, foundations, and governmental agencies interested in the evaluation of educational programs and projects (Joint Committee on Standards for Educational Evaluation, 1981). Although the latter work was prepared to improve evaluations of educational practice, the principles it sets forth apply to program evaluations in all types of settings.

This chapter includes material based on statements of ethical conduct in research, as well as descriptions of good program evaluation practices. The reason for combining these two issues in this chapter lies in the authors' belief that ethics in evaluation means more than honesty with money and data and respect for research subjects. We believe that evaluators have the responsibility to provide clear, useful, and accurate evaluation reports to the organizations for which they work. Furthermore, the evaluator has a responsibility to society to work in a way that has the potential to improve services for people. Ethics are more complicated for evaluators working in settings designed to help people than for basic researchers working on issues with little immediate relevance to organizations. This is not meant to imply that basic research is irrelevant to the needs of society. We simply mean that errors in basic research are less likely to be used in a setting that could harm people. Many steps intervene between the statement of a finding in a basic research study and an application; these steps serve as checks to identify erroneous findings. In contrast, poorly done evaluations have affected the provision of services to needy people, disrupted the staffs of service organizations, and encouraged the use of harmful experimental medical treatments. For these reasons, we view ethics in evaluation as including all aspects of conducting an evaluation—from initial planning through presentation of the results to interested parties.

The beginning evaluator can use statements of ethical principles to guide the planning, conduct, and reporting of evaluations. There may well be crucial choices required at all stages of a program evaluation. As Morris Franklin learned, evaluators may perform a very careful evaluation and feel that everything has gone well, only to discover that the dissemination of their findings will violate the ethical standards used to guide their work. Ethical issues for evaluators may be divided into five categories: treating people ethically, recognizing role conflicts, maintaining scientific credibility, serving the needs of possible users of the evaluation, and avoiding negative side effects of evaluations.

ETHICAL ISSUES INVOLVED
IN THE TREATMENT OF PEOPLE

The first responsibility of the evaluator, as it is with the basic researcher, is to protect people from harm. Since harm can be done to people in a variety of ways, concerned evaluators will guard against harm to program participants as well as to the staffs of programs evaluated.

Assignment to Program Groups

Often the first question that will concern an evaluator is whether any harm can come to someone receiving the program that is being evaluated. Although medical, educational, and social service programs are offered with the purpose of helping those who participate, sometimes programs have either no impact, or a negative impact. A controversial evaluation was reported by Sobell and Sobell (1978), who designed a program for alcoholics based on behavioristic principles that theoretically should have permitted alcoholics to drink at a moderate level after treatment. The principles underlying this program contradict the traditional assumption that alcoholics cannot drink without once again becoming dependent on alcohol (Burtle, 1979). It is not unethical to conduct an evaluation on such a project; however, the evaluator working with a treatment team using a disputed procedure should be sure that if the treatment fails, the program participants will receive adequate additional service so that they will not have been harmed by the evaluation. Pendery, Maltzman, and West (1982) have argued that Sobell and Sobell did not conduct sufficient follow-up research on the participants in the evaluation in order to learn whether controlled drinking worked for the participants in the program: Many were back in the hospital within weeks or months of discharge from the controlled drinking therapy. Nevertheless, in the published version of the evaluation, the Sobells implied that this approach to treatment for alcoholism was a viable alternative to the traditional treatment which emphasizes abstinence.

Informed Consent

Another way to protect the participant from harm is to obtain the prior agreement of potential program participants who will take part in the evaluation. This is especially important when the evaluator plans an evaluation based on the random assignment of program participants to different forms of treatment or to the control group not receiving the treatment. When people are asked for their agreement, it is important for them to understand the request—that is, for their consent to be "informed." Informed consent means that potential participants themselves be allowed to make the decision about whether to participate, and that sufficient information about the program be provided to enable them to weigh all alternatives. If the person is misled or not given sufficient information about the risks involved, then informed consent has not been obtained, even if the person has signed an agreement to participate.

Seeking to give enough information to enable people to give informed consent may create an additional ethical dilemma for the evaluator. It may be that a control group, not receiving the new service under study, will feel in competition with the treatment group or, alternatively, will feel

unfairly deprived (Cook and Campbell, 1979). If informed consent procedures have the potential to change the behavior of the nonprogram (or traditional program) group, then the validity of the evaluation will be threatened. There is no clear way to resolve such an ethical tangle. One
approach, adopted by the American Psychological Association, is to consider the costs involved to the participants being studied. For example,
Mexican-American women applying for family planning services were randomly assigned to a treatment group (oral contraceptives) or to a control
group (dummy, look-alike pills) (Bok, 1974). The high costs of being in the
control group, ten pregnancies, argues that these women should have been
given complete information about this study. Such gross violations of ethical principles in research and evaluation are far less frequent in recent
years than they were in the past.

Confidentiality

Information gathered during the course of an evaluation is to be
treated with the utmost care. Whether the information is about program
participants or employees, evaluators violate ethical principles if they conduct the research in a manner that violates people's privacy. This point was
discussed in the previous chapter and will be stressed again in the chapter
on the use of monitoring systems.

ROLE CONFLICTS FACING
EVALUATORS

Evaluators gather data for the purpose of placing a value on plans for, the
implementation of, or the outcome of programs. Since people serving on
the staff of these programs earn their living as well as gain psychological
rewards from their work, it should not be surprising that the evaluation
process will create conflicts for those involved in evaluating the quality of
the services or procedures provided. The most common conflicts arise (a)
because most in-house evaluators are part of the management team of the
organization, but the work of evaluators involves many groups other than
managers; (b) because evaluators seek to be as objective as they can but yet
are often called upon to be advocates for the organization; and (c) because
consultant evaluators need to win contracts to do research in order to maintain the financial health of their company, even when it is hard to complete
the evaluation with the desirable scientific rigor. Each of these role conflicts
are discussed more fully below.

The term *stakeholder* refers to those people who are involved with the
program under evaluation—as clients, administrators, staff, and so on
(Gold, 1983). The term comes from the idea that those who support or

benefit from an endeavor have a stake in its success. Thus, the clients served by a program have a stake in the outcome of an evaluation; if the program is suspended, they may lose a needed service. The staffs of programs want their work recognized and need the income their jobs generate. A publicly funded program will have stakeholders in the government, and even the taxpaying public has a stake, regardless of whether people are aware of either the specific program or the evaluation that is being conducted. Other stakeholders can be identified by the reader. Evaluators ideally will serve all the relevant stakeholders, even though evaluators are usually employed by only one of the stakeholders—the organization management, in the case of the typical in-house evaluator, or a governmental agency, in the case of many consultant evaluators. In an important sense, a large proportion of evaluators' ethical dilemmas arises from conflicts of interest among the stakeholders involved with a program. Before conducting an evaluation, it is wise to consider all the people who might be affected by the outcome. As is stated in Chapter 2, it is crucial to form a clear idea of who wants a program evaluated before beginning an evaluation. However, the evaluator will have a better understanding of ethical issues if the needs of all the stakeholders are considered, whether they want an evaluation or not.

To illustrate the process of identifying the stakeholders of a program, consider the case of an evaluator charged with conducting an evaluation of a new method of sentencing convicted criminals. A state governor proposed and the legislature passed a sentencing procedure for certain crimes called "Class X crimes." The legislation was passed because there is a widely held opinion that the sentencing practices of judges are too lenient and are quite different from judge to judge. The legislation, in effect, took the question of length of jail sentence out of the judges' hands for certain crimes: A defendant judged guilty of a Class X crime now faced a sentence determined by law. Who were the stakeholders in this situation?

First, the state legislature that commissioned the evaluation was a stakeholder, since it wrote the laws that was being evaluated. The governor had a stake in the outcome of the study, since he proposed the law. The governor would want all evaluations of his work to be favorable in order to enhance his chances of reelection. Those state legislators who favored the law likewise desired a favorable finding. In contrast, some legislators who opposed the law may have preferred to see their position vindicated by a finding that the law had not had its intended effect. All the citizens who look to the courts to assist in the job of preventing dangerous individuals from committing additional crimes had an interest in this work. Judges, too, had a stake in the findings of the study, since it was their day-to-day behavior that was being studied. Prison officials needed to be aware of evaluation findings, especially with respect to the possible influence of the new sentencing procedures on their facilities. Police officers also were interested to learn how the new sentencing procedures had been implemented. Defense lawyers, defendants, and the state attorney's office also had stakes in the outcome of the evaluation, since their strategies depend on how sentences are determined. Clearly, many groups care about the findings of program evaluations.

Effective evaluators take the range of stakeholders into account as they plan, conduct, and report their work. The conflicting expectations of different stakeholders can lead to ethical difficulties for evaluators. Anticipating these and other conflicts can spell the difference between intolerable problems—resulting in the evaluation becoming a political "football"—and a carefully planned, even if controversial, evaluation.

Evaluators should try to minimize conflicts among the wants of various stakeholders before the evaluation begins, since they are subject to less pressure if they can negotiate questions such as: Who will have access to results? What information is to be used? How would different patterns of data be interpreted? and so on. If the study is begun without settling these issues, the probability that different groups will manipulate the evaluation to suit their own purposes is increased. At times jealousies and disputes about ownership of information have made it impossible to conduct a credible evaluation. Stakeholders who do not want an evaluation conducted benefit from such an outcome; however, all others lose.

THE SCIENTIFIC QUALITY
OF THE EVALUATION

Once the possibility of harm to program participants is minimized and potential role conflicts are explored, the evaluator can turn to ethical issues associated with the scientific quality of the evaluation project. It is the authors' view that conducting evaluations which are invalid for the purpose for which they were commissioned is just as unethical as, for example, not protecting the confidentiality of information obtained from participants. The next sections cover the ethical ramifications of four of the most frequently found threats to the scientific validity of evaluations.

Valid Measurement Instruments

Evaluators in educational and mental health settings frequently use standardized, published tests in measuring the expected outcomes of the program being evaluated. The most well developed tests are the standardized achievement tests designed to estimate a child's progress in school. Because these tests are so well developed, there is a temptation to apply them even when they may not be appropriate to measure the outcomes of a program. In other words, one cannot simply ask if a measurement tool is valid:

The most effective evaluators ask if a measurement tool is valid to assess program participants in a specific setting. Choosing an inappropriate way to measure a hypothesized outcome can render an otherwise well-planned study useless or, worse, misleading. For example, an evaluation of a school program on ecology used as an outcome measure a standardized achievement subtest on science, including topics on hygiene, biology, and earth science (Joint Committee, 1981). This subtest was not appropriate for measuring the achievement of the students in the innovative ecology course. The evaluation's negative findings did not reflect the actual results of the program.

Evaluators will make mistakes, just as all people do. However, failing even to consider the specific content of the course and the actual material covered by the selected subtest can be considered unethical conduct on the part of a professional evaluator. It is unlikely that any standardized test exists to measure the achievement of students in an ecology course, because few such courses have been taught until recently: The evaluator should have recognized that. The school district would have been better off had the evaluation not been conducted at all; the program is now saddled with a negative evaluation which—although invalid—must be explained by program supporters.

Skilled Data Collectors

It is likely that a standardized test can be competently administered by people with little training; however, many evaluations use information collected through personal interviews. Interviewing is not an easy job. Good interviewers possess skills and common sense that will permit them to obtain the information needed without injecting biases, and to maintain the good will of the person interviewed. It requires a degree of maturity and a respect for truth to be able to record and report attitudes at variance with one's own. An early study (Rice, 1929) found that two interviewers of destitute men were reporting very different answers to an interview question concerning why these men found themselves in their current condition. One interviewer repeatedly found that the men attributed their problems to alcohol; the other interviewer reported that the men said they were the victims of an unjust society. The fact that the first interviewer favored prohibition while the second was a Marxist suggests that the interviewer's reports were strongly influenced by their own political views.

It is not always easy to obtain the cooperation of the individuals to be interviewed. Guba and Lincoln (1981) note that interviewers need to exercise polite persistence as they seek to interview program participants. Carey (1974) interviewed terminally ill patients as part of an evaluation of hospital care for dying patients. It takes great sensitivity to conduct such interviews without appearing to care more about data than about the personal tragedies of the patients. Children present a very different type of problem. Interviewing children in a compensatory education program designed to improve self-confidence, study habits, and social skills requires patience and the ability to gain the cooperation of the children. An interviewer without experience in working with children may learn very little about their feelings, because children do not respond to the same demands as adults do. Indeed, if young children do not feel respected, they may not say anything at all! An evaluation cannot provide meaningful information with data that are inaccurate or incomplete.

Research Design

One of the themes of this book is that the research design must fit the needs of those who will utilize the information. As later chapters will illustrate, different needs require more or less scientific rigor. However, once a need is articulated, it is unethical to conduct an evaluation if it is known at the outset that the planned evaluation cannot answer the questions that the sponsors of the evaluation put to the evaluator. This seems to be the ethical dilemma faced by Evelyn Marshall, as outlined in the introduction to this chapter. Although her company needs the work, and although the program should be evaluated, it seems unlikely that she can conduct an evaluation to answer the questions the state legislature has presented to her company.

At this point Marshall has at least three alternatives: (1) she could go ahead and do the evaluation, (2) she could decline to conduct the evaluation and hope that an alternative job comes by to keep her productively employed, or (3) she could negotiate on the actual questions to be addressed by the evaluation. The first alternative is unethical, and the second is risky for Marshall; but the third may well prove productive. Frequently sponsors of evaluation are unskilled in research methods and do not know when they have given an evaluator an impossible assignment. It may be that the legislature does not really require an evaluation that traces the causes of any possible changes in parole procedures. What is actually needed may be only a careful documentation of the actual implementation of the new law. If negotiations reveal that implementation is the main issue, Marshall can conduct the evaluation; in fact, she can now do a better job than would have been possible fruitlessly trying to trace causal links.

Adequate Descriptions
of Programs and Procedures

One of the basic characteristics of science is its public nature. Science is to be conducted in such a way that other scientists can evaluate the procedures used and conduct (replicate) the same research. Only in this way can errors in research be detected. Frequently evaluations are not described in sufficient detail to permit others to fully understand either the program or the evaluation procedures. Patton (1980) illustrated the advantage of describing the program as an aspect of conducting a program evaluation. He found that an evaluation of a program to help economically disadvantaged young mothers learn parenting and financial management skills concluded that the program was ineffective—even though the program was not implemented. If the evaluators had taken the effort to observe and describe the program as put into effect (not just as planned), they would have learned that there was so much political resistance, the program never even occurred. Even when programs are implemented as planned, the program may be so weak that it is unlikely participants will be influenced (Quay, 1979).

Besides describing the program, the evaluation procedures should be presented in enough detail so that others can understand how the evaluator obtained and analyzed information. As will be mentioned later, all interested parties will not want to know every detail. However, such detailed reports should be available to others who want to implement the program, or who want to compare evaluations conducted in different settings. If it is impossible to compare evaluations because they are inadequately reported, one might wonder if the report writers were clear in their own minds about what was done.

In general, it is crucial that the evaluation be interpretable. Data sources and research design must be relevant to the purposes of the evaluation; data collectors need to be sufficiently skilled to provide accurate data; and others should have access to a detailed description of the program and the evaluation procedures.

RECOGNIZING THE NEEDS
OF ALL STAKEHOLDERS

The concept of stakeholders was introduced above in the context of potential role conflicts for evaluators. Considering the different stakeholders is also important for making an evaluation as useful as possible for all those who may use or be influenced by the evaluation.

Program Managers Are
Concerned With Efficiency

Those who are responsible for managing an organization are concerned about the efficiency of its services and operations. Profit-making firms must produce goods and services in an efficient manner; otherwise, competing firms will be able to serve customers at a lesser cost. In time inefficient firms will go out of business or be bought out by more efficient ones. Nonprofit human service agencies do not operate on the same principles as profit-making firms; however, effective managers still strive to provide the maximum amount of service possible to clients, students, or patients in their agencies. The most important aspect of an evaluation in a manager's judgment may frequently be information on the efficiency of the program. A later chapter will discuss the cost-benefit questions so important to managers.

An Evaluation Can Help the Staff

The needs of the staff will be best served if the evaluation can provide practical guidance, improving the effectiveness with which they serve clients, students, patients, or customers. An evaluation of the flow of information through a large division of a firm may reveal inefficiencies. If the staff is provided with viable alternatives to the current procedures, they will have been well served by the evaluation. A study of physician residents in a large hospital detected gaps in the services the residents provided to patients (Posavac, Carey, and Marin, 1980). For example, residents did not make good use of the social support services (for example, social work and chaplaincy) provided by the hospital for patients, and they had difficulty in maximizing the comfort of dying patients whose diseases could not be cured. Residents desiring to improve their skills could make use of this information by accepting appropriate training.

Obviously, recommendations that are not accompanied by an estimate of the resources required to carry them out are not realistic. Evaluators also know that an evaluation is a good vehicle for giving staff members recognition for good work. Evaluations that are unnecessarily one-sided neglect some legitimate needs of the staff—an important stakeholder group in an in-house evaluation.

Clients Can Be Served by an Evaluation

An effective evaluation must also consider the program participants. Clients frequently have no voice in the planning or implementation of either programs or evaluations. Upon reflection, this fact seems almost bizarre: The group most affected by programs is the least consulted. However, clients are not unified, they seldom have spokespersons, and they do not hire evaluators. Among the ways evaluators can fulfill their responsibility to clients is to compare the needs of the program participants with the services offered, to help the staff and manager better understand the needs of participants, and to structure recommendations around the clients' needs. It is not unknown for recommendations to be made without an adequate understanding of the client population. The needs of the manager and the staff have sometimes taken precedence over those of the client.

Another aspect of the stake students, patients, trainees, and so forth have in an evaluation is their interest in continuing to receive service during the evaluation. It is usually impossible to conduct an evaluation without causing any disruption in the work of the staff and in service to participants. Ethical concerns for the needs of program participants require that service disruption be minimized.

Community Members
as Stakeholders

Most service agencies receive some of their financial support from the community by way of taxation or contributions, or indirectly through reductions in property taxes. In some ways the community is in the same position as the client population: The community is dispersed and does not have easily identifiable spokespersons. Perhaps the most ambitious approach to involving the community in the evaluation process is the citizen evaluation model developed for the National Institute of Mental Health (NIMH) (Zinober and Dinkel, 1981). Following procedures and using materials prepared by NIMH, community citizens can evaluate community mental health centers themselves. This approach is one way to ensure that the stake of the community will be recognized. While this endeavor requires the commitment of citizens, it can—and has—been done (Albright, 1982).

Financial Backers

Human service agencies usually have the financial support of government bodies, charitable organizations, or foundations. In business organizations there are many management layers between an evaluator and the ultimate financial backers; however, costs and profits will be considered at all levels of the organization and will be a part of all evaluations. Groups that put up the money certainly have a stake in the success of the programs they support. Frequently governmental offices and foundations commission evaluations of programs receiving their support. In these instances their interests are probably well protected. Ethically planned in-house evaluations should also reflect the interests of the groups that supply the financial backing for the service agencies.

Figure 4.1 illustrates how stakeholders' views can lead to different conclusions, even when evaluating the same information.

AVOIDING POSSIBLE NEGATIVE
SIDE EFFECTS OF EVALUATION
PROCEDURES

Evaluators face a number of ethical issues related to the applied nature of their research. The ethical issues covered in this section are less central to the conduct of basic research; however, in the applied research arena these

Differences in the views of various stakeholders are illustrated in the controversy over "workfare" programs, which require applicants for welfare to hold part-time, temporary jobs. The idea is that welfare recipients should do some work for the assistance they require. While they continue to look for steady work, they spend a week or two a month in public or nonprofit organizations doing jobs that would not have been filled by a regular employee.

Some critics say the program is shortsighted, that the people do not learn real work skills, and that the state does not adequately supervise these temporary "employees." Other critics say workfare merely requires welfare applicants to "sing for your supper," making welfare programs punitive. A public aid official counters by saying that some workfare participants need workfare to learn that holding a job requires coming to work, staying all day, not hitting anyone, and bathing before they go to work. Nonprofit service organizations report that the day-care, janitorial, and food service assistance they get through workfare has improved their services to other low-income people.

An evaluator would be hard pressed to gather data that would be acceptable to all stakeholders, because there are fundamental value conflicts that data will not resolve. (Source: Brotman, 1983.)

FIGURE 4.1. An illustration of how stakeholders' values can conflict.

questions can take on immense importance both for evaluators and for the stakeholders affected by the evaluation study.

Can Someone be Hurt
by Inaccurate Findings?

Inaccurate findings can either show falsely positive findings—erroneously suggesting that the program is effective—or falsely negative findings—erroneously suggesting that the program is not effective. When such false conclusions are due to random statistical variation, the first false finding is called a Type I error, and the second is termed a Type II error. Such false conclusions can also be made when insufficient attention is paid to the design of an evaluation. Without careful thought, evaluations sometimes focus on the wrong variables or use too short a time span to show either positive or negative effects. At other times an evaluator's enthusiasm for a program may lead to falsely optimistic conclusions.

The possibly misleading work on alcoholism treatment by Sobell and Sobell (1978) has already been discussed in the light of the follow-up study done by Pendery, Maltzman, and West (1982). It is possible that the treatment of alcoholics at other institutions may have been changed when therapists read of the apparently favorable results the Sobells claimed for the controlled drinking therapy. Basic researchers are cautioned to care for the safety and welfare of the people actually studied in an experiment. In addition, evaluators need to think about how program planners might be affected by the report of an evaluation. Inadvertently encouraging the use of a harmful program due to insufficient care in conducting research is an ethical problem with which basic researchers need rarely be concerned; however, it is often an important issue for evaluators.

In contrast to falsely favorable evaluations, falsely negative evaluations can also harm people by encouraging the elimination of beneficial services. Lazar (1981) described one overlooked aspect of preschool programs such as Head Start. According to Lazar, Head Start, a summer preschool program for economically disadvantaged children, made its strongest contribution to the future school achievement of the children not by what it taught, but by the way it involved mothers in the education of their children. Showing mothers how to work with their children and introducing them to the school system, encouraged them to develop a level of involvement with the education of their children which is often not found among lower-income families. This involvement could have been achieved regardless of the actual content of the summer programs. Evaluations that focused only on the intellectual growth of the children during the eight-week program were too narrow. The falsely negative conclusions could have harmed other children if preschool programs had been eliminated. Comprehensive evaluations of programs such as Head Start have shown them to be effective (Darlington et al., 1980), in contrast to the initial study (Cicarelli, Cooper, and Granger, 1969).

Statistical Type II Errors

Type II errors (concluding that a program is ineffective when it is in fact effective) can occur because the sample of program participants involved in the evaluation was small or just happened to be atypical. Whenever measurements are made on a sample of people rather than on the whole population, and whenever measurement instruments are not perfectly reliable, random variation can produce Type II errors. Evaluators can seldom test whole populations, and the information sources available to evaluators are never perfectly reliable. Basic researchers worry about Type II errors because it is a waste of time to conduct research that yields inaccurate conclusions. However, Type II errors in a basic research study typically cause no harm to others. Evaluators, on the other hand, have an additional worry about random statistical errors: They do not want to falsely conclude that a valued program is ineffective.

Unfortunately, evaluators work in situations that make Type II errors very likely. In an attempt to reduce the demands made on program participants asked to provide data, short surveys may be used and the number of variables may be limited. To reduce the disruption of services, only a few participants may be tested. In other cases there may only be relatively few participants in an expensive program to be evaluated. Or the evaluator may not be given sufficient resources to measure the outcome variables on a large number of participants. In all such cases the possibility of making Type II errors is increased.

Pay Attention to Unplanned Program Effects

Ethical evaluators are careful to examine the programs as implemented, not just as designed. One aspect of this issue is the low level of actual implementation of programs. This point has already been discussed. A second aspect of this issue involves possible negative side effects of a program. Just as physicians are concerned about side effects of medications, evaluators work most effectively when they are alert to unexpected negative features of a program. For example, welfare procedures may demean recipients, prison regulations may cause dependency leading to more difficulty in making decisions after release, and an arbitrary method of introducing improved working conditions may alienate employees. Such outcomes will, of course, never be found in the goals of the program as planned. In fact, program planners and managers might not even anticipate these results. Evaluators can do more useful work if they detect important negative side effects of programs.

Chapman and Risley (1974) described a program whereby children were paid to pick up and turn in litter. The program developers did not expect the children to bring in bags of household garbage from their homes: The program staff refused to pay for these bags. The children then threw the household garbage into nearby yards, certainly an unwanted side effect. The program was revised so that payment was made not for bags full of litter but for cleaning up specified yards. Recognizing a negative side effect led to a better program. Table 4.1 includes some additional negative side effects of policies with desirable goals.

Table 4.1.   Seeking to Achieve Desirable Goals Has Led to Serious Side Effects Unexpected by the Program Developers.

DESIRABLE GOAL	PROGRAM	NEGATIVE SIDE EFFECT
Save gasoline	Reduce size of cars	Increase in injuries during accidents
Reduce auto pollution	Pollution control devices	Reduced gas mileage
Save energy	Burn waste forestry products for heat	Loss of nutrients currently returned to the soil
Improve food production in poor nations	Use fertilizers and farm machinery	Poor farmers who could not afford costs sold farms and became unemployed city dwellers

Unexamined Values Held by the Evaluator

Conflicts between the role of program advocate and the role of evaluator have already been mentioned. The evaluation may also be rendered less valid if values are assumed by the evaluator without examination. Sjoberg (1975) suggests that evaluators typically accept the existing power structure and adopt its values with little reflection. For example, embezzlement is not treated as a major crime because, according to Sjoberg, it is a middle- and upper-class crime. He also suggests that many teenagers are labeled delinquent because they violate the norms of those who hold the power in society. Sjoberg has highlighted an important issue for evaluators, whether or not one agrees with his examples. He has forcefully argued that one cannot serve the needs of all groups with a stake in the evaluation if the evaluator has implicitly adopted the values of the most powerful group involved with the evaluation. Clearly, it is difficult to recognize assumed values. One way to guard against the effects of such implicit values is to avoid working with only the individuals planning or offering the service. Trying to learn what participants seek in the program may yield insights not gained in discussions with professionals.

Other unexamined values may be hidden in statistical analyses. Ball and Bogartz (1970) examined the overall mean achievement of children watching "Sesame Street" and concluded that the series was successful in achieving some of its goals. Cook et al. (1975), however, divided the children on the basis on socioeconomic background and concluded that the program was not effective. Among other things, the program was specifically designed to improve the cognitive skills of children from low socioeconomic areas. One reason the cast includes many members of minority groups is to increase the chances of children from minority groups watching the program. Nevertheless, Cook et al. learned that the cognitive skill gap between lower- and upper-class children who watched "Sesame Street" actually increased. Therefore, although watching the program had a positive impact, it did not provide the special help to disadvantaged children that was a fundamental goal of the program. Without a creative reanalysis of the evaluation, this important—but subtle—finding would have been overlooked. One ethical viewpoint asserts that when benefits are uneven, the least privileged group should benefit the most (Bunda, 1983).

SUMMARY

The major ethical issues involved in conducting research have been described under five topics: the protection of the people studied, the danger of role conflicts, threats to the scientific quality of evaluations, the varying needs of different groups who may be influenced by the evaluation, and negative side effects that may be related to the program or to the way of conducting the evaluation. Special emphasis was given to the applied and political nature of the settings in which program evaluations are conducted. The applied setting creates more ethical dilemmas than the basic research setting. Although these conflicts and limitations require evaluators to exercise considerable care in conducting evaluations, these issues serve to make the role of the evaluator vital and exciting.

STUDY QUESTIONS

1. Analyze the different views of the various stakeholders who would be involved with a teacher evaluation in a college or university.
2. Contrast the dangers of Type I and Type II errors in basic research versus those in program evaluation, with special regard to ethical considerations.
3. Some evaluators do not mention all negative or unfavorable findings in official evaluation reports, but do bring such issues to the attention of program managers during private meetings. What are the pros and cons of this practice?

FURTHER READING

JOINT COMMITTEE ON STANDARDS FOR EDUCATIONAL EVALUATION. 1981. *Standards for evaluations of educational programs, projects, and material.* New York: McGraw-Hill.

PERLOFF, R., AND PERLOFF, E., EDS. 1980. *Values, ethics, and standards in evaluation.* San Francisco: Jossey-Bass.

ROSSI, P. H., ED. 1982. *Standards for evaluation practice.* San Francisco: Jossey-Bass.

part II

EVALUATION
OF NEED
AND PROCESS

In Chapter 1 readers learned of the need for program evaluation and the growing trend toward using evaluation methods to improve and to justify the offering of human service programs. An overview of the evaluator's role vis-à-vis service providers and organization administrators was given in Chapter 2. Measurement principles were discussed in Chapter 3 to emphasize that evaluators are research professionals who know how to approach the quantification of variables important to human services. In Chapter 4 ethical concerns and the evaluator's responsibilities were described.

In Part II the discussion of the specific tasks of evaluators is initiated. Evaluators can make contributions to the administration of programs without actually examining the effectiveness of human services in achieving goals. First, Chapter 5 shows how evaluators can participate in the planning of programs by using their social science skills to help planners find indicators of need and to quantify and summarize these indicators. Second, evaluators can assist in monitoring a program to learn the extent to which it has been implemented as planned. Administrators and representatives of the public want to know: Who gets what services from whom? Program evaluation methods, as illustrated in Chapter 6, can be applied to answer such a question.

5

Evaluation
in Program Planning

What sort of service can a person trained in social science methods provide to planners of human services? How can a program evaluator do anything *before* there is a program? There are three general types of contributions to be made: (1) specifying the needs a program should meet; (2) helping to describe the goals and objectives of the program; and (3) selecting from among various possible programs.

Planning is required before any human service program is begun. Long before the doors of a service agency swing open, some people must shape the service according to their perceptions of the need for it and the best ways to meet those needs. A surprisingly large number of programs have been planned on the basis of little more than an influential person's impression of what a group needs. Whether the program is for alcoholics, malnourished children, or unemployed blue-collar workers, subjective impressions often guide the planning of the program. Before we illustrate the methods an evaluator might use to help the planners of human services, a brief discussion of the problems faced by planning committees may be helpful. These comments are based on observations of meetings of planning committees made up of such human service providers as teachers, social workers, or nurses. Since individuals working in such positions are seldom trained in social science research techniques, evaluators have made valuable contributions to such planning groups.

THE EVALUATOR
AND THE PLANNING
COMMITTEE

What Planning Committees Want
to Accomplish

There are two important general goals: to produce the best possible practical plan and to find a plan with broad-based support. Many planning sessions, however, follow the less than ideal patterns of planning either by administrative fiat or by means of dilatory, boring planning sessions. Both patterns may be caused by the lack of definitive information and the difficulty for any individual to grasp the total set of needs and program possibilities.

Unambiguous information is hard to obtain and, in fact, may not exist. Even experts in an area cannot know what policy is most likely to succeed. Evidence for following a given path can usually be found; however, often there is other evidence supporting a different course. After hearing experts use the expression "on one hand . . . but on the other hand," a Senate committee chairman expressed a desire for "one-armed scientists" (David, 1975). His desire was obviously facetious; however, it illustrates a crucial point—even when information is available, it will seldom point to a single plan to solve a problem.

Planning committees may have difficulty selecting the best plan because human beings are limited in how much information they can use at one time. To consider simultaneously all the variables involved is impossible. Fortunately, methods are available to break a decision down into parts or steps. The jargon word for this process is to *disaggregate* a decision. The suggestion to disaggregate is good advice when making any decision; however, planning committees may persist in grappling with the whole problem without seeing that aspects of the problem can be approached one at a time. The last section of this chapter describes how to disaggregate a decision.

The frustration of not seeing a clearly best way to solve a problem sometimes inhibits planning. When a committee tackles a complex problem, often no one structures the task for the committee. This lack of structure leads various individuals to either engage in small talk or push their own views. Once it becomes clear that the planning committee is not getting anywhere, an administrator may decide what the plans should be. The committee may actually be greatly relieved by such a move.

To be fair, some planning groups do not function well because they have access only to funds earmarked for certain purposes. Such groups work within a rather narrow range of options. However, the planning group still has a critical task; a human service program can take many specific forms, even within a narrow range of options.

Evaluators Can Help Program Planners

It is unfortunate that evaluators are so often consulted only after a program is already in place. Doubly unfortunate is the situation in which the evaluator is consulted after a program is suspected of being ineffective. Well-managed human service organizations are directed by managers who recognize the need for evaluation. Such managers may encourage evaluators to sit in on planning sessions; indeed, planning is much like evaluation. The planner merely uses a future tense (for example, *Will* the program help?), and the evaluator typically uses the past tense (for example, *Did* the program help?). If evaluators are involved early, planners have convenient access to knowledge about what can be evaluated objectively and at what cost. Such collaboration is likely to be helpful, because in many human services the innovators are not trained in management, research or in program evaluation methods. In addition, many administrators and planners do not have experience in conceptualizing program objectives in ways that encourage making observations and summarizing information that will provide corrective feedback to the program staff and managers. For example, the goals of many service programs are written in such general terms that it is impossible to know when the goal has been attained and when it has not. For example, the goals of "giving quality medical care," "reducing crime," and "opening meetings to the community" cannot be evaluated as phrased. When do you know "crime" has been "reduced"? What crimes? How much of a reduction would count? One percent? Ten percent? For how long must a reduction last? All these questions (and others) must be answered before a plan can be made and before an evaluation can be initiated.

The next section of this chapter concerns some general issues evaluators should raise in planning sessions. Next, methods of carrying out an assessment of need are described. Last, a method to help planners divide a complex decision into manageable parts is presented.

GENERAL ISSUES TO ADDRESS IN PLANNING

Identifying the Intended Participants

While clearly identifying the population(s) to be served by a program is the most advisable first step in program planning, it is easy to evade this hard task. Some people talk about serving the needs of the "community." As long as a vague term is used, the various people involved in the planning may comfortably continue to "plan" while each holds a different view of the community to be served. Even worse, those without a clear idea of the community assume the others know who the community is. The evaluators can help the planning group to address this question. Nevertheless, they can expect foot dragging, because the task is both hard and anxiety arousing. This is so because once a choice is made among the possibilities, a commitment is involved; it is not difficult to hide weak plans in vague descriptions.

Carefully identifying those to be served is crucial—the needs of one group are different from the needs of another group. Further, an approach that may work with one group may not be effective with a different one. For example: Junior high school students have different social and academic needs than senior high school students; repeat offenders are less likely to benefit from a program that may benefit teenagers who have been convicted of one crime, although both may be correctly identified as "juvenile delinquents"; people from more privileged economic backgrounds probably expect human services to be housed in more attractive settings than do people used to less plush housing; and an elderly population needs different services from a mental health center than do teenage runaways.

One way to force oneself to be specific and clear is to put ideas down on paper and permit someone else to react to them. A chart summarizing the characteristics of a target population may be useful. A hospital planning an ambulatory care center may define the following groups as the target populations: the elderly; indigent or near-indigent families; children of all families requiring immunizations and other routine care; and newcomers to the local community. It is possible to obtain estimates of the sizes of these groups from local governments and census reports, as illustrated later in this chapter.

Identifying the Needs to be Met

Successful programs seek to alleviate real problems that are recognized by the population to be served. Certainly, planners of human service programs are likely to do a better job if they know what the target population needs. There is a critical difference between the needs felt by a population and the needs professionals attribute to the population. If the target population does not recognize a need, the program will have to include an educational aspect. The staffs of screening and treatment programs for high blood pressure deal daily with people who do not recognize a need for care. When the disease first develops, elevated blood pressure usually does not produce felt symptoms; in addition, the treatment does have undesirable side effects (*Medical World News,* 1977). Because people expect to feel better, not worse, after taking medicine, many reject the treatment. A rejected treatment means a program failure, even though the medication is effective in prolonging the lives of the hypertensive patients by reducing the likelihood of strokes and other cardiovascular diseases.

A university English professor provides a second example of the disappointing results of not realizing that a target population may not construe a problem in the same way as a professional offering a service. She reasoned as follows: (1) Many college students do not write very well, and professors in many fields agree that improvement would be desirable; (2) English professors have only limited contact with students, compared to professors in the students' major fields; therefore (3) one way to improve student writing is to improve the ability of non-English faculty to grade, evaluate, and improve the writing done for non-English courses. She developed a series of workshops for non-English department faculty members involving a number of her departmental colleagues and obtained funds from the college dean for a guest speaker. The flaw in her plans was very basic. It was wrong to assume that people who complain want to act upon their complaints. Although many college professors complain about student writing ability, relatively few may be ready to involve themselves actively in the grading and counseling required to encourage improvement. Consequently, the attendance at the workshops and the lecture was primarily from the English department; non-English department faculty could be counted on the fingers of one hand. As a matter of fact, there were more graduate student evaluators present to observe the first workshop than there were faculty members from departments other than English. Other workshops were then canceled. The point should be clear: Programs can be effective only when they meet real needs and when the target population agrees that it has those needs.

In assessing the need for a human service, it is very important to be objective—the extent of need is easy to overestimate. Nurses were concerned about the large number of stroke patients in a medium-sized hospital. They felt they were unable to meet these patients' needs without a special stroke unit. Because of these concerns, the administrators cooperated in a study of the severity of stroke patients in their hospital. It quickly became clear that there were actually very few stroke patients in the hospital. Those few admitted with possible strokes were usually discharged with much less severe diagnoses. In spite of the subjective feelings of many of the people on the staff of that hospital, there was no way to justify the added expense of a special stroke unit. The administration needed to deal with the concern of the staff, but in ways other than the institution of a new unit.

Another reason for objectivity is that the no nonsense people who are responsible for funding human service projects will be more likely to respond to clear plans designed to meet objectively determined needs. If the project just described had found that a large number of stroke patients were being treated at the hospital and that many of these patients were being discharged with greater disabilities than those suffered by patients of other hospitals, then the response of the hospital's administrators would have been more favorable to requests for a new service unit.

The Program's Resources

An evaluation of a proposed program will include an evaluation of the type of staff required. What training and experience should the staff members have? Will their training fit the actual needs of the people to be served? Is their work planned to use their talents effectively? Effective people may ultimately be ineffective if placed in situations for which they were not trained or if the situation restricts the use of their skills.

The staff must be housed in adequate facilities. If they lack appropriate areas in which to meet program participants as individuals or as groups, the program may be impossible to deliver. Work-training programs must have up-to-date equipment, or the training will not be useful to the trainees. The location of the facilities is also important; public transportation may be a necessity for the people to be served.

Expectations for the Program

Evaluators can also help planning committees specify the goals and objectives of the program. Program sponsors and funders are increasingly asking for a careful description of the objectives of new programs (Wholey, 1981). Without this emphasis it is next to impossible to determine whether the service was offered as planned or whether the service achieved what it was set up to do. Goals and objectives need to be described in ways that permit one to recognize when they have been achieved and when they have not. Otherwise, people cannot be held accountable for their work.

There are several levels at which goals can be written. Marshall (1979) illustrates these different levels for a manager who wanted to install a computerized inventory system. At one level her goals could be phrased in terms of obtaining the necessary hardware, programs, and training for her employees by certain dates. At a second level her goals would concern the actual functioning of her new inventory system. These goals might refer to the shortened time required to locate inventory items, and fewer items being out of stock. Third, her list of goals should take note of the actual purpose of the new inventory system: Customers should be more satisfied with her firm, and business should improve. Marshall emphasizes that planners should keep this third level of outcome goals clearly in mind as they work. Since there may be many ways to achieve better customer satisfaction, planners should not limit themselves to only one method before examining alternatives. However, once a course of action is selected, statements of goals at all levels are appropriate for good planning and for developing an accountability system. Figure 5.1 includes several examples of ways to state objectives.

Evaluators not only help in developing statements of goals and objectives for planners, but they are also called upon to help estimate the degree of success the program will have in achieving these goals (Wholey, 1981).

VARIOUS LEVELS AT WHICH GOALS CAN BE WRITTEN

Level 1. An example of goals that refer to the accquisition of basic hardware and personnel for computerizing an inventory control system. This is a "start-up" objective. Nothing can happen without this being achieved.

The system will be installed in all forty-two companies in a six-year period—four in the first year, six in the second, and eight each year after.

Level 2. The ways to recognize the inventory system as working well are included in this second level of goal statements. The achievement of Level 1 goals does not guarantee achievement of Level 2 goals.

The system can handle 15,000 inventory items.

Items can be located using the system in an average of ten seconds, with no more than 5 percent of searches taking more than thirty seconds.

Level 3. Although achieving goals at the first two levels is crucial for the ultimate success of the project, there are additional goals that should be considered. The real reason for computerizing an inventory system is to make a difference for customers. These goals reflect whether the customers are getting better service from the company.

Delivery times will be reduced.

There will be 50 percent fewer items out of stock as compared to the current system.

Formal customer complaints about out-of-stock items and slow responses to customer requests for information will be reduced by 50 percent.

FIGURE 5.1. Objectives for a program should refer to all levels of the program. Implementation, function, and outcome goals are reflected in this illustration. (Adapted from Marshall, 1979.)

On the basis of completed evaluations, personal experience, and theoretical understanding, evaluators can help to explore the possibilities that a planned program can be put in place, that it will attract cooperation from the community, and that it will lead to the improvements hoped for. It is not unusual for programs to be implemented that are simply too weak to have the impact planners thought likely (Sechrest, West, Phillips, Redner, and Yeaton, 1979). For example, can a summer in a preschool program such as Head Start realistically be expected to provide the basic skills needed for doing schoolwork, when a child has spent five years in a severely impoverished home? Can twelve hours of psychological counseling really affect a prisoner's ability to get and hold a job after release? This approach to examining a program during the planning stages has been called *evaluability assessment* (Wholey, 1981) and *preformative evaluation* (Scriven, 1981). The last section of this chapter describes how to systematize these expectations.

When it appears that a program will be insufficient to meet the needs it is designed to serve, two paths are open. On one hand, the program's goals could be scaled down. It may be better to strive to meet realistic goals than to fail to meet overly optimistic ones. On the other hand, the program could be strengthened. Both paths may require that the entire program be reconsidered. Program sponsors might not be satisfied with scaling down their expectations, but strengthening the program may require the expenditure of more funds than the sponsors wish to provide. The evaluator's contribution to a better program is important in the long run; however, in the short run the suggestion that a program might not be sufficient for its purposes will not be joyfully received. Nevertheless, program plans examined in this way are likely to be more successful.

INFORMATION SOURCES FOR
THE ASSESSMENT OF NEED

People who have participated in planning committees have complained that so much is unknown that their job is close to impossible. No one can make the planning committee's job easy; however, there are a number of techniques for gathering information that can reduce some of the planners' confusion. Sources of information that have proved useful include census data relevant to the need for human services, existing community agencies serving similar problems, surveys of residents of the community to be served, and knowledgeable people in the community, often called *key informants*.

Census Data

Census data are available for many years. Some of the items in the census surveys are relevant to program planning. This source has much to recommend it for use in program planning: It is usually considered reliable and valid; it is public when in summary form; and it is relatively inexpensive as compared to other types of data. The indexes in Figure 5.2 were derived from census information. This information was part of a needs assessment study utilized in a plan to expand mental health facilities in a group of rural counties. By comparing these indexes with similar variables for the whole state and for the nation, the extent of needs could be estimated. Census data will not be useful when planning a program in a rapidly expanding locality or within an organization.

Similar or Related Existing
Services

Before launching a new facility or initiating a new program to provide additional services, the planning group should make an inventory of existing agencies in the area that offer similar or related services. Such a survey will help to avoid the duplication of services and to locate key informants who can provide good estimates of certain community needs. For

Age distribution of population
Percentage of teenagers not in school
Percentage of black teenagers not in school
Percentage of working mothers of children under 18
Percentage of working mothers of preschool children
Percentage of aged persons living alone
Percentage of aged persons in poverty[a]
Percentage of extremely crowded housing units[b] without
    plumbing facilities
Percentage of large households[c] with low income
Percentage of female-headed families with children
Percentage of disabled persons not in institutions
Percentage of disabled persons not in institutions and unable to work

[a] *Based on local income levels*

[b] *More than one person per room*

[c] *Six or more persons*

FIGURE 5.2: Census data used in the needs assessment study prepared for the Spoon River Community Mental Health Center. (Source: *Community Mental Health Plan, Spoon River, Illinois*; Spoon River Community Mental Health Center, Inc., 1977.)

example, there are a variety of sources where people seek the emotional support that could be provided by a mental health center. Clergy and physicians probably deal with more such people than do psychologists and psychiatrists (see Posavac and Hartung, 1977). There is a wide range of estimates of the percentage of people seeing physicians who basically are not physically ill. Some estimates are as high as two-thirds of all patients. The clergy of certain religious denominations spend much time with parish members experiencing crises. Thus, members of the clergy and physicians would be good key informants in plans for developing new mental health services.

Number of People Receiving
a Service

Once the facilities and personnel currently offering a service are identified, an empirical study of the number of people who are being treated or served is often conducted. There are at least two approaches to estimating the number of people receiving a service. The most direct approach is to survey the appropriate individuals in the area. Physicians and clergy could be asked how many people they have served during the last month(s) who may require attention for certain mental health problems. The problem list would be kept short, because classifying people into a few categories would be less subject to error than asking informants to use finely discriminated categories. One needs survey presented only three categories: mental illness (defined very broadly to include "problems in living"), drug abuse, and alcohol problems. Specific services to children and to elderly adults are being stressed more than in the past. A persons-under-treatment survey may include a gross age categorization, such as seventeen and under, eighteen to sixty-four, and sixty-five and over.

The number of people actually in programs can be ascertained from the existing programs. These values will often be more accurate than estimated values. Medical and mental health programs must keep accurate records, although such records will not be flawless. Programs filling social and recreational needs, such as park programs or centers for senior citizens, probably will have far less accurate records.

Since additional services are being planned, the number of people who were referred to other agencies would be of interest. Also of interest would be estimates of the numbers of people the current care giver would have liked to have referred to another service or agency but could not, because the service did not exist in or near the community. Such information is important; some individuals are already in appropriate programs, but others may be receiving services that are not closely related to their needs.

When estimating need for any type of program, the distinction between incidence of a problem and prevalence of a problem is worth making. Incidence refers to the number of times a problem is experienced. Prevalence refers to the number of people who have the problem at a given time. For example, the incidence rate of the common cold is high; many people get one during a year, perhaps more than once a year. However, people usually recover in several days, so the prevalence at any one time is low. The distinction is important: A response to a problem will be different depending on whether the problem is viewed as widespread, but temporary, or less widespread, but long lasting. For example, attempts to help unemployed people will be different if one believes that most unemployed individuals are merely between jobs rather than that unemployed people are likely to be out of work for a long period of time.

Simply documenting a need is not sufficient to show that people will leave the care giver from whom they currently obtain services. People do not view care givers as readily interchangeable—trust develops slowly. Offering a service for which there is an objective need is not the same as offering a service that people would prefer over what they currently use. The continued use of native healers by some Spanish-American residents of cities in the United States is an example of a preference for what is known over services offered by public agencies (Adler and Stone, 1979).

It is important to repeat a word of caution: Informants, even quite knowledgeable ones, often overestimate need. Therefore, estimated needs must not be considered as actual needs without collaborative evidence. Estimated needs are not worthless values; however, they should be treated as estimates.

Community Resident Survey

The residents of a community have certain attitudes toward the development of human services and toward the particular services needed. Their attitudes can be part of the planning. If the service is relevant to all citizens, the community should ideally be surveyed systematically to obtain a representative sample of the opinions of the residents. Obtaining a truly representative sample is extremely difficult, and thus expensive. Avoiding clearly biased samples, however, is possible if the planner is careful in the selection of community respondents. Interviewing only professionals, only low-income residents, or only elderly people would render the results quite useless. A compromise might be possible by using intact groups that are likely to be fairly representative of the community. Such a course would not be expensive, because intact groups completing a survey do not require much time from a survey administrator. Public schools and church groups are two sources of respondents that may be available to a planning group. Depending on the nature of the program being planned, special groups of likely users could be sought. For example, medical planners would want to contact emergency rooms and outpatient clinics. Because parenting programs are more likely to be used by new parents, the names of families with babies might be obtained from hospitals or churches. (Some facilities may not be willing to provide names, in order to protect the privacy of their members or patients.)

The form of the community survey requires some care in construction. When constructing a survey, it is important to remember its purpose: to assess the need for a service, the acceptability of a particular service, and the willingness of people to use the program or facility. Some surveys, however, are set up in such a way that a very high response in favor of the proposed facility is guaranteed. In attitude measurement this bias is called *acquiescence*. Acquiescence refers to the tendency of people to say yes to questions if the questions at all encourage such an answer. Some needs surveys have essentially listed various services and asked if such services "should" be available to people in the community who need it. Imagine being asked:

> Do you think (your hometown) should have an emergency service that provides immediate counseling any time of the day or night for people who are having a crisis with personal or family problems?
>
> Do you think it would be helpful to you to learn more about mental illness and where to get mental health services, or to be able to handle a specific situation?

Wouldn't you answer yes to these questions? Most people would. There is nothing terribly wrong about the questions in themselves, but there are some additional types of items that should be added to this type of question.

The lack of a measure of intended behavior and the silence about costs of the services are among the reasons the above questions are not sufficient for a needs assessment. People can agree that a service *should* exist but feel that the need for it is so small that they are unwilling to devote more than a token amount of money to it. If this were the case, a marked degree of assent to a question of need would be quite misleading. If few want to pay for a service, the fact that many think it should be available is irrelevant.

Another useful approach to an assessment of need is to estimate what use people intend to make of a service. If the assessment of need concerned mental health programs, the survey constructor would be careful not to ask personal questions respondents would be unwilling to answer honestly. The survey should seek to estimate whether individuals have looked for a similar service for themselves or for someone they know.

For some services the community survey would be especially helpful. For example, many burglaries and acts of vandalism go unreported because the victims feel there is little hope of regaining the stolen goods or that it is too much trouble to report the problem. If the community survey revealed that such hopelessness was widespread, the need for programs of help might be even more compelling than the crime statistics themselves.

Whether a planned program is large or small, the principles described above can be used in assessments of need. The need for programs within large organizations, such as faculty development, student counseling, worker safety programs, and special hospital programs are among the kinds of small-scale programs for which needs should be documented before beginning the program. For each of these programs, a survey of those currently offering similar services, estimates of the number of those receiving similar services, and a survey of potential users would be valuable approaches to gathering information about need.

A DECISION THEORY APPROACH TO PLANNING: THE MULTI-ATTRIBUTE UTILITY (MAUT) METHOD

Having identified the general issues to be addressed in planning, and having described some of the tools for the assessment of need, we can now consider a practical approach by which evaluators can assist planners in choosing among possible programs. The method described in the remainder of this chapter is the Multi-Attribute Utility (MAUT) Method (Edwards, Guttentag, and Snapper, 1975). This method is a technique derived from decision theory, which has been used for program planning, especially for allocating resources to competing human service programs. The method can also be adapted to making decisions of any kind, for example, in the purchase of new equipment, the choice of a new career, or personnel selection. However, in this book attention is focused on the use of the MAUT method for program planning. After first examining the basic purpose and design of the MAUT method, we shall outline and illustrate the method itself.

Basic Purpose and Design of the MAUT Method

The basic purpose of the MAUT method is to disaggregate a decision—that is, to separate the elements of a complicated decision and evaluate each element separately. Instead of approaching a decision from a global viewpoint and beginning with a debate about the merits of competing programs, decision makers begin by reaching agreement on what they are trying to accomplish through the available programs. Having agreed on their overall goals, they then develop a consensus on the criteria to be used in judging the desirability of the competing programs. After having established this common ground, they can debate the merits of the programs in the light of the criteria established. This approach will in many cases narrow the focus to the exact area of disagreement and highlight the basic agreement among the planners.

A simplified version of decision disaggregation might be described as follows:

1. Decide on the appropriate criteria on which to base a decision. These criteria are values that the decision makers wish to maximize through the program. These criteria will guide their choice among available programs.
2. Weight the criteria to reflect their subjective importance to the decision makers. This procedure determines the relative importance of the values of the decision makers.
3. Evaluate each possible program on the basis of each criterion. This step enables the decision makers to pinpoint the strengths and weaknesses of each alternative program.
4. Combine the evaluations made on the basis of individual criteria into an overall judgment. This step shows the overall desirability or utility of each program.

Consider the example of a high school graduate choosing between attending College A and College B. A college experience may be viewed as a program to facilitate personal growth. Rather than trying to make the decision by stepping back and choosing a college on the basis of overall feelings, the student might choose to disaggregate the decision in the manner outlined in Figure 5.3. The student first identifies the criteria that reflect his or her values with respect to a college. In this instance the student

Criteria in choosing a college (values)	Weight of criteria (importance)	Rating of options	
		College A	College B
Attending a college with:			
An acceptable cost	3	8	6
A good academic reputation	2	7	8
An attractive location	2	4	5
Good social opportunities	1	9	5

Computing desirability

College A's desirability: 3(8) + 2(7) + 2(4) + 1(9) = 55
College B's desirability: 3(6) + 2(8) + 2(5) + 1(5) = 49

Decision: Choose College A

FIGURE 5.3: Disaggregation of the selection of a college.

identified acceptable cost, good academic reputation, attractive location, and good social opportunities.

Second, the student weighted the criteria to reflect their relative importance. As seen in Figure 5.3, the item called social opportunities was ranked last and given a weight of 1. Location and academic reputation of the college were considered to be of equal importance, and both were thought to be twice as important as social opportunities. Therefore, they were given a weight of 2. Finally, cost was judged to be the most important item and was given a weight of 3, which indicates that it is three times as important as social opportunities and half again as important as both location and academic reputation.

Third, each college was rated on a scale from 1 to 10 on each of the four criteria. The table shows that College A was judged more desirable on cost and social opportunities, while College B was judged more desirable on academic reputation and location.

Finally, the overall desirability (utility) of each college was determined in a quantitative manner by multiplying the rating on each criterion by its weight and adding the products for each college. The sum of the products equaled 55 for College A and 49 for College B. The decision was to choose College A.

When more than one decision maker is involved in a decision, the decision disaggregation method provides a system for combining their input in a manner that minimizes conflict. The decision makers begin by establishing common ground, agreeing on the criteria and the relative value of each before debating the merits of the available options. This procedure disciplines the discussion by identifying the areas of potential disagreement; that is, whether there is a difference in priority of values, in estimates of how much each option will maximize the values, or in both areas.

For example, suppose that in the above illustration the student's mother and father were to share in the selection of a college with their son or daughter. Rather than beginning the discussion with the parents declaring their preference for College B and the student opting for College A, they would begin by discussing their values and trying to agree on priorities before discussing the merits of either school. It would then become clear whether there was a conflict of values or rather a conflict on how well each college was judged to fulfill a common set of values.

The decision disaggregation method of decision making is really not a new concept; rather, it is an old idea with new terminology and extended application. Benjamin Franklin may have been among the earliest people to use a simplified MAUT approach in decision making (Dawes and Corrigan, 1974). In a letter to his friend Joseph Priestly dated September 19, 1772, Franklin suggested the following procedure for arriving at decisions:

> My way is to divide half a sheet of paper by a line into two columns; writing over the one *Pro*, and over the other *Con*. Then, during three or four days consideration, I put down under the different heads short hints of the different motives that at different times occur to me *for* and *against* the measure. When I have thus got them all together in one view, I endeavor to estimate the respective weights . . . [to] find at length where the balance lies. . . . And, though the weight of reasons cannot be taken with the precision of algebraic quantities, yet, when each is thus considered, separately and comparatively, and the whole matter lies before me, I think I can judge better, and am less liable to make a rash step; and in fact, I have found great advantage for this kind of equation, in what may be called *moral* or *prudential algebra* (Dawes and Corrigan, 1974, p. 95).

What Franklin called "prudential algebra" is a simplified MAUT approach, although he places less stress on the quantitative analysis and more on the qualitiative analysis of various arguments for and against a given measure.

Ten Steps of the MAUT Method

There are ten steps to the MAUT approach to measuring the relative usefulness of action alternatives. Edwards (1977) described the steps in detail. The steps are briefly summarized and explained below.

Step 1: Identify the organization whose utilities are to be maximized.

In other words, what is the organization or person for whom the evaluation is being conducted? In the above example, the person for whom the evaluation was being conducted would be the student planning to attend college.

Step 2: Identify the issue or issues to which the utilities needed are relevant.

That is, what is the purpose of the evaluation? What decision is the organization or individual addressing? In the above example the decision to be addressed is which college to attend.

Step 3: Identify the entities to be evaluated.

The "entities to be evaluated" are the options or choices the organization or individual has at hand. The options may be action alternatives or programs designed to meet an organizational need. For example, should the high school graduate attend College A or College B?

Step 4: Identify the relevant dimensions of value.

The "relevant dimensions of value" are the criteria on which the organization or individual will focus in order to make a choice between competing options or courses of action. They reflect organizational values as they are applied to the decision at hand. The dimensions should be clear and specific enough so that all the planners will understand them in the same way. In our example the cost of college might be further defined as tuition plus transportation and room and board, so that the statistics gathered on Colleges A and B would be comparable.

Finally, the criteria should be concrete enough to allow for accurate measurement. In our example "an acceptable cost" is the criterion that can be most objectively measured, and "good social opportunities" is a poorer criterion, since it must be measured in a vague, more subjective manner.

Step 5: Rank the dimensions in order of importance.

After the dimensions have been selected in Step 4, the organizational representatives rank the dimensions in order of importance. Disagreement between representatives is almost certain at this step, and this disagreement should be resolved through discussion and consensus. It should be made clear that the order can, and probably will, be altered later on during the discussions that take place during Step 6. In the example "an acceptable cost" was rated first, "good academic reputation" second, "an attractive location" third, and "good social opportunities" fourth.

Step 6: Rate dimensions in importance, preserving ratios.

The process begins by assigning the least important dimension a rating of 10. (The figure 10 is arbitrary, but allows for fine grading of subsequent dimensions while still retaining integer numbers.) Then the next least-important dimension is considered. If this dimension is considered to be twice as important as the previous one, it is given a rating of 20. If it is only half again as important, it is assigned a rating of 15. In fact, the representatives may decide that the second dimension rated is really no more important than the first dimension rated and give it a rating of 10 also, or even reverse the order of importance in light of further discussion. These ratings are called "weights" in Steps 7 to 9. As the process continues, many changes are likely to be made both in ranking and rating of dimensions. Such changes are acceptable and often desirable. Because the college-choice example was deliberately simplified, the refinements of this and the following steps were not used in the manner described.

Step 7: Sum the importance weights, divide each by the sum, and multiply by 100.

This is purely a computational step so that the ratings of all the dimensions will add up to 100. Edwards refers to this process as "normalizing" the weights. This process provides a clearer picture of the relative values of the weights given to each dimension, and makes subsequent calculation easier to manage.

During Step 7 the representatives will be able to recognize the reason for not including too many dimensions under Step 4. If there are too many dimensions, some will end up with trivially small weights that will, in effect, eliminate their impact on the decision. About six dimensions are ordinarily adequate and manageable. Lower-ranked dimensions can also end up with trivial weights if more highly ranked dimensions are carelessly judged to be five or six times more important than the lower-ranked ones.

Step 8: Measure the location of the entity being evaluated on each dimension.

These "measurements" are judgments and usually are very subjective estimates. At times objective data may be available. Edwards suggests asking each representative to estimate the probability on a 0-to-100 scale that a given option will maximize each dimension. In other words, if a program is judged to have a high probability of fostering the value represented on a certain dimension, it might be assigned a .70 probability. If the program has a low probability of fostering the same value, it might be given a .20 probability. It is likely that all available options will be thought to have merit on each dimension of value. Therefore, it will seldom be appropriate to use 0. These estimates indicate how useful a course of action is in achieving the desired objectives. Thus, these probabilities are called utilities in discussions of the analysis of decisions.

Once again, there will probably be divergence of estimates by different representatives. However, through the MAUT process common ground has previously been established through agreement on the dimensions and their relative weights. As a result, disagreement is now narrowed to the estimate of each option's probability of maximizing a given dimension of value.

Step 9: Calculate utilities for entities.

The equation is

$$U_i = \sum_j w_j u_{ij}$$

Remember that the sum of w_j equals 100. U_i is the aggregate utility for entity i; w_j is the normalized importance weight of dimension j from Step 7; and u_{ij} is the rescaled position of entity i on dimension j from Step 8 (Guttentag and Snapper, 1974, p. 58).

Stated simply, the total utility of each program or action alternative is obtained by multiplying the importance weight for each dimension (from Step 7) by the probability rating of an option on that dimension (from Step 8) and summing the products.

Step 10: Decide.

If a single action alternative is to be chosen, the rule is simple: Maximize U_i. If a subset of alternatives is to be chosen, then the subset for which the sum of all U_i's is a maximum is best (Guttentag and Snapper, 1974).

If the decision makers want only one program and are indifferent to cost, the best decision will be the program with the highest aggregate utility, U_i. Since costs are usually important, the MAUT user needs to choose a method to handle costs. Cost can be handled in more than one manner. In the college-choice example, cost was a value dimension. If cost is not introduced as a value dimension, then the utility of each option is considered in light of the budget available. It may be possible to fund the two best options or programs. If the cost of the program with the highest utility exceeds the budget, then the program next in priority might be chosen. The problem of relating program plans, outcomes, and costs is complex. Chapter 11 discusses the problem in greater detail.

An Application of the MAUT Method

To understand more fully the ten steps of the MAUT method as described above, consider the example of a large manufacturing firm that is concerned with high turnover among its employees. The firm would like to build loyalty and trust among its employees so that there would be greater stability in the work force. The president of the firm invites the firm's four vice-presidents to meet and to suggest what steps should be taken. Suppose that one of the vice-presidents, who has been reading about decision making, suggests that they disaggregate their task. The vice-presidents decide to use the MAUT method to approach the problem.

Step 1.

The organization whose utilities are to be maximized is the manufacturing firm. The firm will be represented by the vice-presidents.

Step 2.

The issue to which the utilities are relevant is how the firm can best build the loyalty and trust of its employees.

Step 3.

When the vice-presidents meet for the first time, they identify the available options or action alternatives. Let us suppose that they identify four possible courses of action:

- Presidential visits to employees in their work areas
- "Skip-one" contact sessions (where employees have the chance to discuss their work life with their own supervisor's supervisor
- Training the supervisors and all management personnel to develop better supervisory skills
- Career-planning sessions for all employees

Step 4 and Step 5.

Next, the vice-presidents identify the following six dimensions of values that would guide their choice and then rank them (*Step 5*) in the following order:

1. Personalization of relationships
2. Increased input by employees into the decision-making process
3. Removal of fear of retribution from the communication network
4. Increased job self-determination
5. Assurance to employees that the company followed through on previous employee recommendations
6. Clarification of company goals

Step 6.

Next, the vice-presidents proceed to assign weights to each dimension. They give dimension 6 a value of 10 and then decide that dimension 5 is of equal importance; therefore, dimension 5 is also given a value of 10. Dimension 4 is considered and judged to be twice as important as either dimension 5 or 6; dimension 4, therefore, is given a weight of 20. In like manner, dimensions 3, 2, and 1 are assigned weights of 30, 45, and 55, respectively.

The weights are normalized by dividing each by the sum of the six weights and then multiplying by 100. This process results in the following normalized weights:

Dimension	Raw Weight	Normalized Weight
1	55	32
2	45	26
3	30	18
4	20	12
5	10	6
6	10	6
	170	100

Step 8.

The group discusses the probability of each value dimension being maximized by each option. For example, option 1 (presidential visits) is given a .25 probability of maximizing dimension 1 (personalization or relationships); option 2 (skip-one contact sessions) is given a .50 probability; option 3 (training of supervisors), a .65 probability; and option 4 (career-planning sessions), a .50 probability. The process is repeated for the remaining five dimensions. The probabilities are all given in Figure 5.4.

Step 9.

Utilities are calculated for each option by multiplying the weight of each dimension by its probability estimate. For example, option 3 receives the highest utility score: $32(.65) + 26(.85) + 18(.80) + 12(.50) + 6(.40) + 6(.80) = 70.50$. Option 2 ranks second, with a utility score of 59; option 1 ranks third, with a utility score of 38. Finally, option 4 is last, with a score of 35. These calculations are summarized in Figure 5.4.

Step 10.

Decide. In the supposition that a training program for supervisors (option 3) would consume all the available money and resources, the vice-presidents would probably recommend to the president that only option 3 be implemented. However, if enough resources are available to implement option 2 (skip-one contact sessions) as well, then option 2 might be recommended along with option 3. The skip-one contact sessions received a utility score (59) that was not too far behind the score for a training program for supervisors (70).

Options (specific action proposals)		Dimensions (Values) to be maximized						Utility	Final rank
	Weights =	1 32	2 26	3 18	4 12	5 6	6 6		
1. Presidential visits to employees in their work area	Probabilities =	.25	.30	.75	.00	.70	.70	37.70	3
	Wts. × Probabilities =	8.00	7.80	13.50	0	4.20	4.20		
2. Skip-one contact sessions	Probabilities =	.50	.60	.75	.50	.50	.70	58.30	2
	Wts. × Probabilities =	16.00	15.60	13.50	6.00	3.00	4.20		
3. Training of supervisors and management personnel to develop better supervisory skills	Probabilities =	.65	.85	.80	.50	.40	.80	70.50	1
	Wts. × Probabilities =	20.80	22.10	14.40	6.00	2.40	4.80		
4. Career-planning sessions for all employees	Probabilities =	.50	.15	.20	.75	.10	.10	33.70	4
	Wts. × Probabilities =	16.00	3.90	3.60	9.00	.60	.60		

FIGURE 5.4 Multi-attribute utility (MAUT) worksheet.

In the supposition that there are not enough resources available for option 3 (training for supervisors), then option 2 would be recommended as the best choice within the firm's budget. The remaining two options (presidential visits and career planning) received utility scores of 37.70 and 33.70, respectively, and are clearly judged to be less effective than either options 3 or 2.

Rather than rely solely on the recommendation of the vice-presidents, the president might be well advised to seek input from other groups within the plant who would be affected by the decision. For example, the president might have a group representing first-line management and another group representing nonmanagerial employees meet separately to use the MAUT method to address the question of building employee trust and loyalty. If both groups arrive at the same conclusion as the vice-presidents, the president would have greater certainty that a supervisory training program would be accepted.

Use of the MAUT Model to Guide Evaluation

Not only is the MAUT model a guide to decision making but it also provides a means of focusing evaluation on the area where decisions must be made. Suppose that in the example just given, the president decides to proceed with a program to train supervisors and management personnel. However, the president questions how correct the vice-presidents were in the high probability (80 percent) they assigned to the effectiveness of the training of supervisors in removing fear of retribution from the communication network. The evaluation team can then focus its efforts on clarifying the degree to which fear of retribution is removed through supervisor training.

Subsequent evaluation will be needed to estimate the probability that the program did achieve its goal on one or more value dimensions. This could either confirm the wisdom of the choice of a given option or make the decision makers review their commitment to that option.

SUMMARY

After discussing general issues in planning and the tools for assessment of need, this chapter presented an example of the decision theory approach to planning. Evaluators who have the opportunity to cooperate with planning committees in selecting programs in this manner will have gained valuable background information and will develop personal rapport that will facilitate subsequent program evaluation.

STUDY QUESTIONS

1. Assume that the following questions appeared in a community survey. Discuss the strong and weak points of each.
   a. Is it important that (your town) have a program for gifted children in the public schools?
   b. Would you use a nutrition information service if it were available in (your town)?
   c. Have you ever sought counseling help for yourself or for someone else?
2. A key informant survey on the nutritional needs of the children of a particular community included the individuals listed below. Describe the degree to which each is a good or a poor source for information on the nutritional level of children of the community.
   a. The mayor
   b. The members of the city council
   c. A private-practice physician
   d. The school nurse
   e. A restaurant owner
   f. The truant officer
   g. Day-care center teachers
   h. Elementary school teachers
   i. Senior high school teachers
3. Assume that your college has a $50,000 grant to reduce crime on campus. Consider what sources of information about needs could be used. Then list the objectives such a program might attempt to achieve. Next list some possible specific actions that might be followed (for example, publicity campaign, new locks, escort service, and so on). Finally, draw up a MAUT decision matrix to choose among the possible programs.
4. Assume that you are chairperson of the local school board. Because a recent tax referendum has failed, the board must choose between discontinuing a remedial reading program and dropping an advanced program for gifted children. As board chairperson, how would you approach the decision, using the MAUT method?
5. Prepare an illustrative MAUT decision matrix as in Figure 5.4 to disaggregate a choice you must make or have recently made.

FURTHER READING

Additional information on needs assessment is available in

ATTKISSON, C.C.; HARGREAVES, W.A.; HOROWITZ, M.J.; AND SORENSEN, J.E., EDS. 1978. *Evaluation of human service programs.* New York: Academic Press. For special emphasis, see Chapter by BELL, R.A.; NGUYEN, T.D.; WARHEIT, G.J.; AND BUHL, J.M., Service utilization, social indicator, and citizen survey approaches to human service need assessment, and Chapter by SIEGAL, L.M.; ATTKISSON, C.C.; AND CARSON, L.G., Need identification and planning in the community context.

WARHEIT, G.J.; BELL, R.A.; AND SCHWAB, J.J. 1974. *Planning for change: Needs assessment approaches.* Gainesville, Fla.: University of Florida.

The Multi-Attribute Utility Model and other aids to decision making are described in

EDWARDS, W.; GUTTENTAG, M.; AND SNAPPER, K. 1975. A decision-theoretic approach to evaluation research. In *Handbook of evaluation research,* vol. 1., ed. E.L. Struening and M. Guttentag. Beverley Hills, Calif.: Sage.
RAIFFA, H. 1968. *Decision analysis: Introductory lectures on choices under uncertainty.* Reading, Mass.: Addison-Wesley.

Carey has adapted the MAUT method to the selection of chief executive officers in organizations. The method is called the Weighted Value Assessment System.

CAREY, R.G. 1979. Selecting hospital leaders through shared decision making. *Hospital Progress,* November, pp. 53–55.

6

Monitoring the Operation
of Programs

Program monitoring "... is the least acknowledged but probably most practiced category of evaluation" (ERS Standards Committee, 1982, p. 10). The most basic form of program evaluation is an examination of the program itself—its activities, the population it serves, and how it functions. Program monitoring includes an assessment of how much effort in the form of human and physical resources is invested in the program and whether the effort is expended as planned. The evaluation of effort is important; a program without sufficient resources cannot be expected to influence the participants in the program, and a program planned to meet one problem will be less useful when applied to a different problem.

An evaluation of the activities of a program cannot reveal whether the clients actually benefit from the program. Evaluation of the degree of successful outcome ultimately achieved requires an approach that goes beyond the methods described in this chapter. The methods illustrated here are called administrative monitoring (Poister, 1982). Monitoring that is related to goals and objectives of programs and agencies has been labeled performance monitoring. Relating staff work to goals is discussed in Chapters 7 through 10.

A well-planned, well-staffed, and well-housed program may not function effectively. Evaluators commissioned to assess the quality of a program will also inquire into its day-to-day performance. Businesses evaluate their performance by counting cash receipts at the end of the day and by performing inventories of stock at regular intervals. Human service managers need measures of activity similar to those available to commercial firms.

The problem, of course, is that the ultimate products of human service programs, well-functioning people, are not nearly as objectively measured or as concrete as store inventories.

The place to begin is to ask whether the human service program has been implemented as planned. If well-designed advertisements encouraging seat belt use are not actually published or broadcast, there is no reason to evaluate the impact of the material. If drug abusers do not attend a drug abuse program, there is little need to ask whether the program reduced drug abuse. Systematic methods have only recently been developed to monitor medical care, counseling and psychotherapy, training, and other forms of human services. Some of these methods assess the degree to which previously specified optimal procedures are followed. In this chapter we do not address the question of following optimal procedures; that question is pursued in Chapter 7. At this point evaluation is limited to a description of the services that are actually delivered.

Managers need such information to facilitate their planning and decision making, to anticipate problems, and to justify the existence of the program. For example, if it is discovered that a population receiving assistance is not the one targeted, then the program is not serving the need it was designed to meet and may have to be altered. Striking differences in the contributions of different staff members or an unusually heavy client dropout rate would be other problems important to detect. Managers can act to correct problems only if they have adequate information. Thus, program monitoring usually serves a formative function for program managers. Without accurate information, problems may become apparent too late to be corrected.

THE PROGRAM AUDIT
AS A MEANS OF PROGRAM
EVALUATION

Some evaluators have come to use the term *audit,* taken from accounting terminology, to describe the process of quantifying the amount of services rendered and the identity of program participants (Sells, 1975). Others simply refer to this activity as monitoring a program (Mechanic, 1975). To keep the term separate from the functions of accountants, the term *audit of services* is used to refer to a systematic examination of program inputs, or the effort put into a program.

Evaluators who conduct an audit of services gather information so that they can describe the program. A description of the program includes a profile of the clients coming into the program, a summary of the services given, workloads of the staff members, and sometimes clients' evaluations of the program. Program directors and staff sometimes believe they do not need quantified information to summarize the type and amount of services they provide and to whom these services are given. However, it is common knowledge among evaluators that the subjective feelings of staff members are often in error.

In several studies in which the authors have participated, program staffs have been very wrong in describing the population served by the program. In an evaluation of an innovative organization of nursing on a hospital unit (Carey, 1979), the staff said that 90 percent of the patients would have one of three major problems: respiratory illnesses, diabetes, or hypertension. As part of the evaluation, the diagnoses of the patients on the unit were recorded. It turned out that only 20 percent of the patients were diagnosed as having one of these three ailments. Is it possible that service could be improved if the nurses realized that they were actually serving a very heterogeneous patient population? An educational program designed for a relatively homogeneous patient population cannot be very effective when given to a group containing individuals with many unique needs.

The description of the population served and the services rendered by a program fills several needs. The immediate needs of management may be most obvious. In order to manage a human service program effectively, it is necessary to know who receives what service from whom, and when the service is given. Managers fill their roles better the more they are able to anticipate and avoid crises.

There are additional purposes, however. An audit of services is a necessary prelude to rigorous study of the outcome of services. Planning for future growth or redistribution of resources is a third reason for an audit of services. Knowing what is currently done provides a way to plan rationally.

Information suitable for planning or for use as a base line before a rigorous evaluation may be gathered through a modest audit of services conducted between two specific dates. In contrast, management needs require an ongoing information system and may well require the development of a system to obtain information routinely. The limited approach provides a snapshot of the program; the ongoing method provides a motion picture of the program. An examination of the program's records for a limited time period is undertaken to answer some particular questions about the level and types of services given; such information can give the planner and manager some directions to follow in program planning. On the other hand, repeated descriptions of a program over fairly short time periods, such as one month, permit closer monitoring and allow adjustments to be made in the way the program is run.

As with most dichotomies, this contrast of special, limited audits with extended, routinized audits may break down in practice. However, the distinction is useful; programs have different needs at different times. If a manager needs information that is gathered repeatedly over short time intervals, an approach requiring hand retrieval of data would be overly expensive and slow. On the other hand, a small program may not be sophisticated enough to require a complex information system; in such cases a simpler, less ambitious procedure would be used. Both forms of process evaluation will be illustrated at the end of the chapter. One case study illustrates an audit of a state's alcoholism services at a particular time. The second illustrates the repeated monitoring of services of a drug abuse hotline. Some writers in program evaluation view the development of management information systems as a major part of the role of in-house program evaluators (for example, see Attkisson et al., 1978).

WHAT SHOULD BE SUMMARIZED IN AN AUDIT OF SERVICES

There is no formula for selecting and gathering the information required to describe a program. Programs differ in the types of people served, the services given, and the type of institution offering the services. Evaluators bear in mind several points as they prepare an audit of services. These points are not explicit guides as to which information to gather or which procedures to use. Rather, they help evaluators focus on the issues that need to be addressed.

Relevant Information

The information gathered must be central to the purpose of the audit. Important information includes material useful to set staff levels, satisfy accreditation criteria, and plan for space needs. Effective evaluators attempt to gather only information that is relevant to describing the program and how it functions. Many characteristics of clients and programs are not central to program decisions. Evaluators may find many potentially interesting hypotheses to explore while doing an evaluation, such as, Is birth order related to the probability of becoming a juvenile delinquent? This question might well be important for theories of social development. If evaluators have the time to study issues of basic research, they may seek to explore some of these hypotheses. However, every bit of additional information recorded in an audit increases the cost of data collection and analysis.

Actual State of Program

A second point important to an audit is that it must describe the actual state of the current program. Evaluators are careful to distinguish between the program as described and the program as administered. Many programs that look very good on paper fail, not because they were designed poorly but because the staff or the participants did not actually follow the design or the procedure as planned. In a large university with many commuting students, an attempt was made to help freshmen become part of university life. In one program groups of eight to twelve freshmen were invited into faculty homes for social evenings. A number of enthusiastic faculty members volunteered to take part in the program. One of the major findings of the evaluation was that in spite of this early enthusiasm on the part of the faculty, 40 percent of the faculty did not actually invite the students whose names they were given. Second, among the students who did receive invitations, 60 percent declined to attend. One particular faculty member, who did not request that students respond to the invitation, prepared a fairly generous buffet dinner—only to discover as the evening passed that not one student was going to come. This program to involve students in the life of the campus did not need to be evaluated with an experimental design as planned. Merely noting the number of faculty who did not invite the students whose names they were given and the proportion of students who did not accept the invitations that were made was enough to show that the program was not being carried out. The program itself was very unlikely to reduce the number of freshman dropouts or to improve student morale. Without a careful study of the implementation of the program, administrative officers concerned with freshman dropout problems would have been at a loss to understand just what went wrong with the program.

The information necessary to describe the services rendered include (1) the type of service offered by the program (such as job training, group therapy, immunizations); (2) the extensiveness of the program (such as hours of training or therapy, skills to be learned, location of the program, facilities); and (3) the number of people participating in the service, especially the proportion of people completing the program.

The Providers of Services

The preparation of an audit of services should include a description of who gives the services. In large hospital settings many care givers—such as physicians, nurses, and physical therapists—are licensed by the state for the particular job. In other human service settings, especially where pay is low, people with limited training are involved in giving the service. Counseling programs for drug addicts or former addicts are sometimes staffed by people who are neither trained nor psychologically equipped for the positions they are filling. It is also possible that the staff may be overqualified. An evaluation of a project staffed by volunteer lawyers to help ex-convicts readjust to community life found mixed results—the released prisoners looked to the volunteers for legal aid, not for general readjustment help.

Thus, the legal training of the volunteers stood in the way of a truly effective program, in spite of sincere efforts (Berman, 1978).

Program Participants

A fourth major part of an audit includes a description of those who receive the services. If a program was well planned, the population to be served would have been specified carefully and the program tailored to meet the needs of that group. An audit should document the identity and the needs of the people using the service and compare these findings to the program plans. In other words, the fit between the program and the needs of those using it can be examined. If the fit is not good, changes or redirections for the program can be considered. If the agency never actually defined the group to be served, a description of the people using the agency may be especially enlightening.

The people using the program are routinely described by gender and age. The choice of additional information to be presented depends on the specific nature of the program. Such information may include where the people live, the major problems for which they are seeking help, the source of referral, ethnic background, and so forth.

The ease or difficulty people have in obtaining the service is an aspect of the description of those receiving the service. Unfortunately, this information is seldom in agency files. It would be necessary to prepare a short survey to administer to people using the service. Questions asked should cover how much time elapsed between initial contact and first appointment, the mode of transportation used, parking availability (if required), and time necessary to wait for care. In preparing such a survey, one must be aware of differences in ease of access that are related to variables such as time of day (morning versus afternoon versus evening), day of the week (workdays versus weekends), type of service, and welfare status of the individual. It is unlikely that a facility would need to gather all this information routinely. Obtaining it soon after beginning the program and at later time periods as the facility changes or expands would be sufficient.

When audits are reported, evaluators have come to expect to be told that the results of the audit (and this is true of any evaluation for that matter) were already known. It is a common human tendency to assimilate new information without realizing that it does conflict with what was previously expected. An accomplished evaluator will not reveal the findings of evaluations before obtaining some information on what the staff and director expect the audit to show. Only in this way will an evaluator actually know whether the audit produced "nothing new" or whether the results did indeed yield new material. After all, evaluators must be concerned about their own egos once in a while. (Case Study 6.1 illustrates a retrospective audit of the services to a select population—alcoholic native Alaskans.)

AN APPROACH TO PROVIDING
REPEATED AUDITS

When setting out to prepare a method of providing periodic reports describing the way an agency functions, the evaluator needs to have a hand in designing the agency's records. Instead of using existing files, the evaluator can help the agency design recording and filing procedures that will be useful for evaluation and for routine agency needs. When records are designed for use in evaluations, it is quite economical to prepare the type of reports described in this chapter.

The Existing Records
of a Program

It would be impossible to perform an empirical evaluation of effort without adequate records. However, it is no secret that the records of human service agencies are often in abysmal condition. Inadequate records are frequent even in hospitals, where sloppy handwriting has resulted in fatal drug overdoses and the amputation of a healthy leg instead of a diseased one (Dixon, 1977). Why are charts and records in such poor condition? Record keeping is a dull and time-consuming task. Individuals attracted to human service occupations often view record keeping as time taken away from clients, students, or patients. In the very short run, that view may be correct. Furthermore, records were less important in the recent past, when impressionistic evaluations of success and effort were sufficient evaluations in many settings. The existence of this and other books on evaluation methods shows that impressionistic evaluations are no longer accepted as sufficient by regulatory and accrediting agencies. We hope the reader will also see that in the long run well-kept records (and evaluation, in general) will result in more effective attention to human service program participants.

Evaluators helping an agency to develop an ongoing plan for documenting the provision of services will probably first ask what material is available in the records as currently maintained. However, even agencies with highly detailed and carefully maintained records may not have all the information useful for program evaluation purposes. Such records often contain long narrative accounts of progress or disability. The reason narrative records are not useful is that they lack a common frame of reference.

This lack is caused in part by the different points of view people adopt in defining success in human services. For example, the care giver, the program participant, and the community tend to define success in quite different terms. In the area of mental health, these different perspectives are often quite evident. People in the local community are distressed by public acting-out behavior. Communities do not want individuals around who wear unusual clothing, argue frequently with neighbors or shopkeepers, or tell passersby about hallucinations. The larger society wants individuals to keep up their living quarters, hold jobs, and, in general, behave responsibly. If mental health counseling or the provision of tranquilizers can keep people looking and acting relatively normal, society will consider the service successful and effective.

Therapists, on the other hand, have traditionally been less interested in day-to-day responsible behavior than in personality structure and emotional health. They would not view therapy as effective if it only assisted people to cope better or to conform passively to social norms. Instead, they would desire to detect greater autonomy, greater self-actualization, less guilt, and more frequent assertiveness. These are behaviors that are largely not observable by the community and not relevant to its evaluation of a mental health center.

Individuals receiving therapy may have an altogether different set of standards. They may evaluate therapy on the basis of whether they feel better about themselves. It is quite possible for clients to find a mode of adjustment that is acceptable to themselves but that would not satisfy the therapist or many members of the community.

Strupp and Handley (1977) have discussed these three points of view in more detail, especially with regard to negative outcomes in therapy. When individuals differ in their relative emphasis on these three points of view, free narrative reports will not be very useful to the evaluator. If the therapists also differ in theoretical orientations (such as Freudian versus behaviorist versus medical), the narratives will be even more difficult to compare and to summarize.

Increasing the Usefulness of Records

It is first necessary for the program director and other information users to develop a list of essential information useful in managing and evaluating the program. A point repeatedly stressed in this book is that information is gathered only when it is useful. If there are legal requirements to obtain certain information, or if decisions are to be made on the basis of the information, then it should be gathered. Otherwise, the material need not be recorded, unless it is suspected that negative side effects are occurring.

Information should not be gathered simply to fill folders in file cabinets. Methods of summarizing the information must be developed to increase the usefulness of files. In different contexts staff or managers have confidently assured evaluators that certain information was "in the files"— unfortunately, many files are incomplete. However, the major point is that in-the-files information is not useful information. Retrieving material from client folders is a time-consuming task. Further, it is a sensitive task: The privacy of the clients must be maintained. It is more efficient to develop a system that permits the routine summary of participant descriptors (that is, age, sex, disability) and service provided without manually going through file folders that often contain personal material important to the client and the care giver but irrelevant to the evaluator.

How Records Can Be Used
in Process Evaluations

One useful approach might be to prepare monthly summaries of all new clients. Figure 6.1 is a form that could be used when people initially request counseling at a center offering outpatient counseling. It contains much of the same information many counselors request. Regardless of the size of the facility, a sheet such as this would become the first entry in the individual's file. Notice that the center personnel add some information themselves, such as an identification number[1] and a problem code. Otherwise, the form could be self-administered.

To use this information most easily and effectively, it is necessary to have the material entered into a computer system. In order to maintain the client's privacy, it is necessary to have some of the material in Figure 6.1 on a second copy in a form that is not easily identifiable. A second copy can be obtained using two printed forms with carbon paper bound between the pages. Confidentiality can be maintained by making it impossible for the client's name, street address, telephone number, and other traceable material to print through. The information would be identified by the number added by the intake worker or secretary before the copies are sent to a data analyst. Figure 6.1 includes spaces to code type of problem(s) leading to a request for counseling.

The specific information to be gathered will depend on the needs of the particular human service agency preparing the system. Figure 6.2 contains a list of items that agencies would want to consider in preparing forms for gathering information about new clients.

Simply having some of the information in Figures 6.1 and 6.2 summarized each month or quarter would yield a more complete description of new clients than many agencies traditionally have available. For each calendar or fiscal year, the individual reports could be combined into a yearly profile of new clients.

Figure 6.3 is an illustrative new client report for a given month. The report includes information important to a particular center. For example,

[1]Recently colleges and social service agencies, among other groups, have begun using social security numbers for identification purposes. Using social security numbers, however, means that unscrupulous people can more easily match up an agency's records with other information about an individual (*Time,* July 18, 1977).

PLEASE COMPLETE THIS FORM AND RETURN IT TO THE SECRETARY IN THE ENVELOPE PROVIDED. THE INFORMATION YOU GIVE US IS CONFIDENTIAL AND WILL BE CAREFULLY SECURED.

Name _____   Please do not write in boxes below:

Address _____   □ □ □ □ □ □ □

_____ zip _____   □ □ — □ □ — □ □

Telephone _____

Marital Status: (Circle one)
  1. Never married 2. Married now 3. Widowed 4. Divorced/Annulled 5. Separated

Sex:
  1. Female   2. Male   3. Couple application

Age: _____   Age of spouse if married now: _____

Who referred you to the center? (Circle one)
  1. Myself, friend, family   4. Hospital   7. Another agency
  2. Another client   5. Physician   8. Other _____
  3. Clergyman   6. Psychiatrist   _____

What problem(s) has prompted you to consider counseling at this center?   □ □
_____   □ □
_____   □ □
_____   □ □

What form of counseling are you most interested in at this time? (Circle one)
  1. Individual   2. Family   3. Marital   4. Group

Who lives in your immediate family?
     Adults (give their relationship to you) _____   □ □
                                            _____   □ □
     Children (give ages)   _____   □ □
                                            _____   □ □

Have you previously received counseling from some other agency or counselor?
  1. Yes
  2. No

If "Yes" and if you do enter therapy with a counselor from the center, may we contact this person or agency about you?
  1. No
  2. Yes (Give name of counselor) _____

     Please sign _____

Where are you employed? _____

Please give the name and address of any insurance company that will meet part of your expenses at the center.

Name _____ Address _____ Ident. No. _____

FIGURE 6.1 An application form for potential clients of an outpatient counseling center.

Initial Information
Name
Address
Sex
Age
Educational level
Marital status
Family description
Ethnic background
Referral source
Problem(s) leading to request for services
Previous participation in similar human services programs
Insurance coverage
Veteran's benefits
Welfare status
Dates: Of initial application
         When formal participation begun

Some information will be unique to the type of agency involved. For example:

Mental health services:	Previous hospitalizations
	Type and extent of therapy
	Current medication
	Previous diagnoses
	Alcoholism/Drug user
	Functional life status
	Identity of previous therapist
Criminal justice programs:	Status with court system
	Type of previous programs
	Location of programs
	Voluntary or forced participation
Job-training programs:	Jobs held, length of previous employment
	Income
	Reason for unemployment
	Types of previous job-training programs
	Location of programs
Educational programs:	School attending
	Grade level
	IQ or other standardized tests
	Location of previous programs

Ongoing information
Amount of service rendered (hours of therapy, courses completed, skills mastered)
When service given
Identity of care giver(s)
Functional status or adjustment during and at termination of service
Reason for termination
Degree of self-support
Fees charged
Referral made

FIGURE 6.2 Types of information an agency might include in the basic descriptive information gathered about those seeking service, as well as the type of information added as the service is given.

NEW CLIENTS FOR MAY 1984

GENDER AND AGE OF NEW CLIENTS

		N	%	AGE
INDIVIDUAL CLIENTS	FEMALE	98	65	34
	MALE	30	20	27
COUPLES (TWO PEOPLE)		11	15	32
		---	---	--
TOTAL NEW CLIENTS		139	100	32

MARITAL STATUS AND GENDER

	FEMALE	MALE
NEVER MARRIED	28	12
MARRIED NOW	48	15
WIDOWED	3	0
DIVORCED,ANNULED	15	3
SEPARATED	4	0

SOURCES OF REFERRAL

	N	%
SELF,FRIEND, FAMILY	27	19
ANOTHER CLIENT	5	4
CLERGY	67	48
HOSPITAL	15	17
PSYCHIATRIST	2	1
ANOTHER SOURCE	3	2

PROBLEM CODE

	N	%
MARITAL PROBLEMS	80	58
INDIVIDUAL ADJUSTMENT ISSUES	128	92
PROBLEMS AT WORK	30	22
PROBLEMS AT SCHOOL	8	6
PROBLEMS WITH CHILDREN	62	45
ALCOHOLISM, DRUG USE	28	20
UNDIAGNOSED PHYSICAL SYMPTOMS	16	12

SERVICE SOUGHT

	N	%
INDIVIDUAL THERAPY	82	59
FAMILY THERAPY	15	11
MARITAL THERAPY	32	23
GROUP THERAPY	10	7

NUMBER(%) HAVING PREVIOUS PSYCHOTHERAPY   45 (32%)

NUMBER(%) EMPLOYED   92 (66%)

FIGURE 6.3 An illustrative monthly report describing applicants for outpatient counseling.

one counseling center with which we are familiar seeks to be of service to community clergy when they are faced with parish members who have emotional problems that cannot be handled by brief supportive counseling. A variable included in a hypothetical report of new clients for this center would be source of referral. This center can document that it is fulfilling one of its goals by showing that a large proportion of its referrals do indeed come from clergy. Age, sex, apparent problem, type of therapy desired, and location of residence are useful types of information in judging whether an agency is serving the population it was designed to serve.

The value of having summaries such as that shown in Figure 6.3 would be apparent to anyone who has worked in a large organization—it is necessary to let people know what you are doing. Program managers can more easily justify the continued existence of their programs if they are able to provide documentation of the number of people served, as well as brief demographic descriptions and the reasons clients give for seeking the service. Having information available also facilitates responding to requests for information. Frequently government agencies request material that may be available only by searching through the files. Chapman (1976) reported that the need to quickly prepare an extensive survey precipitated a crisis in a mental health center because much necessary information was not easily available. The crisis ultimately led the center to prepare an information system capable of routinely summarizing client characteristics as well as much additional information.

Following the Course of Service

The course of a service can be followed by preparing standard forms with spaces in which therapists can record certain information after each client contact. This short contact report does not take the place of the therapists' process notes, which are normally for the personal use of the therapist. Figure 6.4 is an example of such a contact report. The identification number would be used to match this report with other information about a particular client, such as information gathered at the beginning of therapy and from previous contact reports. The therapist number and therapy type are useful for documenting workload. The functional status ratings could be based on the procedure described in Chapter 3 (see Figure 3.2). Including the charges on this form would facilitate an automated billing system. Information about referral can be noted on this form, and a therapist may also indicate that a formal end of therapy has occurred.

To make more efficient use of the contact report in Figure 6.4, there should be copies for the therapist, the client, and the data analyst. All three copies could be made simultaneously. The client's copy and the data center's copy would not include all the information included in the therapist's copy. The copy for data processing would not include any of the printed labels included in Figure 6.4; it would not even indicate that the report referred to a therapy session. Figure 6.5 includes just the numbers and instructions for coding. The name of the client is not included; however, the identification number is. The client's version of the form is shown in Figure 6.6. It includes the client's name and center number (to facilitate access to records if a question should occur), the charge for services, the name of a referral (if any), the time of next appointment (if any), and the therapist's signature. These contact reports provide information useful for the management of a program.

FIGURE 6.4 An illustrative form for a therapist to use after each therapy session with a client. This copy would be kept by the center.

FIGURE 6.5 The way the information in Figure 6.4 would be transmitted to the person responsible for analyzing the information for future use.

FIGURE 6.6 The client's copy of the therapist's form illustrated in Figure 6.4 would contain the information shown above.

A monthly report of clients who have ended their association with the center could follow a format similar to that of Figure 6.7. Information about the amount and type of service received,[2] mean functional status at the beginning and at the end of therapy, amount of charges, number of referrals, and the type of termination occurring could be summarized and related to the demographic information previously obtained. Examining just the information in Figure 6.7, the director and staff can learn that about one-quarter of the clients apparently reject the services offered. This conclusion can be drawn from the fact that 24 percent of the clients accept two or less units of counseling and that 29 percent of the clients leave without the therapist's agreement. A director would probably seek to lower these proportions. The illustrative reports offer some clues about how to approach such a goal. The lower part of the report shows that older clients rejected therapy more frequently than younger clients did. Approaches to older clients could become a topic for in-service training at this center. Material presented later in this chapter will provide further suggestions for the director who seeks to lower the proportion of clients who receive little care at this center.

A monthly report can also be prepared for each therapist. Such re-

---

[2]A unit of service can be considered as one 50-minute period of individual psychotherapy or two 50-minute periods of group therapy. Other settings, of course, would require different units of service.

```
REPORT OF TERMINATED CLIENTS IN MAY 1984

CASES TERMINATED IN MAY: 84

    TYPE OF TERMINATION        N      %
                              ---    ---
      MUTUAL CONSENT           67     68
      CLIENT DECISION          24     29
      THERAPIST DECISION        3      4

    UNITS OF SERVICE RENDERED   N      %
                              ---    ---
      2 OR LESS                20     24
      3 TO 6                   14     17
      7 TO 15                  36     43
      16 TO 30                 13     15
      OVER 30                   1      1
```

RATINGS OF FUNCTIONAL STATUS

| LEVEL | CLIENTS AT EACH FUNCTIONAL LEVEL | |
	WHEN THERAPY BEGAN	AT TERMINATION
DYSFUNCTIONAL: 1	0(0%)	0(0%)
DYSFUNCTIONAL: 2	0(0%)	1(1%)
DYSFUNCTIONAL: 3	2(2%)	0(0%)
DYSFUNCTIONAL: 4	25(30%)	3(4%)
FUNCTIONAL: 5	41(49%)	2(2%)
FUNCTIONAL: 6	8(10%)	7(8%)
FUNCTIONAL: 7	6(7%)	4(5%)
FUNCTIONAL: 8	2(2%)	21(25%)
FUNCTIONAL: 9	0(0%)	46(55%)
MEAN FUNCTIONAL STATUS	5.00	8.05

TYPE OF TERMINATION AND AGE OF CLIENT

	UNDER 29	30 AND OVER
MUTUAL CONSENT	25(76%)	32(63%)
CLIENT DECISION	6(18%)	18(35%)
THERAPIST DECISION	2(6%)	1(2%)
ALL	33(100%)	51(100%)

UNITS OF SERVICE AND AGE OF CLIENT

	UNDER 29	30 AND OVER
2 OR LESS	5(15%)	15(29%)
3 TO 6	7(21%)	7(14%)
7 TO 15	14(42%)	22(43%)
16 TO 30	6(18%)	7(14%)
OVER 30	1(3%)	0(0%)
ALL	33(100%)	51(100%)

FIGURE 6.7 A report on the clients terminated during one month, including characteristics of services rendered to these clients.

ports would provide the therapists with information about their work as compared to that of the other therapists as a group. People working in human services seldom have quantified information on how their work compares to that of others in their own field or institution. However, the value of feedback in improving one's performance has repeatedly been demonstrated. Seligman and Darley (1977), for example, showed that residential use of electricity could be reduced over 10 percent simply by providing consumers, on a weekly basis, with information on how much electricity was used. Other examples of the value of feedback were given in Chapter 1 of this text.

A report format that could provide information for the individual therapist is given in Figure 6.8. This example describes the therapist's caseload and the amount of service rendered during the month in question. Note that therapist Helper has some problems. He had a higher proportion of clients drop out during the previous month than did the other therapists in the center. Of more importance, this hypothetical report shows that those who quit had received less service than was given to other clients before termination. This therapist also has a relatively large number of inactive clients, that is, clients who have not received any service for ninety days or more. The report politely requests that therapist Helper terminate these clients or see if they are still interested in continuing therapy. Last, there is a frequency table of ratings of psychological function of Helper's clients who officially ended their contact with the center during the last month.

Program changes or procedural changes can be planned to remedy any deficiencies found. What sorts of questions might therapist Helper want to discuss with his director? It seems that he is losing many clients after only one or two counseling sessions. Everyone has a string of bad luck once in a while. If Helper's record does not improve and he continues to lose clients prematurely, he should seek some assistance in improving his manner of relating to clients. Perhaps he is too judgmental; perhaps new clients need more direction during the first sessions. Ideally, noting undesirable characteristics early in a therapist's career should permit improvements in the therapist's techniques before poor practices are deeply ingrained. Also, it is to a therapist's advantage to learn of problems before hearsay and rumor define his or her therapy as below average in quality (House, 1976). Prue et al. (1980) described how feedback to staff improved the performance of workers at a state hospital. Feedback on treatment activities was a cost-effective method of improving service to the patients.

A Threatening Use of Process Evaluation

Gathering the type of information requested in Figures 6.1 and 6.4 permits the presentation of information in a way that can be very controversial. No one enjoys being evaluated. Nevertheless, so long as the process

```
REPORT FOR THERAPIST HELPER
```

	HELPER	OTHER THERAPISTS
TOTAL CASE LOAD ON JUNE 1, 1984	64	433
ACTIVE CASES	49(76%)	364(84%)
INACTIVE CASES	15(24%)	69(16%)
(NOT SERVED IN 90 DAYS)		

```
THE NAMES OF YOUR INACTIVE CLIENTS ARE:

    ARCHIBALD, L      NORRIS, M M
    BEST, B           OVERMAN, S
    BOULDER, M M      PAKOWSKI, M M
    ERNEST, G         RASMUSSEN, P
    GRAND, K          THOMAS, A
    HANSEN, M M       TRAVERSE, P
    MORRISON, S       WILSON, G
    NARWELL, B
```

```
PLEASE FILE A TERMINATION NOTICE OR A REFERRAL NOTICE, OR HAVE AN
APPOINTMENT WITH EACH OF THESE INACTIVE CLIENTS BY JULY 31, 1984.
```

	HELPER	OTHER THERAPISTS
TERMINATED CASES IN MAY		
TERMINATED BY MUTUAL CONSENT	10(48%)	47(75%)
TERMINATED BY CLIENT DECISION	9(43%)	15(24%)
TERMINATED BY THERAPIST	2(10%)	1(1%)
NUMBER OF THERAPY SESSIONS WITH CLIENTS TERMINATED IN MAY 1984 (MEDIAN)	4.0	7.5

```
RATINGS OF THE FUNCTIONAL STATUS OF TERMINATED CLIENTS WERE:
```

LEVEL	CLIENTS AT EACH FUNCTIONAL LEVEL	
	HELPER	OTHER THERAPISTS
DYSFUNCTIONAL: 1	0(0%)	0(0%)
DYSFUNCTIONAL: 2	0(0%)	1(1%)
DYSFUNCTIONAL: 3	0(0%)	0(0%)
DYSFUNCTIONAL: 4	2(10%)	1(1%)
FUNCTIONAL: 5	1(5%)	1(1%)
FUNCTIONAL: 6	1(5%)	6(10%)
FUNCTIONAL: 7	2(10%)	2(3%)
FUNCTIONAL: 8	4(20%)	17(27%)
FUNCTIONAL: 9	11(52%)	35(56%)

FIGURE 6.8 A possible format for feedback to individual therapists.

evaluation is only on a facilitywide basis, staff members may "grin and bear it." If the information available about an individual care giver is released only to that person, the controversy may concern merely the time and expense of the information system. However, the information generated by the methods just described permits numerical comparisons to be made among individual therapists. Most staff members dislike having their work compared to that of others in this way. Although such evaluations will be resisted, a manager needs objective comparative information. If staff members offer quite different services, obviously such comparative reports are more difficult to prepare. For example, crisis counselors, outpatient therapists, and inpatient group leaders cannot easily be compared to one another. However, when many individuals perform much the same tasks, contrasts among individuals become possible. In general, information on individual staff members should never be released in a general report. Individuals can be given their own data, which they can compare to summary data from the whole facility; however, only the director has a right to information on each individual staff member.

In Figure 6.9 the work of each therapist is summarized in one line. Contrasts among the therapists are invited. Those with very low or very high caseloads and those with many inactive clients can be easily noted. If there are particular therapists who lose a disproportionate number of clients early in the course of counseling (and thus often deliver only a minimal service to these clients), they can be readily identified. See, for example, the information on Helper.

Therapist Helper has the largest proportion of inactive clients and loses more than anyone else before three counseling sessions. However, Helper rates his clients as functioning higher than all other therapists except Nelson. There are at least two interpretations of these findings. One, Helper has been assigned clients who do not really need counseling. He correctly sees them as generally functioning well and does not provide unnecessary counseling. Two, Helper is not providing counseling that is seen as helpful by the clients. Although they drop out, Helper rates their functioning "good" as a way of justifying his high rate of client loss. The first interpretation is tenable if the pattern does not continue. However, if clients are assigned at random or to whomever has an opening and the pattern continues, the second interpretation appears more likely. Such a negative evaluation does not mean that Helper should be dismissed. It may mean that Helper should have some in-service training; perhaps his approach in setting the stage for counseling is not appropriate to the population utilizing this center. Such possibilities should be explored and may resolve the situation. If so, Helper will be a better counselor and his clients will be better served.

Even though initial objections to process evaluation as presented in Figure 6.9 are likely to be numerous and intense, there are important advantages to preparing such materials. We believe that accurate information is better than impressionistic information of unknown accuracy. What is to be gained by giving the program director the sort of information in Figure 6.9? The director's chief responsibility is to facilitate the delivery of quality human services—psychotherapy in this example. If a therapist is performing markedly less well than others, clients are being shortchanged when they are assigned to that therapist. It would be best if therapists took the initiative in approaching the director for help in improving their work.

CURRENT CASES AS OF JUNE 1, 1984   TERMINATED CASES IN MAY 1984

THERAPIST	ACTIVE CASES			INACTIVE CASES			N	FUNCTIONAL STATUS % ABOVE 7	% SEEN LESS THAN 3 TIMES	MEDIAN NUMBER OF VISITS
	N	% OF CENTER CASES	FUNCTIONAL STATUS (MEAN)	N	% OF CENTER CASES	FUNCTIONAL STATUS (MEAN)				
ABRAMS	39	11	6.5	4	7	6.3	6	100	33	6
COULDER	29	8	7.2	0	0	DNA	9	89	22	7
GREGORY	43	12	6.8	9	15	5.9	4	75	25	8
HELPER	49	13	6.7	15	25	6.7	21	71	48	4
MATTHEWS	28	8	6.5	1	2	6.0	6	50	17	9
NELSON	29	8	7.0	6	10	7.2	5	80	0	6
NICOLET	36	10	6.6	8	13	6.2	8	75	12	6
PETROVICH	38	10	7.1	10	17	5.9	5	80	0	7
RUDOV	19	5	7.1	1	2	5.0	4	100	0	9
VINCENT	35	10	6.5	4	7	6.3	10	80	20	7
WILLIAMS	20	5	5.9	2	3	6.5	6	100	17	8
ALL	365	100	6.6	60	100	5.4	84	80	24	7

FIGURE 6.9 A report permitting the center director to spot problems and to suggest ways to improve services given.

However, if the individual does not approach the director, the director's job requires approaching the individual. The reason for providing this information frequently—once a month or once a quarter—is to encourage improvement before a situation becomes intolerable.

Figure 6.9 should be supplemented with an accounting of time spent on various activities. For example, if therapists Rudov and Williams are devoting much time to community work, to administration, or to in-service training, their rather low caseloads are readily understandable. As an exercise, readers might try to prepare a form for therapists to use in accounting for their time. Categories of activities would include individual therapy, group therapy, administration, education, and community service. How might such report forms be designed? How might Figure 6.9 be extended to include this new information?

As with any type of information, a report such as Figure 6.9 can be misused. Critics fear providing summaries of information usually hidden in files allows such data to be used in a vindictive manner. Most evaluators believe that providing more information will reduce the opportunities for directors to behave tyrannically. Most unfair managers restrict information, just as despotic rulers control the media in the nations they govern. Nevertheless, certain precautions can be built into the system to circumvent some possible misuses of the information. For example, the system can be designed to minimize the possibility of acceptable variations in personal style appearing as deficiencies. Some therapists may encourage clients to leave therapy sooner than other therapists do. They may do this because of personal and theoretical convictions, not because of inadequate therapeutic skills. An information system should be planned in a way that does not confuse therapy designed to be short term with rejected therapy. In Figure 6.9 we sought to avoid this confusion by separately reporting the number of clients terminating after one or two counseling sessions. Even those who plan on short-term therapy expect to retain clients beyond two sessions.

Implementing an Information System

In 1976 Chapman stated that a computer-based information system is not cost effective in agencies or programs with ten or fewer care givers serving one thousand or fewer people in a year. However, the development of personal computers and the extraordinary drop in the cost of computer memory (Toong and Gupta, 1982) has made such rules of thumb obsolete. The type of reports illustrated in this chapter can easily be produced by desk-top computers such as those manufactured by Apple and IBM (among others) that use what are called database programs. The software for developing the tables illustrated in Figures 6.7, 6.8, and 6.9 is available for less than $300. Using such programs does not require any programming experience. (A computer, of course, could also be used to handle other aspects of managing an agency, such as billing, filing, or accounting.) The system described in this chapter is relatively simple. An even simpler one for a telephone hotline service is described in Case Study 6.2. Examples of more complex information systems can be found in Chapman (1976).

If done poorly, monitoring services can be expensive, disruptive, and unpleasant experiences for all involved. If done well, such evaluations of effort can provide feedback on performance that often enhances growth. Kreitner (1977) has called such feedback *informational feedback.* There are other forms of feedback, such as *corrective feedback,* that are also useful in helping people to improve their performance. Although automated systems such as those described in this chapter provide very valuable sources of feedback, managers should not permit these and similar systems to be the only source of feedback given to staff members.

AVOIDING MAJOR PROBLEMS
IN IMPLEMENTING AN
INFORMATION SYSTEM

Problems in implementing an information system may arise because people are naturally hesitant to try something new and suspect the motives of anyone gathering information. In addition, the evaluator may fall into some traps that will make the task all the harder.

Avoid the Duplication
of Records

Human service staffs will not happily cooperate with an information system that duplicates information already reported and stored elsewhere (Stull, 1977). Few agencies exist without any records. When introducing an information system, it would be undesirable simply to impose the system as an addition to the existing recording procedures. Instead, integrating the information required by the old system with the automation of the new system would be preferable.

It is likely that staff members may question the accuracy of an automated system. The fact that staff cannot describe the population they serve in quantitative terms may mean that they will at times be surprised at the content of the summaries of information gathered. Kivens and Bolin (1977) report that such surprises led some service providers to keep their own records for a time as a check on a new information system. If staff want to duplicate records for their own satisfaction, that is no problem. However, the evaluator should avoid requesting program staff to provide information for overlapping record systems.

Avoid Narrow-minded
Technology

Once a computerized system is considered, there is a temptation to concentrate on the technology of the system and to overlook the needs of the users. Lucas (1975) writes that information systems fail when user needs take a back seat to the technology of an information system. To avoid this problem, the users must be involved in the design of the system. The information that is needed, the manner of summarizing it, the frequency of reports, and other issues should all be determined with the people who will use the information. The evaluator may be enthusiastic about getting the system operating and experienced in producing elegant work. However, learning what will be useful requires patient work with the staff and administrators. Although a completed information system is not chiseled in granite, it is very expensive to change if someone thinks of a new bit of information after the system is operational. Involving users early and thoroughly will minimize the possibility of producing an expensive product that no one really wants.

Avoid Serving the Needs of Only
One Group

Different people fill different roles in an organization. They have different informational needs because their responsibilities are different (Patton, 1978). Hawkins, Roffman, and Osborne (1978) describe the diverse informational needs of judges, probation officers, and program planners in reference to drug user programs. In other settings evaluators should know that the needs of the accounting department will differ from those of the billing department, which in turn will differ from the needs of service delivery staff. By working closely with only one or two such groups, the evaluator runs the risk of providing information useful only to some groups. When that happens, the information system will be seen as irrelevant by those whose needs remain unmet. Furthermore, these people will begrudge giving information. The quality of information supplied can only be eroded when the system is not respected and valued. There is no substitute for understanding the organizational roles of all potential users.

SUMMARY

Human service agencies can begin an evaluation with a systematic description of their programs, the amount of service given, and the identity of those receiving the services. Such a process evaluation permits an accounting of how the agency's funds were expended and a comparison between the program as designed and the program as implemented. This sort of evaluation can be invaluable for showing what aspect of a program needs additional effort or why a program never had the impact intended. Also, the need to complete accrediting agency and government surveys can be met more easily if process evaluations are planned before the requests for information are made.

The two general approaches to process evaluation were illustrated: a summary of effort over a given time period and a systematized information system to permit repeated summaries of effort on a monthly or quarterly basis. The former requires a manual search through existing files that are often not designed with evaluation procedures in mind. If problems are found, even this kind of evaluation can lead to plans for improvement. When records are designed to facilitate evaluations, ongoing or repeated evaluations of effort are possible.

STUDY QUESTIONS

1. How does program monitoring fit into the schematic diagram in Figure 1.1.?
2. Explain the relationships between program monitoring and formative and summative evaluations.
3. People sometimes object to an evaluation of effort on the grounds that it reveals nothing about the quality of the service rendered. This statement is true. Why does this criticism not negate the reasons for doing the types of evaluations described in this chapter?
4. Suppose you managed a telephone sales office. Twenty people make telephone calls to potential buyers of educational films. If these potential buyers are interested in previewing a film, it is mailed to them. They either pay for it or return it in seven days. How would you develop a monitoring system to keep track of what your employees are doing? How would you measure their success? What type of indexes of success would be important?
5. Improve the form given in Case Study 6.2 for ease of use. Think about how easy or how hard it is to use the form and how convenient it would be to transfer the information to a computer.

FURTHER READING

In the late 1970s several publications appeared that are useful to mental health systems employees who wish to initiate and use thorough process evaluations. Although the content of many of these manuals is taken from mental health settings, the principles in these texts are applicable regardless of the settings in which an evaluator works. These materials also provide considerable help in organizing information into meaningful presentation formats.

CARTER, D. E., AND NEWMAN, F. L. 1976. *A client-oriented system of mental health service delivery and program management.* DHEW Publication No. (ADM) 76-307. Rockville, Md.: U.S. Department of Health, Education, and Welfare.

CHAPMAN, R. L. 1976. *The design of management information systems for mental health organizations: A primer.* Rockville, Md.: National Institute of Mental Health.

HARGREAVES, W. A.; ATTKISSON, C. C.; AND SORENSON, J. D., EDS. 1977. *Resource materials for community mental health program evaluation.* 2nd ed. DHEW Publication No. (ADM) 77-328. Rockville, Md.: U.S. Department of Health, Education, and Welfare. See Part III for materials on management information systems.

HAGEDORN, H. J.; BECK, K. J.; NEUBERT, S. F.; AND WERLIN, S. H. 1976. *A working manual of simple evaluation techniques for community mental health centers.* DHEW Publication No. (ADM) 76-404. Rockville, Md.: U.S. Department of Health, Education, and Welfare.

CASE STUDY 6.1   An Audit of Current Quality of Services

Understanding the current state of a service program is important for several reasons. To meet management and planning needs, managers must know what services are being offered. Without such information, it is impossible to plan in an intelligent manner. This audit study using existing records revealed clear inadequacies in the practices of alcoholism treatment programs and, by implication, suggested concrete ways in which services would be improved.

AN EVALUATION OF ALCOHOLISM TREATMENT SERVICES FOR ALASKAN NATIVES*

Sheldon I. Miller, M.D.

Associate Director, Department of Psychiatry
Cuyahoga County Hospital, Cleveland, Ohio

Edward Helmick, M.P.H.

Project Director, Alaskan Native Board of Health
Anchorage, Alaska

Lawrence Berg, B.A.

Associate Director

Paul Nutting, M.D.

Program Development Officer

*Condensed with permission from *Hospital and Community Psychiatry* 23 (1975): 829–31. Copyright 1975 by the American Psychiatric Association.

Gregory Shorr, M.D.

Program Development Officer
Office of Research and Development
Indian Health Service
Tucson, Arizona

Alcoholism and alcohol-associated delinquency and violence are increasing problems in Alaska, particularly in the urban centers and the transitional native communities. The purpose of the study was to describe services available to Alaskan natives and to assess the degree to which the health system was responding to clients with drinking problems.

The evaluation was an assessment and analysis of the degree to which the service agencies were responding to clients with drinking problems. The study focused on the delivery system rather than on treatment outcome. This methodology differs from the traditional evaluation approach, which is outcome oriented and focuses on the results of treatment.

Our basic plan was to examine the management of clients or patients with a recognized alcohol problem in both medical facilities and alcoholism programs throughout the state to determine if problems of alcohol abuse were being solved or prevented in a logical manner. The problem-solving process was defined as including information gathering, or assessment of severity and review of related problems; development of a treatment plan based on information gathered; and a follow-up and evaluation of treatment. These elements of the problem-solving process were used as standards of care in evaluating alcoholism services.

The review instrument was a flow sheet, which presented a logical sequence for evaluating the problem-solving process. In addition, the review instrument attempted to gather some information on the types of treatment in use and the severity of the problems seen in each treatment category. For the latter, alcoholism was defined along a continuum, with the well individual at the beginning and death secondary to alcoholism at the end. The intermediate states were drawn, in part, from the American Psychiatric Association's *Diagnostic and Statistical Manual.*

Members of the Alaskan Native Health Board selected twelve medical facilities and twenty alcoholism programs to be studied. The medical facilities included all of the U.S. Public Health Service's Alaska Area Native Health Service Hospitals, three of their clinics, and two locally managed hospitals that provide health care to Alaskan natives under contract and serve areas with a high prevalence of drinking problems among natives. There were twenty alcoholism programs in the state at the time the evaluation was planned.

A one-year study period, from July 1, 1971, to June 30, 1972, was chosen. A six-month period was added for follow-up of those cases occurring during the last six months of the study year. Charts of patients or clients over ten years old were reviewed. The audit at each agency ended after twenty-five charts were found in which the care provider recognized that the patient had a drinking problem.

A total of 4,435 charts were reviewed at the twelve medical facilities, and 637 were reviewed at the twenty alcoholism programs, bringing the total number of charts reviewed to 5,072. The data from the medical facilities and the alcoholism programs were kept separate since the medical facilities are charged with treating a variety of diseases including alcoholism, and alcoholism programs are expected to treat alcoholism only.

Medical Facility Data

The review of charts for all individuals over ten years old (4,435) revealed that 291 patients were recognized by the care provider as having a drinking problem. In many instances, the medical system's response to 291 problem users of alcohol left a great deal to be desired; in other cases it adequately answered certain needs. One area of deficiency was information gathering. For only 97 of the 291 charts was there enough information for the investigator to assess the severity of the problem, and for only 89 charts did the chart keeper make such an assessment. That indicates that in 2 percent of the charts reviewed, information was gathered but was not assimilated and used by the care provider.

Although alcoholism is a complex medical and social problem, in only 56 of the 291 charts reviewed was there any attempt made to outline related problems—social, economic, or psychological—influencing the comprehensive care of an alcoholic. The medical system did treat the presenting physical complaint, both alcohol-related and nonalcohol-related, in 94 percent, or 274, of the patients. It should be pointed out, however, that for 6 percent, or 17 of the patients who were recognized as needing physical treatment, no such treatment was given.

Although the system responded to a high percentage of the needs for treatment of presenting medical complaints, it did not do so well in relation to the basic problems of alcoholism. The maximum estimate of problem drinkers in medical facilities for whom a treatment plan for problems other than the presenting physical problem was developed was 148. It should be pointed out here that many of these individuals for whom a treatment plan was developed entered into the plan without having first been evaluated either as to the severity of their drinking problem or for alcohol-related problems. A minimum estimate of the percentage of patients for whom there was no assessment of severity and related problems, but for whom a treatment plan was developed, was 57 percent of the 148 patients.

A crucial factor in the continuing treatment of the patient is an evaluation of that treatment, and the first step in evaluation is a follow-up of the patient. For only 40 of the 274 patients with a treatment plan was there a documentation of follow-up. And for only 22 was there an attempt at follow-up to evaluate the outcome of the treatment plan. Of the 22 who were evaluated, a negative result was noted for nine. In none of those cases, however, was an alternative treatment plan developed. Thus it can be estimated from the medical facility data that a treatment plan will be developed, followed up, and its impact evaluated for only 8 percent of the recognized problem drinkers.

In the process of evaluating the function of the system, we noted the types of treatment used as well as the frequency with which information that would permit the assessment of the stage of severity was gathered. Unfortunately, even when severity was noted, the data were often insufficient to allow placement of the patient into one of the stages.

The treatment methods for the 274 patients were clearly noted. The most common form of treatment was the direct care of alcohol-related medical complications, which occurred for 76 percent of all identified problem drinkers. The second most common form of treatment was individual counseling, which was used for 22 percent of all the identified problem drinkers. Thirteen percent of the patients were referred to a detoxification unit, and 11 percent were given tranquilizers. (Percentages total more than 100 because some patients received more than one treatment at a time.)

Alcoholism Program Data

The data from the alcoholism programs are based on 484 patients recognized by the care provider as having a drinking problem. The assessment of severity of the alcohol problem was audited on two parameters. First, a maximum estimate was made of the percent of charts in which some degree of assessment of severity could be made by the investigator. In 55.2 percent of the charts that was possible. However, on the other parameter—whether the care provider himself made an assessment of severity—a maximum level was calculated to be 40.5 percent.

A comprehensive evaluation of the patient should involve a review of related problems, and a maximum estimate of the number of charts in which that occurred was 275, or 56.8 percent. For 433 patients, or 88.4 percent, a treatment plan was developed. As with the medical facilities, however, we found that treatment was often formulated without sufficient assessment. For 234 of the patients with a treatment plan, there had been no assessment of severity or of related alcoholism problems.

Follow-up occurred with only 124, or 29 percent, of the patients with a treatment plan. Of those patients who were followed up, the evaluation of 82 was documented. Thirty-nine of those evaluated had negative results, and for only eight was an alternative plan initiated. Thus in the alcoholism programs it can be estimated that a treatment plan will be developed, followed up, and its impact evaluated for only 16.7 percent of the recognized problem drinkers.

During the review of clients of the alcoholism agencies, efforts were made to determine the most common forms of treatment. They were somewhat different from those used by the medical facilities. Sixty-two percent of the clients received individual counseling, 32 percent went to halfway houses, 29 percent received group counseling, and 15 percent were referred to Alcoholics Anonymous. In addition, several other treatments were used, including detoxification, inpatient psychiatric hospitalization, and sleep-off centers. (Again the figures total more than 100 percent because more than one treatment modality was used for some patients.)

Conclusions and Observations

Although this study was conducted by chart review and therefore may not fully reflect actual practice in all cases, serious deficits in the health systems' response to alcoholism and problem drinking were found. The fact that the records might not reflect actual practice is in itself a serious deficit. Since any individual care provider could, for a variety of reasons, become unavailable to the client, the record becomes an important factor in providing continuity of care. Use of an accurate record is also the only way to audit the health system and to determine whether a system is functioning for a given client.

The absence of even an attempt at a record system is, therefore, a further indictment of the quality of the care offered by the provider. When records are written, information must be organized, processed, and understood by the therapist. Absence of a record raises the question of whether the provider was unable to understand and interpret the information gained from the patient. It might be said that inferior or missing records, rather than raising a question about the validity of a quality-of-care study based on chart review, are in themselves one of the more serious deficits that such a study could find.

The records reviewed indicate a failure to provide the basic components of care that are routinely expected in the treatment of other health problems. Alcoholism seems to be viewed as a single entity rather than as a chronic illness with various levels of severity. The complex nonmedical problems so important in the development of alcoholism and the treatment given the alcoholic are identified only on occasion. While clients and patients are treated for the problem, they frequently are not evaluated, and the treatment method may be determined by program needs, not by client needs.

It must be emphasized that the results of this study are presented in summary form. Some programs did quite well, but for the individual with a drinking problem seeking any help available, that is of little benefit. Generally the quality of the delivery system is poor. The presence of alcoholism seems to put an individual not only at high risk for the development of a variety of problems, but also at high risk of entering a treatment setting that will fail to systematically deliver the service needed to either prevent progression or find and treat current problems.

CASE STUDY 6.2   A System for Routinely Describing and Reporting Services Given

In this case study the authors describe a simple system for evaluating the services provided by a telephone crisis intervention service. Note the reasons the authors list for developing the system and the criteria of a good reporting system.

A PRACTICAL REPORTING AND EVALUATION SYSTEM FOR INTERVENTION PROGRAMS: GUIDING PRINCIPLES AND POTENTIAL USES*

David Zalkind, PH.D.
Harvey Zelon, M.P.H.
Mary Moore, DR.P.H.
Arnold Kaluzny, PH.D.

*Department of Health Administration
University of North Carolina School of Public Health*

Local government officials and directors of local human service agencies such as the United Fund are increasingly being asked to recognize the importance of and provide funding for crisis intervention programs. Often called "telephone hotlines," "suicide prevention centers," or "emergency aid services," crisis intervention programs are becoming one of the most prevalent types of human services programs across the country. While funding is currently available from the federal government through the National Institute of Mental Health, the National Institute of Drug Abuse, and the National Institute of Alcohol Abuse and Alcoholism, most of these small crisis intervention programs are faced with the reality of requesting additional support from local government authorities or United Fund agencies.

To justify their request for funds, a viable record and reporting system is needed. The purpose of this paper is to outline a series of general principles critical to the

*Condensed with permission from the *American Journal of Public Health* 67 (1977): 370–73. Copyright 1977 by the *American Journal of Public Health*.

design of a recording and reporting system and then describe a system based on these principles that can be developed and/or modified for intervention programs. In addition, the paper briefly describes a simple evaluation approach, essentially based on data generated by the reporting system, supplemented by a minimal amount of program operations data. The system discussed here was developed for intervention-level drug abuse programs by the Department of Health Administration, School of Public Health at the University of North Carolina at Chapel Hill under contract to the North Carolina Drug Commission.

The Basic Principles

The basic principles of developing a recording and reporting system for intervention programs are presented below:

1. Determine what decisions program directors are likely to have to make.
2. Determine what information program directors feel would aid them in decision making, and in what format(s) that information would be most useful. (Mock-up tables displaying such information should be developed to help ensure that the desired information will appear in a useful form.)
3. Determine specifically what data need to be collected for use in the tables.
4. Determine what information is either mandatory or prudent to report to other agencies.
5. Develop a simple reporting format. Considerable time should be spent at this stage to ensure that the format is complete and functional. Most intervention programs need a form that can be filled out at the time of contact between the program staff member or volunteer and the client. A form that is too complicated or time-consuming would be dysfunctional, as would one that left out valuable information. Recognize that early drafts of the form will need revision as experience with the system is gained.
6. If there is to be computerization of the system, design the recording forms to be self-coding. If data tabulation is to be done by hand, do not be too ambitious with regard to data that will need to be cross-tabulated.
7. Let the recording form for a client contact serve a dual purpose. When the recording form is done in duplicate, using a carbon, one copy can become part of the client record system. The other copy (minus any client identifiers or other confidential information) may be used for constructing program reports.

Using these principles, the program director should take time to carefully consider his/her decision-making patterns before establishing a reporting and recording system. Determining what decisions need to be made and the information needed to make them increases the survival potential of the agency as well as potentially minimizing funding problems.

A Simple System

A reduced copy of the second page of the client contact form that was developed is given in Figure 6.10. Each form consists of two pages joined at the bottom. The form is self-carboned so information recorded on the top page is automatically reproduced on the second page. However, the bottom page is longer than the top page (8½" by 14" as opposed to 8½") to permit the inclusion of additional information. In Figure 6.10, the sections for client and caller identifier, and problem notes will ap-

INTERVENTION PROGRAM CONTACT REPORTING FORM

Caller Identifier: _____ Client Identifier: _____

Problem Notes: (Four inches of space was provided here.)

. . . .

Staff Identifier _____
                                    Name   Number

PROGRAM CODAP# _____

_____ Staff Type: 1. Paid 2. Volunteer

_____ Date (Month, Day, Year)

_____ Time (Hour, Minute)

_____ Time: AM   PM

_____ Time Spent (minutes)

_____ Contact by: 1. Phone 2. Walk-in 3. Offsite

_____ Contact Status 1. First Contact
                            2. Prior Contact

Presenting Problem(s) and Service(s) Provided:

| Problems | Services | | | | Crisis |
| | Into | Refer | Counsel | Other | (YN) |
	1	2	3	4	
_____	_____	_____	_____	_____	_____
_____	_____	_____	_____	_____	_____
_____	_____	_____	_____	_____	_____
_____	_____	_____	_____	_____	_____
_____	_____	_____	_____	_____	_____
_____	_____	_____	_____	_____	_____

Caller Relationship to client   _____
1. Self 2. Spouse 3. Friend 4. Relative

Client: Age   _____

Client: Sex (M or F)   _____

Client: Race B. W. O-Other. U-Unknown.   _____

Referred to program by: _____
1. Self 2. Individual 3. Agency 4. Other 5. Unknown

If self, learned of program from: _____
1. Media ads 2. Word of mouth 3. Prior client 4. Other

FIGURE 6.10   Client contact reporting form. (continued on next page)

Problem List:

Medical Health Problems	Psycho-Social Problems
10 Veneral Disease	20 Family
11 Pregnancy, Abortion	21 Sex
12 Hepatitis	22 Suicide
13 Drugs	23 School
14 Other	24 Job
15 Other	25 Housing
16 Other	26 Financial
17 Other	27 Legal
18 Other	28 Interpersonal
19 Other	29 Other
	30 Other
	31 Other
	32 Other

_____ If referred, to: 1. Hospital 2. Private _____
Professional 3. Inhouse Name (for your records)
4. MHC 5. Other Agency 6. Other Drug Program

_____ If counseling, type: 1. Individual 2. Family 3. Group

_____ If DRUG related, type(s):

40 HEROIN	48 Anti-depressants	56 Cough and
_____ 41 ILLEGAL	49 Sedatives–Hypnotics	cold
METHADONE	(nonbarbiturates)	remedies (in-
42 Opiod Analgesics	50 AMPHETAMINES (in-	cluding anti-
43 Non-Opiod	cluding combination	histimines)
_____ Analgesics (in-	diet pills)	57 Sedatives
cluding OTC)	51 COCAINE	(i.e., Somi-
44 ALCOHOL	52 MARIJUANA, HASHISH	nex, Nytol)
45 BARBITURATES	53 Hallucinogens	58 Anti-
_____ 46 Major Tran-	54 Delinents (i.e., phen-	infectives
quilizers	cycledine and atropine	59 Cardiovas-
47 Minor Tran-	55 INHALANTS	cular and
quilizers and		Diuretics
Muscle Relaxants		60 Unknown
		61 Other

Sequence Number _____

FIGURE 6.10 *(Cont.)*

pear only on the longer sheet. This sheet is retained within the agency while the top sheet is sent to the central office to be key punched and processed. The central office collects such sheets from participating programs once each month and sends back reports compiled at program, regional, and state levels.

There are fourteen tables that appear in each report. They include: a compilation of contacts made by day of the week and hour (useful for scheduling staff), demographic characteristics of clients (for comparison with target population), and self-referral information source (for estimating effectiveness of different publicity efforts).

However, the information in the report tables is not sufficient to answer all questions, particularly those related to evaluation of the intervention program. Additional information is required.

Summary

The continued existence of intervention programs is contingent on the ability to answer basic questions such as "What is your program doing?" and "Why should we fund your program?" This paper outlines basic principles and describes a practical reporting and supplemental evaluation system that can be used by administrators of even the smallest intervention program.

part III

EVALUATION OF OUTCOME

Descriptions and illustrations of outcome evaluations make up a large portion of this book. A major purpose of these presentations is to encourage an understanding of the variety of forms an outcome evaluation can take. The selection among these methods is determined by the decisions evaluators and program managers make about the primary purpose of the evaluation.

The first decision is whether the evaluation would be better focused on the degree to which each individual achieves the outcome desired, or whether summary information on groups of participants is more useful. Individualized assessments of outcomes are well suited to evaluations of medical and mental health care and managerial effectiveness. In Chapter 7 several widely used individual goal attainment evaluation methods are introduced.

Drawing up individualized goals is often expensive. Further, such goals are often not required. Many programs are offered to fairly homogeneous groups of people who seek to gain quite similar benefits. Evaluators will probably work with group-based data far more frequently than with individual-based information. Such evaluations are described and illustrated in Chapters 8, 9, and 10. These chapters have been organized so that the simplest form of outcome evaluation is presented first.

A simple examination of the state of program participants after receiving a service will tell program managers and sponsors whether the participants leave a program with acceptable levels of achievement or health. If there are objective program goals that are widely accepted as valid, the simple evaluation designs described in Chapter 8 may be quite satisfactory.

When simple evaluation designs will not suffice, additional information must be gathered to improve the interpretability of the evaluation. Chapter 9 includes three approaches to improving the clarity of interpretations: observing the program participants more than twice; observing additional groups; and measuring additional dependent variables. Of course, these approaches can be combined to produce even better evaluation designs.

When the purpose of an evaluation is to ascertain beyond any doubt whether a program did or did not cause an observed change in the program participants, the methods of Chapter 8 will not be adequate. If the evaluation is carefully planned, the methods of Chapter 9 will often be quite satisfactory. All doubts about causality, however, are most easily eliminated if a true experiment is used to assess the outcome of a program. The advantages of true experiments and the precautions to follow to guarantee that an evaluation designed as an experiment remains an experiment when implemented are the topics of Chapter 10.

Once the outcome of a service program is known, it is possible to ask whether the outcome is worth the cost. In other words, is the program an efficient use of resources? The basic principles of cost-benefit and cost-effectiveness analyses are described in Chapter 11. Since support for social programs has been eroding since the late 1960s, it is likely that cost concerns will become more important in evaluations of human services than they have been in the recent past.

7

Assessing the Achievement of Individualized Goals

Chapter 6 discussed methods used in administrative monitoring. Such methods are frequently quite useful in helping one to understand a program. Nevertheless, the most effective use of information gathered through monitoring procedures requires that comparison be made between the data found and some standard of effectiveness. Poister (1982) called this approach performance monitoring. Without standards of care or service, monitoring can find only, for example, that X units of care were given, or that one staff member sees more clients than another member. Therefore, the question of whether the amount of work done or whether the effort of any staff member is satisfactory cannot be answered using the methods described so far.

Society sets many standards. There are fairly clear and objective fire safety standards, such as: The halls of public buildings must be so many feet wide; exit doors must open out; and furniture must not be placed in exit routes. In schools a specified number of square feet must be provided for children of various grade levels. In counseling settings there may be standards about how many hours of direct service each counselor must offer per week.

More important than standards describing physical structures or effort expended, however, are standards of quality of outcome. The end does justify the means, so long as the means are ethical and responsible. This would be especially true in human service settings; professionals seldom really know what does and what does not reliably work to help people learn, to help them improve emotional health, to help them hold a job, and so on. This chapter focuses on methods that assess the achievement of individualized goals, that is, goals that are prepared for specific individuals or for a specific category of people.

The task of evaluating success in meeting a goal would be relatively easy if the parties involved could agree on objective goals. When such agreement exists, a program can be evaluated simply by observing the group of people experiencing the program. Foxx and Azrin (1973) have described a method of toilet training based on the behaviorist principles of shaping and reward. The goal or criterion of success was the time required to train the child to use a child-sized toilet. Because the goal set for the program—one day—was so much shorter than the time most parents require, there was ready agreement with the goals of the program. For parents who have worked for months to achieve that goal, there is no need to ask whether such an outcome would indicate that the program was successful.[1] A program that far exceeds typical levels of outcome is not difficult to evaluate, especially if a wide consensus endorses the level of outcome achieved. Stanley (1982) made a similar point in a discussion of a program to aid gifted teenagers. He maintained that since very, very few fourteen- to fifteen-year-olds started college, the high success rate of students in a summer math/science program argued for its positive impact. An evaluation did not require a sophisticated design such as those described in later chapters.

However, few outcomes are as striking as that in Foxx and Azrin's work or in Stanley's work, and seldom is consensus so easily achieved. Outcomes are not striking because longstanding behavior is hard to change; change is usually small, even after an effective program (Rossi, 1972). Consensus on ideal outcomes is not likely—people with different viewpoints desire different outcomes. In Chapter 3 the different expectations of the client, the therapist, and the community were described for the case of psychotherapy. Ideal outcomes are also hard to specify because people enter programs with different levels of abilities and, therefore, are likely to complete programs at different levels.

In order to assess the degree to which programs achieve their goals, methods are needed that help the evaluator develop standards and assess whether those standards or objectives were achieved.

This chapter focuses on several techniques used when there is a need to evaluate the degree to which the service approaches predetermined standards of effective work. There are three general methods illustrated: Goal Attainment Scaling, management by objectives, and peer review. These techniques have been found useful in a variety of settings, and they illustrate a number of principles important to evaluation.

---

[1]For those new parents among the readers, Foxx and Azrin did succeed. The mean time required to toilet train the children was 3.9 hours. See Case Study 8.2 for further information on this program.

DEVELOPING OUTCOME GOALS

There are a number of reasons why it is extremely important to have performance goals for human services. In the first place, specifying a goal forces people to become more realistic in their aims. It is very easy to set ambitious but vague goals that are seldom achieved by anyone (House et al., 1978). Often, in perhaps a sincere attempt to persuade decision makers, people describe what *could* be achieved by someone accepting counseling, therapy, job training, or some other human service. When the therapy or training is over and these very optimistic goals have not been achieved, it is fairly easy to rationalize why these goals were not met. It is important to be optimistic, but it is also important to be realistic. Spelling out the specific goals to be achieved is a discipline that helps human service professionals look very carefully and critically at their plans.

A second reason why specified goals are important is that it is hard to know just when a human service should stop. When helping a person learn social skills, write more effectively, or develop marketable job skills, it is possible to see additional room for further improvement, regardless of positive changes that have occurred. Having specific goals prepared ahead of time makes it easier to decide when the service can end.

Third, when goals are specified, the client, other staff members, and third parties such as insurance companies or employers can participate in setting and evaluating the achievement of goals of human services. Psychotherapists, for example, often have been criticized for having private goals and for being the only judge of whether those goals were achieved. Frequently these criticisms are valid. Preparing specific goals and discussing them with the client, with other staff members, and at certain times with employers ensures that many individuals participate in this process.

A fourth reason to set specific goals is that clear goals are in themselves motivating. People work more efficiently when they know what is expected of them. Industrial psychologists have found that difficult but specific goals lead to better performance than do nonspecific goals (such as "Do the best you can"), easy goals, or no goals at all (Locke, 1968; Yukl and Latham, 1978). McCarthy (1978) used goals to reduce carelessness in a textile plant. Dicken (1978), a nurse, writes that goal setting is a motivator for patients recovering from serious illnesses. Burns (1977) found that setting goals was effective in improving the performance of school principals. Most workers and students are happier, more productive, and more satisfied when they know what is expected of them. Realistic but challenging goals can provide human service personnel with considerable help in their work.

Finally, goals are important because managers need to monitor performance. Lohr, Brook, and Kaufman (1980) comment on the widely differing quality of care provided by physicians, even when the procedures involve elementary medical care. Moeller (1982) makes a similar observation, blaming poor performance on lapses of attention, carelessness, and poor follow-through—not on lack of knowledge.

Problems in Setting Performance Goals

There are certainly many problems in setting goals for any human service facility. One of the major problems students raise when goal setting is first described to them is: What is to keep people from setting very low goals, therefore guaranteeing that they will always achieve and often exceed those goals? If the mere achievement of goals was all that was important, this would be a damning criticism of this approach to program evaluation. However, just as athletes cannot set unrealistic goals that they can easily achieve, neither can human service care givers. In both cases other people are involved in evaluating the validity of the goals. Counselors whose only goal is to prevent clients from committing suicide would probably achieve that goal with more than 99.9 percent of their clients; if, however, therapists must share these goals with other staff members and with the client, then this very minimal goal will be challenged and rejected as meaningless for the vast majority of clients seeking counseling. It is likely that if clients and other staff members share in the development of human service goals, a balance will be found between the ambition to achieve overly challenging goals and the temptation to set easy-to-achieve goals.

A second problem that people raise when they first consider explicit goal setting is that it renders the care giver's job harder to do. Very often in health care settings, if therapists or nurses are asked what their goals are, they usually say to provide good medical care so that people can get better. Colleges set goals such as training educated and cultured men and women. Such goals cannot be challenged. However, they are so general that it is impossible to know to what extent the goal is ever achieved. Setting explicit goals will make the care giver's job somewhat harder. However, if human service agencies hope to be perceived as helpful and expect to be paid for their efforts, they will have to show that they are planning services or curricula carefully, that they usually achieve what they expect, and finally that what they expect is accepted as worthwhile by patients, trainees, clients, and the institutions or individuals paying for the service.

The Approaches to Be Presented

This text will explicitly discuss two approaches to goal construction. One of these approaches is that developed by Kiresuk, called Goal Attainment Scaling (Lund and Kiresuk, 1979; Kiresuk and Sherman, 1968). The second approach discussed is called management by objectives (McConkey, 1975). Goal Attainment Scaling (GAS) and management by objectives

(MBO) are actually quite similar; however, the person whose behavior is described in the goals is different for the two approaches. MBO concentrates on the manager's behavior, whereas GAS concentrates on the behavior of a client of a human service facility. There are other forms of goal setting for clients, patients, and managers. GAS and MBO, however, are widely used and well known and are good illustrations of the value of an individualized goal-setting approach to evaluation. Finally, peer review, a method of monitoring quality of work popular in health care settings, will be described.

INDIVIDUAL TREATMENT GOALS

Constructing individual treatment goals is important as a discipline, as an evaluation strategy, and as a means of encouraging communication between client and therapist. Explicitly recording goals requires much more discipline and thought from the therapist than simply saying, "We'll do the best we can." As an evaluation strategy, the preparation of explicit goals is important because the quality of intended care and actual care can then be compared among various approaches or organizations. Finally, sensitive care givers realize that their goals may not be the same as those held by the client. For example, a couple seeking marital counseling may, by chance, select a counselor who concludes that divorce is the only option and directs the counseling toward having the couple accept divorce and carry it out as smoothly as possible. Another couple with the same level of difficulties may select a counselor, just by chance, whose goal is to avoid a divorce at all costs. It seems important that clients and therapists discuss goals ahead of time to minimize this chance aspect from the counseling relationship. Communication is also to be encouraged between client and therapist so that time is not wasted on minor problems or on repeatedly following the whims of client or therapist while forgetting the major problems.

What is required in the construction of individual outcome goals? First, goals must be explicit, and they must be recorded. Second, they must be realistic yet ambitious. The balance between realism and ambition is likely to be achieved when the goals are constructed in cooperation with the client and in consultation with other staff members. Third, the goals must be reviewed; as therapy progresses, the client may become dissatisfied with the original goals and wish to revise them. On the other hand, the client may become satisfied in having achieved the goals and desire to end therapy. Or the client may realize that those goals have been achieved and may wish to construct new goals that would have seemed overly ambitious when therapy began.

Goal Attainment Scaling

Goal Attainment Scaling goes beyond what has been discussed in the preceding paragraphs: It permits measurement of the *degree* of attainment of the outcomes desired, regardless of the unique needs of an individual client. Making such measurements requires some ingenuity, because human service goals are often difficult to quantify. However, obtaining a quantified index of success is an advantage, since comparisons among treatments and institutions then become possible.

In selecting the goals for a therapy relationship, the initial discussion with clients must center on why they have requested therapy and what they would like to get out of it. Therapists will at the same time discuss what they feel can be expected and, if all goes well, what might be possible. In the initial one or two interviews, clients and therapists should be able to agree on some outcome goals for the therapy.

It is possible that the therapist may have some additional goals that would be important for a client to achieve but that the client would not be prepared to accept as legitimate goals during the early stages of counseling. One can easily imagine a psychotherapist being struck by the abrasiveness or the manipulating manner of a new client. Few people enter therapy because they are dissatisfied with their abrasiveness or their manipulative approach to social relations. It may be possible as counseling progresses that clients might begin to sense that one of their own characteristics is involved in the problems that brought them to counseling. At that time they may wish to include it as a goal in their therapy. Thus, there is a place for goals that the therapist may not wish to share immediately with the client. However, having made this point, the reader considering the use of GAS should remember that GAS goals must be shared to obtain the method's full usefulness.

After the goals have been stated and recorded, GAS requires that each goal be weighted by its relative importance. In general, the client is to cooperate with the therapist in rating the importance of these goals. One of the easier procedures to use in rating the importance is to assign some arbitrary value to the least important goal. A value of 10 is easy to work with. The therapist and client must then decide how much more important the next goal is. Perhaps that goal would have a weight or value of 20 because they agreed it was twice as important as the least important goal. In this way numerical values can be applied to the goals that therapist and client agree are central to this therapeutic relationship. (This weighting process is identical to that described for use with the MAUT model in Chapter 5.)

An Example of the Use of GAS

If a school counselor was going to begin a counseling relationship with a student in academic and disciplinary trouble, several school-related goals might be set up to guide the counseling. Perhaps the student wants to achieve higher grades, to be sent less frequently to the principal's office for discipline, and to improve his or her reading speed.

Once the dimensions have been specified, the next step is to describe the state the student is expected to be in by the end of some time period, if counseling goes normally. Then the most unfavorable and the most favorable outcomes are described. The dimensions and the descriptions are the basis of the GAS grid. For example, a D student may be expected to improve to a C level: The worst outcome would be to fail; the most favorable outcome would be to obtain B's and A's. In terms of improving reading speed, the worst outcome would be to stay the same, since it seems unlikely that reading speed would drop during the following several months. On the basis of standard test scores, the counselor feels that the student could double his or her reading speed if real effort were expended. Finally, suppose that the student was being sent to the principal's office an average of six times a month when counseling began. The worst outcome would be even more discipline problems; the most favorable outcome would be no discipline problems. These scales and descriptions are shown in Figure 7.1.

The values recorded to the right of the various outcome levels are equivalent to z-scores.[2] The expected outcome is valued at 0 because the mean of a set of numbers has a z-score of 0. The most favorable outcome is expected to occur only 5 times out of 100, so it has a z-score of 2. Finally, the least favorable outcome, also expected 5 times out of 100, is valued at −2. The two less extreme outcomes are assigned z-scores of +1 and −1.

To take full advantage of the method would require assigning importance weights to the three scales. If we assume that the student was in danger of being expelled for behavioral problems, scale 3 would be weighted most heavily, and reading speed would be least important. The counselor assigned reading speed a weight of 10. Grades were felt to be 50 percent more important, so scale 2 was weighted 15. Finally, fewer trips to the principal was weighted 20. These weights do not add up to any set value, since only their relative values are important.

The beginning level of the student is checked on the grid. After counseling, an asterisk was added to record what the student achieved during counseling. Numerical values can be calculated using the weights and the scale attainment levels associated with each level of outcome. The formula given by Kiresuk to calculate a standard (T) score analogous to the standard scores on personality tests is

$$T = 50 + \frac{10\Sigma\ w_j x_j}{\sqrt{(1 - \rho)\Sigma w_j^2 + \rho(\Sigma w_j)^2}}$$

In the formula, w_j is the weight assigned to the scales, x_j is the attainment level on the scales, and ρ refers to the average scale intercorrelation, which

[2]Standard scores such as z-scores are described in any statistics textbook.

Level of outcome	Value of outcome	Scale 1: school grades Weight: 15	Scale 2: reading speed Weight: 10	Scale 3: trips to principal Weight: 20
Most unfavorable	−2	D− or F	75 wpm ✓	7+
Less than expected	−1	D✓	100 wpm	4-7✓
Expected level	0	C− or C*	150 wpm*	2-3
More than expected	+1	C+ or B−	200 wpm	1*
Most favorable	+2	B or A	250+ wpm	0

Check marks refer to levels at the beginning of counseling. T = 33.53

Asterisks refer to levels at the end of counseling. T = 52.99

FIGURE 7.1:   Example of a goal attainment grid using objective individualized levels of goal attainment. (Adapted from Garwick, 1973.)

is assumed to be .30. For our hypothetical student, the initial value of T was found by substituting the attainment levels before counseling as follows:

$$T = 50 + \frac{10[15(-1) + 10(-2) + 20(-1)]}{\sqrt{(1 - .30)(15^2 + 10^2 + 20^2) + .30(15 + 10 + 20)^2}}$$

Carrying out the calculations, we find that the student began at a level of 33.53.

If the student remains in counseling and tries to adjust more successfully to school, the student is expected to improve to 50. Any better achievement will result in a score above 50. Assume that the asterisks in Figure 7.1 indicate the level of the student at the end of the school year. If the counselor calculates the goal attainment level after counseling, a value of 52.99 would be found. Thus, the student did a bit better than was expected and is functioning quite a bit better than at the start of counseling.

The use of GAS is a valuable discipline for counselors. Although calculating the T-values for a single client provides little useful information not already available from the grid itself, comparisons of outcomes among programs or types of approaches to counseling can be made if GAS is used routinely. Often individual therapists receive their GAS results plus a summary of the overall average attainment levels of the rest of the staff. In this way therapists learn how effective they are in comparison with other therapists, without the possible embarrassment caused by general release of each therapist's average attainment level.

The question of who does the final outcome rating is critical. In the example of a junior high school student, the outcomes are objective and very easy to assess. The question of outcome assessment is far more difficult when outcomes are stated in terms of less dependence or less manipulativeness. An example grid for counseling requiring such scales is given in Figure 7.2. In such situations periodic follow-up by raters other than the therapist is probably required to use GAS in order to contrast treatment types or to evaluate the competence of individual therapists.

MANAGEMENT BY OBJECTIVES

One of the current approaches to management that is receiving a great deal of attention and is being applied in many human service facilities is management by objectives (often abbreviated MBO) (Gerstenfeld, 1977). The approach used in MBO was first suggested in the mid-1950s by Drucker (1954) and McGregor (1960). Their approaches stressed the following three points: (1) Organizational goals must be clearly established and communicated to all managers in the organization; (2) the managers of the organization are to set individual goals that conform to the intent of the organization's goals; and (3) periodic review of the degree to which managers are achieving their objectives is necessary.

This is not a book on management; therefore, we cannot go into management procedures in great detail. However, the program evaluator should have some familiarity with this well-known and widely used management technique.

The initiation of MBO requires commitment of the whole organization to the MBO approach. Top levels of management set their own goals; however, it is important to notice that in the MBO approach, all managers are involved in some way in the goal setting. Goals are not imposed on anyone but are developed jointly by managers and their supervisors.

Performance must be reviewed or, in our terms, evaluated. Managers must receive feedback and evaluation on the degree to which they are meeting their goals. Such evaluation assumes that all managers have some freedom in developing their approaches to achieving the goals of their units. If the managers had no freedom to choose how to approach meeting the goals, then one could hardly hold them accountable for the success or failure of their own unit.

In one study managers said that the most important advantage of MBO was that it improved planning and organization of work. The second most important advantage was in helping managers understand the goals of the organization and their responsibilities in meeting those goals (Sloan

FIGURE 7.2: An example of goal attainment scaling when outcomes are hard to quantify. The level at intake is marked with a check and yields a value of 29.4. The level at follow-up is marked with an asterisk and yields a value of 62.2. The difference between these values is the Goal Attainment Change Score of 32.8. (Reprinted with permission from T. J. Kiresuk, "Goal Attainment Scaling at a County Mental Health Service," *Evaluation*, Monograph No. 1, 1973, p. 15. Copyright 1973, The Program Evaluation Project.)

and Schrieber, 1971). Moore and Staton (1981) reported similar findings with city managers who said that MBO was effective in clarifying their goals.

Like all management and all evaluation procedures, MBO has some disadvantages as well. A repeated objection to MBO concerns the amount of time consumed in completing the paperwork and in developing the goals themselves. It is likely, however, with any systematic procedure of keeping records and developing goals, that the time commitments will decrease as people become familiar with the system.

Preparing MBO Goals

The central step in developing a workable MBO plan is the statement of goals, or objectives. Such objectives must refer to observable organizational behavior and be compatible with the organization's overall objectives, regardless of the level of management preparing them. Some examples can be based on the case study of alcoholism treatment for native Alaskans (Case Study 6.1).

The reader may remember that there were a number of problems in assessing severity of alcoholism, in treatment planning, and in follow-up procedures. For example, in only 283 out of 775 cases of alcoholism did the therapist assess the severity of the problem.

Objectives that could be written following the search of records are:

- The severity of the alcohol problem of every client is to be assessed by the care giver before a treatment plan is developed.
- A review of the client's related problems must be made during intake procedures.
- Assessment of treatment effectiveness must be attempted.
- When follow-up proves that the treatment did not result in improvement, alternative treatment plans should be used.

Achievement of these goals should be facilitated for the care givers. Every staff member whose performance on these goals will be monitored must have participated in planning them and must know that management will be directed by these goals. A casual presentation of goals is insufficient to assure a wide understanding of them. Perhaps care givers could have the importance of these goals discussed with them individually. A minimal requirement would be that each manager discuss the importance of these goals with the staff.

Institutionalizing MBO Goals

One way to institutionalize these goals would be to develop some formal procedures that incorporate them. If these goals were incorporated into a record form that was used at all institutions, the communication of these goals would be carried out. Although it may seem that a new form is a minimal response to these clear needs, using a form that requests information about the client's condition, the planned treatment, and the timing of follow-up may be sufficient to change the care giver's behavior to meet the goals we have suggested above.

Figure 7.3 is the form that was developed by the Alaskan Native Health Board as a first step in improving care for people needing alcoholism treatment. Persons gathering intake data from new clients would be required to assess the severity of the problem by completing the form. Because the form requires a description of the plan for treatment, one cannot complete the form unless there is a plan for treatment. There is also a section of the intake form that is filled in after treatment, when follow-up is attempted. One cannot require therapists to contact all clients after treatment; however, one can require documentation of an attempt to contact the client. If care givers fill in this form completely and accurately, they will have achieved the objectives described above.

The Native Health Board also had a long-range goal in mind in developing this form. They discovered in their process evaluation that it was impossible to compare the effectiveness of any one institution with another; records of the clients' needs for treatment and the outcome of treatment were not available—or else the records were so different from one another that comparisons were impossible. The use of this standard form in all alcoholism treatment facilities in the state made possible comparisons among facilities. In addition, the use of a common form made it easier for a client to move from one facility to another. A common problem that human service givers face is the number of clients who are lost to the program. Many clients change homes or for personal reasons wish to seek service at a different facility. The use of a common form permits the facilities to keep track of transient clients. Such long-range goals may conceivably be developed by the health board for the whole state.

PEER REVIEW

The methods described so far have focused on monitoring the organization's procedures (Chapter 6) and on the success of the organization's service (GAS and MBO). However, neither approach is primarily designed to examine the skill or judgment of the care givers or managers in achieving desired outcomes. Neither approach can directly isolate inadequate work nor provide clues to guide the improvement of work. In both medical and psychotherapeutic settings, the trend is toward requiring some sort of outcome review that can document patterns of good and poor care (Drude and Nelson, 1982; Jacobs, Christoffel, and Dixon, 1976; Markson and Allen, 1976).

FACTORS WHICH MAY INDICATE SEVERITY OF DRINKING PROBLEM		SYMPTOMS – DISABILITY INDEX			INSTRUCTIONS: STAGES REFER TO FACTORS PRESENT IN LAST THREE MONTHS ONLY. CHECK APPROPRIATE BOXES. WRITE ADDITIONAL INFORMATION ON REVERSE SIDE.		
		STAGE 0	STAGE 1	STAGE 2	STAGE 3	STAGE 4	STAGE 5
PHYSICAL	APPARENT INTOXICATION & ADDICTION	None	Alcohol abuse averages less than once per month	Alcohol abuse averages more than once per month	Evidence of addiction Can't go more than one day without drinking and/or DT's		
PHYSICAL	INJURIES DUE TO INTOXICATION	None	Only one alcohol related injury in the past 3 months that required medical att'n.	More than one injury in the past 3 months that required medical attention.			
PHYSICAL	PATHOLOGIC CHANGES (This section may be completed by a physician)	None	None	Preclinical target organ damage	Symptomatic target organ damage	Irreversible liver damage	Irreversible brain damage
SOCIAL	FAMILY RELATIONSHIPS	No problems related to alcohol abuse	Some quarrels related to alcohol abuse (with spouse, parents, etc.)		Breakage of family ties because of alcohol abuse (divorce, drinker leaves home, etc.)		
SOCIAL	NON-FAMILY RELATIONSHIPS	Usually does not associate with alcohol abusers		Usually associates with alcohol abusers	Only associates with alcohol abusers		
ECON.	EDUCATIONAL/ VOCATIONAL	No problems with school, job, or employability related to alcohol abuse	Some problems with school, job or employability related to alcohol abuse.	Threatened with expulsion from school or loss of job because of alcohol abuse.	Out of school or unemployed because of alcohol abuse.		

PERSONAL DATA

NAME_____
Last   First   Initial

Individual's Agency Number_____

Social Security Number_____

Birthdate ___/___/___ Sex: Male____ Female____
month day year

Race: White____ Indian____ Other____
Black____ Oriental____ Unknown____

Marital Status: Married____ Widowed____ Divorced____
Single____ Separated____ Unknown____

INFORMATION ABOUT THIS CONTACT

Ambulatory care ☐ or Institutional care ☐

First contact_____ Recontact_____

Appointment_____ Walk-in_____ Home Visit_____

Referral from_____

Who is seen
Individual with drinking problem_____
Family members or others (name-relationships) -

PROBLEMS WHICH MAY CONTRIBUTE TO ALCOHOL ABUSE

	Yes No	Plan For: Past Three Months	Today and/or Future
1. Physical Disabilities			
2. Psychiatric Problems			
Social Problems			
3. Vocational/Educational			
4. Family			
5. Housing			
6. Legal			
7. Financial			
8. Other (specify)			

Physical / Psychiatric Diagnosis

TREATMENT PLAN FOR ALCOHOL ABUSE

Counselling

	Plan For: Past Three Months	Today and/or Future
20. Individual - Insight		
Supportive		
21. Group Insight		
Supportive		
22. Family Therapy		
23. Behavior Therapy		
24. Alcoholics Anonymous		
25. Counseling for family members		
26. Other (specify)		

Institutional Admission

	Past Three Months	Plan For: Today and/or Future
9. Sleep-off Ctr.		
10. Halfway House		
11. Jail		
12. Med. Hospital		
13. Psych. Hosp.		
14. Nursing Home		
15. Other (specify)		

Medical Treatment of Alcohol Abuse

16. Antabuse		
17. Tranquilizer		
18. Detoxification		
19. Other (specify)		

FUTURE CARE
Follow-up at this Agency
1. None
2. or_____ visits a month here
Referred to other Agencies
Names of Agencies_____

NO TREATMENT PLANNED

Agency_____

Signature of Therapist and Job Description_____

Today's date ___/___/___
month day year

27. Individual refuses care
28. Individual's family refuses care for themselves
29. Care deferred until next visit
30. Other (specify)

CASE CLOSED ON THIS VISIT
31. Planned_____ or Unplanned_____
Closure by:
32. Individual_____
33. Therapist_____ 34. Both_____

FIGURE 7.3: A form to promote better treatment for alcoholism. (Reprinted with permission from E. Helmick et al., "A Monitoring and Evaluation Plan for Alcoholism Programs," *British Journal of Addictions* 70 (1975): 371. Copyright 1975, Longman Group, LTD.

Peer review refers to any system whereby peers of care givers (physicians or psychotherapists) examine the techniques used and outcome produced in treating patients or clients. Sometimes these systems are called quality assurance, quality control, or utilization reviews. Without acceptable peer reviews, hospitals risk the loss of their accreditation.

Peer reviews can serve different purposes and can vary in their thoroughness and the degree to which they intrude into the care giver's behavior. The least thorough and least intrusive peer reviews may simply consist of a staff meeting at which therapists voluntarily describe cases and their plans for treatment. The comments of other staff members fill an educational function and serve as a way to help the care giver obtain new points of view. If the procedure is voluntary, and if the advice does not have to be followed, the reviews may be done only infrequently, and they may have limited impact on the behavior of the care giver.

Newman and Luft (1974) described how a community mental health center met the problem of unacceptably high costs for psychotherapy through a peer review process. The center's administrators did not want to develop a harsh, conflict-prone system to control costs, but they did feel costs were out of control. The most direct cause of high costs was the amount of therapy hours provided. It was decided to introduce peer review panels whose approval was necessary if therapists intended to provide tax-supported counseling for more than six sessions. To obtain such approval, the therapist was required to make a case presentation to a three-member panel justifying the longer therapy. In order to minimize hostility and the perception of coercion, the reviews were organized so as to increase the potential educational benefits of the review. Note that this approach is not threatening to the therapists, because the only information the panel obtains is from the therapists themselves.

How well does the system seem to work, and how well are the reviews received by the therapists? Luft (1979) reports that the review system has resulted in fewer treatment sessions per patient and that clients spend fewer months as active patients of the center. The most striking effect has been the reduction in the number of very long-term patients.

Many therapists report that they have come to value the assistance they receive from the review panels. (In fact, Luft found that that system has been received far more favorably than the administration had expected.) The therapists believe that only a few patients required more therapy than they received, and a survey of patients revealed a high level of agreement between therapists and patients about improvement and about whether there was a need for additional therapy. Most patients and therapists agreed that sufficient therapy had been obtained.

Overall, the therapists feel that the review procedure has been an aid to their professional growth. Those who most frequently utilize the panels seem to be influenced in their nonreviewed cases as well. Only a small proportion of therapists feel that the review procedure has interfered with their work.

A more thorough review procedure would require an examination of the actual content of the therapy sessions or the medical care given. Psychotherapy peer review can be based on tape recordings of counseling sessions. Experienced clinicians report that most clients do not appear to be disturbed by the tape or cassette recorder. A major difficulty with reviewing tapes is the time involved. A less desirable alternative would be to review the counselor's notes on a case. Unfortunately, a counselor's notes are subjective, and reviewing them would also require much time. There probably is no good *and* practical way to review the content of more than a small proportion of counseling sessions.

SUMMARY

The common thread tying together the methods in this chapter is that criteria describing good outcomes of human services can be developed. Services can be evaluated by comparing the actual outcome observed with standards of good outcome. The outcome-oriented methods in this chapter differ from those in the following chapters in that the methods presented here can be applied only when outcome is assessed on an individual basis; those in the following chapters utilize statistical procedures requiring data based on groups. Because of this individual emphasis, these methods are applicable in settings in which an individual's ideal behavior can be described. Thus, these methods are useful in counseling, rehabilitation, and medical facilities in which the client's or patient's outcome is assessed, as well as in all management settings in which the manager's achievement is of interest.

STUDY QUESTIONS

1. Construct a GAS Grid (Figure 7.1) for a college student who wants help in learning to study more effectively. Imagine a student who is not doing well in school. What are some things he or she might do differently? Make up specific goals that student could follow in trying to improve study habits.
2. Discuss the problem of maintaining confidentiality of records when peer review procedures are used in mental health settings.
3. Most of the following objectives are too vague for use in performance monitoring. Make them more objective. One objective is too ambitious. Make it more realistic.
   a. Improve the level of community mental health
   b. Conduct in-service training workshops
   c. Reduce the waiting time for new clients seeking care

    d.   Have all people referred to a second agency actually make contact with that second agency

4.   What is to keep a psychotherapist from setting GAS goals that will be easy to meet?

5.   Answer this objection to GAS: "The method forces me to harden my treatment plans, but I think I should remain flexible. In fact, my clinical experience indicates that the flexible clinician is far more helpful than one who makes hard-and-fast plans or sets inflexible goals for therapy."

6.   Among the goals that a university wished its graduates to achieve were

    a.   Reflection and critical judgment

    b.   Passion for justice

    c.   Enjoyment of life in its highest forms

On the basis of what was presented in this chapter, what would a program evaluator say about these goals? How could an evaluator go about learning whether these goals were achieved?

FURTHER READING

Evaluators considering the use of GAS should obtain materials from

Technical Assistance and Program Evaluation
1609 11th Avenue, South
Minneapolis, MN 55404

The center provides guides, conducts workshops, and even has produced videotapes about the use of GAS.

For further information on MBO, the following materials are helpful.

McCONKEY, D. D. 1975. *MBO for nonprofit organizations.* New York: AMACON.
MORRISSEY, G. L. 1970. *Management by objectives and results.* Reading, Mass.: Addison-Wesley.

A helpful book for preparing objective goal statements—whether GAS, MBO, or another system is chosen—would be

MAGER, R. F. 1972. *Goal analysis.* Belmont, Calif.: Fearon.

8

Nonexperimental Approaches to Outcome Evaluation

Chapter 7 focused on the achievement of outcomes for individuals. Medical care, psychotherapy, and managerial achievement can often be evaluated using that approach. However, the measurement of individual outcomes and a comparison with individualized goals may not be a feasible approach to evaluation in many settings. A neighborhood crime prevention program, a new way of admitting patients to a hospital, and a class for diabetic senior citizens have goals that apply equally to all people using the program. Therefore, such programs can be better evaluated using information describing group performance rather than measures of the degree to which specific individuals achieve goals. This section of the text focuses on the analysis of data gathered from groups for the purpose of evaluating the outcome of human service programs. The chapters begin with the simplest approaches and progress to the more complex and more scientifically rigorous. Each approach, regardless of its scientific rigor, has its place in program evaluation. However, the usefulness of a particular approach depends on the questions the evaluator is seeking to answer.

As indicated in the chapter titles, when evaluators are commissioned to learn if a program caused an outcome, they choose a more rigorous research design than when commissioned to show merely that clients leave a program at a certain level of competency or health.

As these chapters progress, the questions each approach can address—as well as the misuses of each approach—will be described and illustrated. The reader should develop a sense of the purpose of careful experimental design and see how each level of control is introduced to increase the clarity of the interpretation of the data.

SINGLE-GROUP DESIGNS

One Set of Observations

When teachers, nurses, administrators, or judges inquire into the success of some social service program, they frequently use the simplest form of outcome evaluation. Basically, they want to know how the program participants are faring after the service has been provided. Do the members of a job-training group have jobs three months after receiving job skills training? What percentage of smoking clinic participants are in fact not smoking one month after the program? The first step in deciding if a program is useful is to learn if the participants finish the program with a level of achievement that matches the program's implicit or explicit goals. This simple form of evaluation requires that a set of systematic observations be made of one group at some specified time after completion of the program. This simple posttest-only assessment of outcome will show the staff and the evaluators whether the participants finish the program at a low, medium, or high level of achievement. For example, the rearrest rate for released first-time felons may be 5 percent, 15 percent, 30 percent, or 75 percent. If the program is to help ex-convicts avoid further trouble with the law, but nearly all fail to do so, then there may be no need to evaluate any further. Program improvements should precede any further outcome evaluation. On the other hand, if program "graduates" do have a low rate of recidivism, the staff *may* have an effective program which should be studied more thoroughly. Still, evaluators would not even know whether the program participants improved during the program. To learn whether people improved requires a more complex design.

One Group—Two Sets
of Observations

If the question the evaluators are seeking to answer cannot be addressed through one set of observations made some time after the completion of the program, then a more complex research design should be considered. The pretest-posttest design is used when the evaluators want to ascertain that the participants improved while being served by a program designed to help them. The program might have caused such an improvement; however, the pretest-posttest approach to data collection is not sufficient to permit such a conclusion.

The reasons why causal interpretations may not be permitted have been labeled "threats to internal validity" in the classic work by Campbell and Stanley (1963). *Internal validity* refers to the interpretability of the data in light of the way the observations were made. For example, showing that people who complete a reading program do indeed read well or, for that matter, better than they did a month before does not mean that the program itself led to the improvement. This caution is especially serious when only a small portion of those who began the program actually complete it. A plausible alternative interpretation is that the most motivated learned, but the program is unsuccessful for most people. In order to evaluate the adequacy of various approaches to outcome evaluation, a detailed understanding of the threats to internal validity is critical. As the reader will see, the posttest-only and the pretest-posttest approaches are very deficient in terms of internal validity. As more complex designs are presented, various plausible alternative interpretations will be eliminated until finally the only plausible cause of change is the human service program itself.

The questions that can be answered by simple, nonexperimental approaches to outcome evaluations are summarized in Figure 8.1. This figure and others in the following chapters reflect the idea that the evaluation design should be based on the questions to be answered and on the resources involved with the program—not on a priori assumptions adopted from basic research practices (Cronbach, 1982). When programs are relatively inexpensive, not harmful to participants, and fairly standard, absolutely airtight evaluations are not needed (Smith, 1981). The bulk of this chapter is devoted to the appropriate uses of the pretest-posttest design and the rea-

FIGURE 8.1 Single-group evaluation designs and the questions they can answer.

Name and symbolization[a] of the evaluation design	Questions that can be answered
Posttest Only X O	How well are the participants functioning at the end of the program? Are minimum standards of outcome being achieved?
Pretest-Posttest O X O	Both of the above questions. How much do participants change during their participation in the program?

[a] *Throughout this text, the notation adopted by Campbell and Stanley (1963) will be used. The program is symbolized as X and an observation by O.*

sons why care must be exercised when interpreting the results of pretest-posttest evaluations.

USES OF THE
PRETEST-POSTTEST
DESIGN

Did the Program Participants
Change?

Before describing the various reasons unrelated to the program that may explain why participants change, some statistical tests necessary to show that participants did change are presented. Statistical tests distinguish between random variation and systematic variation. In other words, statistical methods permit us to decide whether the observed improvement between pretest and posttest is large enough to indicate that some real change occurred in the participants, or whether the change is so small that it cannot be distinguished from such chance influences as the participants' health, mood, care in completing the forms, transient level of motivation, or liking for the interviewer. If unexplained chance variation is so large that one cannot be certain that participants did change, for whatever reason, there is no point in examining the data any further to learn whether the program could have affected the participants (Winch and Campbell, 1969). When statistical tests are discussed, the concern is not about internal validity, but merely about the differences (or lack of differences) between two numbers, such as two means. This is called a question of conclusion validity (Cook and Campbell, 1979).

A statistical test for continuous variables. The required analysis depends on the nature of the measures of program success used. Frequently evaluations employ measures yielding continuous scales. For example, measures of psychological or physical function (such as depression, academic achievement, or minutes of unassisted walking) are treated as continuous variables with equal intervals. Income level, length of employment, and credits for good prison behavior are further examples of variables that can be treated as continuous. For such variables, program success is indicated by the mean value attained by a group of participants.

The correct statistical test for the pretest-posttest evaluation design using continuous variables is the correlated-groups t-test (McCall, 1975). This test is also called the matched-group t-test. This analysis is correct whenever the data from the pretest and the posttest are not independent; that is, each pretest value is associated with a posttest value. The most frequent use of this method occurs when the same people are tested before and after a program. People make closer matches with themselves than with anyone else.

The major advantage of the correlated-groups *t*-test is the recognition that a person with a low pretest score can hardly be expected to achieve at the same level or to do as well as another person with a relatively high pretest. In a sense, this analysis tests whether the *changes* that were observed are reliably greater than zero. Such changes may occur when a person goes from a low pretest to a moderate posttest or from a moderate pretest to a high posttest, among other possibilities. The standard form of the *t*-test for randomly assigned independent groups is less likely to detect changes than the correlated-groups analysis.

Much more will be presented about statistical analysis in later chapters; however, the presentations are not a substitute for a statistics text. The statistical procedures are presented as a way to remind the reader about previous course work and as a way to help the reader apply statistical methods to program evaluation.

A statistical test for categorical variables. In some evaluations program participants are classified into categories, such as employed or not, at home or in a nursing home, or rearrested or not. For categorization data, the measures of program success are best expressed as a proportion or a percentage. For example, program success could be expressed as: 57 percent are able to live independently; 68 percent are employed after job training; or 15 percent are back in jail after twelve months.

If the measure of success is a percentage or a proportion of the participants achieving some goal, then nonparametric tests are to be used. Suppose a program was designed to assist ex-convicts recently released from prison to obtain and retain employment. One measure of success of such a program would be an increase in the number of participants holding jobs. If nineteen had jobs when the program began and forty-one were employed after two months in the program, the evaluators might wish to learn whether these numbers are reliably different. (Remember, finding a significant difference is only the first step in analysis. It means that the program *might* have caused a change, not that it did. A significant difference should be followed up with a more rigorous evaluation if a question of the cause of the change needs to be answered.)

Because these values refer to the same individuals, a nonparametric test applicable to a test-retest situation is needed. The McNemar test for the significance of changes (Siegel, 1956) was designed for this purpose. To conduct this test, it is necessary to know the number of ex-convicts who had jobs before the program but lost them, and the number who did not have jobs before but had jobs afterward. These are the people who changed, and clearly the program staff wants more participants to move from unem-

	Employed after the program (N = 41)	Unemployed after the program (N = 84)
Employed before *the program* (N = 19)	14	5
Unemployed before *the program* (N = 106)	27	79

[a] *Illustrative data*

FIGURE 8.2 Number of persons employed and unemployed before and after a job-training program for 125 ex-convicts.[a]

ployed to employed rather than the reverse. Suppose the program served 125 people and that the pre- and postprogram employment status is as indicated in Figure 8.2. The 19 employed before the training (14+5) appear in the upper half of the table. The 41 employed after the program appear on the left half of the table (14+27). To test if more people gained jobs than lost them, the number of people in the lower left cell, 27, should reliably exceed the number in the upper right cell, 5. The McNemar test contrasts 27 with 5, using a χ^2 (*df*=1) as follows:

$$\chi^2 = \frac{(27 - 5)^2}{(27 + 5)} = 15.12$$

Because this value exceeds the tabled χ^2 value (2.71), the evaluators may conclude that the increased number of employed program participants was large enough to be reliable—more ex-convicts are indeed employed after the program than before. If there are three, four, or five levels of program success, there are other nonparametric tests that would be appropriate. Readers are directed to discussions of gamma and Spearman's rank-order correlation in Davis (1971) and McCall (1975), respectively.

Did the Participants Change Enough?

If the change from pretest to posttest is statistically significant, evaluators face another issue: Did participants change *enough* to demonstrate a real effect in their daily lives? Singh, Greer, and Hammond (1977) found that the outcome of a classroom program on civic responsibility was an increase of three points on a ninety-two-point attitude test. The authors concluded that the amount of change, although statistically significant, was not large enough to have a practical impact on the children's behavior.

If evaluators want program evaluation findings to have an impact on decisions, they will be sensitive to the issue of meaningful change, not just statistically significant change. Many texts on statistics do not devote much attention to the question of the actual size of the differences between two values. Consequently, many students feel their job is complete after they have performed a statistical test and found a statistically significant difference. Applied social scientists, however, cannot stop at the point of reporting a "significant" finding. The sponsors of human services want to know if the participants are in any *practical* way better for having participated in the program. It is true that these questions are easier to raise than to answer. However, these are important questions, and they will be answered by someone—perhaps by an administrator, a funding agency, or a newspaper reporter.

For in-house evaluators performing a simple evaluation, the best approach to use in addressing the question of importance of the findings is consultation with the program's stakeholders after measures have been chosen but before data are collected. For example, would a job-training program be a success if only 10 percent of trainees found employment after three months? Would 25 percent be sufficient? Seventy-five percent? Would a mental health program be satisfied if depressed clients improved five percentile points relative to normative values? Or would a fifteen-point improvement be required to demonstrate that the improvement was satisfactory? In addition to the program staff, there are other groups who have an interest in the achievement of a program—for example, community groups, funding agencies, and program participants. The minimum amount of change necessary to define the outcome of a program as a success cannot be fully specified without considering the costs necessary to achieve that outcome. The relationship between the outcome and the costs of a program can be analyzed using the simple forms of cost-benefit and cost-effectiveness analyses discussed in Chapter 11.

Relating Change to Services and Participant Characteristics

The discussion of the pretest-posttest design to this point has concentrated on methods to use in documenting the possible improvement of program participants. Another approach to evaluation is to relate the amount of service received to the degree of improvement observed. Although such research may be open to the criticism that the results can be interpreted in various ways, it can be very useful in certain situations. For example, a very important study in the history of medical research followed the strategy of relating the patient's condition to the amount of treatment received. In 1835 Pierre Louis (Eisenberg, 1977) reported his study comparing the amount of blood let from patients with their progress in recovering from "inflammation" (pneumonia). Early-nineteenth-century medical theory led to the expectation that the more blood let, the better the treatment and the more likely a recovery. Louis measured the volume of blood drawn from the patients. He then compared these values to the course of their illnesses. He found that a patient's prognosis was not related to volume of blood taken. This finding was an important influence on the medical practice of that time and contributed to the eventual discrediting of bloodletting as a form of medical treatment. Louis was unable to conclude anything about the cause or the proper treatment of pneumonia, but he did identify a useless treatment.

Another reason to do an evaluation even if it is unable to identify the cause of change is to search for characteristics of the participants that might be related to achieving program goals. Do men experience better outcomes than women? Do members of minority groups complete the program as frequently as majority-group clients? Is age related to outcome? These questions can be explored, tentatively to be sure, using a simple research design. If policy-relevant relationships are found between outcome and a characteristic of participants, that variable would be involved in any future studies. The findings may even have immediate impact if a program appears to have a good effect on some segments of the target population but little effect on other segments.

Although it is quite easy to discuss the idea that personal and service characteristics may be related to success in a program, the statistical method of relating improvement to other variables is often misunderstood. The most intuitive approach is to subtract pretest scores from posttest scores, label the difference "improvement," and correlate the improvement scores with age, number of units of service received, and any other variables of interest. This "obvious" method is not desirable. To understand this point fully requires more advanced statistical sophistication than readers are assumed to have. The basic concept involved concerns the reason why improvement is more likely for some participants than for others. On the average, people who initially score low on a measure are more likely to improve than people who initially get high scores. Students know that it is generally harder to improve on a B+ than on a C−. This observation is related to the concept of regression to the mean, which will be discussed shortly.

Nunnally (1975) comments that one should avoid using change scores because they are based on shaky statistical assumptions. Further, the complex methods suggested to deal with change scores are hard to explain to others and are controversial, even among experts. Nunnally makes one exception to this warning: When the evaluator is interested in relating change to some characteristic of the program participants, change scores may be used. For example, since the length of some human services, such as psychotherapy, is not standardized as is (for example) a school year, an evaluator might want to relate improvement to the amount of service received.

The best way to relate improvement or change to the amount of service received or to some characteristic of the program participant when information is available only from the group receiving the program is to use residualized change scores. Judd and Kenny (1981) call this approach regression adjustment. This approach is illustrated here because introductory texts do not cover the method. To calculate a residualized change score, it is necessary first to calculate a regression equation that uses the pretest to predict the posttest. Even though program participants improved on a variable, it is likely that those who were better off on the pretest will, on the average, be better off on the posttest. Thus, we usualy expect a positive correlation between a pretest and a posttest. Figure 8.3 includes hypothetical data which will be used to illustrate the calculation of residualized change scores. Imagine a job-training program consisting of twenty training sessions. The correlation between the pretest and the posttest given in this figure is .47. The goal of the evaluator is to correlate job skills improvement with amount of training received.

FIGURE 8.3 Hypothetical data illustrating how change can be correlated with amount of service, adjusting for differences among program participants at the start of a program.

PROGRAM PARTICIPANT	SKILL LEVEL BEFORE	SKILL LEVEL AFTER	CHANGE	RESIDUAL AFTER	TRAINING SESSIONS	RESIDUAL SESSIONS
1	24	26	2	−0.54	16	−2.26
2	23	29	6	3.12	18	−0.13
3	19	26	7	2.73	20	2.40
4	18	27	9	4.39	19	1.53
5	20	19	− 1	4.92	16	−1.73
6	24	31	7	4.46	20	1.74
7	25	22	− 3	−5.19	15	−3.39
8	24	25	1	−1.54	19	0.74
9	21	22	1	−2.58	19	1.14
10	14	16	2	−4.01	14	−2.94
11	14	26	12	5.99	20	3.06
12	21	30	9	5.42	19	1.14
13	18	22	4	−0.61	19	1.53
14	16	15	− 1	−6.31	13	−4.20
15	23	26	3	0.12	19	0.87
16	14	13	− 1	−7.01	17	0.06
17	23	26	3	0.12	19	0.87
18	19	29	10	5.73	20	2.40
19	17	28	11	6.04	19	1.67
20	16	27	11	5.69	18	0.80
21	14	15	1	−5.01	14	−2.94
22	22	21	− 1	−4.23	19	1.00
23	25	26	1	−1.19	19	0.61
24	23	19	− 4	−6.88	15	−3.13
25	21	27	6	2.42	17	−0.86
26	22	29	7	3.77	18	0.00

To do this analysis, the pretest is treated as the predictor, or independent variable (usually denoted as X in regression formulas), and the posttest is treated as the criterion, or dependent variable (usually denoted as Y in regression formulas). The regression equation calculated to relate the two tests is

$$\text{Posttest}_i' = 10.86 + .65 \text{ Pretest}_i$$

The posttest score that is expected for each participant is calculated using the regression equation. For example, the value of the first person's pretest, 24, would lead one to expect a posttest score of 26.54. The difference between the actual posttest and the calculated posttest is the residualized change, -0.54. That is, on the basis of the relationship between the pretest and the posttest, person A showed a change 0.54 units lower than was expected. To correlate this measure of change with amount of service received, it is also necessary to use the pretest as a predictor of number of training sessions attended; that is, the service unit variable must also be adjusted for the individual differences in pretest score. In this phase of the analysis, the measure of service is treated as the dependent variable (the Y). Amounts of service received as predicted by the pretest is given by the equation

$$\text{Service}_i' = 15.08 + .13 \text{ Pretest}_i$$

Expected service is calculated for each person. Then the difference between actual service and expected service is found. The residual of number of sessions has been adjusted to reflect the fact that there was a nonzero correlation between the pretest and the number of training sessions attended. (If the pretest and the number of sessions had not been correlated, this step would not have had an effect on the analysis) Finally, a correlation is found between residualized change and the residuals of units of service. The correlation between the two columns of residuals is .65. This indicates that more improvement was shown by those program participants who received more units of service, even when adjusted for differences in pretest scores. The same strategy can be used to correlate personality, background, or demographic information with improvements by substituting the variable of interest in place of training sessions in this illustration.

This is an internal analysis for the purpose of learning something about differential improvement levels. In this hypothetical program we know that improvement occurred and that, on the average, the more sessions attended, the more improvement. However, the causes of improvement cannot be discerned on the basis of this analysis. The reasons for caution in interpreting the causes of improvement are described in the balance of this chapter.

THREATS TO INTERNAL VALIDITY

Once a statistically significant improvement has been found that is large enough to be nontrivial, evaluators need to eliminate explanations of the change that are not due to the program. For example, sixth-grade children will do better on a task requiring precise eye-hand coordination than they did as second graders. Is this a result of primary school (the "program") or the result of maturation? Maturation is an alternative explanation that cannot be eliminated in this situation, and one that forbids attributing the cause of the change solely to the effect of grade school education. Such alternative explanations of research results were labeled "threats to internal validity" by Campbell and Stanley (1963). As mentioned above, the reasons why participants achieve a certain level of outcome cannot be unambiguously attributed to the program when either a posttest-only or a pretest-posttest approach is used. However, it is important to know why these single-group approaches fail internal validity considerations. As this and the next two chapters progress, different methods will be described to eliminate plausible nonprogram explanations of change. Only when the nonprogram explanations are eliminated, can the cause of change be attributed to the program.

Actual but Nonprogram-related Changes in the Participants

Two threats to internal validity refer to *real* changes that occur in program participants due to influences not related to the program. *Maturation* refers to natural changes in people that can be expected solely due to the passage of time. The most obvious example is a child growing older. *History* refers to events happening in the community, society, or even the entire world that will change the behavior of the participants of a program. Events such as an election, a recession, or a war may all influence the measures of program success.

Maturation. Children can perform more complex tasks simply because they get older; people get more tired the longer they have gone without sleep; and there are predictable general patterns to the developmental processes of adults and elderly people. If an evaluation utilizes variables that can be expected to change merely with the passage of time, maturation could be a plausible explanation for the changes that occur between the time of the pretest and the time of the posttest. In other words, the evaluator may well have found that real change occurred during the course of a program; however, the reason for the change is that the program lasted x number of months and thus the participants are x months older and x months more experienced—not that the participants gained anything from the program.

The existence of maturation-based changes does not mean that maturation is the *only* explanation of the changes observed. Nor do plausible, alternative hypotheses mean that the program had no effect. Interpretations would be easier if the evaluator could learn how much of the change was due to maturation and how much was due to the program. Using the pretest-posttest design, this separation cannot be made. Methods to estimate the change due to maturation involve testing other groups of participants or potential participants as well as testing over a greater number of time periods.

History.   History refers to any specific event that occurs between the pretest and the posttest that affects the people in the program. For example, a recession may make even the most well-designed program to help people find jobs look like a dud. On the other hand, an economic recovery would make a similar but poorly run program look like a winner. These concurrent national economic changes are plausible alternative interpretations of any changes found among the participants of employment programs. All nonprogram events or series of events that affect the participants would provide plausible alternative explanations.

Some of the same approaches used to account for maturational effects can help isolate historical effects: Test additional groups and test at additional times. However, maturation is more predictable and stable than is history. Unexpected events can occur at any time or may not occur at all during a given evaluation. Evaluators should be sensitive to societal or organizational changes that may affect an evaluation. In addition, Cook and Campbell (1979) discuss the influence of events occurring in a particular group under the term *local history*. Events such as staff being involved in personal feuds, the presence of a particularly influential individual in a program group, or a local community disaster cannot be accounted for by any evaluation research design unless the evaluation is replicated a number of times in different settings.

Who Was Observed

Three threats to internal validity must be considered when the participants in a program are not a random or representative sample of the people who might benefit. These three threats are called *selection, mortality,* and *regression*.

Selection.   Participation in a human service program is voluntary. Even when prisoners or parolees are forced to participate, the level of meaningful participation is voluntary. Thus, the people obtaining a service are different from those not obtaining it. In the posttest-only form of evaluation, the process of self-selection may mean that the participants were already quite healthy when they began the program. The fact that the posttest detects a desirable state tells the staff nothing about the effectiveness of the program. It is true that sometimes an evaluation of a program is based only on the end result for the people completing the program. Clearly, these individuals chose to complete the program and do not represent the effect of the program on all for whom the program was designed.

The pretest-posttest approach to evaluation is much stronger in controlling the unwanted effects of self-selection. By measuring the participants before the program, the possible change can be documented. Centra (1977) has reported that the college teachers most likely to be involved in faculty development programs are "good teachers who want to be better." After a faculty development program, most of these teachers, the program participants, will be quite good teachers. Their competence will tell us nothing about the quality of the program—these teachers were good to start with. However, observations of their achievements before the program will permit an estimation of the amount of improvement.

Mortality.   The posttest-only design is also inadequate when participant dropout is a problem. People differ in whether they will begin a program (selection), and they differ in whether they will complete a program (dropout). Campbell and Stanley (1963) use the term *mortality* to refer to dropping out of a program for whatever reason. Students drop courses they do not like or find too challenging; people in therapy quit when they learn that personal growth is hard; and in medical settings some patients in programs do actually die.

The level of achievement observed at the end of a program may indicate how well the program functioned, how good the people were when they started, or how motivated the people were who stayed until the end. As a general rule, those who stay are more prepared for the program than are those who drop out. Failing students are more likely to drop a course than are those earning B's and A's. Patients who die were probably the least likely to benefit from a health care program. Without a pretest the evaluator will not know how much dropping out there was nor what sort of individuals dropped out. A director of a small drug user program informally mentioned that his program had a 90 percent success rate. Upon inquiry, however, it was learned that only about 10 percent of those who start the program are there at the end. Having success with 9 out of the 100 people who begin the program is markedly different from having a 90 percent success rate.

As with selection, the pretest-posttest design handles participant mortality fairly well. By pretesting, the evaluators know who has dropped out and how they compared to those who remained. The pretest-posttest design enables evaluators to know when high preprogram achievement and participant dropout are not plausible explanations for the good level of outcome observed at the end of the program.

Regression.   The threat to internal validity labeled *regression to the mean* is one of the hardest threats to understand. This is true probably because some statistical thinking is required to understand this threat. However, as with most basic statistics, many people already understand regression to the mean at the conceptual level, even though they may not apply it consistently.

Kahneman and Tversky (1974) report that airplane pilot trainers have a practice that illustrates how people can be misled by the effects of regression. If you think carefully about the example, you will see what regression means and why its effects are often undetected. It is said that after a particularly good landing, the trainers do not compliment the trainee, because when such a compliment is given, the next landing is usually done less well. On the other hand, after a poor landing the trainers severely reprimand the trainee in order to elicit a better landing on the next try. It is clear that the empirical observations are true—complimented exceptionally good landings are often followed by less good ones, and reprimanded bad landings are often followed by better ones. However, let us see why the compliments and the reprimands have nothing to do with the quality of the following landing.

Imagine learning a complex task. Initially, performance level fluctuates—sometimes better, sometimes worse. What goes into the better performances? At least two things: the degree of skill achieved, and luck or chance. Flight trainees know they should touch the plane down with the nose up, but they do not yet sense the precise moment to lower the wing flaps and at the same time adjust the elevators to achieve the proper touchdown angle (Caidin, 1960). Sometimes they do it too soon, and sometimes too late. Because these errors are largely due to chance, the likelihood of doing everything correctly at the precise second for two consecutive landings is low. Similarly, the likelihood of badly estimating the precise instant two times in a row is also low. Therefore, the likelihood of two consecutive good landings is low for pilot trainees. In other words, an observer (or a trainer) should *not* expect two consecutive good landings by a novice trainee, regardless of what is said or not said by the trainer.

The essentials of the effects of regression to the mean can be further illustrated with a rather silly but instructive example. Choose twenty pennies and flip each six times, recording the number of heads flipped for each penny. Select the penny that produced the most "excessive" heads (five or six heads can be considered excessive). Reprimand the penny for producing too many heads. Then flip that penny six more times to see if the reprimand had the desired effect. If the penny yields fewer heads than it did during the first set of six flips, the penny is behaving in the way it was urged to behave. On the average, the reprimand will appear to have been effective 98 percent of the time if the penny originally produced six out of six heads, and 89 percent of the time if the first result had been five out of six heads. The binomial distribution permits the calculation of these percentages (Hays, 1963).

In summary, regression to the mean warns that whenever a performance level is extreme, the next performance is likely to be less extreme. This principle applies to emotional adjustment as well as to learning to fly airplanes and flipping pennies. If the people who currently are the most depressed are included in a therapy group, it is very likely that in three months they will be as a group less depressed. This does not mean they will be at a healthy level of adjustment. Most likely, they will still be more depressed than the general population. However, some of the transient random events that caused the worst depression will have passed, and as a group the most depressed people will be less depressed than they were before.

Is regression a threat to the internal validity of the pretest-posttest evaluation design? Not necessarily, but it often is. If individuals who are representative of some intact group are tested before and after a program, then regression is not a problem for evaluations following this evaluation design. For example, if all children in a school are given a special reading curriculum, regression will not be a threat to internal validity. However, if only the children reading at the lowest levels on the pretest are included, regression will be a threat to the correct interpretation of the pretest-posttest change. The reasons why children are low in a single test include poor reading skills; but the reasons also include such chance things as poor guessing, breaking a pencil point, having a cold, misunderstanding directions, worrying about a sick sister, or planning recess games. A day, a week, or a semester later on a second test, these events will not be experienced by exactly the same individuals. Generally, these retest scores will be higher than those on the first test for the children who previously had scored the worst. Also, these retest scores will be lower for those who previously scored the best.

Regression is often a plausible alternative hypothesis for pretest-posttest change when human service programs are aimed at those people who are in need of help. Remedial programs are not prepared for everyone, but rather for those who have fallen behind: reading very poorly, earning a low income, feeling emotional distress, and so forth. Sometimes a screening test to select people for the program is also used as the pretest in an evaluation plan. For example, students reading the most poorly on a test are placed in a reading improvement program, and a second administration of the same test or of a parallel form is compared to the preprogram test scores. This is a poor practice; regression is a very plausible alternate explanation for at least part of the improvement. Improvement in such an evaluation cannot be interpreted. On the other hand, if poor readers or troubled clients get worse (that is, go downhill when regression effects were likely to improve their level), then the evaluation can be interpreted. The correct interpretation is that the program has failed.

The Methods of Obtaining Observations

There are two additional plausible hypotheses discussed by Campbell and Stanley: *testing* and *instrumentation* effects. At times these can make the interpretations of outcome evaluations ambiguous. These threats to interpretation are generated by the evaluators themselves and by their observation methods.

Testing. The effect of testing refers to changes in behavior due to the observation techniques. First, two administrations of a test or survey may differ simply as a function of the respondent's increased familiarity with the tool at the second administration. Ability scores increase reliably on the second administration for people unfamiliar with the test (Anastasi, 1982). People interviewing for jobs gain from the experience and can present themselves better on subsequent interviews.

A second aspect of the effects of testing is called reactivity. People behave differently when they know they are being observed, as compared to when there is no observer or when people are not aware of an observer. This concept was discussed in Chapter 3; however, it is worth recalling. Clients, patients, prisoners, schoolchildren, and so on will be affected when they know someone is recording their behavior, opinions, or feelings. Observation techniques vary in how reactive they are.

The pretest-posttest design is clearly weak in the control of testing effects. If program participants were unfamiliar with the observation procedures, scores might change on the second test. The direction of change that should be expected due to repeated testing does not seem clear except for ability and achievement tests, on which improvement is usually expected. The research design itself does not create reactivity if both pretest and posttest can be done in an equivalent and nonreactive fashion.

Instrumentation. The last threat to internal validity to be discussed refers to the use of measurement procedures themselves. Most college instructors know they are not totally consistent when grading essay examinations. There is a real potential for standards to change as the instructor becomes familiar with written examinations. The standards may become higher or lower.[1] If a pretest-posttest design uses measures that are not thoroughly objective, it would be wise not to score the pretest until after the posttest is administered. Then shuffle the tests together and have them scored by someone who does not know which are pretests and which are posttests.

If the measures require observations that must be made before and after the program, the examiners may become more and more skilled as they gain experience. Thus, the posttests may go much more smoothly than the pretests. If so, a change in instrumentation becomes a viable alternative to concluding that the program had an effect. In such situations the examiner will be most effective if highly experienced before the pretest is administered.

The Interactions of These Threats

Over and above the influences of these seven threats to internal validity, it is possible for our interpretations to be confused by the joint influence of two of these threats. For example, the parents who seek out special educational opportunities for their children (self-selection) may have children who are developing more rapidly than those of parents who do not seek special help for their children (different rates of maturation). This situation would be called a selection-by-maturation interaction. More will be said about this threat when more complex evaluation designs are discussed in later chapters.

The threats to internal validity refer to reasons why an observed change may not be caused by the program or human service that the group obtained between the pretest and the posttest. Internal validity is thus the most basic concern of evaluators who are examining whether a program was responsible for an observed improvement.[2] As noted above, obtaining strong evidence of causal relationships is not the sole reason for conducting an evaluation. However, if evidence for causality is needed, and if there are plausible explanations based on the types of influences just described, the evaluator may well avoid conducting an evaluation using these basic designs.

---

[1]One way to minimize these changes is to read all answers before assigning any grades. Only then are grades assigned. When there are a number of questions, there is a way to minimize the effect of the instrumentation change. Grade all answers to the first question, shuffle the papers and grade all answers to the second question, and so on. Even if standards change, the likelihood of individual total test scores being systematically affected is very low.

[2]If there is no "improvement," there usually is nothing to explain, except in rare circumstances where a loss of function is expected without intervention. A program for arthritic patients is an example of a service in which the goal is to avoid deterioration. Such programs hope at best to maintain abilities, not to cure.

CHANCE AND CREATIVITY
IN SINGLE-GROUP DESIGNS

Threats to internal validity explain why some data collection procedures forbid interpretations of a causal connection between the program and the observed condition of those who received the program. The ways the data are analyzed can also create misinterpretations. Taking advantage of chance and developing creative interpretations can make an evaluation appear insightful when it is not. Because evaluators want to conduct valid research, being aware of these misleading practices is important.

Students and professionals not experienced in research methodology often engage in a practice that fosters inaccurate conclusions. This is the practice of "fishing" for statistically significant relationships among a large number of outcome variables and variables describing the people (such as sex, age, ethnic background). Fishing is often done by repeatedly subdividing the sample of program participants and comparing the ad hoc groups on the outcome measures. For example, if participants are divided by gender and the means of the outcome measures of the two groups are compared, then divided on the basis of age, then ethnic background, and so forth, some of the comparisons will reveal differences that may indeed be significant, but just by chance. Finding significant differences just by chance is a Type I error. If a large number of relationships are studied, some will appear to be strong, just as flipping a large number of coins six times each will reveal that certain coins appear to be biased toward heads or tails. The same coins, if retested by flipping them six more times each, will be found to be unbiased. Unfortunately, when performing evaluations, new observations cannot be obtained as easily as flipping coins several additional times.

The second reason erroneous, chance relationships are not discovered is that *once the data are examined,* the evaluator or the program staff can usually make sense out of the results. Once a young graduate student presented a senior professor with findings that seemed markedly at variance with the professor's own research.[3] The professor quickly interpreted the results in a way that coincided nicely with the professor's work. A week later the student discovered that the computer program was malfunctioning and the initial results were meaningless. This anecdote has a happy ending: When the results were correctly analyzed, they were as originally expected, quite compatible with previous work. The point to remember is that reasonably creative people can make sense out of nearly any finding *once the information is presented.* This ability, coupled with the practice of gathering many variables and "fishing" for results, can lead to erroneous findings that appear to be well thought out.

[3]The first author of this book was the student, but the senior professor must remain anonymous.

A nearly foolproof manner of discovering which results are simply Type I errors is to repeat the research. In controlled laboratory social science research, replication is not that difficult. However, because program evaluation often disrupts the service setting, it is seldom replicated. A more practical approach involves collecting only the information that can be used and having rational or theoretical reasons for the planned analyses. In addition, unexpected findings are best treated as very tentative, especially if they are embedded in a large number of analyses that are statistically nonsignificant. Finally, be very suspicious of surprising findings that require a number of assumptions or elaborate theorizing to understand. The professor mentioned above was only able to interpret the computer-generated nonsense by making elaborate and novel, although plausible, assumptions.

USEFULNESS OF SINGLE-GROUP DESIGNS

When there are specified standards for the outcome of a human service program, and when the participants do not drop out, the pretest-posttest design may be sufficient to document the program's success. However, even when standards are not available, the reader should not gain the impression that these approaches do not have any legitimate uses. These single-group designs are less intrusive and less expensive than more ambitious designs and require far less effort to complete than the methods described in later chapters. Thus, these designs can serve a very important function in the evaluator's toolbox as first steps in planning rigorous program evaluations. Single group evaluations serve at least three purposes: (1) to assess the likely usefulness of more rigorous evaluations; (2) to search for promising variables related to success in the program; and (3) to "soften up" the facility for more rigorous evaluation in the future.

Assessing the Usefulness of Further Evaluations

Before embarking on a rigorous plan that will control for all the plausible alternative interpretations, a single-group design would serve to show whether there is any improvement to interpret. If no program participants have jobs for which they were trained, it is likely that no further research is needed to evaluate a job-training program. The program failed, period. No statistical analyses are necessary. If participants finished at a good level, the pretest-posttest design may show that the people improved during the program. This finding may well satisfy some users of program evaluation reports. Also, the finding of reliable improvement may justify a more complex evaluation. Lenihan (1977) used a simple design as a first step in learning whether the use of the phone helped pretrial defendants to raise bond. Showing that 22 percent of the defendants who used a phone that was available on an experimental basis did raise bail suggested that a more rigorous evaluation could be worth the expense. Had only 2 or 3 percent been able to raise bail, the possible effect of the phone would have been very small, and no further study would have been done.

Correlating Improvement with Other Variables

The use of the pretest-posttest design and change scores permits improvement to be related to the amount of service obtained and to characteristics of the program participants. It may be that a program offered to a very needy population primarily benefits people who are relatively well-off. Thus, the good achievement found by a posttest design was due to the already-competent people who selected themselves for the program. If so, further work is unnecessary. On the other hand, the good level at the end of the program may really indicate a general improvement in most participants. Perhaps the improvement is due to the impact of the program. Further work would be merited.

Preparing the Facility for Further Evaluation

A third reason for conducting an evaluation using only the program participants as respondents is to help staff accept the idea of evaluation. As described in earlier chapters, human service providers—from paraprofessional counselors, to teachers, to physicians—are now beginning to recognize that their work can and will be evaluated. This realization does not come easily, because the quality of human services is hard to quantify. However, if evaluators begin their work with less threatening approaches, they have better chances of leading service providers to see the usefulness of evaluation and to value the contribution of evaluators.

The methods described in this and the previous chapters are among the least threatening. There is no possibility that the research could show that unserved people do as well as people who got the service—a very frightening possibility to staff members. There are studies indicating that in some situations people who receive counseling are not much better off than similar people not counseled (see Ellsworth, 1975, p. 242). However, evaluators who suggest that counseling does not work are not going to find that the counseling staff readily welcomes their services. Less threatening— but still an unwelcome possibility—is the finding that an alternative service is just as beneficial to program participants. If the alternative service is less expensive, a comparison of people in the two groups could create anxiety for the staff of the more expensive program. This anxiety will be manifested in roadblocks to the study, hostility, and general uncooperativeness.

Just this type of response occurred during an in-house evaluation of a hospital program. The director of the program was very cooperative in initiating and implementing a study of the patients in his program. He displayed considerable openness to evaluation, saying such things as, "Maybe we don't help people as much as we think we do—we should know that"; and "If a patient is institutionalized after leaving here, we have failed." However, when the evaluators proposed increasing the rigor of the evaluation by gathering data from a neighboring hospital without a similar program, the director seemed to change his position. Such a comparison could conceivably have shown that similar patients regained as much ability as those in the director's expensive program. He now said, "The additional data is unnecessary since the value of these programs is well known and fully documented." The expanded study went on anyway. His negative attitudes dissolved when it became clear that the neighboring hospital had surprisingly few patients with the necessary diagnosis and that those who were available were much milder than those served in the program. Because the two groups of patients were not compatible, the study could not threaten the program. Cooperativeness and cordial relations returned.

Rational use of resources requires that ultimately such comparative studies be done. But they should not be done in a way that leaves the staff demoralized or bitter. In-house evaluators who try to force methodologically rigorous evaluations on staff and who are unable to see the value of approaches with less-than-precise experimental control will find their work undervalued and their influence on the program diminished. Beginning in a nonthreatening way permits evaluators to gain the confidence of staff members. We do not intend to devalue the more rigorous approaches. The point stressed here is that less rigorous studies can also be useful.

SUMMARY

This chapter emphasizes two major points. First, a careful understanding of the needs of the users of an evaluation may indicate that a simple research design is able to serve quite well to answer these needs at a particular time. Evaluators perform unnecessary work when they insist on giving users more than they want or can use. The second major idea concerns the conceptual tools useful to understand why simple single-group evaluation designs cannot answer certain questions often important to administrators and to those responsible for financial support of a program. These conceptual tools have been called threats to internal validity and have become part of the vocabulary of social scientists in recent decades. Evaluators can use this conceptual scheme to select the research design most appropriate to answer the questions put to them by those needing services and programs evaluated.

STUDY QUESTIONS

1. Not many years ago, when a child had frequent bouts of sore throat, family doctors recommended removing the child's tonsils. Typically, the child's health improved afterwards. If parents and doctors attributed the improved health to the effects of the operation, what threats to internal validity were ignored?

2. Some fifty elementary school children witnessed a brutal murder on the way to school in a suburb of a large city. The school officials worked with a social worker, a school psychologist, and others in an attempt to help the children deal with their emotions, to avoid long-term ill effects, and to help parents with their children. A year after the tragedy, there appeared to be no serious aftereffects. What assumptions are necessary to call this program a success?

3. Watch newspapers and news programs for instances in which the reporter's approach to drawing conclusions is, in essence, a posttest-only research design. For example, find reports similar to the one described in question number 2. What threats to internal validity were ignored in the reports you found?

4. Politicians are notorious for attributing any improvements in government affairs to their own efforts, and any deteriorating affairs to the policies of others. Find or recall examples. What threats to internal validity most typically operate in government affairs?

5. Why can a smoking control clinic be evaluated using a one-group pretest-posttest study? It is also possible to gather useful follow-up data to evaluate the program. What index of success could be used to summarize effectiveness if participants could be observed only after the program?

FURTHER READING

Internal validity is discussed more fully in the following works.

CAMPBELL, D. T., AND STANLEY, J. C. 1963. *Experimental and quasi-experimental designs for research*. Chicago: Rand-McNally.
COOK, T. D., AND CAMPBELL, D. T. 1979. *Quasi-experimentation: Design and analysis for field settings*. Chicago: Rand-McNally.

For a review of Type I errors that often occur when "fishing" randomly for relationships, and for a review of regression principles, see any statistics textbook. The book listed below is a well-received introductory text.

McCALL, R. B. 1980. *Fundamental statistics for psychology*. 3rd ed. New York: Harcourt Brace Jovanovich.

Change scores are discussed thoroughly in the following sources.

JUDD, C. M., AND KENNY, D. A. 1981. *Estimating the effects of social interventions.* New York: Cambridge University Press.

NUNNALLY, J. C. 1975. The study of change in evaluation research: Principles concerning measurement, experimental design, and analysis. In *Handbook of evaluation research,* vol. 1, ed. E. L. Struening and M. Guttentag. Beverly Hills, Calif.: Sage.

CASE STUDY 8.1   A Program for Psychosomatics

To avoid appearing overly critical of the work of others, the first case study is from the authors' own research. The report is excerpted from an evaluation of an inpatient program for psychosomatic individuals in acute need of medical treatment. The essence of the pretest-posttest design is illustrated. Readers ought to be able to find numerous weaknesses in this case study related to uncontrolled threats to internal validity. The original evaluation controlled for some of these weaknesses, since it included more variables, a comparison group, an additional testing time, and a consideration of costs. Nevertheless, even this simplified version of the study could have provided unit managers and hospital administrators with some basic information. The unit was well received by many patients, and they—as well as their spouses—felt improvement was experienced.

EVALUATION OF THE MEDICAL ECOLOGY PROGRAM

Raymond G. Carey and Emil J. Posavac

Summary and Conclusion

The major issue of the evaluation concerned whether the patients in the Medical Ecology Program (MEP) improved in their psychological functioning. Multiple measures were used, and all indicated improvement. In answer to direct questions about the benefit they received, about 80 percent of the patients who completed the program said they received much benefit and were glad they participated in the program. All self-descriptive measures by the patients (such as anxiety, depression, fatigue) indicated substantial improvement between admission and the ninety-day follow-up. Physicians and program counselors agreed that there was substantial improvement in the level of psychological functioning. Significant others (usually spouses) reported some improvement from admission to follow-up, although not as much improvement as the patients reported.

A second issue dealt with how much program patients improved as compared to similar patients who received other modes of treatment. Normative data were available for the rating scales used by the significant others describing the changes that occurred in outpatients receiving psychotherapy. The patients who completed the program changed on the average as much as the patients represented in these change norms.

On the basis of this limited study, the MEP appears to serve a population of patients who respond favorably to the program and who show improvement to the same extent as patients receiving psychotherapy only.

Background

The ecology program.   The Medical Ecology Program was developed to serve the needs of people with physical dysfunctions whose medical treatment is "impeded or complicated by emotional factors." In addition, the unit serves psychiatric patients with somatopsychic illnesses who need acute medical treatment and other patients who have emotional difficulty in accepting or adjusting to their illnesses provided they require acute medical care.

Patients in the program receive medical care as other hospital medical patients, and they participate in the three-week program. The program consists of: (1) twice-weekly lecture/discussions on the relationships between emotions and health; (2) twice-weekly medical lectures; (3) weekly religious discussion/lecture sessions; (4) weekly movie/discussions; (5) twice-weekly group counseling/psychotherapy; (6) thrice-weekly individual counseling/psychotherapy; and (7) therapeutic recreation and occupational therapy three to five times per week. There are additional services available as needed. Spouses and family members are included in a weekly orientation program.

Every patient is assigned to one of several program counselors who is responsible for the patient's participation in and understanding of the program. Program counselors provide the inpatient counseling/psychotherapy sessions and plan for outpatient follow-up services.

The purpose of the study.   The JCAH medical audit system used at the hospital selects patient charts for peer review on the basis of a disease entity or the type of procedure used. Special programs serving a wide variety of diagnoses, such as the MEP does, are not compatible with the JCAH audit system. Therefore, a specially prepared evaluation was requested for the MEP. Because the major thrust of the program focused on improved psychological functioning, the evaluation focused on those goals. Quality of medical care was not examined.

Method

The authors met with the director and the staff of the MEP during the late summer and fall. These meetings familiarized the authors with the goals of the program, which are largely reflected in the Outpatient Progress Report sent to the physicians of participants in the Outpatient Program. These goals include: reductions in anxiety, relief from depression, improved self-image, increased sense of responsibility, improved family life, and decreased concern with medical condition.

Selection of measures.   The discussion of goals resulted in agreement on the selection of research instruments to measure success in achieving program goals. The measures included:

The Profile of Mood States (POMS) for use at admission and follow-up.
A specially constructed Patient Survey for use at discharge and follow-up.
The Global Assessment Rating Scale (GARS) for use at admission and discharge.
The Personal Adjustment and Role Skill (PARS) for use at admission and follow-up.

As can be seen, multiple measures were used to gather data from a variety of sources—the patient, relatives, and professionals. These instruments and the times at which they were administered are described in the following paragraphs. [The original report described the measures at this point.]

Collection of data.   Patients were asked to provide data at admission, discharge, and ninety days after discharge. Within a day or two after admission, the unit secretary gave the admission surveys to the program counselor, who asked the patient to complete the surveys. All of the measures listed above except GARS and PARS were included in this packet. A blank GARS form for the physician was placed in the patient's chart, and the program counselors completed GARS forms as soon as they became acquainted with their patients. The spouse or other appropriate relative was asked by the program counselor to complete the pretreatment PARS scales. If the relative could not be contacted personally, the PARS form was mailed.

At discharge, the MEP patients responded to a number of direct questions about their experiences on the unit. The physician and program counselor were again each asked to complete the GARS.

Ninety days after discharge, the former patients were mailed the same set of measures completed at admission and the direct questions about their participation in the program. The person completing the pretreatment PARS was mailed the posttreatment form. Follow-up telephone calls were made by the Office of Evaluation and Research to those patients and relatives who did not return the material within ten days.

Description of the patients.   Patients admitted to MEP between June 1 and November 30 were eligible for the study. During these months there were 112 program patients and 92 nonprogram patients on the unit. Of the 69 patients who agreed to participate, 63 completed the admission materials, 58 completed the discharge survey, and 38 the follow-up materials. Of the 69 patients who provided at least some information, most were women (84 percent) and middle-aged (median age = thirty-eight years). A large minority (42 percent) were taking antianxiety medication, 23 percent were prescribed major tranquilizers, and 29 percent were prescribed antidepressants. The length of stay ranged from three to sixty-six days. The median stay equaled the program's planned length, twenty-one days.

The sixty-nine MEP patients in the study were 62 percent of the program patients during the period of the study. The forty-three program patients not represented either refused to participate or were discharged soon after admission. These forty-three unrepresented program patients and the ninety-two nonprogram patients averaged approximately seven days on the unit.

	Time of report	
Survey item	Discharge (N = 58)	Three-month follow-up (N = 37)
GLAD they participated in the program	88%	86%
Reporting MUCH benefit from the program	78%	70%
Reporting MUCH relief from presenting medical symptoms	50%	47%
Reporting having learned MUCH about physical symptoms and emotions	79%	73%
Reporting the ultimate causes of their physical problems were half or more emotional	86%	81%

FIGURE 8.4 Percentage of patients responding favorably about their experiences in the Medical Ecology Program (MEP).

Results: Do the Patients Improve?

Direct questions about the MEP.   Figure 8.4 contains the percentage of patients who responded favorably when asked about their experiences in the MEP. Nearly nine out of ten patients reported they were glad they participated in the program. The patients also believed they learned much about their physical symptoms and emotional lives (79 percent). The table shows that the positive feelings about the program held up over the three-month period between discharge and follow-up.

Patient self-descriptions.   Figure 8.5 contains the various self-reports of the patients. Substantial improvement in mood including anxiety and depression can be seen when admission and follow-up levels are compared. This improvement is not an artifact caused by the drop out of respondents from admission to discharge because the correlated-groups *t*-tests were used. This analysis used only the data from those who completed both the admission and follow-up ratings. If at all misleading, Figure 8.5 may slightly underestimate the amount of improvement reported by the patients.

Evaluation of improvement by others.   The evaluation of the patients' psychological improvement as made by others is not as consistent as that indicated by the direct questions or the self-descriptions. Figure 8.5 contains the mean ratings from the PARS scales at admission and at follow-up. On all but one PARS scale, the change is toward better adjustment; however, there are only few changes that are large enough to achieve statistical significance. The anxiety-depression scale shows a sizable drop, and the confusion and the outside (of home) social scales also show some improvement. Relationship to children indicated a slight worsening. The other differences were not large enough to be viewed as reliable. Overall, the relatives did report less anxiety and depression, but they did not report the thorough improvement that was shown in the self-report measures.

	Time of rating	
	Admission	*Follow-up*
Self-report using POMS		
Tension-anxiety	18.6	10.9**
Depression	23.3	10.5**
Anger-hostility	12.0	8.0*
Vigor	11.0	14.7**
Fatigue	14.4	8.5**
Confusion	12.3	7.7**
Evaluation by relatives using the PARS scales		
Interpersonal relations	13.6	14.2
Anxiety-depression	13.9	9.7*
Confusion	11.8	9.3*
Alcohol/drugs	5.5	4.9
Household management	12.0	13.7
Relationship to children	12.1	10.0
Outside social	6.2	8.1*
Employment	6.9	5.9

Note: Means showing better adjustment are underlined. Sixty–three patients filled out the POMS at admission, 38 at the follow-up. Fifty–three spouses completed the PARS at admission, 26 at the follow-up; however, scales that are gender-specific were answered by fewer spouses.

* *p* < .05

** *p* < .01

FIGURE 8.5   Means of the self-report and relative-completed measures.

The global psychological functioning rating by the physicians and the program counselors showed substantial and highly significant improvement. At admission patients were rated at about fifty, indicating that approximately half were viewed as having moderate symptoms causing some difficulty in functioning and about half as having serious symptomatology requiring treatment. The GARS discharge ratings in the sixties described patients with "mild symptoms" who are generally functioning well and who would not be considered sick by untrained people.

How Much Do MEP Patients Improve Compared to Similar Patients?

It seems clear that MEP patients improve. A further question concerns the amount of improvement relative to other patients who are treated differently. One approach to answering this question was available. The manual for the PARS scales provides change norms. "Change norms" give the follow-up PARS ratings that can be expected for all possible admission ratings. Using the change norms, one can determine if the amount of change reported by the relatives of the MEP patients is more or less than that observed in other populations. Without going into detail, the improvements observed for the MEP patients are quite similar to that found among either outpatient psychiatric clinic patients or hospitalized psychiatric patients.

CASE STUDY 8.2   Toilet Training Children

When the behavior of people who do not receive a program is well known, an evaluator need not conduct an evaluation of any more complexity than a pretest-posttest design. In this case study the common frustration of parents seeking to toilet train their children was evidence that a rapid method of training children would be an improvement over standard practices.

DRY PANTS: A RAPID METHOD OF TOILET TRAINING CHILDREN*

R. M. Foxx and N. H. Azrin

Although all normal children seem to learn eventually to toilet train themselves, parental "common sense" procedures have resulted in no more benefit than has occurred without training. For example, Madsen et al. (1969) found that parental training for one month reduced accidents by only 5 percent, which is about the same insignificant decrease that they obtained without any toilet training. In view of this failure of training efforts, the common attitude of permissiveness regarding toileting (Spock, 1968) is understandable and justified. One can understand why this permissive view of toilet training as an exercise in futility has recurred about every decade for the past sixty years.

Recently, a method has been developed for rapidly training the retarded to toilet train themselves without prompting (Azrin, Sneed, and Foxx, 1973). The success of those efforts indicated that similar and even more rapid training might be achieved with normal children by use of that general method. The present study evaluated a modification of that method with a group of nonretarded children.

Method

Children.   Thirty-four children were selected for training, twenty-two boys and twelve girls. Because the training procedure required the child to be capable of responding to verbal instructions, a screening test was devised for ascertaining a potential trainee's instructional responsiveness.

*Condensed with permission from *Behavior Research and Therapy* 11 (1973). 435–42. Copyright 1973, Pergamon Press, Ltd.

General rationale.   The general method was to provide an intensive learning experience that maximized the factors known to be important for learning; then to fade out these factors once learning had occurred. The learning factors maximized were a distraction-free environment, a large number of trials, consideration of the component responses, operant reinforcement for correct responses, a variety of reinforcers, quality of the reinforcers, frequency of reinforcement, manual guidance, verbal instruction, immediacy of reinforcement, immediacy of detection of incorrect responses, and negative reinforcement for the incorrect response.[4]

Results

Reduction of accidents.   Figure 8.6 shows the number of accidents before and after training for the 34 children. The mothers had recorded the number of accidents by counting the number of times the child had to be changed each day during the week preceding and following training. Following training, the parents were contacted every month for four months by telephone or by a personal visit from one of the trainers. Prior to training, the children averaged about six accidents per day per child. Within the first post-training week, accidents had decreased by 97 percent to 0.2 accidents per day per child, or about one per week. This near-zero level of accidents endured during the entire four-month follow-up period and applied to bowel movements as well as urinations. A within-subject comparison of the children's pre- and post-training accidents by the Wilcoxin Matched-Pairs Signed Ranks Test showed a significant ($p < 0.01$) reduction of accidents for the very first day after training and for each month of the post-training period.

Training time.   The mean training time was 3.9 hours; the median time was 3.5 hours, and the range was one-half hour to 14 hours. Training was considered complete when the child toileted himself completely and with no prompts. The older children, aged twenty-six to thirty-six months, were trained in a training time of about 2.25 hours. The twenty to twenty-five-month old group had a mean training time of about 5 hours.

Parent   reaction.   The   parents   characteristically   expressed   disbelieving pleasure.

Reaction of the children.   Most of the children reacted to the training program as if it were a very pleasant experience, hugging and kissing the trainer.

Bedwetting.   None of the children was given specific training for bedwetting (enuresis). Yet, the mothers of ten children (about 30 percent) reported that their child stopped wetting at night during the entire first week immediately following the daytime training. Follow-up checks showed that all ten of these children continued to stay dry at night during the four-month follow-up period.

[4]A lengthy discussion of the program has been omitted in this condensation.

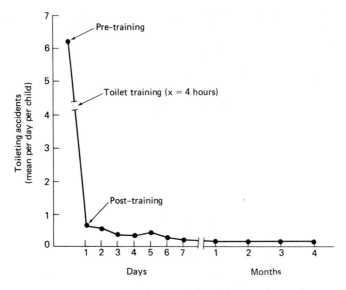

FIGURE 8.6 The effect of the Dry Pants toilet training procedure on the frequency of toileting accidents, both bladder and bowel, of 34 normal children. The toilet training period is shown as an interruption in the curve and required an average of 4 hours per child. The Pre-Training data point represents the children's accident rate per day during the week prior to training. Data points are given for the first 7 days after training and monthly thereafter. Each datum point is the average number of accidents per day per child.

Discussion

The results showed that the training program was an effective method of training normal children to toilet themselves without any prompting. All thirty-four children were trained. Training was accomplished rapidly, requiring an average of only 4 hours per child and only about 2 hours for children older than twenty-six months. The accidents quickly decreased to a near-zero level and remained near zero during the four-month follow-up. Bowel training and bladder training were accomplished concurrently with no need for a differential training procedure. An incidental benefit was that bedwetting (enuresis) was also eliminated for about one-third of the children. Successful training was achieved even for children as young as twenty months, for problem children who resisted any type of training, and for children who did not speak. The training program appeared to be a pleasant experience for the children.

The present results demonstrate that toilet training is not a futile exercise; training can be achieved by intensive learning procedures, as was also indicated by recent reinforcement studies (Madsen et al., 1969). Consequently, one can no longer defend an attitude of fatalistic permissiveness on the grounds that bladder and bowel control cannot be hastened. A permissive attitude would still be justified if the training effort produced an enduring negative emotional attitude. The results showed the converse: the children who were negative prior to training were described as more pleasant and cooperative after training. Overall, we suggest that training be deferred until a child is twenty months of age because the training effort for the average child below that age might counterbalance the convenience of having him trained.

REFERENCES

AZRIN, N. H.; SNEED, T. J.; AND FOXX, R. M. 1973. Dry bed: A rapid method of eliminating bedwetting (enuresis) of the retarded. *Behavior Research and Therapy* 11: 427–34.

MADSEN, C. H.; HOFFMAN, M.; THOMAS, D. R.; KOROPSAK, E.; and MADSEN, C. K. 1969. Comparisons of toilet training techniques. In *Social learning in childhood,* ed. D. M. Gelfand. Belmont, Calif.: Brooks/Cole.

SPOCK, B. 1968. *Baby and child care.* Rev. ed. New York: Pocket Books.

9

Quasi-Experimental Approaches to Outcome Evaluation

The previous chapter demonstrated how very simple research designs can answer important questions for the evaluator and for users of evaluations. However, early in that chapter it was stressed that these designs can seldom help evaluators identify the cause of changes in program participants. Whenever program administrators and governmental agencies commission evaluators to discover the cause of such changes, evaluations of greater complexity must be designed. In order to show that something causes something else, it is necessary to demonstrate (1) that the cause precedes the supposed effect in time; (2) that the cause covaries with the effect; and (3) that no other alternative explanations of the effect exist except the assumed cause. It is easy to satisfy the first criterion, and the second criterion is not that difficult to test either. Both can be demonstrated using the methods described in Chapter 8. The third, however, is much more difficult and is the focus of this and the following chapters.

In this chapter various methods are presented that possess greater internal validity than the simple methods described in Chapter 8. The validity of outcome evaluations seeking to demonstrate causal relationships can be increased by (1) observing the participants at additional times before and after the program; (2) observing additional people who have not received the program; and (3) using a variety of variables, some expected to be influenced by the program and others not expected to be affected. These methods have been labeled quasi-experiments by Campbell and Stanley (1963); although these methods do not achieve the airtight control of true experiments, quasi-experiments control for many biases and, can thus, yield highly interpretable evaluations—if carefully planned.

DISTINGUISHING CHANGE
FROM RANDOM FLUCTUATIONS

Increasing the number of observations across time is one approach to reducing the chances that an observed change was due to a nonprogram source. All behaviors show random variation over time. The number of crimes on a given day or week is not a constant, nor is it a uniformly decreasing or increasing variable. Although there are some predictable influences on the number of crimes committed (for example, cold weather inhibits crime, warmer weather seems to encourage it), the causes of most changes in the day-to-day crime rate are unknown. Nevertheless, the popular media often act as though such causes were known and effective remedial action well understood.

In July 1975, a few days after several thousand police officers were laid off in New York City, there were two days in which an abnormally high number of murders occurred: Nine murders occurred on July 8, eight on July 9. These two high-crime days were contrasted with the average for the year—four per day. Were newspapers correct in attributing the cause of these additional murders to the reductions in the size of the police force (see Egelhof, 1975)?

The first criterion necessary for a causal conclusion was met: The police were laid off before the murders. However, it is not known if murder covaries with size of police force, and alternative interpretations of the observed number of murders were not even considered. Without some information about the normal variation from day to day, it is hard to know whether eight or nine murders is unusual on a summer day. No information was provided about the weather. It may have been unusually hot. Did the murder rate stay that high after July 9? Without this additional information it is impossible to draw even the most tentative conclusions about the effect, if any, of the reduction in number of police officers on murder rate. Ignoring these threats to internal validity can lead to quite erroneous interpretations of the causal relations between two events. As was mentioned before and will be stressed again, it is even possible that an effective program will look ineffective if possible explanations of change are ignored.

A second and frequently cited example of the possibility of misunderstanding a phenomenon when given limited information occurred in Connecticut during the 1950s (Campbell, 1969). In 1955 there were approximately 14.2 automobile accident fatalities per 100,000 residents. This was a record rate and was especially high compared to the 1954 rate. The governor initiated a crackdown on speeding during 1956. The fatality rate in 1956 dropped to about 12.2 per 100,000. Could the governor justifiably claim that the measures he took were responsible for the reduction in fatalities? Readers might stop for a moment to develop an answer to that question.

The way to decide if the governor could take credit for the drop requires information about fatalities before the crackdown year as well as after the crucial year. The number of fatalities before the record in 1955 may show that fatalities per year were systematically rising in response to the number of autos per resident on Connecticut roads and the number of miles driven per auto. Because accidents increase when the number of cars increases, a steady increase in fatalities, while undesirable, may be unavoidable in this situation. A program to reduce fatalities would be up against strong forces and could be expected to yield few results.

A second alternative would be that the record rate in 1955 was simply a statistical artifact. Perhaps a few very tragic but fortunately infrequent multifatality accidents occurred during the same year. Or perhaps especially bad weather occurred just before or just after holidays when many drivers were on the road. Because consecutive years of such coincidences are unlikely, a remedy for the high fatality rate is quite likely to appear to succeed, regardless of how well or poorly conceived.

The actual fatality rates for the years before and after the Connecticut speeding crackdown were reported by Campbell (1969) and are given in Figure 9.1. The reader can see that the 1955 rate does appear to be a discrepant value, even though the magnitude of fluctuations from year to year is markedly large. This example will be discussed in more detail later in this chapter. The point of interest here is that looking at accident rates over a number of time periods permits a much better informed conclusion than merely examining the rates just before and just after the introduction of the treatment.

A third example of the usefulness of examining information over a number of time intervals is provided by Rheinstein (1959), who examined the effects of tightening divorce laws in Germany in 1900. The divorce rate dropped dramatically after the change, and even dropped slightly the following year. A complex analysis revealed that the law had an impact; however, examining the divorce rate over a longer period (from 1902 to 1914) revealed that within four years the rate was equal to that in 1899, and by 1914 the rate was nearly double that of 1899. Mazur-Hart and Berman (1977) examined divorce in the context of a relaxation of legal requirements. They found that the introduction of no-fault divorce laws also had no impact on divorce rate in a midwestern state.

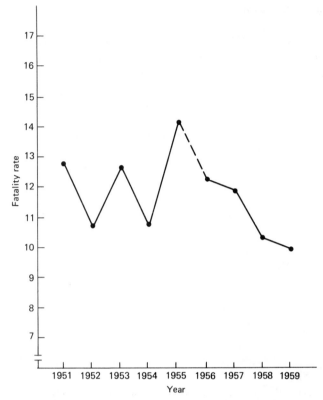

FIGURE 9.1 Automobile accident fatality rate for Connecticut by year, before and after the beginning of a crackdown on speeding drivers. (D. T. Campbell, "Reforms as Experiments," *American Psychologist* 24 (1969): 419. Copyright 1969, by the American Psychological Association. Adapted by permission of the author.)

Time-Series Design

In recent years considerable attention has been given to the use of information across many time intervals. These approaches have come to be called time-series analyses. Influences fostering this interest have come from economics at a macro level and from behavior analysis at a micro level. Economists have used information over long time periods, seeking to learn the effects of policy changes on such variables as income level, industrial output, and employment. On a very different scale, behavior analysis research has utilized objective measurement of a single individual over many time periods, during which various interventions were begun and stopped. Once again, the unit of analysis—in this case a single person—is not appropriate for most evaluations; however, the importance the behavior analyst places on obtaining stable base-line measurement before an intervention and on documenting both change and the maintenance of change have become one of the concerns of program evaluators. A study done in this tradition will illustrate the behavioral analysis approach to program evaluation (see Case Study 9.1).

It is worth noting that the data of the economist and the behavior analyst are more similar to each other than might be supposed merely by considering the units of analysis used. Whether referring to a country or to a single child, the researcher obtains one value or makes one observation for each "subject" for each variable during each time interval studied. For example, for the economist there is only one unemployment level in the nation per time period, one GNP, and one inflation rate. For the behavior analyst there is only one index of a specific abnormal behavior per time period. Thus, writers can refer to "single subject" research in both cases.

Time-series designs as applied to program evaluation received strong encouragement from the work of Campbell and Stanley (1963), who gave them an important place among their quasi-experimental designs. Collecting data over many time periods is a way of satisfying some of the internal validity tests described in the previous chapter. Because maturation effects can be traced during the time periods before and after the intervention, the likelihood of confusing the program's effect with maturation effects is greatly reduced when using a time-series design rather than a pretest-posttest design. Similarly, the effects of history will be more easily detected using a time-series design than when an evaluation is performed using observations at only one or two time periods. By examining the reaction of the dependent variables to historical events, it is possible, at least at a qualitative level, to distinguish the effects of the program from the impact of major nonprogram influences.

A time-series approach to program evaluation minimally includes the following characteristics: (1) A single unit is defined, and (2) quantitative observations are made (3) over a number of time intervals (4) that precede and follow some controlled or natural intervention (Knapp, 1977). In the language of experimental design, the unit observed (person, group, or nation) serves as its own control.

Program evaluators, unlike economists, use time-series designs almost exclusively when a definite intervention has occurred at a specific time. The design is often called an interrupted time series (Caporaso, 1973); and the evaluator's job is to learn whether the interruption—that is, the human service intervention—had an impact. Figure 9.2 illustrates this design in symbols.

There are a number of possible outcomes observable in a graph of a program's outcome plotted over time intervals. Figure 9.3 illustrates some of these possibilities. Each part of the figure is plotted with time intervals

NAME AND SYMBOLIZATION	QUESTIONS THAT CAN BE ANSWERED USING THIS DESIGN FOR A PROGRAM EVALUATION
Interrupted time series O - O - . . . O - X - O - . . . - O - O	All the questions in Figure 8.1 Are there maturational trends that might explain an improvement? Do historical events cause the dependent variable to change?
Pretest-posttest with a nonequivalent control group O - X - O O - - O	All the questions in Figure 8.1 Is change more than the effect of history, maturation, testing, selection, or mortality?

FIGURE 9.2 Simple quasi-experimental designs for program evaluation.

FIGURE 9.3 Some illustrative possible patterns of a criterion of program success plotted over time. Time of the program or intervention is indicated by the dashed vertical line.

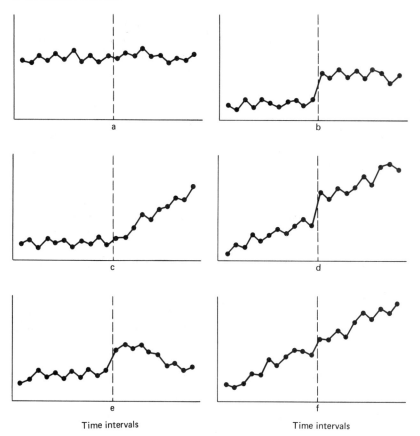

a

b

c

d

e

f

Time intervals

Time intervals

209

along the abscissa, and magnitude of the outcome-dependent variable on the ordinate. Figure 9.3a illustrates no effect of the intervention: There appears to be no out-of-the-ordinary change in the observations after the program. In contrast, Figure 9.3b illustrates what is usually the most hoped for result of an interrupted time-series analysis. The graph shows a marked increase from a fairly stable level before the intervention, and the criterion remains fairly stable afterwards. One might expect this sort of result from an effective training program that increased the skills of employees or from the introduction of labor-saving devices. Clearly, the method can be used when the intervention is designed to lower variables as well as to raise them. Accident rates and failure rates are examples of variables one would like to see drop.

Figures 9.3c to 9.3f all show some sort of an increase after the intervention, but their interpretations are much less clear. Figure 9.3c shows an increase in slope after the intervention. The variable being measured began to increase over time after the intervention; however, there was no immediate impact as in 9.3b. An influence, such as television viewing or improved nutrition, whose impact is diffuse and cumulative might produce the result in Figure 9.3c. In 9.3d there is a localized increase apparently due to the intervention superimposed on a general increasing trend.

In Figure 9.3e there appears to be an effect due to the intervention; however, it seems to be temporary. Many new programs are introduced with much publicity, and the deeply involved staff members want the program to work. Perhaps extra staff effort is responsible for the immediate impact. However, once the program is part of the regular procedure and the extra effort is no longer extended, the outcome achieved returns to its former levels. Schnelle and colleagues (1978) showed that a helicopter patrol decreased crime in a high-crime area. However, the authors questioned whether the effect would hold up if the experiment was to be continued beyond the initial trial period. It is possible that although the *novelty* of the helicopter patrol served to frighten potential thieves and thus to lower crime for a short period, the airborne patrol's inherent effectiveness is not strong.

A possible pitfall for an evaluator could exist when a situation occurs such as that illustrated in Figure 9.3f. Here a steady increase over time is observed. A naive approach to the analysis would be to contrast the mean of the time periods before the intervention with the mean of the time periods after. This contrast may be statistically significant, but it does not help one understand the effect of the intervention.

Analysis of Time-Series Design

Rigorous analysis of interrupted time-series design is beyond the scope of this book. The methods now accepted are described by Gottman and Glass (1978); however, advanced statistical sophistication is required to understand and use these methods. For readers of this book, some steps that fall short of the most correct and complete analysis may be taken that will help in interpreting time series data.

First, when the effects of the intervention are striking, statistical analyses may be unnecessary. Case Study 9.1, concerning the safety of sanitation workers, illustrates a situation in which the change in the dependent measure, the criterion of success, is so strong and so closely related to the intervention that one can conclude that the program had a positive effect. Similarly, McCarthy (1978) found a strong effect from a daily posting of the number of high bobbins in a textile plant. High bobbins lead to tangles and lost production time, but their incidence can be greatly reduced by additional employee care. The feedback and the workers' attempts to meet the posted goals resulted in a dramatically reduced rate of malfunction. A graph of the number of high bobbins showed a dramatic drop after feedback was initiated. Furthermore, when McCarthy temporarily removed the feedback procedure, the number of high bobbins began to climb. Reinstatement of the feedback brought the number back down again. It is hard to argue with the interpretation that the feedback caused the results.

There are other examples of time-series records that are not as easy to interpret. The literature on medical education shows that resident physicians on the average order more laboratory tests for hospital patients than do community physicians who have more experience (for example, Dixon and Laszlo, 1974). To learn whether this finding held for a specific community hospital, a plot of the number of laboratory tests per month was made beginning three years before a major expansion of the hospital's residency programs and one year after. Because neither the hospital's size nor its utilization rate changed systematically during the four-year period, the influence of these variables was ignored. The most striking observation was a steady increase in the average number of laboratory tests compared to the previous month. This increase of an additional five hundred tests per month was observed throughout the time period. However, the increase that occurred between the month before the program was expanded and the first month of the expanded program was about ten thousand. Because the steady monthly increase resumed after this big jump—that is, the graph resembled Figure 9.3d—the evaluators felt safe in attributing the cause of the increase to the fact that young residents were now ordering the bulk of the laboratory tests.[1] The effect of the residents on laboratory tests seemed clear, and the interpretation fit published reports on the topic. However, the interpretation was not as compelling as the effect of feedback on high bobbins described above. The residency program could not be introduced, removed, and then reintroduced as McCarthy did in manipulating the high bobbin feedback.

[1]Partially on the basis of this sudden jump, the program director instituted procedures to reduce the excessive use of laboratory tests by residents.

Finally, there are situations in which there is a valid question about the interpretation of the results of a time-series design. Figure 9.1, showing the results of the crackdown on speeding, cannot be validly interpreted using the informal examination methods described here. Cook and Campbell (1979) report that recent analyses support the belief that the program had a reliable (that is, statistically significant) effect. The methods necessary to make that interpretation require mathematical skills beyond those assumed for readers of this text and beyond those possessed by most active evaluators. It is likely, however, that program evaluators will use these methods (for example, Gottman and Glass, 1978; McCleary and Hay, 1980) to a greater extent in the future.

One aid to visual inspection of a time-series graph has been provided by Tukey (1977). He suggests that the graph be smoothed by plotting the median of three adjacent points in place of each observation. Suppose that the following observations were made for a fifteen-month period: 30, 22, 40, 17, 35, 25, (Intervention), 45, 23, 55, 42, 35, 52, and 43. Plot these values. Now take the median of 30, 22, and 40. Plot 30 for month 2. Take the median of 22, 40, and 17. Plot 22 for month 3. Continue for the entire time series. When you are finished, you will see that the graph has been smoothed, so that the change that was caused by the intervention can be clearly seen. This technique is most useful when the intervention leads to a lasting, large change but the change is masked by large random fluctuations among time intervals.

OBSERVING OTHER GROUPS

Nonequivalent Control Group Design

The simple time-series design increases the interpretability of an evaluation by extending the periods of observations over time. Another approach is to increase the number of groups observed. If the pretest-posttest design could be duplicated with another group that did not receive the program, a potentially good research design would result. So long as the groups are comparable, nearly all the internal validity tests are satisfied by this design, called nonequivalent control group design (diagrammed in Figure 9.2). Nonequivalent control groups may also be called comparison groups.

The evaluator expects to observe a larger improvement between pretest and posttest for the program group than for the comparison group, as illustrated in Figure 9.4. The correct statistical tool to analyze the data from such a design is the two groups by two time periods analysis of variance, with repeated measures over time periods (Kirk, 1968).[2] If the program

[2]Other names for this design are the split-plot factorial or mixed designs.

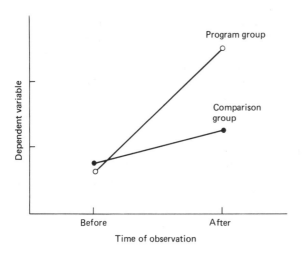

FIGURE 9.4 Hypothetical results of a nonequivalent control (comparison) group design.

was successful and the group means followed the pattern in Figure 9.4, the analysis of variance would reveal a significant interaction between group and testing period.

Including the comparison group permits a distinction to be made between the effects of the program and the several alternative plausible interpretations of change. Because the comparison group has been tested at the same time periods as the program group, both groups have had the same amount of time to mature. Historical forces have presumably affected the groups equally. Because both groups would have been tested twice, testing effects should be equivalent. Finally, the rates of participant loss between pretest and posttest can be examined to be sure they are similar. Nonequivalent control group designs are especially useful when part of an organization is exposed to the program while other parts are not. Since selection to the program is not in the hands of the participants, and since the participants' level of need does not determine eligibility, the comparability of the groups is quite good. Unfortunately, as will be shown below, these favorable conditions are not often met.

Weakness of the Design

Clearly, the major weakness in all nonequivalent control group designs is in selecting a comparison group not sufficiently similar to the program group to permit drawing valid interpretations. For example, it is possible that those who choose to be in the program may be maturing at a different rate than those in the comparison group. Parents who seek out special programs for their children may also be devoting more attention to the children at home than are parents who do not seek out special programs. Campbell and Stanley (1963) called this threat to internal validity a "selection-by-maturity interaction." Another problem will arise if the program participants are chosen because of extreme scores on the pretest, and the comparison group is selected from others with less extreme scores. If so, as mentioned in Chapter 8, the results may be distorted by regression effects.

A way out of the problems caused by using a nonequivalent control group research design is often sought by matching the comparison groups with the program group—that is, the people forming the comparison group are chosen because they resemble the program participants on income level, objective test score, rated adjustment, locality of residence, or other criteria. While matching is often used to select comparison groups for quasi-experiments, it is a controversial way to form such groups.

The widely cited evaluation of Head Start (Cicarelli, Cooper, and Granger, 1969) has been criticized for its use of matching (Campbell and Erlebacher, 1970). Head Start is a program for disadvantaged children offered in the summer or during the year prior to beginning first grade. The program was designed for the preschool children most lacking in school-relevant skills and attitudes. In addition, nutritional and medical goals were involved in the program.

When Head Start was selected for evaluation, it was already widely accepted and offered in many communities (Datta, 1976b); therefore, the program could not be withheld from any group of children. The evaluation utilized a posttest-only design with national samples of children, some in Head Start programs and some matched samples not in Head Start. The evaluation compared achievement on standard tests of Head Start children in first, second, and third grades with similar non–Head Start children and concluded that Head Start was largely a failure. Critics have attacked the methodology utilized in this evaluation on a number of grounds; however, the focus of the present discussion is on regression effects that likely lie behind the conclusions of the Head Start evaluation.

Because the population of children available for the non–Head Start comparison group was less disadvantaged than the children in the Head Start group, those children selected as matches could not be equivalent to the children in Head Start. In order to find children qualifying for Head Start who had cognitive achievement scores similar to those of children not qualifying, either or both of the following points had to have been true: (1) The comparison group was selected from among the less able children not qualified for Head Start; or (2) the experimental group was selected from among the more able children who attended Head Start.

To understand the effects of regression toward the mean, it is important to understand why the previous statement is true. Once a group is selected on the basis of need for a national program, there is no other group that can be found that is just like the people in the program. Thus, no perfect comparison group exists. However, on some variables (for example, family income, school grades, test scores) there will be overlap among the members of the two groups. Who will overlap? The people in the "needy" group who overlap with the "not needy" group *must* be among the relatively better-off among the "needy" people. Those in the "not needy" group who overlap with the "needy" children *must* be among the least well-off among the "not needy" people.

Consider an artificial, but illustrative example. Suppose a teacher wanted to provide a special spelling program for all the second graders. If the teacher wanted a comparison group, he or she could find some third graders who scored as low as the second graders. Are these groups equivalent? Probably not. These third graders would have been selected from the lower portion of a population that, in general, is more capable than the second-grade experimental group. What will happen upon retesting the groups in evaluation? Because no spelling test is completely reliable, the low-scoring third graders in the comparison group will look as though they improved, not only because they learned some new words but also because they are regressing toward the mean of third graders. This regression will make the second graders' improvement due to the program appear smaller and less impressive than it may actually have been.

In other words, the groups of children have different influences raising their scores. The program children will probably show an improvement because the new program has affected them and because they matured a bit. The comparison children will improve because of exposure to the regular spelling classes, added maturity, *and* regression. Campbell and Erlebacher (1970) assert that the Head Start evaluation was biased in just the way this hypothetical teacher's evaluation would be biased. Because human service programs typically produce small improvements, the size of the regression effects might even exceed the program's effect. In fact, Campbell and Erlebacher (1970) argue that regression artifacts may make compensatory education look harmful when, in fact, the programs may have had a small positive influence.[3]

The moral of this section is simply the following: The nonequivalent control group design is especially sensitive to regression effects when the groups are systematically different on some dimensions. In compensatory education evaluations a systematic preprogram difference between experimental and comparison groups is likely to be found. It should be noted that if the program effect was massive and the program children improved markedly, the evaluation may reveal that the program was effective. Nonetheless, the size of the effect will still be underestimated. On the other

---

[3]There is no controversy over whether regression occurred in this evaluation; however, the size of the likely regression effects is hotly disputed (see Cicarelli, 1970; Evans and Schiller, 1970).

hand, when similar groups do exist, the nonequivalent comparison group design is quite powerful and very useful.

OBSERVING OTHER
DEPENDENT VARIABLES

At this point the methods described in Chapter 8 have been expanded to include observations of the program participants at many times and to include observations of groups other than the program participants. It is possible to increase the validity of interpretations by observing additional dependent variables that are not expected to be changed by the program, or at least are expected to be changed only marginally. Consider a remedial reading program offered during the summer vacation for children reading below their grade level. A pretest-posttest design would be markedly strengthened by testing the children before and after on arithmetic as well as vocabulary, grammar, and reading speed. All extraneous influences such as self-selection, history, and testing effects that may affect reading scores will also affect arithmetic scores. Thus, if scores on reading increase but those on arithmetic do not, the conclusion that the program is effective is fairly safe. As long as the children were not selected for the program on the basis of the pretest, regression is not a viable alternative interpretation of the cause of the change.

There is a problem with this approach. The added dependent measures must be similar to the major dependent measure without being strongly influenced by the program. In the example above, if the children did read better, it might be expected that they will do better on a written, standardized arithmetic test than they did before the program. It is hard to imagine additional dependent measures that (1) would be affected by the same threats to internal validity as the outcome measure but (2) would not be affected by the program. Cook, Cook, and Mark (1977) suggest that these difficulties mean that this "nonequivalent dependent variable" design is best used as an adjunct to other methods, not as the major evaluation design.

COMBINING METHODS
TO INCREASE INTERNAL
VALIDITY

Time-Series and Nonequivalent
Comparison Groups

The most interpretable quasi-experimental designs are those that combine the approaches mentioned above into one evaluation. If a group similar to the program participants can be found, the simple time-series de-

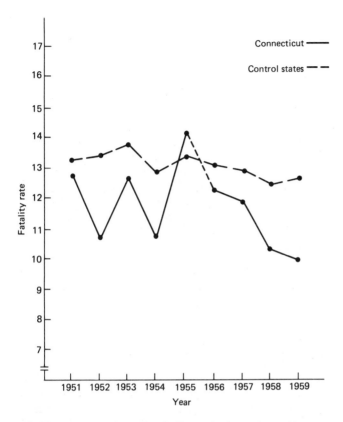

FIGURE 9.5 Automobile accident fatality rate for Connecticut and for comparable states. (D. T. Campbell, "Reforms as experiments," *American Psychologist* 24 (1969): 419. Copyright 1969 by the American Psychological Association. Reprinted by permission of the author.)

sign is considerably strengthened. The analysis of the Connecticut speeding crackdown mentioned earlier was made possible by examining the fatality rates of four neighboring states. Figure 9.5 contrasts the average of these four states' fatality figures with Connecticut's fatality rate. As can be seen in the figure, there seems to be a general trend toward a lower fatality rate in all five states; however, Connecticut's 1957–1959 rates are increasingly divergent from those of the neighboring states. Although regression toward the mean is a plausible alternative interpretation of the drop from 1955 to 1956, the continued favorable trend is hard to explain if the crackdown, which was kept in force during the following years, did not have an effect. Riecken and Boruch (1974) state that tests of significance are less important than a qualitative understanding of the various threats to the validity of causal conclusions about the impact of the intervention. However, methods to be used for precise analyses are being developed (see Gottman and Glass, 1978).

FIGURE 9.6 Hypothetical results of an interrupted time-series design with switching replications.

A key to drawing valid interpretations from observations lies in being able to repeat the observations. If a study can be replicated, one can be much more sure of conclusions than if it cannot be. The time-series design with a comparison group that receives the same intervention as the experimental group but at a later time provides additional safeguards against validity threats. Figure 9.6 illustrates the ideal pattern of results from such a study. Cook and Campbell (1979) call this design an "interrupted time series with switching replications." If the observations fit the pattern in Figure 9.6, little in the way of statistical analysis needs to be done. Unfortunately, many societal changes are also occurring during the time of the observations, so that the dependent variables do not fall into an easily interpreted pattern. Case Study 9.1 is a successful example of a time-series design with switching replications in an evaluation of a solution to a municipal problem.

Time-Series and Nonequivalent Dependent Variables

Another improvement in the time-series design involves the use of nonequivalent dependent variables. Ross (1973) provided information on a 1967 crackdown on drunken drivers in Britain. Because the intervention was nationwide and because similar information from other countries

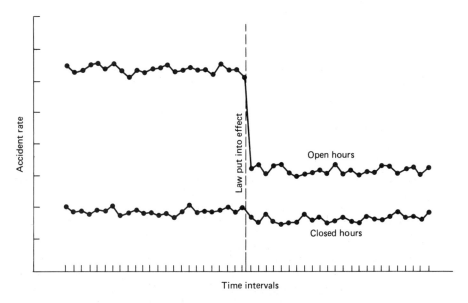

FIGURE 9.7 Illustrative outcome from a time-series analysis using two dependent variables, one likely to be more affected by the program than the other.

might not be comparable, relevant, or available, a nonequivalent dependent measure was sought. A feature of the laws introduced in 1967 was that pubs could be open only certain hours. Because people drinking at home are less likely to be driving than are those drinking in pubs, one way to evaluate the impact of the program was to divide the traffic fatalities into those occurring during pub hours and those occurring when the pubs were closed. These variables satisfy the requirements of the nonequivalent dependent measures approach, because historical trends that would affect drivers during pub hours should also affect drivers at other times. Severe weather, increased police vigilance, and improved record keeping, for example, would affect both accident rates equally. The data followed the pattern presented in Figure 9.7. A dramatic drop in casualties was observed during pub hours after the introduction of the breathalyzer, but no drop was found during other hours.

The Patch-Up Design

Cook and Campbell (1979) use the term *patch-up design* to describe a method that illustrates the essence of the quasi-experimental approach. Being aware of the threats to internal validity that are most likely to affect an evaluation, evaluators may decide to add comparison groups specifically designed to control for certain influences, until the most plausible competing interpretations are eliminated.

The dean of a college of arts and sciences in a medium-sized university requested an evaluation of a junior year abroad program sponsored and supervised by his college. The report was needed for a board of trustees meeting scheduled in six weeks. Clearly, there was no opportunity for a time-series design. (As mentioned in earlier chapters, it is not unusual for evaluators to work under considerable time pressure.) The research was planned around the obvious comparison—college seniors who studied abroad versus seniors who studied at the parent campus. In this comparison selection is one threat to internal validity that cannot be ignored. Students who decide to go abroad for a year are clearly different from those who remain at home. An approach to estimating the preexisting differences between these two groups is to test individuals before they leave. A pretest-posttest design was impossible due to the short time allotted for the study. Because the decision to study abroad is costly and requires much planning, sophomore students sign up rather early for the program. By comparing seniors who have been abroad with sophomores arranging to go abroad, the self-selection threat is negated, because both groups have selected themselves to go abroad. However, now a second threat to internal validity becomes a problem. Sophomores are less mature than seniors. Two years in age may not be that critical for middle-aged or elderly people, but two years may make quite a difference in an evaluation of a program for college students. By adding one more group, sophomores who did not intend to study abroad, the major threats to the internal validity of this evaluation were covered.

The design is summarized in Figure 9.8. If self-selection was related to higher scores on the dependent measures, one would expect the groups in the upper row to have higher scores. If maturation led to higher scores, those in the right-hand column should have higher scores. If the program had an impact, then the upper-right-hand group, the self-selected seniors,

FIGURE 9.8 Hypothetical mean scores on a measure of international understanding for the students in the junior year abroad evaluation. A program effect is indicated by these means.

		Maturation Level	
		Sophomores	Seniors
	Students who will study or have studied abroad	50	65 (Experimental group)
Self-selection			
	Students who have not studied and will not study abroad	40	45

should have especially high scores as illustrated. Unfortunately, the sophomores planning to spend the year abroad were very hard to find, and only three were tested. Therefore, the means in Figure 9.8 are hypothetical.

A more complicated patch-up design was described by Lawler and Hackman (1969). They wished to evaluate the success of having custodial employees design their own incentive plan to reduce absenteeism. The authors believed that an incentive plan would work only if the employees designed it themselves. The authors had to use intact, existing work groups; therefore, some form of the nonequivalent control group design had to be used. Three intact work teams making up the experimental group developed their plans in consultation with the experimenters. The first comparison group had an incentive plan similar to that developed by the experimental group, but it was imposed upon them by management. Including this group enabled the evaluators to distinguish between the effect of an *employee*-designed incentive plan and the incentive itself. A second comparison group simply met with the experimenters to talk about the work and absenteeism. This group was necessary to show that any reduction in absenteeism would have been due more to the incentive plan than to the discussions with industrial psychologists. Finally, a comparison group with no incentive plan and no discussion was added.

The data were analyzed using a time-series analysis because (1) the rate of absenteeism may change slowly, and (2) absenteeism is a very natural variable to be calculated on a weekly basis—whether or not there is a program. Comparing the rate of absenteeism for the twelve weeks before the intervention with the rate during the twelve weeks afterwards showed that the participant employees improved from 12 percent absent to 6 percent, while the rates for the other groups did not change. Note that without each of the control groups (just as in junior year abroad study), some alternative interpretation would have been plausible. The comparison groups were selected to counter specific, plausible interpretations of any improvement in the absenteeism rate of the experimental group.

There are other threats to internal validity with which the design does not deal because they were not plausible in this study. For example, instrumentation refers to possible changes in measures of outcome or success such as those that occur when staff become more vigilant or experienced because of interest in the evaluation. Because job absenteeism is a critical variable in work settings, the development of a program is unlikely to make any changes in the measurement of absenteeism.

SUMMARY

The use of quasi-experimental research designs in program evaluation is widespread. These approaches are often compatible with the need to minimize disruption in organizations and the need of evaluators to obtain sufficient information to permit the isolation of probable causes of changes in program participants. However, the use of quasi-experimental research designs is not straightforward; the evaluator needs to consider which specific threats to internal validity must be accounted for in each evaluation. Anticipating just which threats are likely to be problems can cause headaches for evaluators: There are no standard approaches to designing quasi-experimental evaluations. Often the correct statistical methods to use in analyzing a quasi-experimental evaluation are controversial. One of the most promising quasi-experimental methods, the interrupted time-series design, is receiving considerable theoretical study. New analytical methods are likely to become widely known in future years.

STUDY QUESTIONS

1. Explain which threats to internal validity are not covered by an evaluation of a parole program in which male parolees are tested before and after the program and are compared to a sample of men living in the same neighborhoods as the parolees.

2. Assume that reading levels in a school district were steadily declining over recent years and that a new reading program was implemented to counter this trend. After two years the reading levels continued to decline, but the superintendent announced that the program was a success because reading levels would have declined even more without the program. What would be necessary to evaluate the validity of such an announcement? Think of the minimum amount and the least expensive sources of such information.

3. Suppose a new medical treatment were offered to residents of an upper-middle-class suburb. As a comparison group, similarly aged patients with the same diagnosis were found in a county hospital providing free care to welfare families. Evaluate this nonequivalent control group evaluation design.

4. A problem with quasi-experimental evaluations is that often a particular set of results can be interpreted, but a different set cannot. For example, assume a service to a disadvantaged group resulted in improved performance on some variable. If the postprogram performance of this disadvantaged group is better than that observed in the middle-class comparison group, the interpretation of the evaluation is clear. However, if postprogram performance of the disadvantaged group is lower than that of the middle-class comparison group, then there are many more possible interpretations. Explain these statements.

FURTHER READING

Cook, T. D., and Campbell, D. T. 1979. *Quasi-experimentation.* Chicago: Rand McNally.

McCleary, R., and Hay, R. A., Jr. 1980. *Applied time series analysis for social sciences.* Beverly Hills, Calif.: Sage.

CASE STUDY 9.1   A Program to Increase the Job-Related Safety of Sanitation Workers

The use of an interrupted time-series design is illustrated in this evaluation. An intervention was introduced to one group, while a second group served as a comparison group. Later, when the intervention was introduced to the second group, the first was used as the comparison group. This design, called the *interrupted time-series design with switching replications,* is one of the most powerful quasi-experimental research designs. It is useful when an intervention or a human service must be given to all members of an already-formed group or not at all, and there is at least one other group that can be given the service at a later date. This case study also illustrates some aspects of the responsibilities of program evaluators to report their findings to all concerned (see Chapter 12) and to encourage the use of the results of program evaluations (see Chapter 13).

EVALUATING MUNICIPAL POLICY: AN ANALYSIS OF A REFUSE PACKAGING PROGRAM*

Trevor F. Stokes and Stephen B. Fawcett

Proposed changes in city service operations are often not subjected to formal pilot testing prior to their implementation. The present study examined the effectiveness of one proposed change in the operation of a city sanitation service, that is, the modification of refuse packaging requirements. This research resulted from consultation with officials of the Sanitation Worker's Association on various problems within the sanitation department. Issues of concern to the workers and city management included the packaging of refuse by city residents, the quality of sanitation services, the safety of equipment and work procedures, job security, and worker morale. The inadequate packaging of refuse by city residents was a matter of particular concern to the workers.

Method

The study examined the refuse packaging behavior of persons living in 183 residences in Lawrence, Kansas, a community of fifty thousand. These residences were arbitrarily divided into two experimental areas, one on either side of a major city street. There were ninety-four private residences in the West, and eighty-nine in the East.

Observation.   Before the sanitation crew collected refuse, packaging violations were counted each collection day in the experimental areas. Observations occurred at the same time each day. An observer was driven by car through each section according to a predetermined route. The car stopped at each residence to

*Condensed with permission from the *Journal of Applied Behavior Analysis* 10 (1977): 391–98. Copyright 1977 by the *Journal of Applied Behavior Analysis.*

allow counting of violations. Observation of individual residences was always concluded prior to the arrival of the crew.

The presence or absence of refuse to be collected was recorded for each residence. Furthermore, if refuse was out, that residence was scored for adherence to the packaging standards. The type and number of violations were scored for residences violating the regulations.

Violation types were predetermined by the city ordinance covering sanitation service. However, the precise wording of the violations [largely omitted in this condensation] adopted for the present study incorporated the concerns of the workers and city management personnel and were defined so as to facilitate reliable observation. These ordinances were designed to ensure the safety of sanitation workers and reduce the likelihood of spilling refuse during collection.

There were six categories of packaging violations:

1. Edge of container (can or bag) more than six feet from the collection point.
2. Refuse extending more than nine inches above the top rim of can.
3. Untied or torn plastic refuse bags.
4. Unacceptable refuse containers (cardboard boxes, paper bags, pasteboard or fiberboard barrels, and wicker baskets).
5. Yard trimmings not tied in bundles less than eighteen inches in diameter and less than four feet long.
6. Loose litter, trash, or garbage greater than two inches in diameter and within six feet of refuse container.

The reliability of observation was assessed on four days (3, 5, 9, and 13) by having the driver of the observation car independently score each residence at the same time as the regular observer. An agreement was scored if both observers agreed to the categorization of a residence. These comparisons yielded the following percentages of interobserver agreement: scoring of violating residences, 98.3 percent; nonviolating residences, 96.9 percent; residences without refuse, 98.6 percent.

Municipal enforcement program. The enforcement program involved instructions and feedback about packaging and contingent collection of refuse appropriately packaged. Instructions consisted of a letter signed by the City Manager and the Superintendent of Sanitation mailed to each resident following the last day of baseline. The letter emphasized the intent of the city to enforce the packaging standards. Attached to the letter was a copy of the standards for packaging garbage and trash that detailed the violation types and provided reasons why these violations reduced the safety and efficiency of the sanitation service. In addition, each letter contained a copy of a violation tag that would be left as a courtesy to residents if part of their refuse was not collected. Feedback consisted of violation notices distributed by the sanitation crewman riding on the back of the truck. These notices, checklists specifying the relevant violation type, were usually attached to the handle of the refuse can. Fifteen to thirty seconds was required to fill in and leave a notice at a violating residence. Nonviolating residences did not receive written feedback. Contingent collection involved collection only of adequately packaged refuse. All refuse failing to meet the minimum standards was not collected until the packaging met the standards.

Experimental Conditions

The effect of the enforcement program was analyzed in a multiple-baseline design across the West and East neighborhoods.

Baseline. Baseline observation in both sections commenced shortly after the City Commission formally gave approval for the study to proceed and directed that the enforcement procedures be implemented in the two test neighborhoods. Additional public notification of the particular neighborhoods involved and the details of the enforcement procedures to be followed (noncollection of inappropriately packaged refuse) appeared in the local newspaper's report of the commission meeting, which also occurred prior to baseline. During baseline, the sanitation crew followed their normal procedures, collecting refuse packaged correctly or incorrectly.

Enforcement program in the West. Following the fifth collection day, a notification letter was mailed to each resident in the West section. The enforcement program was instituted beginning the next collection day and remained in effect through day 15. Baseline conditions remained in effect for the East section.

Enforcement program in the East. Following the tenth collection day, similar notification was provided to residents in the East section. The enforcement program was implemented as of day 11, and remained in effect through day 15.

Follow-up. Following day 15, a letter was sent by the city to each of the 183 residences in the experimental area. This letter thanked the residents for their cooperation in the testing of procedural changes in the Sanitation Department and informed them of the successful conclusion of the study. The sanitation crew was instructed to discontinue the enforcement procedures after day 15 and resume the "normal" baseline conditions. Four weeks later, on day 23, a follow-up observation of packaging violations was made.

Results

Figure 9.9 shows the daily number of violations in the West and East sections. Before enforcement, there were means of 59.4 and 79.9 violations per day in the West and East, respectively. After enforcement, the number of violations was markedly reduced to means of 9.7 and 23.2 per day in the West and East, respectively. These lowered numbers of violations were maintained at a follow-up observation four weeks after completion of the study.

Figure 9.10 shows the daily percentages of residences violating at least once. During the study, a mean of 45 of the 183 residences did not have their refuse out when violations were counted. In the West, a mean of 39.9 percent of residences with refuse out committed at least one violation per day before enforcement, whereas a mean of 12.5 percent of residences violated per day during the enforcement program. Similarly, in the East, the mean percentage of residences violating decreased from 45.4 percent to 22.6 percent. Lowered rates were maintained at the follow-up observation.

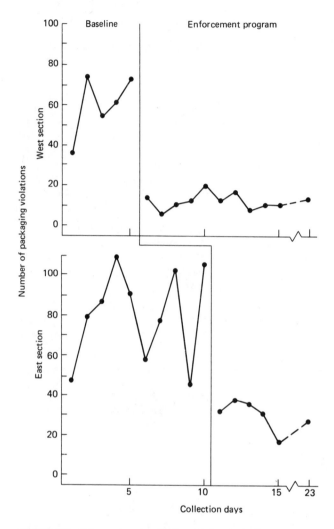

FIGURE 9.9 Daily number of packaging violations in the West and East neighborhoods.

Of the 183 residences studied, 27 (14 percent) never committed a violation during the fifteen collection days (eight weeks) of the study. Of the other 156 residences, which committed at least one violation, 88 percent averaged fewer violations per day during the enforcement period than they had averaged per day during baseline; 6 percent showed no change; and 6 percent showed increased violations. Seventy-four of the 183 residences met the noncollection contingency: 45 residences experienced the contingency on one day, 17 on two days, 7 on three days, 4 on four days, and one residence had refuse not collected on 6 different days. Of course, many residents observed the application of the enforcement contingency to their neighbors.

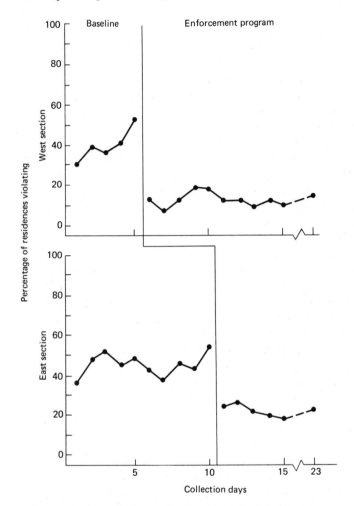

FIGURE 9.10 Daily percentages of residences violating the packaging regulations in the West and East neighborhoods, based on those residences with refuse out.

Discussion

The enforcement program, which consisted of instruction, feedback, and contingent refuse collection, was effective in markedly reducing the number of violations of packaging regulations and the percentage of residences violating. Correlated with these objective data changes, the ratings by the sanitation crew established the social validity of the effects of the enforcement program. The differences between sections in baseline and enforcement levels of violations were mirrored by the men's ratings: refuse was rated as better packaged, safer, and easier to collect. The workers' ratings suggest that these procedures might be a valuable component in a comprehensive safety and efficiency program for sanitation workers.

Fewer than 19 percent of the test neighborhoods' residents complained to the sanitation workers or city officials about the requirements of the enforcement program when part of their refuse was not collected. This type of program will probably always be met with some dissatisfaction, especially when first implemented. In this context, it should be noted that the number of complaints in the study areas did not differ significantly from the rest of the city.

The conduct of policy research is not a simple activity. As with many other research endeavors, the researchers cannot enter the experimental setting, collect their data, and depart cheerfully without regard to the political realities of that setting. Policy research, necessarily, involves close cooperation with both the policy makers and those persons involved in the procedural testing of proposed changes. The Sanitation Workers' Association initiated the present research through their identification of the packaging problem and request for assistance from the authors. The city of Lawrence (through the office of the City Manager) and the workers' association provided the support and political insulation essential for the conduct of the research. The authors formulated the details of the municipal enforcement program in consultation with local residents, the sanitation workers, and city management personnel. They also developed the experimental procedure, design, and measurement system. Through the City Manager, a request to conduct a pilot testing of the possible policy changes was submitted to the city commission. Such approval was given, and the research was then conducted.

Following the completion of the study, the research findings were discussed with sanitation workers and city management personnel with the aim of formulating a proposal for city-wide implementation of the test procedures. The research data and an implementation plan that were similar to the procedures of this study were then submitted to the policymaking body, the elected city commission. After considering the authors' report, the commission adopted the recommendations: a new refuse packaging ordinance was passed. This new ordinance incorporated the old specifications for refuse packaging, but also included the new enforcement provisions tested in the present study. The city management personnel were then instructed to implement the new policy.

In summary, the municipal enforcement program decreased the number of refuse packaging violations in the test neighborhoods. The data formed the nucleus of a recommendation of change in one area of public policy. Thus, the present study described an inexpensive and effective application of contingencies to ameliorate a municipal problem, and provided an example of the contribution of applied behavior analysis to the data-based determination of public policy.

CASE STUDY 9.2   Helmets and Motorcycle Accident Fatalities

The effects of legislation are very hard to evaluate; the laws apply to large units (states), and seldom are perfect comparison states available. This case study utilized the records of sixteen states in a study of the effectiveness of laws requiring motorcyclists to wear crash helmets. Because the states did not adopt laws simultaneously, the study compared fatality rates before and after the laws were passed, regardless of the actual date of passage. There are a number of possible explanations of the results. Readers should exercise their critical skills to find the threats to internal validity that may not be covered by the research design.

HELMET LAWS REDUCE FATALITIES*

Motorcyclist helmet use laws are reducing fatalities in motorcycle crashes, according to a recent study of the effectiveness of these laws. The study, which was conducted by Leon Robertson, senior behavioral scientist for the Insurance Institute for Highway Safety, examined the effects of helmet use in terms of compliance with the laws and their effects on fatalities.

The highway safety program standards adopted by the National Highway Traffic Safety Administration include a requirement that states implement all standards,

*Condensed from Insurance Institute for Highway Safety, *Status Report* 10 (November 5, 1975): 1–3.

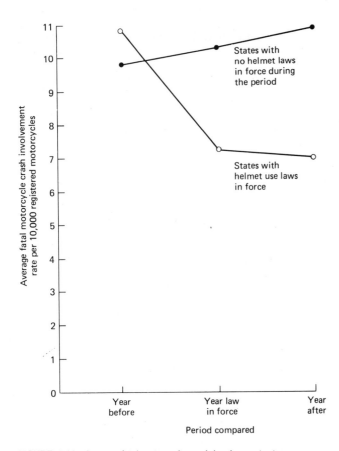

FIGURE 9.11 Average fatal motorcycle crash involvement rates per 10,000 registered motorcycles of 8 states that have helmet use laws and 8 matched comparison states that did not have helmet use laws during the same periods.

including motorcycle helmet use laws, or face loss of all federal highway safety program funds and a portion of federal highway construction funds. Only three states had motorcycle use laws prior to 1967; during 1967–1969 an additional thirty-seven states enacted such laws in accordance with the federal requirement. Currently all but two states, California and Illinois, have such laws. Utah's law, however, applies only at speeds above 35 miles per hour.

To determine the effect of helmet use laws on motorcyclist fatalities, the Institute's study compared the fatal crash involvement rates in eight states (Arizona, Colorado, Idaho, Kansas, Kentucky, Louisiana, Maryland, and Minnesota) that adopted helmet laws with those of similar states (California, New Mexico, Montana, Virginia, Mississippi, West Virginia, and Iowa) that had no such laws during a comparable period.

The study found that the "average fatal involvement rate for the eight states that enacted helmet use laws declined from more than 10 per 10,000 registered motorcycles the year before the laws' enactments to about 7 per 10,000 registered motorcycles, both in the years of enactments and the following years. In contrast, the average fatal involvement rate in the eight matched states that enacted no helmet laws at the time that their comparison state did so remained at about 10 per 10,000 registered motorcycles throughout the period studied" (see Figure 9.11).

During the study, observations of helmet use were conducted along heavily traveled roadways in Atlanta and Baltimore, where helmet use laws are in effect, and in Chicago and Los Angeles, where there are no such laws. In Atlanta and Baltimore, "virtually all of the riders . . . were using helmets." In Los Angeles, more than 60 percent of the riders were using helmets, "but only 25 percent of Illinois riders were using them." The study noted that these findings do "not necessarily mean that these states had high use immediately upon enactment of their laws, nor that all states with such laws have the same experience."

10

Analysis of Causes of Change

The previous chapter described various approaches to reducing the number of plausible interpretations of change observed in program participants. Such interpretations include many possible sources of bias as well as the effect of the program itself. The biases refer to the ideas summarized in the threats to internal validity—self-selection into the program by those who would benefit, general community or societal changes that overshadow all effects of the program, and the reactive effects of making observations, among other factors. The ways of separating these biases from program effects involved observing the participants at a number of time intervals and observing both the relevant dependent measures and dependent measures not likely to change due to the program. In addition, observations of intact groups not experiencing the program can improve interpretability if the groups studied are similar to the program participants. Even when carefully designed quasi-experimental evaluations are conducted, there usually remains a lingering doubt that some influence other than the program led to the improvement observed. Perhaps the people forming the nonequivalent control group were different from the experimental group in some way that was not considered in planning the evaluation. Perhaps the people in the nonequivalent control group were less motivated or reacted to the observations differently than the program participants.

The only way to put these doubts to rest is to adopt a research strategy that accounts for all the possible threats to internal validity. The only method that will do this is the classic experimental design utilizing random assignment of participants to the program or to a control group. This chapter reviews the need for experimentation as a tool in program evaluation, describes the most opportune times to introduce experimentation, and makes practical suggestions for meeting the problems of conducting experimental research in organizational settings.

EXPERIMENTATION
IN PROGRAM EVALUATION

The Logic of Experimentation

Before discussing details of experimentation, a brief review of the logic of randomized experimental design may be useful. A true experiment refers to an evaluation based on observations of people who are randomly assigned to the program group or to some control group. In the previous chapter quasi-experimental methods were presented that are useful when evaluators do not have the administrative power to assign people to particular experiences. In such settings evaluators utilize preexisting intact groups; however, such intact groups were formed for reasons other than the need for an unambiguously interpreted evaluation. Because such groups exist of their own accord, it is very likely that the groups will be different on many variables.

Deniston and Rosenstock (1973) showed that neither a nonexperimental nor a quasi-experimental design validly estimated the effectiveness of a treatment program for rheumatoid arthritics. The cyclical nature of the severity of this illness creates large biases in any design other than an experimental one. In other words, threats to internal validity (particularly regression to the mean) could not be handled by a quasi-experiment when studying this population. No group can be used effectively as a nonequivalent control group for a study of the value of treatment for rheumatoid arthritis. Although this is an unusual population, Deniston and Rosenstock make the general point that even when evaluators recognize a potential source of bias, they may be unable to control for it—short of forming the groups themselves through random assignment. When done on a completely random basis, the treatment and control groups are comparable, since they do not differ systematically before the program begins.

Setting up truly equivalent experimental and control groups requires a nonbiased method of assigning the participants to the groups. Often evaluators believe that random assignment is impossible, when in fact it is a possibility, even within the strictures of functioning organizations. Carey (1979) evaluated the reorganization of a nursing service, taking advantage of a natural random assignment procedure. One of two medical floors of a large hospital was redesigned around a more personalized nursing concept. Assignment of new patients to rooms (and consequently to floors) was made on the basis of bed availability by admitting personnel unaware of the research and uninvolved in nursing organization. Because severity of illness and physician practice determine length of stay, the floor on which a bed is available in a hospital operating near capacity is a random factor. Thus, with no disruption of hospital routine, randomly assigned equivalent groups were obtained. Because the groups were not formed in a biased fashion (for example, physician preference for a floor, or assignment of the more severely ill to one of the floors), the results could be interpreted without concern for many of the threats to internal validity.

Boruch and Rindskopf (1977) liken a randomized experiment to an aspirin for evaluators; the evaluator is thereby relieved of the headaches involved in trying to identify and estimate the sizes of the biases that are present in nonrandomized evaluations such as the nonequivalent group design. The discussion of the patch-up design suggested that the evaluator introduce control groups to measure the impact of the identified biases. Although this is a good approach, there are times when the biases are recognized too late in the course of the evaluation. Further, there will be times when a comparison group needed to eliminate a particular threat to internal validity will be unavailable. Various statistical methods are used to remove the biases when randomization is not possible. However, the use of these methods is controversial and can lead to incorrect conclusions. Campbell and Erlebacher (1970) point out that evaluations using these statistical corrections might make a program look successful when it is not, or unsuccessful when it is successful. Boruch (1975) and others have shown that the statistical methods cannot correct for biases in basic evaluation designs whenever the variables describing group differences are imperfectly measured. Because measurements of academic achievement, emotional adjustment, criminal recidivism, productivity, and so forth, are never perfectly reliable, the statistical adjustments fail to remove all biases.

Experimental Designs

Figure 10.1 includes diagrams of several experimental designs. Each of the groups in the research designs is formed by randomly assigning possible participants to receive the program (the experimental group) or not to receive it (the control group). The most simple form of the true experiment, diagramed in the top section of the figure, employs observations after the program is delivered, but uses no pretests. Because the groups are formed randomly, there is no necessity to use a pretest to show that the groups were equivalent before receiving the program. Such pretests are advisable, if not essential, when preexisting groups are used for an evaluation, as in the quasi-experimental, nonequivalent control group design. As

Experimental design	Symbolic representation*	Questions that can be answered
Posttest-only control group	X O O	Did the program cause a change in the program participants?
Two-by-two factorial	O X O Y O X Y O	Did either or both of the aspects of the program cause a change in the program participants? Is there something about having the two aspects of the program given together that creates an especially favorable climate for change? Or, do X and Y interfere with each other?
Solomon four group	O X O O O O X O	Did the program cause a change in the program participants?
Time series with random assignment to groups	X O O O O O O X O O O O O O X O O O	Did the program cause a change in the program participants? Did the effect of the program hold up over time?

* *The program is represented by X or Y; observations are represented by O.*

FIGURE 10.1 Evaluation designs utilizing random assignment to groups, and the questions these designs can answer.

pointed out in Chapter 9, without pretests the evaluator and the information users would never know if the program and the nonequivalent comparison groups were indeed comparable before the program group was influenced by the program. This is not an issue when true control groups are used.

At times a program can be divided into two parts that might be provided separately or together as a unit. In such a case the posttest design can be enlarged, as the second entry of Figure 10.1 shows. An evaluation using this design and the best method of analyzing it will be discussed later in this chapter.

A brief review of the threats to internal validity can illustrate the power of random assignment to distinguish between the effect of the program and nonprogram causes of participant change. There is no reason to believe that the groups differ in maturation rates or levels or that they experience different historical influences. The groups have not selected themselves into the program being evaluated. Since participants did not begin at different levels of health, adjustment, achievement, and so forth, regression to the mean is not a viable threat. Both groups have equivalent testing experiences. The possibility of instrumentation changes exist in evaluation projects, especially when observations are made over an extended period of time. The possibility of the meaning of scores changing as observers gain more experience with the research instruments or get tired of the project must also be considered. The potential problems caused by participant dropout after the evaluation has begun are no worse than with other designs.

In spite of the power of randomization to assure that the control and experimental groups will not be systematically different, some evaluators may feel more comfortable with pretests for both groups. Also, having pretests for experimental and control groups might help in communicating the findings to others who do not understand the advantages of randomization. For these reasons, the third design is given in the figure. The four-group design is not in any theoretical way better than the two-group design with posttests only. Flay and Best (1982), however, warn evaluators that randomization may fail in practice. If that happens, having pretest data can help to preserve the usefulness of the evaluation.

The use of pretests has a cost, however. Often the act of observation is reactive, especially in social settings. It is possible that the pretest may sensitize the program participants to the influences of the program, thus ensuring that the program will work only when the pretest is given. If this is true, then the pretest becomes part of the program. There is nothing at all wrong with including a pretest as part of any program; however, it is easy to forget that the pretest may cause the participants to react differently than they would have had the pretest not been given. In Campbell and Stanley's terminology (1963), adding pretests to the first design weakens its external validity because the pretest may have interacted with the program to cause the observed change. If testing is expensive, it is unlikely that program designers will want to incorporate the testing procedure into the program, even though the evaluation only showed that the pretest *and* the program lead to change—not that the program alone leads to change. The third design, using four groups, takes care of all these concerns.

The advantages of time-series designs can be added to the experimental method by making repeated observations at regular intervals. In this way evaluators can learn whether the program's impact held up across time. The last design in Figure 10.1 is especially useful if follow-up assessments are desired and if the program is implemented on a staggered basis. The built-in replication provided by this design is a very attractive feature.

This discussion is not meant to imply that there are only four experimental designs. Many options are possible, depending on the needs of the evaluations. These four designs are described in order to illustrate the types of possibilities that are available to the evaluator.

OBJECTIONS
TO EXPERIMENTATION

When evaluators fail to use experimental methods, the reasons may be related to frequently voiced objections to experimental methodology. It is important for evaluators to be familiar with these objections, lest they encounter them for the first time while planning an evaluation or, even worse, after random assignment to programs has already begun.

Don't Experiment on Me!

People rightly are not anxious to have someone use them in a poorly thought out experiment. Unfortunately, experimentation has sometimes been unjustly associated with activities such as the CIA and Army "experiments" on the effects of hallucinogenic drugs (*Time,* August 4, 1975). The media do not use the word *experiment* in the careful way experimental design textbooks do. Consequently, it is not surprising when people not trained in social science methodology equate experiments to evaluate the effects of a social program or a medical treatment with the covert administration of dangerous drugs to unsuspecting people and other undisciplined approaches to learning about behavior. Evaluators planning an experiment will be careful to treat the question of experimentation with respect. The advantages of experimentation should be stressed. Furthermore, the fact that the program or service has been carefully planned by competent personnel should be clear to possible volunteers and committees overseeing the research.

Clinical Prerogatives

Often people are hesitant to become involved in experimentation because they want the best service available for their problem, be it a health, emotional, educational, or any other problem. They feel that because human service providers are trained and paid to choose the service most likely to help a person, random assignment to a control group means they are missing out on what they really need. In a similar fashion, service providers usually feel able to select the best care for a person in need or to select the people most likely to benefit from a service program. When they feel this way, the service provider is not likely to endorse an evaluation requiring random assignment to groups.

The fact of the matter is that in many ways people in need get a particular form of service on a fairly random basis. Different counselors follow various theories of counseling. Physicians do not follow set treatment patterns. Different cities draw up quite different welfare programs. Judges do not assign identical sentences to people convicted of the same crimes. The reasons why a particular person experiences a particular form of counseling, medical treatment, or job training are often unrelated to clinical insight.

It is quite natural for service staff to believe that they know best about the selection of treatments. The literature on clinical judgment and decision making also suggests that it is not unusual for staff to believe that the selection of a particular treatment is appropriate, when in fact it is worthless or even harmful to people (Gilbert, Light, and Mosteller, 1975). These misperceptions occur because we remember successes and fulfilled expectations; we often explain away and forget observations that do not fit our expectations (Chapman and Chapman, 1967, 1969). Highly prejudiced individuals remember incidents in which a minority member commits a social gaffe but quickly forget or sympathize with a person from a higher-status group committing a similar misstep (see Allport, 1954). Partisan fans see more rule infractions by the opposing team than by their own team (Hastorf and Cantril, 1954).

It takes a considerable amount of tact to convince service providers that their clinical judgment may not always be valid. Providing examples of nonrandomized studies that were later invalidated by randomized research may help service providers see the possibility of misperceptions and the advantages of unambiguous documentation of service effectiveness. In Chapter 2 we described the necessity of encouraging the development of an experimental orientation among program managers and staff. Campbell (1969) suggested that society should approach new human service programs as if they were experiments—treating a failure of a well-conceived program as an indication of our incomplete understanding of human nature, not as an indication of the low motivation or the incompetence of the staff. Admittedly, this philosophy is not practiced as often as it might be. Some human service providers act as though a negative evaluation means they are incompetent; and therefore they develop rationalizations whenever particular individuals do not seem to benefit from the service provided. Few teachers examine their own performance when a student does not pass an examination. By explaining away all failures, the program staff avoids the opportunity for growth that is provided by unfulfilled expectations. At these times evaluators feel the full force of the conflict between their skeptical role toward service programs and the providers' confidence in the effectiveness of the services given.

Time and Effort Involved

Anyone who has conducted research in an organization knows that research requires a commitment of time and effort. Evaluators should not agree to conduct a research project if they do not have the resources to carry it through promptly. Nevertheless, it takes only a little additional work to conduct an experiment rather than a noncontrolled evaluation. Planning and obtaining approval for an experiment requires more time and perseverance than a pretest-posttest single-group evaluation. However, once approval has been obtained, data collection, analysis, and presentation require the same amount of time, regardless of the quality of the evaluation design. Some care is required of the evaluator to be sure the experiment is not corrupted. These concerns will be discussed in the last section of the chapter.

THE COSTS OF *NOT* DOING AN EXPERIMENT

Performing a randomized experiment in a service delivery setting requires a lot of effort and tenacity on the part of the evaluator. In addition, the staff is inconvenienced because, at a minimum, additional forms must be completed. At worst, the staff may feel threatened and treat the evaluator with hostility. It is worth it? Gilbert, Light, and Mosteller (1975) point out that too often the costs of experimentation are not evaluated properly. Instead of considering the costs in absolute terms, planners should compare them with the costs of *not* doing an experiment. Gilbert, Light, and Mosteller describe several medical procedures that became widely accepted on the basis of observational, nonexperimental studies. For example, in 1964 there were approximately one thousand treatment units being used to freeze duodenal ulcers in the United States for ten thousand patients. After a careful randomized experiment, the treatment was discarded. Although the study that finally showed the treatment to be worthless was expensive, the cost of the worthless treatment was expensive as well. The cost of bloodletting, previously mentioned, was also high. Patients in the latter case did not receive a worthless treatment, they received a harmful one. The cost of a small-scale experiment would have been miniscule compared to the cost of the mistreatment.

If a quasi-experimental study cannot be clearly interpreted, its cost is largely wasted. A number of writers have found that published, poorly controlled studies often favor a novel treatment. Although these studies may be a little less expensive than a well-controlled study, they actually cost more because of misinformation provided to readers who may seek to duplicate the results with their own clients, students, or patients. The proliferation of misinformation supporting an ineffective program means that people seeking help—who expect to receive the "best treatment—may actually be poorly served. Even those who would have refused to be part of an experiment on the assumption that they would not be treated in the best way possible may end up with something worse than a recognized experimental program—an experimental program that is only assumed to be effective.

Gilbert, Light, and Mosteller (1975) suggest that the alternative to careful clinical trials is "fooling around." A service provider trying an approach supported only by uncontrolled studies often does not inform the client/patient/trainee that the treatment is new and not thoroughly understood. Nor does the service provider seek to obtain informed consent from a client/patient/trainee as an evaluator would when conducting an experiment.

The costs of not doing an experiment, then, are many. Evaluations that seek to identify causes—but cannot—are totally wasteful. Evaluations that mistakenly purport to have found an effective program may encourage the use of ineffective programs. There are many reasons to initiate program evaluation. When the reason is to identify causal relationships between a human service (the independent variable) and outcome (the dependent variable), the cost of an experiment is surprisingly low when compared to the cost of not doing it.

THE MOST DESIRABLE TIMES TO CONDUCT EXPERIMENTS

It is the contention of this text that evaluation should be built into the daily operation of all organizations. Usually such evaluation procedures will not be experiments but rather the administrative-monitoring and performance-monitoring approaches described in Chapters 6 and 7. There are, however, circumstances that are best served by an understanding of cause-effect relationships and that are especially well-suited to experimentation, as the following sections will illustrate.

When a New Program Is Introduced

When a new program is introduced, there are several conditions that are likely to make staff and managers be interested in an experimental evaluation: (1) Responsible people are thinking about change; (2) if the control group receives the old program, it is hard to argue that its participants are being unfairly treated; (3) the program may take some time to implement, thus providing time for an evaluation; and (4) there is a need to document the program's success for internal requirements, as well as to show that it might work elsewhere.

One of the obstacles to good program evaluation is the fear people often have of change. It is only natural to become comfortable doing things in the same way year after year. Thus, an important variable that needs to be considered in planning evaluations is the staff's and administration's openness or readiness to change. Salasin and Davis (1979) have developed a scale to measure the beliefs of the staff about the likelihood that an evaluation (as well as other innovations) will be accepted and will have a positive effect on the organization. When the impetus for change comes from within the program in the form of a plan for a new service, the staff does not require prodding to consider change. Of course, the staff may need to be cautioned that most innovations, even when well planned, are not successful (Gilbert, Light, and Mosteller, 1975).

When beginning a new program, the current form of service can be given to the control group. Whatever needs a group may have, its members receive help from somewhere. It may be from a previous program, from another agency, from family members, or from elsewhere. Because the service to be evaluated is new, it is hard to argue that randomly assigning people to continue receiving the service they have been getting is a deprivation. (People who believe deeply in the new program will raise the argument nonetheless.) The evaluator seeking to assign participants randomly will have an easier time defending the random assignment when a new program is introduced than when the program has been running for several years and is considered standard policy.

The fact that most new programs do not go into effect in all parts of the organization simultaneously is an advantage to evaluators. Human relations seminars for managers, for example, will not be given to all managers at one time. All that is necessary to conduct an experimental evaluation is to develop a random procedure to schedule the managers if there are several groups, each receiving the program at a different time. The essential aspects of this design were diagramed in the fourth entry of Figure 10.1. The delivery of the program at different times permits the formation of multiple control groups and the repeated replication of the experimental evaluation at times one through four. Furthermore, the possibility of follow-up assessment of success is possible. The most desirable outcome of the evaluation would be for the dependent variables to follow the pattern shown in Figure 10.2. If all five groups were to improve a similar amount after receiving the program, and if the groups maintained their posttraining level, alternative, nonprogram explanations of the results would be very hard to support.

In order to conduct this sort of evaluation, it is important for evaluators to have access to organizational plans. All too often evaluators' services are requested after the program is in place or after its implementation is planned. People untrained in social science methods seldom understand the evaluator's request for changes in implementation plans to accommodate the design needs of the evaluation. Because service personnel will have worked hard to gain approval for a new program, they will resist

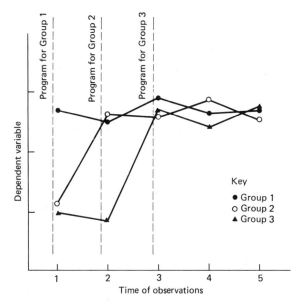

FIGURE 10.2 The most desirable outcome for a three-group design with delayed program participation for Groups 2 and 3. Group 1 received the program before the first observations; Group 2, between the first and second observations; and Group 3, between the second and third observations.

the idea of postponing implementation for the evaluator's sake. Whenever possible, it is far better to be involved in the planning stages than to ask for a change in plans.

A fourth reason why new programs may be evaluated is that there may be less anxiety over the possibility of failure, as compared to the program widely accepted in the organization. Less is at stake if the program does not look perfect, because fewer people have become committed to it.

A fifth reason to document the success of a new program concerns the favorable publicity generated among the general public and among organizations. Employees are likely to feel pride in being associated with an organization that has a reputation as an innovator. Referrals are more likely to be provided if human service personnel in other organizations have respect for an innovating agency.

When Resources Are Scarce

A second circumstance in which experimentation may be accepted is when resources are scarce. If the program cannot be offered to everyone who could possibly use it, some way must be found to decide who will get the program and who will not. The most desirable method—from the evaluator's point of view—is to use random selection to determine who can obtain the service. Riecken and Boruch (1974) report that the general public is remarkably willing to accept the idea of a lottery to determine who does and does not obtain a valuable service. In a real sense a lottery is more fair than a first-come, first-served policy; often those with "connections" are the ones who hear about the program first. Teenagers whose relatives are involved in city government will probably hear about a summer job program before those who must depend on newspapers or other sources for the announcement of application dates and eligibility criteria.

When resources are scarce, many service providers strive to give the program to those most in need. There is no question that such a strategy is in some ways just; however, it is also true that the ways of determining eligibility are not perfectly reliable. In fact, the way in which eligibility is determined is often quite unreliable, with different service providers coming to different conclusions. In cases where the most needy are to get the program, perhaps an agreement can be reached defining a category of uncertain eligibility. Program participants and controls could be selected randomly from this group, and an experiment performed utilizing just the people whose eligibility is uncertain (Crano and Brewer, 1973).

When There Is Controversy About Program Effectiveness

Evaluators who work with a program of uncertain worth enjoy some advantages and must adapt to some disadvantages. While this section stresses the advantages, we must also note the disadvantages.

If service providers disagree about a program, evaluation research will be viewed very critically; contending factions might each seek to recruit the evaluators to their side. The evaluators' behavior may be scruitinized for signs of favoritism. In such situations evaluators would do well to keep everyone informed of plans and to carry out plans in a careful, even-handed manner. Although such scrutiny may make program evaluation somewhat more stressful for the evaluator, the final products may actually be of higher quality—unless evaluators refuse to draw any conclusions from the research. More will be said about handling controversial conclusions in Chapters 12 and 13.

Controversy provides an advantage to evaluators, because controversy over programs can be directed to support an experiment. If some influential people in an organization do not believe in the program, they will not be moved by arguments that it is unjust to deprive a control group of a particular service. If there are others who strongly support the program, it is possible that there will be an institutional battle. In such a case the question of offering the program may be decided on political grounds. If, on the other hand, both sides could agree on what they would accept as evidence of the program's success, the setting for an experiment could well be excellent.

For example, various forms of welfare reform have both proponents and detractors. A number of experiments have been conducted to test whether income supplements would enhance or reduce the willingness of people to seek employment (Kershaw, 1972). Some welfare recipients were randomly assigned to participate in various forms of income maintenance programs or to remain in current programs. Liberal legislators may argue that the people in the control group were being treated unfairly, while conservative legislators might argue that the new program was a giveaway. If program evaluation can supply social science observations to both groups, evaluation will fill a useful role in society. Whether or not welfare is ever designed on the basis of the findings of this research, the level of debate will be raised—and the validity of arguments used will be increased—on the basis of good research (Abt, 1977).

There has been controversy over the question of whether nutritional supplements to malnourished children in tropical areas would have long-term effects on cognitive development (McKay et al., 1978). McKay and his colleagues randomly assigned malnourished children of low socioeconomic status of Cali, Columbia, to receive food supplements beginning at four different times before they reached school age. The four groups received the supplement for periods of forty-five, thirty-four, twenty-six, or ten months before starting school. The authors found that the sooner a nutritional supplement was begun, the more impact there was on cognitive development. However, for all groups there was a positive impact lasting at least one year after the supplements were no longer given. By use of an experiment, the cause of improvement was shown to be due to the nutrition, not to self-selection, regression to the mean, testing effects, or any other nonprogram effects. (This particular experiment was strengthened through the use of two additional untreated groups, one high and one low in socioeconomic status, that were not made up of randomly assigned children.)

When Change Is Desired

Program evaluation utilizing experimental methodology is useful when there is widespread dissatisfaction with current conditions but no consensus about what changes should be instituted. Income maintenance evaluations (Kershaw, 1972) are examples of experiments conducted in response to a desire for change in welfare policies accompanied by uncertainty about what to do. In the 1960s the desire to prevent, or at least to reduce, the rate of school failure of disadvantaged rural and urban children led to a series of experiments with Head Start, a preschool program aimed at teaching cognitive skills and providing medical care and nutritional assistance (Datta, 1976b). On a facility level Carey (1976) took advantage of dissatisfaction with a mandatory counseling requirement for couples seeking sterilization to conduct a randomized experiment in a general hospital. Experimentation as a conscious, rational approach to selecting among alternatives is the prime example of Campbell's concept of the "experimenting society" (1969), in which government and public alike agree to submit proposed changes in human services to experimentation, recognizing that although most innovations do not live up to expectations, the best way to choose among various possibilities is through careful program evaluation.

PRESERVING AN
EXPERIMENTAL DESIGN

Up to this point this chapter has emphasized (1) the advantages of experiments over other approaches as methods to show that a program caused a change in behavior; and (2) the situations that are likely to lead to the acceptance of random assignment to experimental and control groups. As unfortunate as it seems, evaluators cannot rest after planning and getting approval for an experimental design. Once begun, experiments have a way of breaking down without careful shepherding. There are some precautions that can be taken to maximize the integrity of the evaluation so that it will remain an interpretable experiment (Rezmovic, Cook, and Dobson, 1981).

Precautions Before Data
Collection Begins

One of the problems with evaluations is that participants drop out of various groups. If the experimental group is receiving a service, its members are likely to be more easily followed than the control people, who have nothing to gain by staying in contact with the evaluator. It is also possible that participants will drop out of the experimental group if the program makes rigorous demands on participants. Harris and Bruner (1971) sought to measure the impact of a contract weight reduction program involving a cash deposit that would be refunded at a rate of so many dollars ($1.00 or $.50) per pound lost in a given week. In the first experiment 58 percent of the program participants dropped out after random assignment. In the second experiment *all* participants dropped out after random assignment to the program. The evaluation was not without any utility; the dropout rate clearly showed that a program requiring a cash deposit was not acceptable to these overweight people! If the dropout rate is high and dropout is different from group to group, even the most well planned experiment will become uninterpretable.

Perhaps one of the most thorough attempts to minimize treatment-related dropout was carried out in the selection of participants for the New

Jersey Income Maintenance Study. Riecken and Boruch (1974) report that in order to minimize treatment-related dropout, the evaluators explained to possible participants all the levels of income supplement involved in the study and described the information that would be needed from them. Only those people who agreed to provide the information regardless of the group to which they were assigned were retained and randomly assigned to groups.

Few advantages are gained without some accompanying cost. Postponing randomization until some dropout has occurred introduces the possibility that the participants no longer represent the population for whom the program was designed. The people who dropped out because they would not agree to provide information regardless of the group they were in are likely to be different from the people who agreed to all the conditions. It is most likely that those who dropped out included some irresponsible or transient people. It is also possible that some of the most motivated obtained jobs during the initial negotiations and thus were no longer interested in the program. Income maintenance programs, if incorporated into the welfare system, would be provided to all who qualified through low incomes—not only to those who would agree to cooperate in an experiment on income maintenance. If a large proportion of possible participants refused to cooperate with the research, those who refused may have been quite different from those who agreed to cooperate. If so, then conclusions drawn from the experiment may not apply to more than a fraction of the population. What appears to be a successful program may only be successful with some. Sound experiments whose results cannot be applied to other locations or populations are said to lack external validity (Campbell and Stanley, 1963).

A way to counter this threat to generalization is to compare those who refuse to participate with those who do participate. When evaluating a welfare program, a considerable amount of information is available about those who do and do not cooperate. If such variables as age, income, or education do indeed differ between the groups, the usefulness of the evaluation is reduced. If, on the other hand, the groups do not differ on such variables and the proportion of dropouts is small, the conclusions drawn from the experiment can be trusted.

Precautions While the Experiment Is Occurring

Even after the experiment has begun, evaluators must remain close to the data-gathering procedure in order to be sure that agreed-upon procedures are being followed. Cook and Campbell (1979) describe additional threats to internal validity (not presented in Chapter 8) that can occur after

an experiment has been designed and begun; each of the five serves to reduce the interpretability of an experiment.

First, *diffusion or imitation of the program* can occur when the controls
learn about the program and, in effect, administer it to themselves. Straw
(1978) described a weight reduction program in general terms to all volunteers before random assignment. One member of the control group (randomly assigned to receive the program at a later time) used the brief verbal
description to design her own weight reduction program. By imitating the
program, she achieved a greater weight reduction than any of the people in
the experimental group.

Second, *attempts to compensate the control group* occur when staff or managers seek to give the members of the control group some special service to
make up for their not being in the experimental group receiving the program. Posavac (1974) was evaluating an information/counseling program
for postcoronary inpatients. Part way through the evaluation, he learned
that nurses were distributing a short book to control patients who were the
most insistent about getting more information. The nurses had difficulty
accepting the requirement that controls not be given the program textbook
until after the predischarge assessment of knowledge and attitudes. Successful compensation will result in a negative evaluation, because compensation will tend to make the experimental and control groups equivalent on
the outcome measures. A way to discourage such compensation is to point
out that compensating the controls can serve to reduce the likelihood of
finding support for the program and, consequently, reduce the probability
of the program being offered in the future. Thus, if the program is actually
effective, compensation of the controls could result in the loss of a
worthwhile service for people who need it.

Third, control groups sometimes feel a *rivalry with the experimental
group*. Rahe (1978) experienced this problem in an evaluation of an exercise program for Navy fliers. The program was designed to increase the
fitness of the fliers in an attempt to lower physiological stress reactions
when landing on an aircraft carrier. Because the groups were all aboard a
single ship, some of the controls heard about the program and were observed working out on the exercycles in order to "score" as well on the
physiological outcome measures as the pilots in the experimental group.

A threat whose effects are opposite to rivalry is *resentful demoralization*
of those not in the program group. It is possible that people in a control
group will learn that there is a group receiving what they may consider is a
valuable service. One can easily imagine an experimental job skills program
offered to some applicants for welfare. Those without the program may
feel that the others have an unfair advantage in obtaining work and, consequently, reduce their job-hunting efforts. If they did react this way, the demoralization alone could make it appear that the program was effective.

247 Analysis of Causes of Change

The first three threats serve to make the experimental and control groups similar. The fourth may lead to greater differences between groups. *Local history* is a threat that can have either effect. Local history refers to events that occur to members of one group in an experiment. This may be a threat when participants are tested in groups, even though randomly assigned individually to control or experimental conditions. The possibility exists that one member of the group may affect the others in a way that will either enhance or reduce group differences. One member of an elementary school class may act out during testing and affect the scores of the other children. If the class is part of the experimental group, group differences could be reduced. If the class belongs to the control group, the controls might appear even less accomplished due to this one student. Thus, local history could bias the evaluation to favor the control group or the experimental group. The way to avoid the effect of local history is to deliver the program and assess its effectiveness to many small groups (or even to individuals), not just to a small number of large groups.

There is no substitute for an evaluator keeping close track of the data-gathering process. Although close personal attention is time consuming, the delegation of duties to program staff or to people not really involved with the evaluation process may lead to situations that destroy the usefulness of the evaluation. Competent data collection requires commitment to the task. Data gathered by people hired just for data collection have been falsified even by well-trained individuals (Rezmovic, Cook, and Dobson, 1981). There is no substitute for careful supervision of data collectors.

METHODS OF ANALYZING EXPERIMENTS

T-Test

Because random assignment to groups removes the reasons for administering a pretest, the standard form of the *t*-test is the most appropriate statistical test of a simple two-group evaluation. The pretest was introduced only when random assignment was impossible and it was necessary to demonstrate that the control and experimental groups were indeed reasonably equivalent. Any standard elementary statistics text will present an example of the use of this analysis (for example, McCall, 1975).

Simple Analysis of Variance

If the evaluation employs three or more groups, such as would occur when a control group is contrasted with participants in two versions of a program, simple (one-way) analysis of variance is the best statistical test to use. Analysis of variance simultaneously compares the means of three or more groups to learn whether at least one of them is different from the others.

For example, a school system may want to learn whether a tutoring program helps poor readers. In addition, it may be of interest to learn if the value of the tutoring is increased when a short programmed study guide is provided along with the tutoring. If three groups are randomly formed and reading scores obtained at the end of a semester, both program groups would be expected to read better than the control group. Analysis of variance will show whether one or more of the groups produced a mean reliably above the control group.

Of course, evaluators want to know more than just that the group means differed. They want to know whether program group A was reliably better than group B, or whether the program groups were equally effective and were both better than the control group. To do these analyses requires statistical techniques usually not covered in introductory statistics courses. Planned comparisons using the Newman-Keuls or the Tukey procedures are discussed in Kirk (1968).

Complex Analysis of Variance

Sometimes the evaluator wants to determine if two approaches to a problem are each effective, and in addition, whether using both approaches simultaneously is even more effective. Landes (1973) studied the effects of two approaches to reduce the anxiety of children hospitalized for tonsilectomies. The important dependent measures were physiological and behavioral signs of anxiety. Two approaches to reduce anxiety were available. One focused on the children, and the second on the mother. Four random groups were formed. The control group was provided no service other than the normal efforts of the surgeon, pediatrician, and nurse to reduce the child's or the mother's anxiety. One program group of children watched a puppet show about tonsils and hospital stays. The mothers of a second program group attended a group session to explain procedures to them, on the hypothesis that well-informed, less tense mothers would have less anxious children. The third program group watched the puppet show, and their mothers attended the group session to learn about procedures.

The results of this experiment were examined using a complex analysis of variance. Instead of treating the experiment as a four-group design, it can be considered a two-by-two design, as illustrated in Figure 10.3. There is a distinct advantage to analyzing the results as a two-by-two design rather than using a simple analysis of variance. First, one can examine the effect of the puppet show and the effect of the mothers' group separately. In essence, the analysis combines the control group and program group B and compares the overall mean of those two groups to the overall mean of

	Did not attend mothers' group	Attended mothers' group
No puppet show	Control group	Program group B
Puppet show	Program group A	Program group C

FIGURE 10.3 A two-by-two factorial evaluation design best analyzed using complex analysis of variance.

program groups A and C. This comparison reveals whether the puppet show had an effect. Next, the means of the columns of the matrix in Figure 10.3 are found. If these means differ, the efforts with the mothers was effective.

Over and above these comparisons, complex analysis of variance permits one to examine the interaction of the two approaches to the reduction of anxiety. (*Interaction* refers to the joint effect of the two approaches to anxiety reduction.) The graphs in Figure 10.4 provide an illustration of several possible outcomes of a two-by-two factorial design. The graph on the upper left shows no effect; anxiety is the same whether the children see the puppet show or not, and the same level of anxiety is observed whether the mothers participate or not. In the upper right the graph illustrates a reduction for the puppet show but not for the mothers' group. In the lower left both approaches have an effect, and the group with both is the best off. In the lower right, however, there is an interaction between the approaches. In the graph the group with both services is especially calm. In fact, if the means followed this pattern, the children would be more calm than would have been predicted by knowing that both approaches were individually effective.

The reader may recall that the concept of interaction was utilized to isolate the effect of the junior year abroad study in Chapter 9. Readers for whom the idea of interaction is new would do well to compare the example in Figure 10.3 with that in Figure 9.8 in order to be sure the idea is thoroughly understood.

SUMMARY

Whenever program evaluations are designed to determine whether or not a human service program caused any change in the people served, an experimental research design should be considered. It should not, however, be forced on a program or facility that does not support the requirements of experimental research. When implemented, program evaluations based

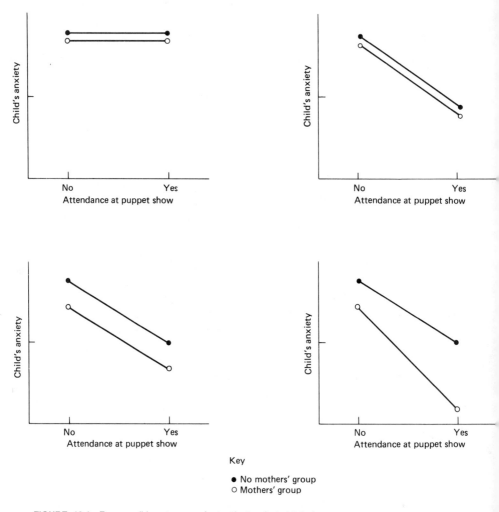

FIGURE 10.4   Four possible outcomes of a two-by-two factorial design. When the lines in the graph are not parallel, the possibility of a significant interaction exists.

on experimental research designs are easier to interpret and to analyze than are the less well controlled evaluations described in Chapter 9. Recall the comment that experimental designs are like aspirins; they reduce the number of headaches experienced by evaluators—reduce, but not eliminate. The most carefully designed evaluations will not be interpretable if they are not carried out as planned. Evaluators recognize that many human service professionals will not fully understand the advantages of the experimental approach and could in all innocence nullify the evaluator's plans. As with all forms of evaluation, someone will need to exercise close supervision over the way the data are collected and the way individuals are assigned to research groups.

STUDY QUESTIONS

1. Why was testing not a viable threat to internal validity in the evaluation of the program to reduce the anxiety of children before surgery?

2. If more program participants than members of the control group drop out of an experimental evaluation, what can be concluded from the evaluation? (Note: The answer "Nothing" is incorrect.)

3. List the advantages and disadvantages of experimental and quasi-experimental evaluation designs. Use parallel columns so that when you are finished with the list, you have a concise way to compare these two approaches.

4. Using language that can be understood by someone without training in statistics and research methods, explain the advantages of experimentation, including random assignment to groups. Imagine you are addressing an elementary school teacher, a nurse, a police officer, or a similar human service staff person. The adequacy of your answer depends on its technical correctness and its appropriateness to the intended audience.

5. Suppose that after an experiment is described (as in question 4 above), someone asks: "If the new program is worth experimenting on, and if the staff feels that the program is good, how can you justify not letting the controls reap the benefits of the program?" What would be an appropriate answer?

FURTHER READING

There are many good sources of material on experimental evaluations.

BORUCH, R. F., and CORDRAY, D. S. 1982. *An appraisal of educational program evaluations: Federal, state, and local agencies.* New York: Cambridge University Press.
GILBERT, J. P.; LIGHT, R. J.; and MOSTELLER, F. 1975. Assessing social innovations: An empirical base for policy. In *Evaluation and experiment,* ed. A. R. Lumsdaine and C. A. Bennett. New York: Academic Press.

The previously cited materials by Donald Campbell and colleagues are useful for this chapter as well.

CAMPBELL, D. T., and STANLEY, J.C. 1963. *Experimental and quasi-experimental designs for research.* Chicago: Rand-McNally.
COOK, T. D., and CAMPBELL, D. T. 1979. *Quasi-experimentation: Design and analysis issues in field settings.* Chicago: Rand-McNally.

CASE STUDY 10.1 Telephones and Raising Bail

The author of this case study took advantage of the introduction of a new program to conduct a true experiment in a criminal justice setting. Note that the evaluator utilized qualitative information obtained from interviews to aid in the interpretation of the quantitative measures. The complete report of this evaluation was cited in Chapter 8 as an example of the use of a nonexperimental design to investigate whether a rigorous evaluation would be useful. You may recall that the introduction of a telephone was associated with an increase in the proportion of detainees released on bond. However, that nonexperimental finding did not constitute proof that the telephone led to the increased rate of releases on bond. The experiment summarized in this case study followed up on the lead provided by the nonexperimental design.

TELEPHONES AND RAISING BAIL*

Kenneth J. Lenihan

Center for Policy Research

Bail is set for many defendants, who are often unable to raise even small amounts—sometimes only $50 or $100 cash, or bonds of $500 to $1,000—and are held in detention until final disposition of their case, which might not come until sixty to ninety days later. Usually, they cannot raise bail because they lack financial resources, but some observers have noted other reasons—in particular, that defendants in custody are cut off from the outside world, so that it is difficult for them to mobilize friends and relatives to raise money on their behalf (Foote, 1955; Suffet, 1965).

With the cooperation of the New York City Department of Corrections, we installed a telephone in The Tombs, a detention prison in lower Manhattan. The telephone was manned by a staff member of The Vera Institute, and Vera paid for its installation and service out of federal funds granted to help solve problems of criminal justice.

Defendants requesting the use of the phone were classified according to the length of time they had already spent in detention and the amount of bail that had been set. Only defendants with bail set at $2,000 or less who had been detained ten days or less were admitted to the experiment. Defendants who qualified were then classified into one of eight categories, according to the amount of bail and the length of time they had been detained so far. Within each classification, defendants were then randomly assigned to either the treatment or control group.

The treatment group was given the opportunity to call the next day; the control group was not allowed to make calls until seven days later. If the telephones were instrumental in raising bail money, it would be reflected in the rates of release and detainment of the two groups. And the treatment group did indeed benefit: 25.4 percent were released on bail within seven days, while only 13.1 percent of the control group were released during the same period ($z = 1.712$; $p < .05$).

This finding was reinforced by what happened to the control group. When, after seven days, the controls were finally given the opportunity to use the phone, their

*Condensed with permission from *Evaluation Quarterly* 1 (1977): 569–86. Copyright 1977, Sage Publications, Inc.

rate of release rose sharply to 24 percent—roughly equivalent to the 25 percent release rate of the treatment group during its first seven days.

After the fourteenth day, three more defendants in the treatment group were released on bail, but no more in the control group.

Although the control group began to close the gap after they started using the phone, they never quite caught up with the treatment group: 33 percent of the treatment group obtained pretrial release on bail; compared with only 28 percent of the control group.

The telephone was installed on the assumption that if a defendant could reach family or friends, he had a better chance to raise bail. The question remained, were defendants really cut off from the outside? To find out, we interviewed the fifty-nine defendants in the treatment group to find out how much contact they had with friends and family after they had been taken into custody. Their responses suggest why the telephone call turned out to be so important.

When an accused man is taken into custody, his first opportunity to reach someone may be by telephone while he is being booked at the police station. Only six of the fifty-nine defendants reported having used the telephone at the station house, and one of these stated that his call did not go through. Moreover, at the station house the accused person does not yet know if the charge will be sustained at arraignment court, if bail will be set and, if so, for how much. So the station house call is not likely to deal with bail, since the facts are unknown, and first offenders may not even be aware that bail is a potential problem.

The next opportunity for contact with outsiders is at arraignment, and only four out of fifty-nine defendants reported that a friend or family member was present in court when they were arraigned.

After arraignment, if bail is not posted immediately, defendants are confined to a detention prison. Here there are three ways in which they may communicate with people on the outside: they may send a letter; they may send a message through a corrections officer; or they may be visited.

Nineteen of fifty-nine defendants reported having written a letter, the most common way of trying to contact someone outside. (Four other defendants said they did not know how to write, six that they were unable to get writing materials.) Only four defendants reported having had a visitor—a number that is understandably low, since a visit to the jail requires prior communication.

Finally, every defendant has the legal right to send a message through a corrections officer. A statement of this right is usually mumbled in a perfunctory manner as the defendant passes through arraignment—whether it is heard or understood is doubtful in many cases. Of the fifty-nine defendants, sixteen tried to send a message through the corrections officer. An officer usually has more requests than he can handle, so some messages simply are not sent. Many others do not get through. Unfortunately, the defendant is never told whether the message was received or what the reply was, if any.

To sum up, almost half of this sample (44 percent) had had no contact at all with the outside, even though they had been in custody for at least four days. One could assume—and many corrections officers did—that this relative failure to make contact with people outside reflected a lack of motivation—yet *every one* of the fifty-nine defendants in the experimental group filled out a request to use the telephone.

Why did the telephone succeed where other forms of contact—notably letters and messages through corrections officers—failed? Perhaps because the telephone more closely approximates direct contact. A message or letter goes in only one direction, but the telephone permits a dialogue, persuasion, a discussion of alternatives—especially about where money might be obtained.

CASE STUDY 10.2 A Preventive Health Program

The authors of this evaluation took advantage of the high demand for a desirable service to conduct a randomized experimental evaluation. As with other case studies, this is a condensed report. It omits references to another control group and a comparison group. As so simplified, the design does not control for a threat to the validity of generalizations drawn from the results of this evaluation. What is that threat, and what can be added to the design that would control for it? Note the authors' comments on the use of randomly selected groups and their decision not to test their hypotheses at the conventional .05 level.

EVALUATION OF A POSITIVE HEALTH CARE PROGRAM*

Jack McKillip and Linda Kamens

Department of Psychology
Southern Illinois University at Carbondale

In this report, we describe one aspect of a comprehensive positive health care program developed by the Student Health Services of Southern Illinois University at Carbondale and directed toward changing students' lifestyles. The project was based on the work of and was organized in consultation with Dr. John C. McCamy (McCamy and Presley, 1975). The importance of lifestyle for health is underscored by the statistics on degenerative diseases; that is, the three top killers of adult Americans are heart attacks, strokes, and cancer. All of these diseases are strongly related to lifestyle, are predictable, and (at least theoretically) are preventable.

The primary assumption underlying the lifestyling program is that health is not a gift or an accident but rather a creative act. The program seeks to lessen susceptibility factors that increase the likelihood of disease and to strengthen resistance factors that lower the possibility of disease by influencing lifestyle in the areas of diet, exercise, stress reduction, and ecological awareness.

Program Description

The lifestyling program consisted of a cultivation session, a weekend workshop, and weekly support/follow-up groups. The cultivation session consisted of a short presentation on the history of the program, a description of the workshop and support/follow-up groups, and an explanation of the time commitment and the purpose of the program's structure. The workshop was a three-day live-in experience involving both cognitive and experiential presentations. The former included presentations on: (1) differences between traditional and preventive models of health; (2) differences between average and normal conceptions of health; (3) the concept of risk factors; and (4) the four areas of health: nutrition, stress, exercise, and environment. The experiential aspects of the program included: (1) techniques to increase awareness of environment in eating and to reduce stress; (2) aerobic and stretching exercises; and (3) a detailed individual disease risk factor analysis.

*Condensed with permission from R. V. Robertson, ed., *Health Care Research in Ilinois*, vol. 2, pp. 352–57. (Springfield, Ill.: Southern Illinois School of Medicine, 1977).

At the end of the workshop, participants set goals for themselves and arranged to meet with their support groups. All participants were given Dr. McCamy's book *Human Life Styling,* a set of log sheets to be filled out daily for the duration of the program, and a feedback questionnaire concerning their reaction to the workshop. Support groups of eight to ten participants met with two staff members weekly for the reinforcement of progress and the sharing of experiences and group problem solving.

Evaluation Design

Since the lifestyling program was a treatment in short supply—there were over two hundred eligible applicants for fifty workshop openings—volunteers were randomly assigned either to the full program group described above or to a no-treatment control group. Prior to randomization, volunteers were grouped on age, sex, and race. Fifty volunteers were assigned to the full program, and sixty-one to the control group. The randomization is, of course, the crucial component of the design, guaranteeing that the groups did not differ systematically prior to the lifestyling program.

Outcome measures.   The evaluation included indicators of both process and impact, but only the latter will be discussed in this paper. Outcome measures were obtained twice, before the program began (prior to randomization) and six months later. These measures included: (1) physiological indicators; (2) attitudinal scales; (3) behavioral scales; and (4) institutional records, for example, incidence of use of the student health service. This report will be concerned exclusively with the self-reported behavior scales.

Procedure.   The actual evaluation was conducted by a team (the authors) who were independent of the Student Health Service staff. The measurement activities were presented as a study of the Student Health Service and not associated with the lifestyle program. All correspondence was handled out of the Department of Psychology, and every attempt was made to keep the lifestyling project and the evaluation separate.

Analysis.   The method of analysis was analysis of covariance[1] of posttest scores with group and sex of respondent as independent variables and age and pretest score as covariates. The analysis compares post-program scores after statistically adjusting for differences due to age and preprogram status. In addition, because of conservative biases built into the full-program group versus the control group comparison, and because the authors generally feel that when testing a new program Type II errors are a greater problem than Type I errors, the alpha level was set at .20.

---

[1]Analysis of covariance is useful when program participants are randomly assigned to groups, and something about the individuals is known to correlate with the outcome measure. For example, in this case study, preprogram attitudes correlated with post-program attitudes; that is, those students relatively more predisposed to following good nutritional habits tended to still be relatively more inclined after the program, even though as a group program participants improved. Analysis of covariance enables the evaluator to perform a more powerful statistical test than is otherwise available. The analysis is complex and cannot be further discussed in this text.

Results

The first concern for analysis was the comparability of groups at the time of posttest. Attrition, that is, failure to complete posttest measurements, was 28 percent for full-program participants and 29 percent for control-group members. Comparisons of demographic characteristics revealed no significant differences between those who did and did not complete the posttest measurements for either group. In addition, analysis of characteristics of the random sample showed the same distribution on age and sex as the experimental groups.

Figure 10.5 presents the pre- and posttest means for the experimental groups and the outcome measures for the random sample for various behavioral measures. Each will be discussed in turn.

The diet scale indicated frequency of eating each of fourteen nonnutritious foods (for example, sweet between-meal snacks) during an average week. Analysis revealed a significant difference between full program and control group on this measure in the direction of a positive program impact ($p < .001$). In addition, a comparison was made between members of the experimental groups (program volunteers) and the random sample.

The exercise scale indicates frequency of involvement in twelve physical activities, for example, jogging, swimming. Although the trend in Figure 10.5 is in the direction of a positive program effect, the differences are not significant.

The stress scale indicates the frequency of engaging in thirteen stress-related activities (for example, making lists of things to do). Analysis revealed significantly less stress for the program group compared to the control group ($p < .13$).

The environmental awareness scale indicates the frequency of involvement in twelve positive environment-improving activities (for example, pick up litter around

FIGURE 10.5 Behavioral outcome measures.

Measure	Range	Test	Full program (N = 36)	Control group (N = 45)
Diet[a]	0–14	Pre	4.4	4.5
		Post	3.4	4.9
Exercise[b]	0–12	Pre	1.7	1.7
		Post	2.0	1.8
Stress[a]	13–65	Pre	32.7	33.8
		Post	34.7	37.3
Environmental awareness[b]	0–12	Pre	3.6	3.7
		Post	4.6	4.2
Alcohol use[a]	1–6	Pre	3.4	3.6
		Post	3.1	3.5
Other drug use[a]	0–4	Pre	.5	.5
		Post	.5	.9
Symptoms[a]	0–71	Pre	12.8	14.5
		Post	6.4	13.2

[a] *The lower the mean, the healthier the behavior.*

[b] *The higher the mean, the healthier the behavior.*

the house, join an environmental group). Although the trend was in the direction of a positive program effect, this difference was not statistically significant.

Two drug-use questions were asked, one indicating the frequency of use of alcohol and the other the use of four other drugs: uppers, downers, hallucinogens, and cocaine. Both alcohol use ($p < .06$) and other drug use ($p < .09$) was lower for the full program than for the control group. The last analysis revealed significantly fewer symptoms for the full program as compared to the control group ($p < .001$).

Conclusions

It is our opinion that the data presented are persuasive evidence of the effectiveness of a positive health care program. While qualifications are in order due to the liberated uses of significance levels, the data suggest that a more detailed examination of the lifestyling model for the design of positive health programs would be worthwhile.

REFERENCE

McCamy, J. C., and Presley, J. 1975. *Human life styling: Keeping whole in the 20th century.* New York: Harper & Row.

11

Analysis of Costs
and Outcomes

The outcomes of human service programs can be fully evaluated only when their costs are considered. Most service providers do not have training in cost accounting and thus often begin work remarkably naive about costs. However, Demone and Harshbarger (1973) state that recommendations for programs whose costs are not estimated are simply statements of philosophy that will not be taken very seriously. Similarly, conclusions about the outcome of a program are not really complete unless the evaluator has discussed the costs of obtaining the outcome. Even an evaluation design that acounts for all threats to internal validity and finds a highly significant amount of improvement may receive a negative evaluation if the costs of obtaining the outcome are prohibitive, or if the outcome could be achieved less expensively using a different program. Being able to relate evaluation activities to cost accounting is becoming a more important aspect of the role of the evaluator (Becker, Harrell, and Kirkhart, 1982).

Cost analysis is not a new idea to commercial people and industrial analysts. The local hardware store manager counts receipts every evening and periodically records costs. By converting transactions into dollars, business people can compare input costs (salaries, inventory, and building costs) with cash receipts. A comparison of these two values tells managers whether they are going into debt or making money. Bookkeeping, of course, is not this simple in practice; however, the principle is straightforward and the unit of analysis (a dollar) is widely accepted. In human service settings the principles are less clear, and the benefits are usually hard to convert into dollars.

Cost analyses are done both after a program has been evaluated and in the planning stage. The topic is presented at this point in order to illustrate how outcomes are related to program costs. When cost analyses are used in planning, costs are estimated and probable levels of outcome are projected on the basis of previous evaluations of similar programs. Conducting cost analyses in the planning stage of program development helps planners select the programs that will provide the best return on investments.

COST ANALYSES

The first step in a cost analysis, whether the program is already functioning or planned, is to divide program costs into categories. It is impossible to estimate the costs of a program as a whole without this breakdown. Popham (1975) presents several ways of conceptualizing costs. His categories include variable versus fixed, incremental versus sunk, recurring versus nonrecurring, and hidden versus obvious.

Variable versus Fixed Costs

All human service facilities must be housed somewhere. If the service requires special equipment, as do medical and dental care and vocational training, the facility cannot easily be used for any other purposes. Also, it is necessary in such services to have a complete set of equipment before treating the first patient or training the first student. Thus, the costs of the facilities and equipment are *fixed costs*. Because of the fixed costs of getting started, there probably is some optimal number of people to serve in order to minimize the fixed costs per person served.

Variable costs are those that will change with the size of the program. The supplies used by the individuals served clearly vary with the size of the program. The costs of maintenance, postage, custodial services, and secretarial assistance are examples of costs that will grow as the program grows to its optimal size.

Incremental versus Sunk Costs

Incremental costs are those that occur as the program continues; *sunk costs* are those that have already been expended. Thus, the distinction is useful only for decisions about continuing or terminating a program; there are no sunk costs for a planned program.

In 1978 the General Accounting Office suggested that it might make financial sense for the Postal Service to abandon a billion-dollar automated system for sorting packages (*Chicago Tribune,* June 14, 1978). It may seem foolish to abandon a billion-dollar system after two years. However, the decision to continue or abandon it should be made on the basis of the cost of running the system as compared to alternative systems. The money already invested (a sunk cost) is irrelevant to the new decision. Writing off the expensive system may be a big waste; however, it is cheaper than continuing to lose even more money. The GAO concluded that the incremental costs of the automated package system exceeded the benefits received; the sunk costs were not considered. Such a decision reflects the popular wisdom that there comes a point at which people seek to "cut their losses" because these losses may simply grow in the future.

Recurring versus Nonrecurring Costs

Recurring costs, as the name suggests, are those that will be due at regular intervals, such as salaries, rents, and utilities. The cost of purchasing equipment is a nonrecurring cost if the equipment is expected to last a number of years before wearing out.

Hidden versus Obvious Costs

In estimating the costs of a new building, no one will forget to include the costs of construction; less obvious costs include furniture, custodial service, lighting, heating, and maintenance. In estimating the costs of expanding staff, salaries will certainly be considered; somewhat hidden but just as real are fringe benefits and other costs, such as the employer's insurance for injured employees or for the careless behavior of employees toward others.

An Example

Figure 11.1 gives the budget of a small Equal Opportunity Program for minority college students. The proposal writers assumed that a small office could be found with furniture in an existing building. The writers did not include maintenance, custodial services, or insurance costs, because these would be the same regardless of what program the university decided to adopt and house in that space. Thus, the budget is for the cost of this program operating in the space available. Note that some costs are recurring (salaries and phone), and others are nonrecurring (typewriter). To make a decision on this proposal, the college administrators must compare this budget with a similar budget from an alternative program, in light of the college's values, goals, and expected benefit from the program.

Direct versus Indirect Costs

Although the terms above—adapted from Popham (1975)—are very helpful for conceptualizing the cost involved in programs, another set of terms is also frequently employed. The distinction between direct and indi-

Director (half-time)	$12,700*
Tutors (graduate student teaching assistants) 3 @ $4,000	12,000
Secretary (half-time)	6,400*
Work-study tutors 3 @ $1,275 (University contribution, 20%; state contribution, 80%)	3,825
	$34,925
Supplies	$ 1,500
Typewriter	1,100
File cabinets	450
Copying	800
Phone	800
	$ 4,650
*Fringe benefits @ 15%	$ 2,865
	$42,440[a]

[a]All costs are in 1984 dollars.

FIGURE 11.1   Proposed first-year budget for an Equal Opportunity Program serving 25 college students.

rect costs is important in understanding the costs of human services (Carter and Newman, 1976). *Direct costs* are those that are incurred in providing services for specific clients. *Indirect costs* are those that cannot be associated with specific clients. For example, the time a social worker spends helping a family obtain assistance from city agencies is a factor in direct costs. The wages (including all fringe benefits) make up the direct cost of the service. The salary of the secretary in the social welfare office who makes the social workers' appointments cannot be related to specific clients. Thus, the cost of secretarial assistance, as crucial as it is in maintaining a service, is not a direct cost but an indirect cost. The facility administrator's salary, telephone bills, amount paid for custodial service, and so forth are all indirect costs. In providing a service program, both direct and indirect costs (also called *overhead*) are incurred, and both must be considered. These costs must then be related to the amount of service given.

The Necessity of Finding Costs

At times agencies supported by public funds have ignored the task of calculating costs per unit of service. Mitlying (1975–76) participated in a cost analysis of a publicly funded alcoholism treatment facility. The agency discovered that the cost (including direct and indirect costs) for each hour of service was $60. (Taking inflation into account, this figure is equivalent to $130 in 1984 dollars.) This figure, which was more than anyone in the agency had expected, was unacceptably high. Regardless of a facility's source of funding, costs should be found and should be divided into direct and indirect costs.

The exact way specific costs are labeled is not standard (Carter and Newman, 1976); however, the distinction is necessary to permit rational decisions about the amount of charges that should be allotted to given clients.

Although the college students in the minority program (see Figure 11.1) will not be billed over and above their tuition, the budget items can be divided into direct and indirect costs. Direct costs include all the tutors' time and probably part of the director's time, because he or she will certainly also be directly involved with the students. Part of the director's time, however, will be spent for indirect services, such as handling correspondence, organizing and supervising the tutors, and finding space for the tutors. Secretarial and office expenses will be indirect costs.

At this point you should have begun to appreciate the basic fact that costs must be considered in planning a program. The discussion should not suggest that estimating costs is easy. Many estimates have been grossly in error. Congress passed a bill to support kidney dialysis for people suffering kidney failure and unable to obtain a kidney transplant (Culliton, 1978). When the bill was approved in 1973, the costs were estimated to be in the low millions. In 1978 the cost was $1 billion, which was half the entire budget for the National Institute of Health. By 1983 the Federal government was paying $1.8 billion per year for dialysis (Wallis, 1983). The failure to provide an accurate estimate of costs led to an unexpectedly large cost to the taxpayer and made it impossible to implement other programs also dealing with pressing health problems.

Further, more detailed presentations of cost analysis can be found in Hagedorn et al. (1976) and Carter and Newman (1976). Although the work by Hagedorn and his colleagues is directed to community mental health center evaluators, the methods presented apply to all human service settings. In addition, this work includes estimates of the time required to carry out the analyses described. Evaluators with limited training in accounting procedures can benefit from this material.

COMPARING OUTCOMES
TO COSTS

Once costs are calculated or estimated, the next step in a cost-benefit analysis is to develop an approach to estimating the benefits of a program. Benefits occur when goals are achieved. Surgeons save lives when they remove diseased appendixes. Because their patients lead normally productive lives afterward, there are considerable benefits to this and many other surgical procedures. Another example of a cost-effective program is the federal attempt to reduce the number of government forms. The commission set up to do this is reported to have saved 350 times as much money as the cost of the commission (Abelson, 1977). A number of cost-benefit analyses have shown the worth of education after high school. Sussna and Heinemann (1972) concluded that the benefits of two-year training in health services were such that the increased earnings were equivalent to putting the cost of education into a bank and obtaining 34 percent interest per year for nursing students and 21 percent interest for laboratory technician students. Clearly, education was a better investment for these students; no savings account can rival such rates of return.

The Essence of Cost-Benefit Analysis

The essential characteristics of cost-benefit analyses illustrated are in a study conducted by Schnelle and colleagues (1978). They sought to evaluate the effectiveness of a helicopter patrol in reducing burglary in a high-crime area. Increasing the number of patrol cars seems to do little to reduce crime (Kelling et al., 1976; Schnelle et al., 1977). However, there was some speculation that a helicopter patrol with its inherently better surveillance ability might reduce burglary. In the city in which the project was done, most burglaries occur during daylight hours and are perpetrated by local youths. Because helicopters can repeatedly observe large areas (in daylight hours), the patrol was expected to frighten off potential burglars.

Schnelle and coworkers used a strategy developed in the field of behavior modification to test the effectiveness of the helicopter. The experiment was divided into five parts. First, a base-line rate of burglaries in the target area was obtained during twenty-one days. Second, the helicopter was introduced for twelve days. The pilot was shown the area and asked to fly low enough to be able to observe suspicious activity. Third, for sixteen days the helicopter did not patrol. Fourth, the helicopter was used again for twelve days. Last, there was no helicopter patrol for eighteen days. Regular car patrol continued during all phases of the experiment.

The burglary rate during the 9 A.M. to 5 P.M. shift was the outcome measure of interest. The experiment was a success in the sense that an average of 1.02 burglaries per day were committed during the periods of regular car patrols (base line) in contrast to an average of only .33 burglaries per day when the helicopter patrol was on duty. However, these data alone did not form a complete evaluation, because the helicopter patrol added to the police department's costs.

Because the helicopter pilot and hanger were already part of the police department, these costs were not considered. However, the costs of additional fuel and maintenance were calculated. These costs were compared to the benefits of lowered amount of goods stolen. Figure 11.2 summarizes the calculation of the benefit-to-cost ratio. The cost of using the helicopter was easy to calculate. The cost of the burglaries was estimated from insurance company material. The fact that the benefit-to-cost ratio was 2.6 indicates that the program was a success. The helicopter patrol did lower crime in an efficient manner.

	Total	Per day
Cost of the program (24 days)	$ 3,032	$126
Cost of the burglaries during no-helicopter patrol periods (55 days)	$27,171	$494
Cost of burglaries during helicopter patrol periods (24 days)	$ 3,853	$161
Benefits (for 24 day program)	$ 8,004	$333
Benefit/cost ratio	--------	$333/$126 = 2.6

* The burglary cost figures were not supplied by Schnelle et al. (1978); however, these costs could be approximated from their report.

FIGURE 11.2   The calculation of the benefit-to-cost ratio of the helicopter patrol.*

Several costs and benefits were not considered. Citizens' feelings of security may have increased (a benefit), but feelings of decreased privacy and irritation at the increased noise may also have occurred (costs). Opportunity costs were not considered because the pilot continued traffic surveillance as before. The benefit of lowered court costs, which occurred because it was necessary to try fewer burglars, was ignored. Also ignored was the fact that fewer burglaries permitted police officers to devote more time to other crime-preventive and investigative work (an additional benefit). Ignoring these benefits and the psychic costs of loss of privacy and of increased noise illustrates an important principle for applied social scientists. Evaluators seek to address the questions directed to them in an efficient manner; once the essential question can be answered, they collect no more data. For Schnelle and his colleagues, the essential question could be answered using costs and benefits that were fairly easy to estimate. Therefore, the evaluators did not concern themselves with the very difficult task of pricing additional benefits. If they had, the benefit-to-cost ratio would have simply increased above 2.6. If the ratio had been less, say 1.1, then the additional benefits of reducing court use and freeing police time might have been priced. Because it was not necessary, it was not done. A theoretical social scientist may want to estimate the "real" benefit-to-cost ratio. An applied social scientist requires only enough information on which to base a practical decision.

Although Schnelle chose to use costs and benefits that were fairly easy to convert into dollars, many cost-benefit studies have found it necessary to quantify costs and benefits that are hard to price. The Army Corps of Engineers has routinely used the recreational value of water projects to help justify construction plans. The dollar benefits of human services are even harder to estimate. If a service prolongs the working life of an employee, some benefits can be calculated. If a job-training program permits some to leave welfare rolls, certain savings can be quantified. But what is the dollar value of better mental health? Of reduced anxiety among cancer patients? Of a 5 percent gain on a standardized reading achievement test for sixth graders? Of increased levels of art and music appreciation? Clearly, these outcomes are worthwhile. But how much they are worth is subject to considerable disagreement.

Military planning provides an even more striking example of the limitations of cost-benefit analysis. How are the "benefits" of a bomb to be calculated? Clearly, the bomb destroys. Benefits, if there are any, accrue to a nation if a war is won. However, the net outcome of a war is negative, not positive, even for the victor. Instead of calculating cost-benefit ratios, one can ask how *effective* the bomb is in fulfilling its purpose. In oversimplified terms, the bigger the hole, the more effective the bomb. Thus, the concept of *cost effectiveness* was developed to use in situations in which the dollar values of benefits are very difficult to quantify.

The Essence
of Cost-Effectiveness Analysis

A bomb could be rated in terms of the size of the hole it makes (expressed in cubic yards) divided by the dollar cost of the bomb. There is no way of deciding if the yard^3/$ figure is good or bad until it is compared to the effectiveness-to-cost ratio of a second bomb. By comparing the two ratios, military planners can choose the bomb providing the bigger bang per buck. This same approach can be utilized in human service agencies whenever improvement can be quantified. If two or more programs effect an improvement on the same variable, the amount of improvement per dollar can be found for each program and a cost-effectiveness evaluation can be made.

Cost-effectiveness analyses are also important in measuring the productivity of businesses. For example, a plant in Ohio that produces titanium routinely calculates three indexes based on effectiveness divided by cost measures. First, pounds of titanium produced divided by number of employees is calculated; second, pounds of titanium are divided by the total assets of the plant; and third, since energy use is so high in the production of titanium, pounds of titanium are divided by the BTU's used in production (Day, 1981). The second of these three indexes is the traditional measure of cost effectiveness; however, the other two indexes help the managers find the aspect of the plant's operation that is responsible for good or poor performance. This example illustrates that evaluators can adapt cost analyses to the needs of the particular organization in which they are working. The measures of outcome and costs will differ from organization to organization.

When Outcome Cannot Be Quantified

The size of a bomb crater can be measured directly. Quantification of improved mental health is hard, but measuring improvements in perceived environmental quality is harder. Measuring increased art appreciation may be impossible. In these instances another approach can be used. Methods that incorporate the subjective value of the decision maker, funders, and the consumers of a program are called *cost-utility analyses* (Levin, 1975). In this case the subjective values and the costs of two or more programs are compared, and the one offering the most apparent (subjective) utility per dollar is chosen. The proposed Equal Opportunity Program (Figure 11.1) would be compared to other proposals in terms of subjective utility, not in terms of quantified effectiveness or benefits. The MAUT procedure described in Chapter 5 is an example of a subjective utility analysis.

SOME DETAILS OF COST ANALYSIS

There are a number of issues to examine when conducting an analysis of costs, which can affect the conclusions of cost-benefit and cost-effectiveness analyses. Although some of these points are details subordinate to the major ideas presented above, these issues are extremely important, both when preparing cost analyses and when evaluating them. We present these points as "issues of concern" because there are no widely accepted formulas for a cost analysis in the human services.

Units of Analysis

The units of the cost analysis should be compatible with the goals of the program. Binner (1977) illustrated how use of two different units can make quite a difference in a cost analysis of inpatient psychiatric treatment. What is the most obvious approach? If there are an average of one hundred patients in a facility and the cost for the year is $912,500, then the cost per patient per day would be $25. Is cost per patient-day a reasonable unit? The way to answer that question is to reflect on the reasons for institutionalizing a person. The goal is to aid patients to function in society, not simply to house them. A better unit than cost per patient-day would be cost per healthy, discharged patient. (For the moment, assume that each patient discharged is able to adjust to society and to earn a living.) The use of cost per patient-day actually encourages a departure from the true goals of institutionalization. Whatever can be done to lower the cost per patient-day will be encouraged, using this unit of analysis. The term *warehouse for people* was coined to describe the practice of developing the cheapest means of keeping people alive. On the other hand, the unit cost per patient discharged alive encourages a return to the real reason for institutionalization.

Note how the unit chosen affects the conclusion drawn from the cost-effectiveness analysis in the following example. Binner cites a state hospital that could house and feed a patient in 1901 for $2.38 per day (corrected to 1974 dollars). The cost per discharged patient in 1901 was $10,309 (1974 dollars). Comparing this hospital to 1974 averages, we find evidence for a 1300 percent increase as well as evidence for a 50 percent decrease in costs since 1901. Can both figures be true? Yes. In 1974 the average cost per patient-day was $30.86 (the 1300 percent increase), and the average cost per alive discharged patient was $5,513 (the 50 percent decrease). Should we be heartened by the decrease or alarmed at the increase? If the goals of the treatment focus on restoring patients to the community, then we should be heartened by the decrease. A comparison of these figures reflects the fact that restoring the ability to live in society requires therapy, community contacts, and medical treatment, among other things. Providing these services raises cost per day but lowers cost per discharged patient; patients are now more likely to return to the community than they were in 1901.

In recent years some nursing homes for disabled elderly people have been the subject of intense criticism for inadequate treatment—poor food, little medical care, few recreational opportunities, limited privacy. Such conditions would be encouraged by the cost per patient-day approach. Although it would not be easy to implement, relating a cost analysis of such facilities to measures of the patients' level of functioning could encourage the facility to help the patients stay healthy and alert (see Kane and Kane, 1978).

There is another complication related to the units of analysis used. At times the meaning of improvement on the variable of interest may change, depending on what level of the variable is involved. For example, it is not necessarily true that an improvement in work skills that leads to an increase in income from $0 to $3,000 is equivalent to an increase from $2,000 to $5,000. The amount of change of motivation and upgrading of skills related to these numerically equal benefits are probably markedly unequal: Changing a person from being unable to hold a job to being able to hold one is probably harder than simply improving a person's skills.

Alternative Uses of Investments

A mistake often made by people informally considering costs is to ignore the component of costs called *opportunity costs*. The most expensive aspect of college education is not the tuition, even at the most exclusive private schools. The cost of tuition is less than the income students could have earned had they been employed rather than attending college. This lost opportunity is a cost of college and should be considered by potential students. Ignoring the cultural, intellectual, and social growth available to college students, people evaluating a college education on the basis of cost alone will ask whether the salaries available to college graduates sufficiently exceed those of high school graduates to allow the college student to make up for this initial deficit of four years' wages. Economists interested in education report that college education in simple dollar terms is more cost effective than simply going to work after high school, although the advantage has eroded in recent years (Freeman and Hollomon, 1975). Further, if people value the conceptual, intellectual, and cultural values of college, these hard-to-quantify benefits add to the advantage of a college education.

A person's time is part of the cost of all human services. However, the time an individual spends waiting for a human service is often not considered a cost of the service, although it should be. Medical care that is ostensibly free is not free if waits of three or more hours are required to obtain it. If people in need of medical care do not have any employment, perhaps the oversight is permissible. However, even then, time spent waiting cannot be devoted to rearing children, preparing meals, or looking for work.

Future Costs and Benefits

A sophisticated cost analysis will include benefits occurring at times in the future. Successful rehabilitation or therapy will enable a person to live with less need of special services in future years. Improvements in work skills, psychological adjustment, and physical health may well have benefits for the children of people served or cared for. The worth of these long-term benefits is, not surprisingly, hard to estimate. Viewing the human services recipient as a member of a family system and a community system is a way to become sensitive to possible secondary benefits of human services. What are some of these secondary benefits? Drug rehabilitation should lead to less crime, because addicts frequently support their habit through theft. If crime is reduced, commercial activity may be encouraged since people might now be more willing to venture into the central business district. Also, the lower the crime rate, the lower the amount the community needs to spend on detection, prosecution, and punishment of criminals.

The noneconomist faces a problem in comparing programs requiring funds and providing benefits at different times in the lives of the program. This is true because the money needed and the benefits available in the future are worth less than the same amount of money and benefits available now. This principle makes perfectly good sense when you ask yourself whether you would rather have $100 now or in twelve months. Ignoring for the moment our normal preference for instant gratification, it makes economic sense to have the money now, because if it is put into a savings account, it will be worth $106 in twelve months. On the basis of this observation, some have criticized state lotteries that spread out $1 million grand prizes over twenty years. The state has the use of some of the money during those years, not the prize winner, so in a real sense, the prize is not worth as much as the promotions promise. The present value of the twentieth $50,000 payment of the million-dollar grand prize is only $10,730, because that sum invested in a readily available 8 percent savings account will yield $50,000 after twenty years. There are some tax advantages in spreading out the awards; however, the basic point remains true.

This text cannot go into the methods used to calculate the current worth of a benefit projected to occur in twenty years. The point to remember is that the cost of programs should include what could be obtained by an alternate use of resources. For example, is it worth spending $100 now in order to receive a benefit of $200 ten years from now? The answer depends entirely on the assumed rate of return for an alternative use of the $100. The amount one could obtain from this other use is the *opportunity cost*. If the rate of return for the latter were 3 percent, the answer to the question above would be yes, because $100 invested at 3 percent will be worth only $131 in ten years. The opportunity cost is less than the benefit. If the rate of return were 8 percent or more, the answer would be no, because $100 invested for ten years at 8 percent will equal $216. It would be better to put the money into an 8 percent savings account than to seek the $200 future benefit.

The interest rate assumed should be realistic. Critics of the cost-benefit analyses provided by the proponents of large-scale water resource projects have asserted that the rates of interest selected are unrealistically low (for example, Hanke and Walker, 1974). If so, the cost of the project would appear lower and the benefit-to-cost ratio would appear higher than they really are. For example, the opportunity cost of a $200 benefit that is ten years away would be $134 if an interest rate of 3 percent were chosen, but it would be $179 if a more realistic figure, 6 percent, were used. It is probably obvious to the reader that fluctuating interest rates greatly complicate these analyses.

Who Bears the Costs and Who Reaps the Benefits?

Many programs are sponsored and paid for by people who do not obtain the benefits. Clearly, the costs of primary education are borne by the whole community, while only the teachers and the children (and their parents) benefit. The community indirectly benefits by gaining a reputation for good schools that attracts and holds residents. The value of homes remains high, and good employees are not likely to move away. A tax increase referendum is more likely to pass if residents believe they benefit at least indirectly by having good schools in their community. Public transit systems are often criticized by people who are required to support the systems through taxes but who never expect to benefit personally from them.

Another clear example of this problem is seen in the development of outpatient surgery procedures. Hospitals are under intense pressure from insurance companies and from the federal and state governments to lower costs or at least limit increases in costs. One response to this pressure is to develop outpatient surgical centers. A patient needing relatively minor surgery does not stay in the hospital overnight. The cost of providing the surgery is markedly lower than traditional practices. However, neither the patient nor the physician benefits from these savings—Medicare, Medicaid, and insurance companies experience the savings. Evans and Robinson (1980) ask what incentive is there for patients and their physicians to use these centers if neither benefits? Evaluators conducting a thorough analysis of costs and benefits will point out the problems in program implementation that will be associated with a discrepancy between who benefits and who pays the costs of programs. Whenever the benefits are enjoyed by people other than those paying for the program, special problems may exist in mobilizing political action to initiate and to maintain the program.

This discussion should serve to sensitize evaluators to the issue of who benefits from programs. However, it is important to note that people voluntarily enter into many contracts from which they hope to receive no dollar benefits. All insurance policies—home, life, health, and car—are designed to provide fairly large amounts of money to those in need after an illness or accident. Clearly, the costs are borne by the majority, who benefit little in terms of dollars. The year-to-year benefit is primarily the peace of mind created by knowing that large expenses will be covered if a misfortune occurs. Most policy holders are satisfied with such assurances and would be delighted never to experience the need to receive a tangible financial benefit from their insurance.

Using Cost-Benefit
and Cost-Effectiveness Analyses

If the benefits of a program can be priced in dollars and a cost-benefit analysis can be done, one approach to program selection is simply to adopt the program having the largest benefit-to-cost ratio. Often, of course, outcomes cannot be valued in dollars. Furthermore, Nagel (1983a) has shown that many decisions involve far more than simply giving or withholding support for a program. Because governmental agencies have predetermined budgets, agency managers are not free to choose a program with the highest benefit-to-cost ratio if the cost exceeds the allotted budget. Instead, managers ideally should seek to obtain the most benefits for the resources they have available. Given the costs of the various programs and the size of the budget, the best program(s) to select might not, *when considered one at a time*, be the most efficient.

If the benefits are expressed in different units, stakeholders and managers can still use analyses relating costs to outcomes to select which programs should be maintained or expanded. The crucial technique is to list all possible courses of action and compare them to each other, taking two at a time. For example, suppose that a program to train 3,000 unskilled workers per year to fill maintenance positions could be funded for ten years for the same cost as a road improvement project that is expected to save five accidental deaths and twenty injuries during the same ten years. If—according to past research and evaluations—both outcomes are equally likely, which course of action should a state legislature chose? This selection can be made without putting prices on jobs, deaths, or injuries. Next, a third program could be compared to this selection. Although evaluators cannot supply data that would lead the legislators to support one program over the other, relating costs to outcomes will illuminate the debate and allow the various stakeholders to see the options more clearly than they could without such analyses. At a time when limitations on the financial resources of governments and other organizations are crucially important, analyses that help decision makers understand the impact of their decisions seem worthwhile.

Major Criticisms of Cost Analyses

There are a number of major criticisms of both cost-benefit and cost-effectiveness analyses. Users of these approaches will profit by being aware of these criticisms, which point up limitations of these useful methods.

Psychic benefits. As mentioned above, improved emotional health is hard enough to price. But what about clean air? Clean streams? An unlittered park? Access to quiet places to walk? One approach would be to study what people are willing to pay to escape environmental deterioration. Another approach is to calculate what must be paid to induce workers to accept employment in dirty, dusty, noisy, or dangerous occupations. These approaches are indirect and probably will never be completely satisfactory.

The value of lives. A second major criticism concerns the approach to valuing lives. Strictly economic analyses based on current or projected earning power place low values on the lives of children and the aged. The present economic value of young children is very low, because children cannot earn anything until ten to fifteen years into the future. However, people clearly do not act as though children are to be evaluated on the basis of economic value. Considerable resources are expended on all children, and especially on sick children. Very ill, premature babies may be hospitalized for months at a cost in the tens of thousands of dollars. In a somewhat similar way, economic analysis fails as an approach to determine the value of the elderly. Those who are unlikely to have a job in the future would have a negative dollar value. Because elderly people also have emotional value to others, this economic value does not reflect the feelings or predict the behavior of others toward the elderly.

An alternative approach to estimating the value of lives is an indirect way, similar to the approaches suggested for pricing the benefits of clean air. An examination of court settlements involving accidental deaths and the amount of money the community will spend to save lives will suggest the dollar values of lives. Abt (1977) reported that in spite of widely discussed large damage awards, American society placed a $10,000 to $20,000 price tag on a year of human life.

Degrades life.   Critics respond to an observation such as Abt's by saying that cost-benefit analysis degrades life by putting a price tag on the priceless: No amount of money can be worth a life, and attempts to put a price on life are inhumane. Social scientists often respond by saying—as Abt did—that reporting what people do does not imply that the reporter (in this case a social scientist) endorses what is reported. The reporter's views, whatever they are, did not cause the courts' decisions. If people believe that society's actions are wrong and that lives should be worth more, then those feelings will become part of the political process.

The amount that is spent on saving lives can vary markedly even within one country. Okrent (1980) cites reports that the French spent $30,000 per life saved through road accident prevention programs, but $1 million per life saved through airplane accident prevention. Expenditures in Great Britain to save lives varied from $10,000 for agricultural workers through $20 million per life for high-rise apartment occupants. Cost-effectiveness analyses are tools to demonstrate these inequities. What is done about the inequities is part of the political process.

Not complete.   Sometimes cost analyses are criticized for being incomplete. This criticism was implied in material already discussed. All benefits cannot be properly priced. Those that cannot should not be assigned an arbitrary or purely speculative price (Levin, 1975). Meaningless values lead to disguised error. Such errors are bigger problems than those caused by incomplete pricing. This incompleteness need not be viewed as a failure of the approach. Cost-benefit analyses are but one aspect of the evaluation of programs, and only a portion of the information evaluated by managers and community representatives.

Nevertheless, costs must be considered; regardless of our values, there are limitations on our resources. Communities must make choices among the various human services that could be offered. Some services will be offered regardless of what a cost-benefit analysis would show: The value assigned to the life of a child transcends the child's economic value. However, many other decisions and choices may be more closely related to dollar benefits. For these decisions and choices, cost analyses will take on more importance, but they still will not be the only inputs considered. And this is as it should be.

Note: There are no case studies in this chapter, because readers of this book are unlikely to conduct cost-benefit or cost-effectiveness analyses without a considerable amount of further study. These approaches require skills that few social science or professional school students (other than economics or business majors) possess. If readers have become sensitized to the need to consider costs and have developed some conceptual tools for analyzing costs, this chapter has been a success.

SUMMARY

Cost accounting is a necessary aspect of operating an organization in either the public or the private sectors. Efficient use of resources requires that costs be categorized as an aid to management and as an aid to making decisions about launching, maintaining, or terminating a service or other organizational activities. The distinctions of variable versus fixed, incremental versus sunk, recurring versus one-time, hidden versus obvious, and direct versus indirect costs all aid evaluators in conceptualizing and describing costs. Being able to measure the results of programs enables evaluators to calculate cost-benefit and cost-effective indexes. To use costs in organizational and governmental decisions it is not necessary to be able to place a price on the results of programs; however, it is necessary to be able to describe the expected results of the expenditure of resources. Stakeholders can then select among the possible uses of governmental or organizational resources. The chapter also included a discussion of several potential problems in the use of costs in program evaluation: using appropriate units of analysis, recognizing opportunity costs, and distinguishing between people who benefit versus those who pay are important concepts for anyone using cost-benefit or cost-effectiveness in evaluation.

STUDY QUESTIONS

1. Pretend you are involved in planning a storefront legal aid program. Draw up a budget for the first year. Take educated guesses as to costs of salaries, rent, supplies, and so on. Label each entry as to whether it is a recurring,

fixed, hidden, or some other type of cost. (Some costs will have more than one label.) Then group the costs into two categories—one for direct costs and one for indirect costs.

2. Compare the following two reading programs using cost-effectiveness analysis. Program A costs $6,000 and results in an average of a six-month reading level increase. Program B costs $13,000 and results in an average gain of eight-months reading achievement. Suppose Program A serves 100 children and Program B serves 300. Which of the two programs is more efficient? (Assume that the children are randomly assigned to programs.)

3. Compare cost-benefit analysis with cost-effectiveness analysis. Think of the different types of decisions that can be made and the kind of information needed to do the analyses. Summarize your comparisons in two columns.

4. The state of medical technology is such that ill or injured people can be unable to do anything—see, hear, talk, read, walk, groom, or dress—but yet be considered alive because their hearts are still beating. While the families of such patients face very large bills, they do not really have their loved one. This problem has ethical, legal, and cost implications (see Fox, 1976). What would a cost-benefit approach have to say about this problem? Think about psychic costs and benefits, opportunity costs, and alternative services to other ill patients before beginning your answer.

FURTHER READING

There are two valuable chapters in a major work on evaluation that has often been cited in this text.

LEVIN, H. M. 1975. Cost-effectiveness analysis in evaluation research. In *Handbook of evaluation research*, vol. 2, ed. M. Guttentag and E. L. Struening, pp. 89–124. Beverly Hills, Calif.: Sage.
ROTHENBERG, J. 1975. Cost-benefit analysis: A methodological exposition. In *Handbook of evaluation research*, vol. 2, ed. M. Guttentag and E. L. Struening, pp. 55–88. Beverly Hills, Calif.: Sage.

Also valuable is:

THOMPSON, M. S. 1980. *Benefit-cost analysis for program evaluation.* Beverly Hills, Calif.: Sage.

Step-by-step procedures specifically directed to the staff and managers of community mental health centers are included in these books.

CARTER, D. E., and NEWMAN, F. L. 1976. *A client-oriented system of mental health service delivery and program management.* Rockville, Md.: National Institute of Mental Health. DHEW Publication No. (ADM) 76–307.
HAGEDORN, H. J.; BECK, K. J.; NEUBERT, S. F.; and WERLIN, S. H. 1976. *A working manual of simple evaluation techniques for community mental health centers.* Rockville, Md.: U.S. Department of Human Resources. Publication No. (ADM) 76–404.

part IV
EFFECTIVE
APPLICATION
OF FINDINGS

"They never read the report! Those who did read it did nothing about the recommendations!" This is the frequent complaint of evaluators who feel that they conducted a sound evaluation of a program and made concrete and useful suggestions but find that decison makers ignore the report and recommendations. At least one young evaluator quit her job in order to call public attention to her findings and her recommendations concerning prison conditions (Solomon, 1975). The question of utilization has received considerable attention from writers in the field of program evaluation. Material from nearly two decades is included in the following sources: Suchman (1967), Weiss and Rein (1970), National Institute of Mental Health (1971), Rossi and Williams (1972), Weiss (1972b, 1973), Davis and Salasin (1975), Posavac (1979), Solomon and Shortell (1981), and Nagel (1983b).

Although devising an effective and appropriate design and writing a clear and meaningful report give evaluators satisfaction, nothing fosters the feeling of psychological success as much as seeing the report effectively utilized. On the other hand, it is disheartening and deflating when a report with substantial and meaningful findings remains in a file drawer, neglected and unused. The final payoff for the professional evaluator is not receiving the check for services rendered, but rather knowing that the evaluation will have an effect on policy and program improvement. The skills involved in bringing about effective application are partly technical, partly psychological, and partly political.

The final two chapters in this book deal with the effective application of findings. When findings are not effectively utilized, it is often difficult to pinpoint the precise reason. The problem could lie with the manner in which the report was written, the way in which the report was presented, the climate in which the report was presented, or any combination of the above.

Chapter 12 contains a discussion of how to write and present an evaluation report in a way that increases the probability that it will be read. Methods that will contribute to a climate conducive to the effective use of evaluation findings are presented in Chapter 13.

12

The Evaluation Report: How to Get it Read

Without effective communication, carefully prepared technical reports are apt to gather dust on agency shelves—never to be read by policy makers or implemented by program administrators. The need for effective communication strategies has received increased attention in recent years (Smith, 1982). A clear, concise, and attractive report enhances the possibilities of effective impact and represents the first step in having findings effectively utilized. After the data have been collected and analyzed, the results must be communicated to multiple audiences, such as program sponsors, program managers, program personnel, program recipients, other researchers, and the public at large. Because not all groups have equivalent needs or equal rights to know all the results, a single version of the report will ordinarily not be appropriate for all readers. Therefore, the quality and quantity of material, as well as the style of presentation, are best tailored to the group addressed. In this chapter suggestions are made about effective writing and presentation of an evaluation report, including the content and style of a report, pitfalls to avoid in reporting, and the manner of report distribution.

THE CONTENT OF A REPORT

The introduction to an evaluation report should describe the setting and nature of the evaluation project. First, the author should describe the program being evaluated, answering such questions as: What is the nature of the program? Who is supervising or delivering program services? How long has the program been in operation? What are the major characteristics of the physical setting in which the intervention takes place?

Second, reports should describe the type(s) of evaluations(s) undertaken. Have the evaluators conducted a needs, process, outcome, or cost-effectiveness study? If the evaluation has a primary and secondary focus, what are they? For example, is the primary focus on outcome evaluation, with secondary attention to cost-effectiveness? If the program has a number of aspects, which aspect is being evaluated?

Third, why was the evaluation commissioned? The general purposes can be described. The evaluation may have been undertaken to maintain accreditation, to improve participant satisfaction, to justify funding, to choose between educational organizations, or to improve public relations.

Fourth, have similar evaluations been undertaken? If so, how does the present evaluation project fit into the literature? What inadequacies (if any) does the evaluator see in previous attempts to evaluate similar programs?

Consider how the above principles are observed in the following excerpt from an in-house report entitled, "Cancer Care Center—An Evaluation of Support to Patients and Relatives," conducted for a large metropolitan teaching hospital (Carey and Posavac, 1977a). The introduction reads as follows:

> On September 1, 1976, the Cancer Care Center of Lutheran General Hospital began accepting patients. The center is a 20-bed unit designed to treat advanced cancer patients utilizing a team approach. Patients are actively treated with the hope of arresting the illness. However, regardless of whether the illness is arrested, the center's overall goal is to help patients cope with their condition and thus to live more effectively than they could otherwise.
>
> The specialized unit was developed because it is believed that cancer patients have needs unlike those of patients with illnesses that are less frightening and less serious than cancer. Further, it is believed that medical care personnel who are particularly interested in the needs of such patients would be better able to help them compared to personnel with no particular interest in cancer care. In order to help patients retain an effective and satisfying lifestyle, the center staff includes a social worker, a chaplain, a nutritionist, and other personnel in addition to physicians and specially selected nurses.
>
> Although most observers would agree that the center's goals are laudable, it is necessary to document the success of the center in meeting its goals. The project described in this report was designed to assess the success of the center in meeting the emotional and personal needs of patients and their relatives. To assess the center's success in improving the various aspects of physical care requires Quality Assurance studies. Quality of medical care is not discussed in this report.

The above introduction contains a brief description of the cancer care program, when it began, various personnel included on the staff, the type of evaluation, and the focus of the study. The review of literature was not mentioned because at the time of the evaluation, medical and nursing journals contained no reports similar to this study. As will be mentioned in the next section, on the style of the report, an effort is made to keep the introduction brief for an in-house report, since readers are fairly familiar with the program. However, for the article that was later submitted for journal publication, the introduction was considerably expanded. A more extended description of the cancer care program and the need for such a program were provided for journal readers. Similarly, reports submitted to agencies responsible for funding the program will also contain more details. Funding agencies like to see detailed information about how the program is carried out.

Who Were the Participants?

The section of an evaluation report following the introduction should deal with methodology. This section should contain both information on program participants and details about the procedure employed. The part dealing with participants should include a description of the target population, the nature of the sampling method used, pertinent demographic material on the sample, and the degree of cooperation obtained from the target population. If the percentages of participants who failed to return surveys or who dropped out of the program are fairly large, some effort should be made to explain their lack of participation.

Consider the following paragraphs from the methods section of the above-mentioned study:

> *Patients studied.* There were three groups of patients studied in preparing this report. A pre-unit comparison group ($N = 67$) was surveyed before the center was opened. After the center was opened two more groups were surveyed. A sample of patients ($N = 52$) who were treated in the specialized center and a group of patients ($N = 53$) with similar diagnoses but treated in regular medical units of the hospital were studied.
>
> Not all cancer patients in the hospital were candidates for the research; however, the same selection procedures were used with all three groups. An experienced nurse examined the chart of every patient discharged with a diagnosis of cancer. Only those patients who were admitted with a diagnosis of cancer could be part of the study. Those admitted without a diagnosis of cancer were eliminated because they could not have been part of the center's program. The following criteria were used to eliminate patients who would have difficulty responding to a survey because they were too sick:
>
> 1.   The chart indicated the patient was close to death,
> 2.   The patient was described as disoriented (i.e., suffering metastasis to brain),
> 3.   The patient was discharged to a nursing home.
>
> In addition, patients over 70 were eliminated because it was expected that many of these patients would find the surveys difficult to complete and might

	Patient group		
Variable	Center	Pre-unit comparison	Post-unit comparison
Number of surveys mailed	52	67	53
Number of usable surveys returned (% return rate)	29 (56%)	38 (57%)	31 (58%)
Age (means)	54.4	54.4	60.2
Sex: Males	31%	45%	36%
Females	69%	55%	64%
Marital status (% married)	62%	84%	81%
Self-reported diagnosis:			
Cancer	90%	90%	67%
Other	10%	10%	33%
Median stay (days)	12	10	13
Number of patients who died before follow-up telephone calls (%)	7 (13%)	9 (13%)	2 (4%)

FIGURE 12.1 Descriptions of the patients in the three cancer treatment groups.

also be suffering from other physical ailments. [Figure 12.1] includes a demographic description of the patients who responded to the surveys in the three groups. Overall, the groups were quite comparable in terms of age, sexual composition, marital status, etc. The one possible difference is found in the different death rates among the patients who were telephoned to inquire about nonreturned surveys. The rate (4%) for the post-unit comparison patients contrasts with the higher values (13%) found for both the Center patients and the pre-unit comparison patients.

Notice that the program patients are carefully described, along with the patients in the two comparison groups. No sampling method was used in this study. However, certain types of patients were eliminated from the study for methodological and humanitarian reasons. Although mention of the two comparison groups introduces the question of evaluation design before the procedure section, this was done to establish the comparability of the groups on the same table that described the patients.

How Was the Evaluation Conducted?

The procedure part of the methodology section appropriately contains material on the evaluation design, methods of data collection, and the operational measures of the dependent variables under investigation. In this section discussion can focus on the details of the experimental or quasi-experimental design chosen, possible biases in data collection and how they were controlled, and the validity and reliability of measures designed specifically for the evaluation. A description of the plan for statistical analysis can either be included in the procedure section or in the beginning of the results section. If a fairly complicated analysis has been selected, then it is advisable to explain the details either in a footnote or in an appendix, especially for an in-house presentation. Comments may be made about the tests for significance or for the degree of association, and about the power of the tests chosen. The amount of detail presented on these items will depend on whether the author is writing a journal article, an in-house report, or a report to a governmental or foundation funding agency. More will be said about this in the section on the style of the report.

In the evaluation we have been describing, the authors chose to place a description of statistical analysis in an appendix so that the flow of the report would not be broken for in-house readers. Read the following paragraph, taken from the appendix, and see whether you agree with that decision.

> Without very sizable numbers of patients in each group, it is not possible to detect small differences among the answers of the three groups tested. With sizes of the groups available, differences among groups would have to have been at least 20 percentage points to be "significant" using standard statistical procedures. For example, if pre-unit care was rated at 72% favorable, the center's care would have to be rated at least at 92% for the statistical test to detect the improvement. Clearly, an improvement of 20% over an already high 72% may be too much to hope for. Because of the problems with such an item-by-item analysis, the data in this study are analyzed on a *set*-of-items basis. The statistical tests used answer the question of whether a set of items has shown *overall* improvement, not whether any given item has shown improvement. The result of this form of analysis is that the reader should *not* view the results of any single item as worthy of particular attention. This is true whether the individual comparison is favorable to the center or unfavorable.

What Was Observed?

In the results section the data shold be presented without lengthy interpretation or discussion. The author should be answering the questions: What happened? What findings appeared? Editorial comments should be saved until the discussion part of the report.

Tables and figures should be brief and simple. All the results for the Cancer Care Center evaluation were presented in three easy-to-read tables (Figures 12.2, 12.3, and 12.4). Notice that in the report's second table (Figure 12.2), containing questions relevant to the evaluation of process, the appropriate comparisons were percentages. In the third table (Figure 12.3) the three groups of patients were compared on the basis of mean scores; percentages were again used to evaluate the attitude of relatives in the

| Questionnaire items | Center | Patients' unit | |
		Pre-unit comparison	Post-unit comparison
1. Were you admitted to your hospital nursing unit in a respectful manner?	96[a]	95	93
2. Were diagnostic tests clearly explained?	82	74	80
3. Were questions about your illness answered to your satisfaction?	82	74	90
4. Were possible side effects of treatments explained before you received the treatments?	92	71	75
5. When you had pain, was something done to relieve it?	96	90	96
6. Did you know why you were given medication?	96	95	90
7. Were you able to sleep at night?	75	58	70
8. Did you receive assistance with your diet?	87	75	68
9. Was someone available when you wanted to talk?	92	88	85
10. Did you share in the planning of your care?	68	50	50
11. Were your family members encouraged to be involved with your day-to-day care?	91	72	68
12. Did you feel the staff was interested in helping you?	100	90	90
13. Was there adequate planning for your needs after discharge? (If not, please explain on the other side.)	92	81	88
14. Because of your stay in the hospital, are you better able to cope emotionally with your illness at home? (If not, please explain what you would have liked done.)	70	81	78

FIGURE 12.2 Percentage of patients answering YES to the questions concerning hospital care.

15. Was the ministry of the chaplain of value to you?	<u>88</u>	61	64
16. In your opinion did the hospital staff communicate well with each other?	89	89	<u>90</u>
17. Was the general atmosphere of your nursing unit depressing?	7	10	<u>3</u>

^a *The most favorable percentage among the three groups is underlined.*

FIGURE 12.2 *(Cont.)*

fourth table (Figure 12.4). In all three tables the most favorable value among the three groups was underlined to facilitate reading.

The text describing the results can be presented very succinctly, as the following example illustrates:

> *Patients' reactions to hospital care.* Before closely examining the results, a few points must be noted. Whenever patients make generally favorable comments about their treatment, innovations of any sort are not likely to greatly improve the patients' ratings of the care received. This fact, called the "ceiling effect," should be borne in mind whenever innovative programs are introduced into a setting that is already well-received. The ceiling effect is often a problem in detecting the positive impact of an innovation here because most patients already view the hospital quite favorably.
>
> The percentages of patients in the three groups who responded favorably to the survey items are summarized in [Figure 12.2]. In no unit did patients evaluate their care in unfavorable terms. In spite of the problem of the ceiling

FIGURE 12.3 Means of the patients' self-described psychological moods (mean scores).

| Profile of mood states (POMS) scale | Patients' unit | | |
	Center	Pre-unit comparison	Post-unit comparison
Tension-anxiety	11.08	11.76	<u>8.84</u>^a
Depression	<u>7.80</u>	10.03	7.84
Anger-hostility	3.40	6.24	<u>3.24</u>
Vigor	12.80	12.47	<u>14.00</u>
Fatigue	10.60	11.65	<u>8.60</u>
Confusion	6.68	7.18	<u>5.68</u>

^a *The most favorable value among the three groups is underlined.*

| | Patients' unit | | |
	Center	Pre-unit comparison	Post-unit comparison
Description of relatives			
Sex of relative: % Male	48	43	56
% Female	52	57	44
Relationship: % Spouse	55	79	68
How much help did you receive from the following personnel?	% reporting having received GREAT help		
Physicians	50	65[a]	58
Nurses	74	51	56
Social workers	39	24	31
Chaplains	38	29	19
Nutritionists (diet counselor)	35	10	27
Physical therapists	44	13	27
Were you disappointed in any of the same hospital personnel?	% reporting disappointment (% YES)		
Physicians	4	6	0
Nurses	0	8	4
Social workers	0	6	4
Chaplains	0	12	4
Nutritionists (diet counselor)	0	10	4
Physical therapists	0	0	0

[a] *The most favorable value among the three groups is underlined.*

FIGURE 12.4 Responses about medical care personnel by the relatives of the cancer treatment patients.

effect, the center's patients described their care in more favorable terms, as compared to the patients in the other two groups. The center's care was evaluated more favorably than the care given the pre-unit group on 15 characteristics, while the reverse occurred only once. The center's care thus was reliably evaluated as better than that obtained before the unit was opened ($\chi^2 = 12.25$, $df = 1$, $p < .001$). In comparing the center's patients with those treated at the same time but on different units, the center's care is again evaluated more favorably on 12 out of 16 characteristics ($\chi^2 = 4.00$, $df = 1$, $p < .0025$). A note about the method of analysis is in the Appendix.

The patients' moods. The mean values for the patients' moods are presented in [Figure 12.3]. On this set of measures center patients were better off than the pre-unit group; however, the post-unit group described themselves as the best off of all. Finding the post-unit group to be the best off was a surprising finding. It may be that this finding is related to the death rate found as a result of calling discharged patients to ask them about the nonreturn of surveys. If the proportion of patients dying within four weeks of going home is an index of seriousness of illness, then it may be that the post-unit group is the most healthy. If so, then their higher values on the POMS may be due to their generally better state of health. This reasoning is supported by the center staff's belief that they treat patients who are in more advanced stages of cancer than other units in the hospital.

Relatives' views of medical care personnel. The relatives' reports of how much help various medical care personnel gave them personally are summarized in [Figure 12.4]. Also in this table are the proportions of relatives who reported disappointment in the various medical care personnel. As in [Figure 12.2], no group of relatives contained a large proportion of disappointed people. The most favorable ratings were given by relatives of the center's patients on nine out of the eleven items ($\chi^2 = 4.45$, $df = 1$, $p < .0025$).

If a program's effects are given as means, it is helpful to include the standard deviations in an appendix. Merely to report that a treatment group differed from the comparison group at a given level of statistical significance does not provide the reader with enough information to evaluate the practical importance of the difference. For example, if an evaluation finds that program and comparison groups averaged 8.55 and 8.19, respectively—but that the pooled standard deviation was 3.92—readers can conclude that the improvement was of little practical use. That is, in most settings staff members would probably not recognize a difference among the groups. Furthermore, if the new program is costly, there is little reason to support it, even if the findings are statistically significant. If, on the other hand, the mean scores had been 11.55 and 8.19, the difference would have been important, since the improvement is over three-fourths of a standard deviation, a fairly respectable improvement (Smith and Glass, 1977; Wortman, 1983).

Other strength-of-association statistics that are useful are the gamma statistics (Davis, 1971; Mueller et al., 1970) and the eta or omega statistics (Hays, 1963). Some comment about the power of the research design to detect a program effect (Cohen, 1982) is also helpful. Although power—1 minus the probability of a Type II error—can be calculated (Boruch and Gomez, 1977; Friedman, 1982) and presented in the report, it is mentioned in few evaluations.

What Action Should Be Considered?

The discussion section should interpret and comment on the results. In the case of a needs evaluation, how strong are the arguments for establishing the given program? In a summative evaluation, what are the arguments for and against continuing the given program? In a formative evaluation, what steps should be taken to improve the program? Is further evaluation indicated? What recommendations are appropriate in light of the results? It is not always easy to say whether the benefits of a given program justify the cost, although the fixed and variable costs of a program can be enumerated. In a cost-effectiveness evaluation the author should indicate whether the findings suggest that the same results could be obtained more economically by a different program.

Consider excerpts from the discussion section of the Cancer Care Center evaluation:

> The overall impact of the Cancer Care Center is positive. Patients and relatives alike view the program in more favorable terms than the care provided in other units of the hospital. The results of the study are unambiguous except for the POMS variables. Previous research has shown that the more discomfort and pain people suffer, the more depressed and, in general, less well-adjusted they seem (Carey, 1974). If the center's patients are indeed in more advanced stages of cancer, the less pleasant moods can be readily understood. To evaluate the impact of the center on patients' moods requires a group of patients just as ill. If the death rates in [Figure 12.1] do reflect the health of patients, then the center patients ought to be compared with the pre-unit group only. If that comparison is made, then the center was successful on all three sets of variables used in this study.
>
> This study has shown that the emotional and educational needs of cancer patients are better met by the program in the Cancer Care Center than by nonspecialized units. The study does not address the question of whether medical care is better in the center than in other units. Such a question can be addressed by a quality assurance study done before the center's organization, contrasted to one with patients only from the center.

Notice that a long discussion section is unnecessary. A cost-benefit analysis was not included, because it was not requested by the decision makers. The discussion section also makes clear what is not evaluated—namely, the quality of the medical care offered to patients in the Cancer Care Center.

The discussion may also include consideration of the adequacy of the program. Is the program sufficiently extensive to serve the people who need it? Is the program sufficiently extensive to deal with the degree of need shown by the people who seek the service (or should be served by it)? Some critics assert that most governmental programs are not funded at levels that can realistically be expected to enable people to resolve their problems (Sechrest et al., 1979). For example, people who cannot hold jobs often need job skill training, emotional counseling, social support, educational services, health services, and so forth for a fairly lengthy period of time. Piecemeal programs providing one of these services will probably have little lasting effect.

Report Outline

It is recommended that evaluators begin the preparation of a report by outlining the points to be covered and the order in which they are to be addressed. The outline can be modified as the report takes final form, and

Evaluation of the Impact of the Physician Residency Program on General Medical Hospital

I. Summary.
II. Introduction
    A. Background of the program
    B. Residency program created important changes in care
    C. Problems in conducting the evaluation
III. Procedure and Method
    A. Data collection
    B. Respondents
    C. Content of the interviews
IV. Results
    A. How respondents evaluate the teaching function of the hospital
        1. Attending physicians reactions
        2. Nonphysician hospital staff evaluations
        3. Residents' views of their programs
    B. Perceptions of the quality of care provided by the residents
        1. Perceptions of technical skills
        2. Interpersonal skills
            a. Staff rapport with residents
            b. Patient rapport with residents
            c. Care of dying patients
            d. Use of hospital nonmedical resource personnel
    C. Organizational changes brought about by the development of the residency program
        1. Increase in number of hospital-based physicians
        2. Development of new outpatient care unit
        3. Conflicts among residents in different specializations
        4. Effects of the program on the cost of medical care
V. Conclusions and Recommendations
    A. Overall comments
    B. Seven recommendations

References
Appendix A. Growth of residency programs at the hospital
Appendix B. Interview forms used with nurses

FIGURE 12.5 Sample in-house evaluation report outline.

can then be used as a table of contents. Figure 12.5 illustrates a report outline that might be used to present the findings of an evaluation of the institutional effects of a physician residency program. Notice that the summary is presented first, not last, as is usually done in a journal article. Program personnel will usually read an evaluation report in its entirety. However, policy makers often want a quick overview before deciding how much time they need to invest in reading a report. If the evaluation detects significant problems, policy makers may decide to study the report carefully in order to evaluate possible approaches to follow in making program improvements.

THE STYLE OF REPORT

In-house Reports versus Journal Articles

As we mentioned above, in-house reports and journal articles differ to some extent on style and emphasis. An in-house report deemphasizes the introduction and methodology sections and emphasizes the discussion and results sections. The reason for this is that in-house readers are familiar with the elements of the program and have no need to know elaborate details of methodology that would enable them to replicate the study. Therefore, they have less interest in the review of the literature, program design, and methodology. In-house readers are most anxious to obtain a general overview of the results of the evaluation and to learn what recommendations were made. For these reasons, the authors of this text suggest putting a 200- to 500-word summary of the salient findings and recommendations at the beginning of an in-house report of ten to twenty pages. The needs of many readers will be met by this summary. Clearly, the summary will be longer for evaluations of wider scope and greater length.

In journal articles, on the other hand, it is appropriate to put considerable emphasis on the introduction and methodology sections. Journal readers, and especially other evaluators, are likely to be interested in theoretical issues, the value of the present evaluation to the particular field of study, and the possibility of replicating the study. These readers would be less interested in the implications for the specific institution where the evaluation was conducted. For these reasons, more details on the experimental design and the statistical analysis of results are appropriate.

Where evaluators have undertaken an ambitious and well-funded evaluation for some large institution, it may be necessary to write a single report for multiple audiences. In this case the report may take the form of two volumes. The first volume will be a short, easy-to-read text listing the main findings and explaining the conclusions and suggestions for action. This volume would be intended for executive use in decision making. The second and more lengthy volume would contain copies of the correspondence that set up the goals, conditions, and financial agreements of the study, as well as extensive methodological details and specialized charts that would have interest only for those needing more detailed information. An example of such a report is the needs and planning evaluation conducted with the help of Arthur D. Little company for the Catholic Hospital Association (1977). Another example is the report of the evaluation of New York

State's drug law. There were actually three published reports of this evaluation: (1) a 33-page conclusion section that would be read by those interested in the overall findings; (2) a 115-page section providing the supporting data for the conclusions; and (3) a 322-page report providing more detailed backup analyses (*The Nation's Toughest Drug Law: Evaluating the New York Experience*, 1978; *Staff Working Papers of the Drug Law Evaluation Project*, 1978).

Quantitative versus Qualitative Style

A *quantitative style* of evaluation puts heavy emphasis on the collection of "hard" data that can be analyzed statistically; a *qualitative style* emphasizes observations either by participants or by outside observers. Both the quantitative and qualitative approaches have their strengths and weaknesses. The quantitative approach, strongly favored by those trained in a social psychological tradition, is usually considered to be more objective and less liable to be influenced by the bias of data collectors. On the other hand, some differences between program and nonprogram participants can be difficult to document using a quantitative approach. However, a trained observer can notice some of the behaviors that statistical data collection methods would find hard to capture.

Qualitative observations have usually been neglected by evaluators trained in a strictly experimental tradition. In recent years there has been a growing reaction to what is seen as an overemphasis on quantitative methodology (Filstead, 1970; Cook and Reichardt, 1979; Guba and Lincoln, 1981). Those who favor more qualitative assessments feel that many program evaluations are unnecessarily and incorrectly pessimistic in their conclusions. These writers believe that evaluators myopically concentrate on readily quantified variables, such as IQ, reading ability, death rates, and income; when such variables do not show the desired improvement, the programs are pronounced failures. Proponents of qualitative evaluation suggest that evaluators ought to step back and observe the overall picture. Enthusiasm, hope, initiative, anger, despair, and anxiety are examples of positive and negative emotions that are often better detected by qualitative observations.

The use of qualitative techniques has proven useful to government policy makers who need prompt and understandable feedback on existing programs and services. Hendricks (1981) has described an innovative evaluation unit in the U.S. Department of Health and Human Services (HSS) that regularly briefs the secretary on the services delivered to clients on a local level. These evaluators make up the Office of Service Delivery Asssessment of HSS. They visit nursing homes, social security offices, community mental health centers, hospitals, Indian reservations, senior cen-

ters, or any other site partially funded by HSS. These evaluators understand rigorous, quantitative evaluation procedures; however, they
recognize that some evaluations must be completed in a matter of weeks in
order to have an impact on policy. Qualitative reports based on interviews
and observations of services answer the need for valid, timely information.

Ideally, both the quantitative and qualitative approaches can be integrated into an evaluation and into the final report. In the evaluation of an
outdoor survival program (Smith et al., 1976), the writers first presented a
quantitative analysis and then included the diary of one of the participants
who experienced the program. The first part of the report is rather dry
reading, but it documents the extent to which the program achieved stated
goals with quantitative operational measures. The second part of the report is a fascinating description of one participant's experience that helps
explain the meaning of the statistics in the quantitative analysis.

Another example is the report that integrated quantitative and qualitative findings of the Kansas City preventive patrol experiment (Kelling et
al., 1976). The study evaluated the widespread belief that the presence or
potential presence of police officers on patrol severely inhibits criminal activity. The report is divided into seven parts. Part one contains the introduction to the study and the major findings. The next three parts of the
report describe the quantitative analysis and contain a description of the
police patrol experiment, data sources, and the experimental findings. The
next two parts of the report contain qualitative observations by police officers regarding police use of time when they have no special assignment and
the attitudes of police officers towards the patrol. The final part presents
the observations and conclusions of the authors.

The Importance of Attractive
Packaging

Whether one is writing an in-house report or a journal article, it is
important to package a report attractively if the authors want it to be read.
First, the authors should use a composition style that is marked by clarity,
succinctness, and cohesiveness. It helps a great deal if each paragraph is
introduced by a topic sentence that summarizes the main idea of the paragraph. Second, good typing will increase attractiveness. Readability can be
enhanced by the layout of material, proper underlining, and arrangement
of tables and figures. A report that has many typing errors makes the
reader wonder whether the authors were as careless in collecting data as
they were in proofreading their manuscript. Third, the report should be as
brief as possible. It is hard to state an absolute length in words or pages for
any section of a report; the length will obviously depend on the scope of a
project. However, the shorter a report, the more likely it is to be read and
used. Reports are also more likely to be read when the authors do not try to
present every peripheral finding in the study but rather exercise discretion

in satisfying the needs of a particular audience. Fourth, color coding various sections of the in-house report can make it more appealing to the eye and can make it easier for the reader to locate material of special interest. Color coding is ordinarily not needed with a short report, but in more extensive presentations it can be of great assistance. For example, if there are a number of appendixes or a series of tables added at the end of a report, these might be printed on different-colored stock than the main body of the text. This would make it easy for the reader to thumb through the report and locate the section where the tables are printed. Finally, if a report is packaged with an attractive cover, it is more likely that readers will pick up the report and read it with interest. Twenty pages of single-spaced type on white bond paper stapled in the left corner are much less attractive to the eye than the same report bound in yellow firm-paper covered with an attractive design on the front. The authors of this text have made it a practice to use a cover that identifies the report as coming from the Office of Evaluation and Research and leaves space for the title of the evaluation, the authors, and the date. Figure 12.6 is the cover design used in one hospital for research and evaluation reports.

PITFALLS IN REPORTING

Overgeneralization from Inadequate Sampling or Return Rate

The first pitfall to avoid in reporting findings is overgeneralization based on inadequate sampling of the total population or inadequate return rate on a survey. For example, if evaluators chose to take a 10 percent sample of a population, some evidence should be presented that this was done in a manner adequate to test the hypotheses or answer the questions posed by the evaluation. Stratified random sampling (that is, sampling that assures various subgroups of the population will be proportionately represented) is a stronger procedure than mere random sampling. However, let us suppose that only approximately one-third of a random sample completed a program being evaluated. This situation represents a sizable dropout of participants. If the data show that the participants who actually did complete the program are much improved compared to a control group who did not receive the program, the evaluator has to be very careful about interpreting the results. It is not legitimate to conclude that the dropouts would have profited as much as those who actually did complete the program.

Consider the results of a national poll conducted by CORPUS, a group that questions traditional views on celibacy for Catholic priests. Questionnaires were sent to 39,097 American priests, including all priests

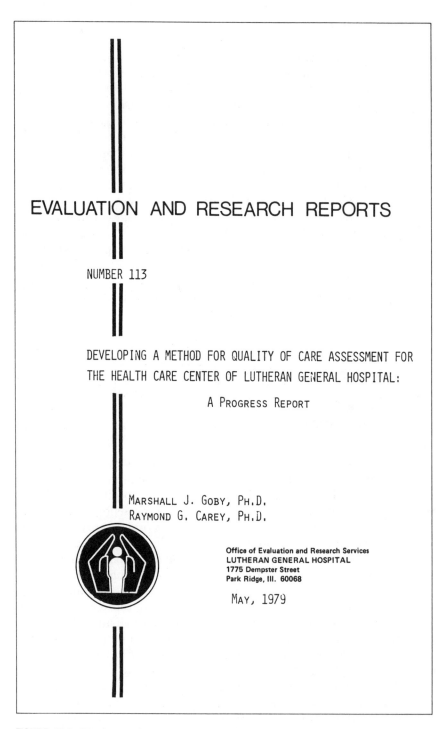

EVALUATION AND RESEARCH REPORTS

NUMBER 113

DEVELOPING A METHOD FOR QUALITY OF CARE ASSESSMENT FOR
THE HEALTH CARE CENTER OF LUTHERAN GENERAL HOSPITAL:

A PROGRESS REPORT

MARSHALL J. GOBY, PH.D.
RAYMOND G. CAREY, PH.D.

Office of Evaluation and Research Services
LUTHERAN GENERAL HOSPITAL
1775 Dempster Street
Park Ridge, Ill. 60068

MAY, 1979

FIGURE 12.6 Sample cover for an evaluation report.

assigned to parish work. Of these, just 6,414 (16.3 percent) responded. Just over half these respondents favored optional celibacy for Catholic priests. The newspaper article reporting the results of the survey carried the following headline: "U.S. priests want celibacy option, active ministry for married clergy." The article further quoted the study director as saying: "The survey results are extremely valid in view of the number of respondents and the general consistency of respondents across the country." On the supposition that the newspaper article accurately quoted the study director, the study director would have to be accused of overgeneralizing on the basis of an inadequate rate of return on the survey. A response rate of 16.3 percent is inadequate to conclude much about the overall opinions of priests in the United States.

As pointed out in Chapter 2, the important issue is the representativeness of a sample, not its size. The evaluators would have been better off to have sampled 4,000 priests (10 percent of the target population) and put more time and effort into obtaining a favorable rate of response.

Conclusions That Are Too Strong for Modest Differences

When evaluators have received a sizable grant for a project or have put a great deal of time and effort into an evaluation, there is a strong desire to demonstrate that their time and money were well spent. This results in pressure on evaluators to read more into their findings than is actually there. In the long run the reputation of evaluators will be enhanced by interpreting findings cautiously. Modest differences between program and control groups should be interpreted as "some evidence" in support of the program, and should not be seen as "demonstrating" or "strongly suggesting" that a program is valuable to the organization sponsoring it.

For example, a health screening clinic wanted to increase the number of people who responded to a mailed announcement of its services. The message on the announcement was changed from a neutral tone to either a threatening ("Your health may be bad") or a positive ("We can help you stay healthy") message. An evaluation of the changes revealed that the threatening message led to fewer responses, while the positive message led to more responses. However, the percentage of people who made appointments only increased from 32 percent to 36 percent (Kirscht, Haefner, and Eveland, 1975)—certainly not a strong effect. If such an innovation had been expensive, it probably would not have been worth doing. It is a fact that many programs have only small effects (Light, 1983). One role of the evaluator is to be sure that people recognize that small effects are likely and that statistically significant effects might be found for programs that are of no practical importance.

Ignoring the Possibility
of Type II Errors

Some evaluators feel that if results do not reach the level of statistical significance, they should be ignored; however, the costs involved in gathering data makes them too expensive to be recklessly ignored (Cronbach, 1975). This is especially true when the sample sizes that are available are so small that detecting statistically significant findings is unlikely. One response to this situation is to observe a larger number of program participants. If this can be done, it is the solution of choice. However, to detect a 5 percent increase over a pretest level of 80 percent favorable with a 10 percent chance of a Type II error (missing a real effect) at a significance level of .05 would require 1,066 observations in each of the comparison and innovative program groups. If the evaluator could tolerate a probability of a Type II error of .50, the required sample sizes drop to 388 (Fleiss, 1973). Obtaining this many respondents is obviously an impossible task for most in-house evaluators. Nevertheless, when evaluating an existing and costly program, evaluators should be reluctant to describe the program as a failure when the probability of not detecting a real improvement is large. (Recall the ethical questions discussed in Chapter 4.) If the evaluator had anticipated this result, the evaluation should not have been undertaken. However, there are many surprises when working in an action setting. For example, the number of people available for testing is often lower than program personnel expected when the evaluation was being planned.

Being cautious about Type II errors is not the same as saying that every nonsignificant interaction must be seen as a "trend." However, when one is guided by strong prior knowledge, or sample size is small, nonsignificant findings can at times justifiably be considered a trend. For example, when a relationship has been predicted on the basis of solid theory or previous evaluations, then the evaluators are more justified in giving serious attention to trends supporting this relationship, even when statistical tests do not yield traditional levels of statistical significance. Trends without such strong a priori support should not be given serious attention until replicated.

Analyzing Specific Rather Than
Total Effects of a Program

When an index of the success of a human service program approaches the maximum possible, detecting a statistically significant improvement on individual criteria is a difficult task. For example, this problem would be experienced by evaluators working in a well-run bank. In such a bank customer satisfaction measures would be highly skewed, with the bulk of responses toward the favorable end of the satisfaction continuum. With respondents answering 80 to 90 percent favorable on individual items, innovative programs designed to give customers better hours, more convenient service, and so on, can seldom raise the level of satisfaction by more than a few percentage points.

In instances such as this, the personnel in an innovative program are usually more concerned with answering the question of whether their new program has an overall positive effect than with knowing whether it was successful on every single criterion. If, indeed, a single criterion was so important that the program would not be a success if it were not achieved, then the researchers must evaluate that program on this single criterion. However, this is often not the case.

One approach to dealing with small effects is to evaluate the program *as a whole,* rather than on a goal-by-goal basis. In this case, rather than evaluating the success of a program by examining each individual standard of success, the evaluators look at the total effect of the program. This was the approach that Carey and Posavac (1979) used in evaluating the Cancer Care Center. (A description of the statistical approach was put in the appendix of the report and was included earlier in this chapter.) Analysis revealed that patients reported better results on thirteen of the proposed seventeen specific goals than either of the two comparison groups. Although the program was not significantly superior to the comparison groups on any individual criterion, the program taken as a whole was demonstrated to be successful. In effect, the evaluators traded evaluative specificity for statistical power. A more detailed explanation of this approach can be found in an article by Posavac and Carey (1978).

Being Honest to the Point of Being Tactless

The final pitfall in reporting is to present the findings in such a blunt fashion that the feelings of the program personnel are injured. It is possible to be honest to the point of being tactless. Negative findings must be presented in a manner that demonstrates a humane concern for the dignity and feelings of people connected with a given program.

For example, in an evaluation of presterilization interviewing conducted by chaplains at a religiously oriented hospital, the findings clearly showed that mandatory pastoral interviewing before sterilization operations did not have great value for most couples in the study (Carey, 1976). However, for many years the chaplains had put a great deal of time and effort into this service. It was important to couch the findings in language that would convey the message but still not place the entire blame for the lack of effect on their skills or efforts. Indeed, lack of effort or skill was not responsible for the negative finding. The evaluator tried to put the findings and focus in a tactful way, as the following excerpt from the discussion section demonstrates:

Follow-up interviews suggested that the failure to find value in the interviews may have been due to the manner in which they were structured and conducted. First, some couples quoted their physician as telling them, "The interview is only a formality," in a tone and manner that indicated that it was a waste of time. The interviews might have been viewed differently if the physician had set the stage for the interview by recommending it as worthwhile and outlining its purpose and nature. Second, some chaplains dislike mandatory interviews. They feel that couples have made up their minds and that nothing is gained in the interview. Chaplains who feel they are conducting a useless interview are likely to communicate this feeling. Finally, the time assigned (15 to 30 minutes) seems inadequate to cover the issues involved.

However, a few couples were clearly in need of help. One of the original 100 couples canceled the operation because they obtained a divorce. Another woman admitted to extreme guilt that she was not handling well. Five spouses said their marriages were unhappy and their sexual relationships were unsatisfying.

In addition, nearly half of the wives reported some degree of anxiety, although this was not necessarily connected with the operation. There is no indication that adequate counseling will be provided by physicians. Only 13 percent of the responding couples saw a physician for counseling, and less than half of these found his counseling of great value. Therefore, in spite of the findings of this study, one should not hastily conclude that mandatory interviews should be dropped without providing an adequate substitute (Carey, 1976, p. 494).

Notice that in this example the evaluator considered the role of the physician in making presterilization interviewing a success, as well as the attitudes of the patients who came in for interviewing. The evaluator also pointed out that some patients, indeed, were in need of counseling, and that the interviews should not be hastily dropped without providing some substitute. As it turned out, this report was well received by the Division of Pastoral Care in the hospital, and hospital policy was modified to make counseling mandatory only for those couples under thirty years of age. This change in policy seemed to concentrate the efforts of the chaplains on the age group where most difficulties were likely to arise. Also, the physicians were urged to make greater efforts to prepare the patients for a more meaningful interview.

MANNER OF DISTRIBUTION

Respecting Both Sponsors and Program Personnel

The manner in which a report is released is almost as important as the quality of the research design and the composition of the report itself. If evaluators wish to see action taken on the basis of their report findings, it is critical to maintain the good will and support of decision makers and of those who wield power in an organization. Consider a situation in which several people feel they have the right to obtain the evaluation report first. Program personnel, the program director, and program sponsors (administration or the funding agency) may be eager to see the results and may be somewhat anxious about the effects the report could have on their work situation. The problem the evaluator faces is how to be sure that none of these groups feels slighted because it was not the first to see the report.

The authors of this text have found it helpful to distinguish between the *final draft* and the *final report*. It seems best to give those who are in immediate operational control of a program the first peek at the findings. This is done by letting them know that they are going to see the final draft on a confidential basis and that their suggestions for clarifying or elaborating on points that are made in the report will be accepted. This preview, however, should not result in the censorship of valid interpretations. This look at the final draft usually has the effect of allaying the anxiety of program directors who are often hoping for the best but expecting the worst. It also gives them a chance to reflect on any surprises that might be in the report.

After meeting with the operational directors of the program and obtaining their comments, the evaluators can incorporate whatever modifications are necessary in assembling the final report. The final report, then, is presented first to the top administration of the organization or institution, who may have funded or at least sponsored the program and the evaluation research. It is important that they are made to feel that they are special people and the first to see what is potentially sensitive information. The failure to do this may mean that the evaluators will lose the administration's support, which is necessary for future evaluation projects, or perhaps not even be invited to conduct further evaluations in the organization.

After presenting the report to the top administration, the order of further release depends largely on the importance of the report and the sensitivity of its contents. Evaluators must be guided by administration with respect to the order and time sequence of distribution. It is possible that administrators can abuse this authority and try to keep the report from being distributed any further, but this is not the ordinary situation in a well-run organization.

Personal Presentation to Key Persons

In presenting both the final draft and the final report, it is strongly suggested that evaluators resist the temptation to simply mail a copy of the report to program personnel or administration. It is recommended that evaluators set up a personal appointment with the key people who will be seeing the draft or report and distribute a copy to them marked "CONFI-

DENTIAL" soon enough for them to be able to read it before the meeting—but not so far ahead that there is danger of the report being leaked to other people within the organization. The purpose of the personal presentation is to give the evaluator first-hand knowledge of which sections of the report need further clarification, of the specific reactions of key persons, and of the likelihood that the latter will take some concrete actions in light of the recommendations. This information, which can be obtained only in a face-to-face meeting, will guide the evaluators in the manner in which they will release the information to other people in the organization and also to those outside the organization. They will know which parts of their report can be shortened, strengthened, or clarified.

Interim Reports

Interim reports are those that are given in the course of an evaluation project before the final report is ready to be released. They are usually unofficial communications about the progress of the evaluation project, the problems being experienced, and, when appropriate, the findings that are beginning to emerge. Interim reports are especially useful in evaluation projects that last a year or more. They help to maintain the interest and enthusiasm of program personnel who focus their attention on the delivery of program services, not on the evaluation. Program personnel can also be thanked for their crucial assistance to date and can be advised about how they might further help data collection.

Distribution Outside
an Organization

Neither program personnel nor sponsors are always enthusiastic about having an evaluation report published outside the confines of their organization or institution. Few evaluations will be entirely positive, and program personnel are as anxious to have outsiders believe only the best about their programs as parents are to have others see only the good aspects of their children. On occasion, program personnel want to be the first ones to write about their program and resent being upstaged by a researcher who publishes before they do.

Evaluators can also be faced with the sensitive situation of balancing their obligation of confidentiality against the obligation to share findings with those who have a need or a right to know. In the case of evaluations that are funded by government, this will rarely be a difficulty, because part of the grant money will be earmarked for publication of results. However, in privately funded evaluations it would be helpful to agree beforehand on ownership of the data and rights of publication. Many private institutions have a research and publication committee or its equivalent that claims the right of censorship over articles published on institutional operations. It is good to clarify the limitations on the rights of the evaluator before the evaluation begins.

If the evaluation is of such a nature that local community or civic groups might be interested in the results, the public relations department of an organization can often be of great help to the evaluators. Public relations personnel can usually give expert advice on which local newspapers would be most interested, on the type of release that would be most appropriate, and on the names of people to contact.

Evaluators will also wish to share their work with the professional community. This involves choosing an appropriate journal for the evaluation report. In writing a journal article, it is important to keep the audience in mind. Some journals are read mainly by program personnel, the people who actually deliver the services; others are read mainly by university teachers and researchers; still other journals appeal to a mixed audience. In any event, it is helpful for evaluators to know the editorial policies, type of audience, and level of professional acceptance of the journals relevant to the field in which they are working.

In addition to the printed media, evaluators may wish to contact others through a presentation to their professional organization. There is a good deal of value in doing this. First, evaluators can keep in touch with professionals of similar interests and promote the sharing of their work. These presentations help others to keep current, because it usually takes over a year before journal articles are published. Second, some evaluators are in the position of having their expenses paid to a meeting only on the condition that they make a presentation. Finally, it may help evaluators to have an additional item on their résumés indicating that they have made a presentation to a society in their field to demonstrate that they are active and productive in their chosen field of expertise.

FEEDBACK TO PARTICIPANTS

In addition to distributing the evaluation report to key personnel within the institution and also to those who have a right or interest in knowing about the findings outside the institution, it is important to keep in mind the obligation of providing feedback to participants. The program would not have existed, nor would the evaluation have been conducted, without the help and cooperation of those people who received the program. In many cases they have a desire to know something about the results of the evaluation, and at times they have a right to know. If evaluators promised participants they would obtain some information on the results of the program, then evaluators should fulfill their pledges. This does not mean the evaluators have to send a complete report to everybody who took part in the program. However, they can give a brief summary of the findings with information on where more details can be obtained.

The manner and time of release of this information to program participants should be approved by the administration or program sponsors. Once again, depending on the nature and sensitivity of the findings, administrators may see potential political problems that have to be addressed in light of the findings. They need time to prepare to address these potential problems before information is released on a wide scale. Releasing the report in a proper fashion provides them with the opportunity and time needed to prepare themselves.

Providing summarized feedback to participants does not have to be an expensive undertaking. Also, it is possible in the course of data collection to sort out the participants who wish to receive some information on the final study from those who do not. For example, in doing survey research the evaluators might ask respondents to include a stamped self-addressed envelope together with their return questionnaire if they wish to receive a copy of the results. In this manner the evaluators can respond to the interest of the participants without unduly increasing the cost of disseminating the report.

SUMMARY

A report will be read when its contents are pertinent; when it is not unnecessarily detailed; when the style is readable and thought-provoking, but not tactless; and when it is distributed in a manner that respects the authority and sensitivities of the organization and its personnel. A well-written report will not necessarily be utilized, but unless it is written well, it has no possibility of having an impact on policy. Creating a climate conducive to effective utilization is the subject of the next chapter.

STUDY QUESTIONS

1. Examine the following means, standard deviations, and group sizes. Comment on the relative practical importance of each finding. (The actual importance will depend on program cost and on the alternate uses of the resources that would be used in the program.)

EVALUATION REPORT	COMPARISON GROUP			PROGRAM GROUP		
	MEAN	S.D.	N	MEAN	S.D.	N
A	51.2	10.6	30	58.7	11.5	30
B	51.2	10.6	10	58.7	11.5	10
C	51.2	22.5	100	58.7	20.5	100
D	5.1	4.0	5	8.6	4.2	5

Calculate a *t*-test for each evaluation. How does statistical significance compare to relative importance?

2.   Under what circumstances do results that fail to reach the level of statistical significance deserve serious attention? When should they be ignored? What is the danger involved in being too permissive toward Type II errors?

3.   Explain why the representativeness of a sample is more important than its size.

4.   Discuss the merits of the quantitative and qualitative style in reporting evaluation findings.

FURTHER READING

EWING, D. 1974. *Writing for results: In business, government, or the professions.* New York: Wiley-Interscience.

SMITH, N. L., ed. 1982. *Communication strategies in evaluation.* Beverly Hills, Calif.: Sage.

13

A Favorable
Evaluation Climate:
How to Encourage
Utilization

The first step in having findings utilized effectively was discussed in the last chapter—namely, writing and presenting a report in a manner that will get it read. In this chapter attention is given to fostering a climate that is conducive to having the report implemented aggressively. This subject is discussed under five headings: (1) encouraging the proper attitude among program staff and policy makers; (2) dealing with negative findings in a constructive fashion; (3) dealing with mixed results; (4) overcoming the obstacles to effective utilization of findings; and (5) improving evaluations.

ENCOURAGING PROPER
ATTITUDE IN STAFF
AND POLICY MAKERS

The realization that not every innovation or creative idea will be a success is the first element of a productive attitude that will contribute to the effective utilization of evaluation findings. Program directors and staff must feel free to innovate; but they must also recognize failure and learn from failures. Accepting the possibility of failure enables individuals to read an evaluation report with a relaxed and open mind rather than with a defensive attitude that prompts them to reject an entire report at the first sign of criticism. It also enables people to set aside less productive ideas and procedures when the evidence is not sufficiently strong to support a certain approach to a problem. Freedom to fail also enables staff to experiment with other approaches to achieve program goals.

The effects of the fear of failure in organizational development (OD) is illustrated in the study by Mirvis and Berg (1977). Organizational development is a relatively new and developing behavioral science that aims at assisting organizations in their efforts at self-improvement. Sometimes this involves introducing complex programs designed to change the structure of an organization, its social climate, or the day-to-day behaviors of specific individuals within the organization. Because of the complexity of the situations addressed by OD programs, mistakes are unavoidable. However, because of pressure to succeed, many failures in OD efforts are ignored or denied, or remain unrecognized. When failures are covered up, it becomes impossible to learn from them. Problems common to OD efforts in many oranizations are considered unique because they have not been publicly described. As a result, some prevailing OD practices go unquestioned and are not improved. Errors in nonroutine situations such as those faced frequently in complex and rapidly changing organizations are neither shameful nor completely avoidable, and patience and persistence may eventually be viewed as the only "right" answers in organizational development. The more fruitful approach is to measure competence not by skill in avoiding errors but by skill in detecting them and acting on the information openly. We must learn to reward those who recognize the risks involved in creating change, and yet still choose to risk, persist, and learn from their errors.

While an atmosphere that respects the freedom to fail is essential for the effective use of findings, it will often be beyond the power of evaluators to foster such an atmosphere where it does not already exist. The attitude of top administration will usually determine whether an organization or program is characterized by a desperate need to make a program work or whether there is a realistic attitude toward the possibility of failure. In healthy organizations administrators understand that innovation entails the possibility that even well-designed and implemented programs may fail. Where a healthy attitude toward failure already exists, evaluators can make the most of it and use every opportunity to underscore and publicize the enlightened attitude of the administration. Where the atmosphere is somewhat clouded and undetermined, evaluators may be able to foster a healthy attitude toward failure by requesting top administration to make some explicit statement to allay the anxiety of timid or insecure program personnel. In those organizations where the need of success is paramount and the fear of failure is rampant, evaluators will very likely be able to do little to bring about a change in attitude that will enable a research report to be received in a productive manner. However, evaluators will rarely be faced with this situation; organizations with a strong fear of failure will not be inclined to sponsor evaluation research in the first place.

Second, personnel should not be led to expect "good" or "bad" news; rather, they should anticipate suggestions for new ways of developing and improving existing programs. It is relatively rare that an existing program will be terminated or continued solely on the basis of an evaluation report. In fact, evaluators are pleased when their report produces any noticeable modification in policy and procedures. However, program personnel tend to be highly involved in their program and are occasionally unduly worried about the continuation of the program in the face of a bad report. As a result, they often look for a one-line answer to the question: Does the evaluation support our program or not? In other words: Does the evaluation bring good news or bad news? Evaluators will have a better opportunity of seeing their findings utilized effectively in those instances in which program personnel understand that every evaluation report brings some good news and some bad news, and that the more important question is: What concrete improvements are suggested by the evaluation report that are feasible for implementation? Evaluators must encourage program personnel to see evaluation as a way to help them improve and modify their program—not as a means to enshrine it or destroy it.

For example, in conducting the evaluation of the physical medicine and rehabilitation unit in a community hospital, the health care delivery team understood from the beginning that the rehabilitation unit was going to stay intact regardless of the outcome of the evaluation. However, they were interested in finding out just how much progress the stroke patients were making during their stay in the unit, and also whether those who had improved during their hospitalization continued to improve, or at least maintained their improvement, after they left the hospital. The results of the study showed that during their hospitalization the stroke patients improved their physical skills (walking, eating, dressing) more than their cognitive skills (speaking, remembering). This information focused the attention of the health care delivery team on improving their efforts to restore cognitive skills. The results also showed that the majority of patients who made progress during their hospitalization maintained their improvement after they left the hospital. The information gave the rehabilitation team a more exact picture of the percentage of those who did not maintain their improvement and enabled them to evaluate whether a follow-up program geared to these patients was needed.

The third way evaluators can promote healthy attitudes is to help program managers be aware of the connection between the findings of the report and their own specific needs. On some occasions program managers fail to see the full value and implications of the report. For example, the chairman of a large department of pastoral care at a religiously oriented hospital commissioned an evaluation of the department in the hope of learning what the patients, nurses, and physicians expected from chaplains and the extent to which patient and staff needs were being met by the chaplains (Carey, 1972). The immediate value of the research was to enable the chaplains to get a clear picture of the differences in expectation among patients of different religious denominations, ages, and marital situations. It also revealed that physicians and nurses had slightly different role expectations for the chaplains than did the patients. Furthermore, many chaplains were surprised to learn that the physicians and nurses placed a higher value on the assistance chaplains gave them in their work than the patients did on the more traditional role of the chaplains. This latter finding was largely due to the very active role the chaplains play at this hospital in assisting the staff to care for patients and family in a time of serious illness and death.

These secondary findings with respect to physicians and nurses turned out to be more valuable than originally expected when later that year representatives from Medicare and certain insurance companies refused to reimburse the hospital for the one dollar a day per patient that was set aside to pay for the care from chaplains. The representatives took the position that these expenses should be disallowed, and the cost of the chaplaincy should be underwritten by the religious organization sponsoring the hospital. They took this position because they assumed that the role of the chaplains was primarily to provide emotional support to a minority of patients who had religious needs. However, the president of the hospital was alert enough to see the application of the evaluation to defend the financing of the chaplaincy program out of patient room costs. The evaluation found that 87 percent of the nurses and 76 percent of the physicians said they found chaplains to be of great help to them personally in their work with patients. Because this was true, it could not be argued that chaplains were assigned primarily to serve a minority of the patient population. The hospital's viewpoint prevailed, largely on the force of the evaluation report. In this instance hospital administrators saw implications of the evaluation report not recognized by the director of the pastoral care program. The most effective evaluators will be alert to practical issues that may be peripheral to the original intent of the evaluation. If they fail to do so, the full implications may go unappreciated—even program managers cannot always be relied upon to see all the values of the evaluation findings.

A final aspect of engendering a proper attitude for a productive use of findings is to phrase conclusions as working hypotheses rather than as definitive generalizations. It would be very satisfying to be able to summarize a report with a clear, succinct statement that settles a question or solves a problem once and for all. When much time, effort, and money are spent on a report, one would like to have something solid to show for the results. However, those who look to an evaluation report to provide definitive conclusions are almost always disappointed.

One of the reasons why conclusions must be seen as working hypotheses is that local conditions do not allow for a generalization that can be applied to every situation. For example, Cronbach (1975) explains that those using personnel tests have long known of the danger in generalizing about how widely specific personnel tests can predict job success. This is true because test validity varies with the particular applicants taking the tests, the conditions of the specific job, and the criteria of job success. To select sales people on the basis of a test found valid in *other* firms is unacceptable in the absence of solid knowledge about how aptitudes interact with the dimensions along which sales jobs vary. For the same reasons, positive results obtained with a new educational program in one community warrant another community trying it; but instead of trusting that those results apply, the next community needs its own local evaluation. Of course, there comes a point when a generalization can be made; then the focus of evaluation can turn from documenting successful outcomes to documenting adequate implementation of the program.

Definitive conclusions are equally hard to arrive at, even in those instances in which a strict experimental design is used. Even with true experiments, program personnel should not be allowed to entertain unrealistically high hopes for a critical experiment. For example, Sloane and his colleagues (1975) conducted one of the best evaluations of psychotherapy ever designed. Groups who received behavior therapy and psychoanalytically oriented psychotherapy were compared with each other and with a control group. The results showed that the target symptoms of all three groups improved significantly, but the two treated groups improved equally well and significantly more than those on a waiting list. However, one year and two years after the initial assessment, all groups were found to be equally and significantly improved. These researchers tried to move beyond the basic question of whether psychotherapy is effective to the question of what type of therapy would be most productive with what kind of patients. Even with an excellent experimental design, the study fell short of giving definitive answers to this question. Nevertheless, the study is a model for future work. More important, it has provided new hypotheses for future investigations that will enable researchers to fine tune their research designs.

DEALING WITH NEGATIVE FINDINGS CONSTRUCTIVELY

Negative findings are disappointing. The temptation is to equate them with failure and to try to rationalize one's way out of the situation by saying, for example, that the program was never fully implemented or that a number of special and unusual cases in the sample affected the outcome. There are more productive ways of dealing with negative findings than rationalizing apparent failures. One such productive approach is to focus on the arguments for continuing a human service program—even if the findings are not supportive—if there are good reasons for continuing the program other than those originally proposed. For example, Waldo and Chiricos (1977) caused some consternation for policy makers who supported growth of a work-release program for prisoners. An analysis to determine whether members of work-release programs and those in a control group differed in recidivism showed that the programs provided no advantage on measures of rehabilitative success. In analyzing and discussing the results, the authors speculated that the work-release program had become an established policy in the absence of empirical justification because it saved money and because it appealed to the common sense of legislators and policy makers. The research, in fact, showed that the program led to no harm. The authors did not argue for the elimination of work-release programs, because such programs might be justified on humanitarian and economic grounds. However, they concluded that policy makers should not attempt to "sell" work release on the basis of its rehabilitative merits but should be prepared to discard it when better programs are demonstrated. The researchers concluded that in the long run legislators (and consequently correctional administrators) are most concerned with economic utility—even in those fields where "changing people" is the presumed mission of the organization.

Common-sense plausibility is another reason for continuing a program in the face of negative findings. When there is considerable agreement on the plausibility of a hypothesis, nonsupportive findings argue for an intensification of research rather than an abandonment of it. Ross (1975) argued in this manner after the evaluation of the Scandinavian laws on drinking and driving failed to support the hypothesis that drunken driving would be deterred by strict laws. According to the deterrence hypothesis, an interrupted time-series analysis of motor vehicles casualty data from Sweden and Norway should have showed change as a result of the initiation of the legal reforms in question. The expectations were not fulfilled. Ross concluded:

> Failure to find support for the deterrence hypothesis does not disprove the hypothesis, which has the merit of common-sense plausibility, but it indicates that the current widespread faith is without firm grounding. From the practical standpoint, it is suggested that the continuation of current policy in Sweden and Norway and its adoption elsewhere, should be more tentative and subjective to more scrutiny and critical evaluation than has been the case to date (p. 286).

Seligman and Hutton (1981) also provide an example of where common-sense plausibility and prior research overrode a no-effect finding. They report an evaluation of the use of a feedback meter to motivate consumers to conserve energy. While the evaluation did not provide any evidence that households with the feedback meter used less energy than households without one, the idea of providing feedback to homeowners through instrumentation is still being promoted. The most obvious reason is that earlier research showed that feedback was effective. Indeed, the prior research was an experimental field study that supported common sense and a theoretical understanding of conservation behaviors.

Another approach to dealing constructively with negative findings is to use no-difference findings to eliminate costly elements of a program. For example, consider the evaluation of presterilization interviewing that was discussed in the previous chapter (Carey, 1976). The policy of the hospital board of trustees was that mandatory interviewing by chaplains or by the local clergy was required before any sterilization operation at that hospital. An evaluation of presterilization interviewing was done by randomly assigning couples who applied for tubal ligations or vasectomies to an interview group and a control group. Results showed no difference in level of anxiety, guilt feelings, or marital adjustment between the interviewed group and the control group. In fact, in some cases hostility was generated in couples who either had a large number of children or who were near the end of their childbearing years and had made a very firm and well thought out decision not to have any more children. The chaplains themselves felt that mandatory interviewing in these circumstances was counterproductive. As a result of the evaluation, the hospital policy on mandatory interviewing was limited to those instances in which the person to be sterilized was under thirty years of age. This change in policy saved a good deal of time and money and at the same time preserved the purpose of the regulation, which was to discourage younger couples from making a hasty decision in regard to sterilization.

No-difference findings have also been used productively in evaluating methods of law enforcement and criminal correction. For example, one innovation after another has been tried, but crime and recidivism rates have not been affected. Glass (1976) comments:

> These no-difference findings, the bane of the experimental scientists, are grist for the evaluator's mill. If cutting reformatory sentences in half does not produce increased recidivism, then shorter sentences are 100 percent more cost-effective [all other things being equal]. . . . Doing as well as in the past but doing it more cheaply is a gain in value as surely as is doing better at a great cost (p. 11).

Using no-difference findings in this manner to eliminate costly aspects of a program must be done carefully. It is crucial that the evaluators demonstrate that they used a good research design, had adequate sampling procedures, and used valid measures of program success. Obviously, it is possible that no-difference findings can result from a poor design, from inadequate number in treatment and control groups, or from inadequate measurement. Nevertheless, with these precautions a negative finding can be transformed into a positive impact on the program.

Finally, even disappointing results can lead to worthwhile changes and improvement in a program, when evaluation efforts are closely linked to the decision-making behavior of program planners and administrators. For example, Smith (1975) evaluated the outcome effectiveness of a new clinical care program for seriously disturbed patients from traditional state hospitals. Outcomes were assessed in terms of social competence and economic cost to the patients and society. The results were very disappointing. Although the increased staff, the increased expenditure, and the community orientation of the new center represented a clear advance in the humanitarian care of the mentally ill, no evidence was found that this new approach substantially altered the social outcome of serious mental disorders or of the disability associated with them. Examination of other outcome studies did not uncover any strong evidence contrary to the negative findings of Smith's investigation. The result of Smith's study was that the center substantially shifted its resources from traditional management techniques (drugs, group psychotherapy) to rehabilitation techniques (teaching useful job skills, skills in daily living, homemaking). Staff were assigned to upgrade community placement facilities and to establish community rehabilitation centers at key locations throughout the region. These new programs were scheduled for another round of evaluation. Unless evaluation had been strongly linked to program planning and administration, as it was at this community mental health center, such shifts in emphasis might not have taken place.

Even in cases in which results are not negative, experience has proven that a strong link between program evaluators and policy makers is essential if results are to be utilized effectively. This link may take the form of liaison individuals or linking situations that translate the needs of policy makers into evaluation research, and evaluation research into practice. Liaison persons are the bridges that give research results maximum impact for nonresearchers. For example, in the field of agriculture, extension agents act as intermediaries between the experimental agriculture stations and farmers. The agricultural extension agents are among the earliest examples of liaison persons who translate research results to the ultimate users. To make effective applications of rapidly developing technology also requires sources of information for potential users. Public Technology, Inc., headquartered in Washington, D.C., transfers research knowledge to such users as urban government, agencies, and organizations who seek to use technology to solve urban problems.

DEALING WITH MIXED RESULTS

The problem of dealing with mixed results—that is, with some findings that support a program and others that do not—is different from dealing with negative findings, when analysis of the data overwhelmingly indicates that the program or treatment under investigation had no practical effects. When there are mixed results, proponents of a program focus attention on those findings that support the program, and those who would like to see the program terminated focus attention on the negative aspects of the evaluation report. The problem of dealing with mixed results is accentuated when politics are involved, when a large number of jobs hangs in the balance, or when many people are rallied to opposing causes. Four approaches for dealing with mixed results and an evaluation of the appropriateness of each are presented here.

Allow Others to Interpret Mixed Results

First, evaluators can report the findings and leave the interpretation to the readers—that is, to policy makers, administrators, or program staff. This can be accomplished by avoiding extended interpretation and discussion of the results in the written report and identifying the difficulties of interpretation only in the oral report, if at all.

This approach may be appropriate in those instances in which an evaluator had an explicit agreement with the sponsors of the research to keep the interpretation of findings to a minimum, and when the role of the evaluator was not to embrace the implementation of the report. However, as we have argued elsewhere, evaluators will ideally have a significant role in program planning. In addition, program personnel correctly expect evaluators to take a position in their analysis and discussion of the mixed results. Evaluators should seldom let the numbers "speak for themselves." Data will be interpreted. If the evaluator does not do the interpreting, others with less objectivity will. The failure of evaluators to take a position and make clear their recommendations suggests either incompetence or a lack of courage.

The Easy Way Out

Evaluators can choose the interpretation they feel is more favorable to the program and emphasize the results in the study that support the favorable interpretation. Where hypotheses in the study were not confirmed, or where the effect was weak, evaluators can tone down unfavorable results by (1) alleging that the outcome measures were unreliable, insensitive, or inappropriate; (2) attributing the lack of statistical significance to the sample;

(3) suggesting that implementation of the program was inadequate due to lack of time, complexity, lack of funds, and so forth; or (4) putting great weight on measures of consumer satisfaction, which is often surprisingly favorable even when more objective results are marginal.

Choosing the more favorable interpretation may be defended in some instances—for example, when the positive findings concern the more critical issues and there is hope that the program personnel will support a follow-up study to clarify the mixed results if they do not lose confidence in the evaluators. However, to espouse the more favorable position out of fear of being criticized by program sponsors, to avoid hurting feelings, or merely to obtain future evaluation funding is not defensible.

The Adversary Approach

Two other approaches to handling mixed results are more professionally responsible and in the long run more valuable, both to the evaluators and to program personnel. The evaluators can use an adversary approach to interpret the results. They can first argue one position and gather all the results in the data that support this interpretation, and they can then take the opposite viewpoint and present the data that support that view. The evaluators can then clearly state which side, if either, they think has the strongest case. If the evaluators cannot decide, they can point this out, along with their suggestions for follow-up research to clarify the ambiguity of the present study.

Another form of the adversary style of presentation would be to ask two independent researchers who had not been connected with the report to study the design and the data collected and then write a position paper supporting each side of the issue. These reviews by researchers representing different viewpoints could then be bound with interpretations of the independent experts and conclude with their own summary and position. The adversary approach has been suggested by some writers (for example, Braithwaite, Patton, and Fang, 1982; Datta, 1976a; Levine, et al., 1978); however, this approach is likely to be relatively expensive, making it unrealistic for the evaluator working in an institution or government office.

Use the Evaluation to Improve
the Program

Perhaps the best way to deal with mixed results is to emphasize that the purpose of the evaluation was not to terminate the program or provide performance appraisals of program managers but rather to help managers and staff improve the program or their conceptualization of the program. In keeping with this line of thought, Nagel (1983b) and Leviton and

Boruch (1983) suggest that utilization is often viewed simplistically because evaluators have not thought through what *might be* utilized from the study. Focusing only on a simple outcome study, utilization can only be a continuation of a good program or a discontinuation of one with weak outcomes. There are other uses of evaluations, however. By thinking through alternatives and basing recommendations on those, there are many degrees of utilization. When the use of evaluations is defined broadly and sufficient time is permitted for knowledge to be used, Leviton and Boruch (1983) find that evaluations are used constructively.

One type of evaluation that is almost guaranteed to produce mixed results, as well as hostility, is an employee work attitudes survey. Among other things, such surveys help managers identify and prioritize problems and monitor the effectiveness of changes and interventions introduced by management. Because there are few units in any organization that do not have some problems and shortcomings, it is not surprising that an employee attitude survey highlights some of these shortcomings for the management team. Some department managers may be hurt and perhaps resentful of what they view as unfair employee criticism. Indeed, they may also resent the evaluators who prepared the employee attitude survey report for having brought them what they consider to be "bad news."

To diffuse the possible negative attitudes on the part of managers and program staff, we have found a useful analogy from the medical field. Managers are asked to view evaluators in the same way physicians view laboratory and other support personnel in a hospital. Physicians have the responsibility for the welfare of their patients and for developing medical care plans to address their patients' illnesses. However, before developing a medical care plan, physicians will have their patients undergo a series of laboratory tests, urine analyses, X-rays, or other diagnostic procedures. In studying the results of these tests, physicians develop a better perspective on the strengths of their patients as well as the underlying causes of the symptoms experienced by patients.

After prescribing a medical regimen for their patients, physicians will once again have their patients undergo a similar series of medical tests to evaluate the effectiveness of their medical care plans. If the results of these posttests do not show that the patient improved, physicians do not interpret the disappointing laboratory findings as attacks on their competence, nor will they harbor resentment toward the laboratory personnel for the negative evaluation reports. Rather, they will conclude that the problem is difficult to diagnose and treat or does not respond quickly to treatment. After studying the implications of the reports, physicians develop alternative treatment plans to address the unrelieved symptoms of their patients. In like manner, managers and program staff can work with evaluators as partners in trying to understand the relative strengths and the weaknesses of their work units or programs. Using this approach, evaluators can be viewed as auxiliary members of the management team, rather than as adversaries.

OBSTACLES TO EFFECTIVE
UTILIZATION OF FINDINGS

In this section four of the more common obstacles to the implementation of findings are discussed. Evaluators will not always be in a position to remove these blocks to the effective use of their findings, but at least they can be aware of their existence and try to work around them where possible.

Lack of Respect of Some
Evaluators for Their Peers

The first block to effective utilization is the acrimonious battles that occasionally arise in the press between evaluation researchers over the interpretation and application of results to sensitive issues or programs. These battles, which sometimes originate from genuine and honest disagreements between researchers, can be carried to an inappropriate intensity and tend to reduce the credibility of all program evaluators. Public policy makers standing on the sideline tend to be dismayed by the accusations of lack of integrity and competence leveled against researchers by members of their own peer group. As a result, administrators and legislators may question the validity of all evaluation research.

Even when differences of opinion between professionals are expressed with mutual respect, it can result in a loss of confidence among those outside a given profession. For example, when physicians or medical experts give a patient conflicting advice regarding the diagnosis or treatment of a medical problem, the patient begins to wonder whether the doctors really know what they are doing. In reality, some problems are very complicated, and medical science does not have all the answers. One cannot expect all physicians to agree on the answers to certain questions. However, physicians profoundly damage respect toward the medical profession when they express their disagreement with another physician's opinion in such a way as to question the physician's competence or integrity. Similarly, when a court reverses the opinion of a lower court, the higher court does not impugn the motivation or competence of the lower court. There is room for legitimate differences in interpretations.

An example of legitimate differences of opinion that have resulted in acrimonious debate between evaluation researchers was the running battle between Pettigrew and Green, on the one hand, and Coleman, on the other, over Coleman's "white flight" thesis and the interpretation of his research on school desegregation in large cities. The highly publicized study

Equality of Educational Opportunity (Coleman et al., 1966), popularly called "The Coleman Report," was in essence a favorable evaluation of court-ordered integration and the busing of students to integrate schools. However, some years later Coleman changed his opinion and wrote:

> In school integration there has been a surprising absence of interest on the part of those formulating and implementing the policy about the overall impact—as opposed to the immediately observable effect—of that policy. The results of these analyses show that the indirect consequences are far from negligible and can sharply reduce or perhaps even in the longer run reverse the intended effect of that policy. . . . The extremely strong reaction of individual whites in moving their children out of a large district engaged in rapid desegregation suggests that in the long run the policies that have been pursued will defeat the purpose of increasing overall contact among races in schools (Coleman, 1976, p. 321).

Pettigrew and Green engaged Coleman in an extended debate over the value of court-ordered school integration. A brief sample of Coleman's remarks about Green and Pettigrew contends that

> . . . on certain questions, there appears to be a kind of conspiracy of silence, and then a rush to the attack when anyone dares to break the silence. I have the impression that if Professors Green and Pettigrew saw the fires in the sky during the riots of 1967, they would have attributed them to an extraordinary display of northern lights. I believe that it does no one any good in the long run for us to blind ourselves to reality, because it is reality, not our fond hopes about it, which measures the effectiveness of government actions (Pettigrew and Green, 1977, p. 407).

Pettigrew and Green accused Coleman of incompetence and ignorance of methodological problems:

> Unfortunately Coleman does not address an array of problems that have been raised about his research. . . .
>
> (a) His research on essentially a demographic problem has been conducted in a demographic vacuum. . . .
> (b) His future projections are inflated by unrealistic assumptions. . . .
> (c) An ecological fallacy is involved in his assertions of individual motivation ("white flight") from gross district-wide data (Pettigrew and Green, 1977, p. 429).

The acrimony between Coleman and social science peers has continued. Commenting on analysis released by Coleman, Hoffer, and Kilgore through the National Opinion Research Center in 1981, Goldberger (1981) concluded: "Upon examination and reflection, Coleman's 'Public and Private Schools' cannot be viewed as a competent scientific report, nor as a responsible effort at policy analysis." The credibility of social science research is hardly enhanced by such exchanges. Need we be surprised if program managers and community representatives hesitate to accept our findings when authorities hold each other in such low repute?

The Weight of Nonempirical Influences

The second obstacle to the effective utilization of findings is the weight of other influences and pressures that compete with the impact of the information in an evaluation report. At times it may seem to evaluators that decision makers are not disposed to give their attention to a report and do not wish to reexamine the policy decisions in view of new information received. However, decision makers may receive a report with an open mind—even with eagerness—and yet find themselves unable to act because they are constrained by economic realities and political pressures.

Bigelow and Ciralo (1975) studied the question of what value there was in collecting information and presenting it to human service administrators. Would information improve their decisions? They studied this question in a large community health center which had thirty management and supervisory personnel. They used three different strategies to try to learn how management was using evaluation feedback. First, they conducted interviews with managers using the Information Use and Decision-Making Questionnaire. Second, they interviewed supervisors when a substantial program modification had been made within their jurisdiction. Third, they introduced a body of data bearing on a program management issue during a meeting of supervisors and than tried to trace the effects over a two-week period. They concluded that managers were disposed to use information, that it affected their intentions to modify programs, and that it resulted in further exploration of a particular management question. The study did not demonstrate that the information resulted in improved performance for the organization. Nevertheless, in the specific instances in which information had, in fact, been introduced, the relative impact of information was appreciable. However, the conclusion that information does have an impact on management had to be qualified by the Heisenberg principle: The very decision making may have resulted in part from participation in the investigation rather than from the input of the feedback data.

Another instance of how other influences and pressures can have a great influence on decision makers is in the issue of guaranteed income as a form of welfare reform (Haveman and Watts, 1976). From the awarding of the original grant for this welfare experiment to submission of the final report in late 1973, a total of six and one-half years elapsed. The four years of the operating phase of the experiment were sandwiched between fourteen months of planning and design and sixteen months of data analyses. The experiment cost about $8 million, about one-third of which went for payments to participating families. In spite of this massive effort, there has been no national movement to modify the present income tax regulation to accommodate a guaranteed income provision. Frankly, no one should have expected a guaranteed income program to develop from the experiment. Public sentiment would have been so overwhelmingly opposed to the idea that legislators would have voted against such a change in the law, even if they were convinced of the merits of the innovation. However, even though public policy has not been changed, the evaluation did alter future debate and discussion of the issue of guaranteed income. Although most economists and politicians would have predicted that even the limited form of guaranteed income used in the study would result in massive malingering and a loss of motivation to work, these theories were not supported. As a result, the loss-of-work-incentives argument was eliminated from the discussion of income maintenance policy. Thus although the evaluation did not change income tax law, it did change the form of the debate.

Preexisting Polarization of Interested Parties

A third block to the effective utilization of findings occurs when opposing factions have been strongly polarized before an evaluation takes place. Recommendations fall on deaf ears when administrators and public representatives have already chosen their position; regardless of the results of an evaluation. As a consequence, they miss important nuances in the findings. A clear example of the effect of polarization can be seen in the interpretations of the evaluation research conducted by Zimring (1975) on the impact of the Federal Gun Control Act of 1968. Gun control legislation is a highly emotional issue. It was unlikely from the beginning that any evaluation would materially change the opinions of many of those aligned on both sides of the issue. Zimring comments on this at the beginning of his report.

> The study will be of little use to the most fervent friends and foes of gun control legislation. It provides data they do not need. Each group uses the Act's presumed failure to confirm views already strongly held. Enthusiasts for strict federal controls see the failure of the law as proof that stricter laws are needed, while opponents see it as evidence that no controls will work. The picture that emerges from available data is more equivocal. There is evidence that the approach adopted by the Act can aid state efforts at strict firearms control, although other resources necessary to achieve this end have never been provided by Congress. There is also reason to believe that the potential impact of the Act is quite limited when measured against the problems it sought to alleviate (p. 133).

Another emotional issue on which some have already decided their position prior to research is the abortion issue. On the one hand, proabortionists place the freedom of the mother above all other values and will not modify this position regardless of the demonstration of harmful effects on society caused by the ready availability of abortion. On the other hand, those who belong to the so-called Right to Life movement place the life of an unborn fetus above all other values and are not about to change this position, even though research shows the harmful effects of back-alley abortions.

The abortion issue is also an example of an issue where other influences and pressures influence decision makers. It is hard for legislators to objectively weigh the evidence of the studies when they are bombarded by letters and public protests on both sides of the issue. In fact, legislators are doing the correct thing in not allowing themselves to be guided merely by the results of sociological or psychological investigations. Policy makers must be alert to the input from the legal profession, philosophers, and medical experts, as well as input from social science studies.

Costs May Exceed Benefits

A final block to the effective utilization of findings is obvious, but worth singling out because of its importance—namely, the cost of programs. Effective evaluators will not ignore cost-benefit and cost-effectiveness considerations. If the value of a program is measured in terms of its benefits per unit of cost, then it is inadequate for evaluators to evaluate programs by measuring either the benefits or the costs alone. Rather, both the benefits and costs must be considered.

Carnoy's (1975) evaluation of the cost effectiveness of educational television (ETV) is an exemplary blend of careful research into both cost and benefits. He concluded that the performance of pupils is not significantly better with ETV than in situations in which teachers are retrained to use more effective curricula. At the same time, the cost of ETV schooling is much higher per pupil than classroom teacher schooling, because teacher retraining costs are usually only a small fraction of the cost of operating a traditional school system.

However, ETV does have the advantage of comparatively rapid implementation. Carnoy showed that ETV cannot be promoted on the grounds that it produces good outcomes because student achievement in ETV settings—although high—is not consistently better than the achievement levels of students in programs that are less expensive. Policy makers, when faced with careful evaluations such as Carnoy presented, can hardly push hard for ETV, even though it can be demonstrated that it has had beneficial results. This is especially true in periods of tight budgets.

METAEVALUATION

Another way to increase the impact of evaluation is to improve the evaluations themselves. Evaluators will be more likely to see their studies effectively utilized when they demonstrate that their work can stand the test of careful analysis and that they themselves are open to growth through constructive criticism. These goals can be realized in part by the practice of evaluating evaluations, or what has been termed metaevaluation.

Various authors have given slightly different meanings to the term *metaevaluation* and have suggested different ways to carry it out. For example, Stufflebeam (1978) distinguishes formative metevaluation from summative metaevaluation. Formative metaevaluation is conducted before an evaluation takes place and is intended as a guide to help evaluators effectively carry out their project by improving the evaluation plan. For example, Stufflebeam described an ambitious formative metaevaluation by a National Institute of Education (NIE) project designed to develop a system for NIE's use in evaluating research and development institutions. The NIE project had two teams prepare alternative evaluation plans and then had a third team evaluate the two plans. Summative metaevaluations are studies of the merits of a completed evaluation. Both formative and summative metaevaluations assess the extent to which an evaluation is technically adequate, useful in guiding decisions, ethical in dealing with people in organizations, and practical in the use of resources. Stufflebeam suggests thirty-four standards as dependent variables for judging the merit of completed evaluations and presents sixty-eight guidelines as procedural suggestions to help evaluators meet the standards. His work provides a detailed outline for those who wish to conduct a metevaluation of their own work or someone else's work.

Cook and Gruder (1978) use the term *metaevaluation* in a slightly different sense than Stufflebeam. They use the term to refer only to the evaluation of empirical evaluations—that is, studies in which data are being, or have been, collected. They exclude from consideration the evaluation of proposed evaluation plans, an activity that Stufflebeam called formative metaevaluation.

Cook and Gruder discuss seven different models of metaevaluation: four that are subsequent to the initial evaluation and three that are simultaneous with it. The three simultaneous models are more complicated and costly, and they are beyond the scope of the present discussion. However, the four models of metaevaluation that can be used subsequent to the primary evaluation are less costly, more practical, and within the consideration of most evaluators. An overview of these four models is presented below.

Model 1

Model 1 is an essay review of an evaluation report. An essay review would include both published reviews and unpublished documents written by in-house or outside consultants at interim stages before the final report is published.

Published reviews would usually concentrate on technical issues such as sampling, measurement, and data analysis. They are particularly useful if, without questioning the data, they bring fresh interpretations to bear on the study. Pettigrew et al. (1973) did this, in part, when they observed that Armor (1972) judged busing a "failure" because his criterion for success was that integration should reduce racial gaps in achievement. Instead, they demonstrated that the absolute achievement levels of blacks had increased, irrespective of what happened to whites. In this approach the data and analyses are accepted as valid, and the issue is one of interpreting the findings. Obviously, only major evaluation studies would receive this scrutiny.

Another type of essay review occurs when a prepublication draft is sent to people with technical and substantive skills and to those likely to oppose the major conclusions of a report. People with differing points of view often interpret phrasing differently than the authors of a report intended. Also, they can provide different, valid ways to interpret findings. Their feedback can be used to modify the final report so that discussion of the report is focused on the implications of the results, rather than on secondary or side issues.

Model 2

The second model of metaevaluation is a review of literature about a specific program. For example, there have been multiple evaluations of prison rehabilitation, psychotherapy, and educational programs. Cook and Gruder suggest that the second model of metaevaluation is best used at an early date to identify approaches to program evaluation that are not fruitful. However, the evaluators can also use this model at the conclusion of their own evaluations to demonstrate the extent to which the major conclusions are supported by other similar evaluations and also to indicate the direction that future research should take.

Multiple evaluations permit more valid and credible research conclusions, especially where clear patterns of convergence emerge. However, it is probably more common that inconsistencies will be found among various evaluations. In these instances no explicit rules exist for combining the results of relevant studies. Light and Smith (1971) have severely criticized the most common method of resolving inconsistencies among different research. They note that most reviewers simply take a vote among the various reports. The "taking a vote" method involves gathering all the studies that have data on a dependent variable and specific independent variable of interest. Three possible outcomes are defined. The relationship between the independent variable and the dependent variable is classified as either significantly positive, significantly negative, or neither—that is, as having no significant relationship in either direction. The number of studies that fall into each of these three categories is then simply tallied, and the category with the most votes is declared the winner and is treated as descriptive of that body of research.

Light and Smith propose *cluster sampling* as an alternative approach to the taking-a-vote method. Clusters are not random samples but rather are subgroups of people or settings. A set of studies investigating a given problem may contain a number of different clusters, not all of which will be present in each study. In the taking-a-vote method, each complete study is the unit of analysis. In cluster sampling the cluster becomes the unit of analysis. Suppose, for example, that the relationship between nursing turnover and a new way of organizing nursing services is evaluated, and that there are five studies based on thirteen hospitals. Suppose that these hospitals can be divided into community hospitals, private teaching hospitals, university hospitals, and VA hospitals. The clusters in this example would be the types of hospitals. In essence, Light and Smith tell us that the program might have different impacts depending on the setting. Thus, before combining the five evaluations of the new style of organization, the possibility of effects due to type of hospital, geographical area, surrounding community, and so forth ought to be explored. If these factors do have an influence on the way the innovative program affects turnover, the metaevaluation will expand our understanding of nursing turnover and programs to reduce it. If these factors are not important, then a positive finding in each of the clusters suggests that the innovation deserves to be implemented widely. Clearly, this approach can be applied to any type of evaluation when there are multiple evaluations of the same innovation carried out in different settings or with groups that differ demographically.

Model 3

The third model of metaevaluation is an empirical reevaluation of a program evaluation; this is perhaps the best-known approach to metaevaluation. The third model consists of the reanalysis of another evaluator's data to test published conclusions or to examine new questions. The reanalysis of the Coleman report by Mosteller and Moynihan (1972) and that of the "Sesame Street" studies by Cook and others (1975) are examples of the third model of metaevaluation. Empirical reevaluation is usually better than an essay review because the former includes the reanalysis of raw data. However, there are also some drawbacks. Empirical reevaluation is seldom timely for the needs of decision makers. Also, it can be misleading if subsequent analyses are conducted on special samples. Nevertheless, evaluators can often lend a great deal of credibility to their report by making the data available to interested researchers for this type of reanalysis.

Model 4

The fourth model of metaevaluation suggested by Cook and Gruder is an empirical reevaluation of multiple data sets about the same program. This model of metaevaluation has been termed meta-analysis by other authors because it consists in the integration of research through statistical analysis of the analyses of several studies. The fourth model is appropriately used in an area that has been heavily researched and where evaluation findings are mixed and controversial. For example, Smith and Glass (1977) conducted a meta-analysis of psychotherapy outcome studies. They coded and statistically integrated the results of nearly four hundred controlled evaluations of psychotherapy. They integrated the magnitude of therapy effects in the various studies by defining the "effect size" as the *mean difference between the treated and control subjects divided by the standard deviation of the control group*. For example, an effect size of +1 indicates that persons at the mean of the control group would be expected to rise to a level equivalent to the eighty-fourth percentile of the control group if they were in the program evaluated. Smith and Glass's findings provide strong evidence of improved adjustment through psychotherapy. On the average, they found that the typical therapy client is better off than 75 percent of untreated individuals. However, they detected only negligible differences in the effects produced by different types of therapy. They concluded that unconditional judgments of the superiority of one or another type of psychotherapy are unjustified. One obvious weakness in this approach is that their sample of nearly four hundred evaluations may not be a representative sample of all the psychotherapy evaluations conducted. It is well known that evaluations with negative findings have a harder time finding a place in journals than do evaluations with positive findings. It is also possible that psychotherapy provided during evaluations is better than psychotherapy provided routinely, when no review or evaluation is being conducted. Therefore, the force of the conclusions might not apply to all psychotherapy.

Light (1983) suggests that meta-analyses will make important contributions to improving evaluation methodology. Wortman (1983) agrees, but he points out that the methodology of meta-analysis itself is still in the developmental stage. In summary, metaevaluation will increase the probability of findings being utilized effectively, because metaevaluation research is a means of improving the quality of evaluation methodology and indirectly testing whether program evaluation delivers what it promises—namely, the accurate representation of the need for a program, a description of the degree to which a program was actualized, and a documentation of the outcomes and the efficiency of various programs.

SUMMARY

Evaluators have become increasingly concerned about the utilization of the information that they provide to organizations and stakeholder groups. When presenting reports, one can improve the chances of information being utilized by encouraging a healthy attitude toward evaluation and developing ways of handling negative and mixed evaluations that will lead to program improvements. The desire to have evaluations lead to program improvement is more likely to be achieved when evaluators are routinely involved with the program in the planning stage (see Chapter 2), all the way through discussions of reactions to completed evaluations, than when evaluators are seen only as technicians who supply data when requested to do so.

STUDY QUESTIONS

1. Discuss some of the negative attitudes that can block the effective utilization of well-conducted evaluations.
2. Should an evaluator argue for the termination of an existing program when an evaluation is predominantly negative? Describe the conditions under which one would so argue, and the conditions under which one would advocate further study.
3. Give an example of how political or economic factors might block the effective utilization of an evaluation report.
4. Explain some of the different meanings that the term *metaevaluation* can have, and give an example of each. What is the value of metaevaluation?

FURTHER READING

EGAN, G., and COWAN, M. A. 1979. *People in systems: A model for development in the human-service professions and education.* Monterey, Calif.: Brooks/Cole.

HAKEL, M. D.; SORCHER, M.; BEER, M.; and MOSES, J. L. 1980. *Making it happen: Designing research with implementation in mind.* Beverly Hills, Calif.: Sage.

HAWKINS, J. D.; ROFFMAN, R. A.; and OSBORNE, P. 1978. Decision makers' judgments: The influence of role, evaluative criteria, and information access. *Evaluation Quarterly* 2: 435–54.

PATTON, M. Q. 1978. *Utilization-focused evaluation.* Beverly Hills, Calif.: Sage.

ZALTMAN, G., and DUNCAN, R. 1977. *Strategies for planned change.* New York: Wiley-Interscience.

Epilogue

This text has sought primarily to provide the groundwork for the development of the technical skills necessary to conduct program evaluations in human services and business settings. The organization of the book reflects the author's view of the most useful approaches to conducting such research. A brief reexamination of the flow chart in Part 1 can give the reader a quick review of the main points of the material covered. The flow chart can also help evaluators explain to staff the services evaluators can provide.

Perhaps equally as important as technical skills are the evaluator's attitudes and orientation toward the role of program evaluator. While these are referred to throughout this book, it may be of help to draw these themes together in this section.

Humility won't hurt. Evaluators work in service settings. These settings are not designed to facilitate the conducting of research. Because of this fact, the evaluator can expect to be seen as filling a marginal role in the service delivery setting. Because the evaluator is always working on someone else's turf, arrogance will effectively block the exercise of even superb technical skills.

Impatience may lead to disappointment. Program and facility administrators have many constituencies, all expecting attention. Program evaluation is only one source of information on which decisions and plans are based. Financial concerns, community pressures, political realities, bureaucratic inertia, and so forth are all powerful influences on program planners and administrators. Evaluators who have patience are less likely to feel ignored and unloved when their recommendations do not receive immediate attention.

Recognize the importance of the evaluator's perspective.   Evaluators have some skills that may be lacking in human service settings. Service staffs focus on individuals and often do not picture the overall program. Evaluators have a social orientation that can provide the staff with a new viewpoint. Administrators, on the other hand, do seek an overall perspective. However, administrators have a far better grasp of financial and other tangible matters than of social variables affecting the patient/client/student/trainee population served. Evaluators can provide information to administrators on social variables that are usually unavailable to administrators.

Focus on practical questions.   People working in human service organizations are seldom concerned about matters of only theoretical interest. Evaluators can work most effectively when they are oriented toward practical questions about the program being studied. Try not to forget that seeking to initiate and sustain change in people's lives is hard work. Faced with pressing human needs and with criticism from governmental bodies and insurance companies for excessive costs and alleged inefficiencies, agency staff and management desire practical assistance.

Work on feasible issues.   If an evaluation is not feasible, do not attempt it. Do not waste your time and that of the staff. However, although it may not be feasible to work on a particular issue, it might be feasible to work on a less ambitious question. For example, if outcomes cannot be handled, it may be possible to develop a procedure to monitor the delivery of service.

Avoid data addiction.   It is tempting to seek to gather a great amount of information about the program or about those served by the program. It might be nice to know everything possible about the program, but there are two compelling reasons to limit the amount of data sought to that which is essential. First, asking for too much information will increase the percentage of potential respondents who will refuse to cooperate and consequently will provide no information. Second, evaluators will often find themselves under too much time pressure to analyze all the data gathered. Thus, the effort of the cooperative respondents will be wasted. If the information is not essential to the evaluation, do not try to gather it.

Evaluators are information channels.   There are many things that can get in the way when new information is presented to potential users. Social science jargon and esoteric analyses can reduce the flow of information to those not acquainted with the jargon or schooled in statistics. Readers and listeners will be bored with a presentation that seems planned to display the evaluator's knowledge and technical skills. Save that for meetings of professional societies. To be effective, presentations to staff should be relevant to the program, and recommendations should be practicable.

Encourage an evaluation orientation. Ideally, evaluation encourages honest relations among staff, clients, administrators, and program sponsors. These groups often act as though all failures could have been avoided. Although all failures cannot be avoided, people can learn from failures. The essence of the concept of the experimenting society is the recognition of the inevitability of failure. Instead of hiding failures or condemning them, help staff and administrators to treat honest attempts as experiments and to learn from failures as well as successes.

Adopt a self-evaluation orientation to your own work. When evaluation results and recommendations seem to be ignored, evaluators will benefit by asking themselves: Was my presentation clear? Did I address the right questions? Were my answers right? At times the honest answer to these questions will be "No." Evaluators are like service staff people in some ways; neither can always avoid failures, and both can learn from their errors.

References

ABELSON, P. H. 1977. Commission on federal paperwork. *Science* 197: 1237.

ABT, C. C. 1977. Applying cost/benefit paradigms to social program evaluations. Paper presented at the meeting of the Evaluation Research Society, October, Washington, D.C.

ADLER, N. E., and STONE, G. C. 1979. Social science perspectives on the health system. In *Health psychology: A handbook*, ed. G. C. Stone, F. Cohen, and N. E. Adler. San Francisco: Jossey-Bass.

ALBRIGHT, J. 1982. Citizen evaluation from the inside. Paper presented at meeting of the Evaluation Research Society, October, Baltimore.

ALLPORT, G. W. 1954. *The nature of prejudice*. Reading, Mass.: Addison-Wesley.

AMERICAN PSYCHOLOGICAL ASSOCIATION. 1982. *Ethical principles in the conduct of research with human participants*. Washington, D.C.: Author.

ANASTASI, A. 1982. *Psychological testing*. 5th ed. New York: Macmillan.

ANDERSON, J. F., and BERDIE, D. R. 1975. Effects on response rate of formal and informal questionnaire follow-up techniques. *Journal of Applied Psychology* 60: 225–57.

ARMOR, D. J. 1972. The evidence on busing. *The Public Interest* 28: 90–126.

ATTKISSON, C. C.; HARGREAVES, W. A.; HOROWITZ, M. J.; and SORENSEN, J. E., eds. 1978. *Evaluation of human service programs*. New York: Academic Press.

BALL, R. M. 1978. National health insurance: Comments on selected issues. *Science* 200: 864–73.

BALL, S., and BOGARTZ, G. A. 1970. *The first year of Sesame Street*. Princeton, N.J.: Educational Testing Service.

BARBOUR, G. P., and WOLFSON, S. M. 1973. Productivity measurement in police crime control. *Public Management* 55: 16, 18, 19.

BECKER, H.; HARRELL, W.; and KIRKHART, K. 1982. Evaluators in grey flannel suits: Implications of changes in roles and evaluation priorities for training evaluators. Paper presented at the meeting of the American Psychological Association, August, Washington, D.C.

BERK, R. A. 1977. Discretionary methodology decisions in applied research. *Sociological Methods and Research* 5: 317–34.

BERK, R. A., and ROSSI, P. H. 1976. Doing good or worse: Evaluation research politically re-examined. *Social Problems,* February, pp. 337–49.

BERMAN, J. J. 1978. An experiment in parole supervision. *Evaluation Quarterly* 2: 71–90.

BIGELOW, D. A., and CIARLO, J. A. 1975. The impact of therapeutic effectiveness data on community health center management: The systems evaluation project. *Community Mental Health Journal* 11: 64–73.

BINNER, P. R. 1977. Outcome measures and cost analysis. In *Emerging developments in mental health evaluation,* ed. W. Neigher, R. Hammer, and G. Landsberg. New York: Argold Press.

BLOM, B., and MOORE, M. 1979. Evaluating mental health services through patient care audits. In *Impacts of program evaluation on mental health care,* ed. E. J. Posavac, Boulder, Colo.: Westview Press.

Blue Shield News. 1977. Routine payment to be discontinued for the following procedures. June, p. 3.

BOK, S. 1974. The ethics of giving placebos. *Scientific American,* 231(5), 17–23.

BORUCH, R. F. 1975. On common contentions about randomized field experiments. In *Experimental testing of public policy,* ed. R. F. Boruch and H. W. Riecken. Boulder, Colo.: Westview Press.

BORUCH, R. F., and CORDRAY, D. S. 1982. *An appraisal of educational program evaluations: Federal, state, and local agencies.* New York: Cambridge University Press.

BORUCH, R. F.; CORDRAY, D. S.; PION, G. M.; and LEVITON, L. C.1983. Recommendations to Congress and their rationale. *Evaluation Review* 7: 5–35.

BORUCH, R. F., and GOMEZ, H. 1977. Sensitivity, bias, and theory in impact evaluations. *Professional Psychology* 8: 411–34.

BORUCH, R. F., and RINDSKOPF, D. 1977. On randomized experiments, approximations to experiments, and data analysis. In *Evaluation research methods,* ed. L. Rutman. Beverly Hills, Calif.: Sage.

BRAITHWAITE, R. L.; PATTON, J. M.; and FANG, W. L. 1982. Evaluating a human service program: Employing the judicial evaluation model. *Evaluation and Program Planning* 5: 81–89.

BROTMAN, B. 1983. 'Workfare': What state terms success others call boondoggle. *Chicago Tribune,* January 2, sec. 3, pp. 1, 4.

BROWN, F. G. 1976. *Principles of educational and psychological testing.* New York: Holt, Rinehart and Winston.

BRYK, A. S., ed. 1983. *Stakeholderbased evaluation.* San Francisco, Calif.: Jossey-Bass.

BUNDA, M. A. 1983. Alternative ethics reflected in education and evaluation. *Evaluation News* 4 (1): 57–58.

BURNS, M. L. 1977. The effects of feedback and commitment to change on the behavior of elementary school principals. *Journal of Applied Behavioral Science* 13: 159–66.

BURTLE, V., ed. 1979. *Women who drink.* Springfield, Ill.: Charles C Thomas.

CAIDIN, M. 1960. *Let's go flying!* New York: Dutton.

CAMPBELL, D. T. 1969. Reforms as experiments. *American Psychologist* 24: 409–29.

CAMPBELL, D. T. 1983. The problem of being scientific in program evaluation. Paper presented at the meeting of the Evaluation Research Society, October, Chicago.

CAMPBELL, D. T.; BORUCH, R. F.; SCHWARTZ, R. D.; and STEINBERG, J. 1977. Confidentiality-preserving modes of access to files and interfile exchange for useful statistical analysis. *Evaluation Quarterly* 1: 269–300.

CAMPBELL, D. T., and ERLEBACHER, A. 1970. How regression artifacts in quasi-experimental evaluations can mistakenly make compensatory education look harmful. In *Compensatory education: A national debate,* ed. J. Hellmuth, pp. 185–210. Vol. 3 of *Disadvantaged child.* New York: Brunner-Mazel.

CAMPBELL, D. T., and STANLEY, J. C. 1963. *Experimental and quasi-experimental designs for research.* Chicago: Rand-McNally.

CAPORASO, J. A. 1973. Quasi-experimental approaches to social science: Perspectives and problems. In *Quasi-experimental approaches: Testing theory and evaluating policy,* ed. J. A. Caporaso and L. L. Roos. Evanston, Ill.: Northwestern University Press.

CAPPER, J. 1983. Marketing evaluation skills and services. *Evaluation News* 4 (2): 57–60.

CAREY, R. G. 1972. *Hospital chaplains: Who needs them?* St. Louis, Mo.: Catholic Hospital Association.

CAREY, R. G. 1974. Emotional adjustment in terminal patients. *Journal of Counseling Psychology* 21: 433–39.

CAREY, R. G. 1976. Presterilization interviewing: An evaluation. *Journal of Counseling Psychology* 23: 492–94.

CAREY, R. G. 1979. Evaluation of a primary nursing unit. *American Journal of Nursing* 79: 1253–55.

CAREY, R. G. 1979. Selecting hospital leaders through shared decision making. *Hospital Progress,* November, pp. 53-55.

CAREY, R. G., and POSAVAC, E. J. 1977a. *Cancer care center: An evaluation of support to patients and relatives.* Park Ridge, Ill.: Lutheran General Hospital.

CAREY, R. G., and POSAVAC, E. J. 1977b. *Evaluation of the Medical Ecology Program.* Park Ridge, Ill.: Lutheran General Hospital.

CAREY, R. G., and POSAVAC, E. J. 1978. Program evaluation of a physical medicine and rehabilitation unit: A new approach. *Archives of Physical Medicine and Rehabilitation* 59: 330–37.

CAREY, R. G., and POSAVAC, E. J. 1979. Holistic care in a cancer care center. *Nursing Research,* 28: 213–16.

CARNOY, M. 1975. The economic costs and returns to educational television. *Economic Development and Cultural Change* 25: 207–48.

CARTER, D. E., and NEWMAN, F. L. 1976. *A client-oriented system of mental health delivery and program management.* Rockville, Md.: National Institute of Mental Health.

CATHOLIC HOSPITAL ASSOCIATION STUDY COMMITTEE. 1977. *Report of the 1977 CHA Study Committee.* St. Louis, Mo.: Catholic Hospital Association.

CENTRA, J. A. 1977. Plusses and minuses for faculty development. *Change* 9(12): 47, 48, 64.

CHAPMAN, C., and RISLEY, T. R. 1974. Anti-litter procedures in an urban high-density area. *Journal of Applied Behavioral Analysis* 7: 377–83.

CHAPMAN, L. J., and CHAPMAN, J. P. 1967. Genesis of popular but erroneous psychodiagnostic signs. *Journal of Abnormal Psychology* 72: 193–204.

CHAPMAN, L. J., and CHAPMAN, J. P. 1969. Illusory correlation as an obstacle to the use of valid psychodiagnostic signs. *Journal of Abnormal Psychology* 74: 271–80.

CHAPMAN, R. L. 1976. *The design of management information systems for mental health organizations: A primer.* Rockville, Md.: National Institute of Mental Health.

CHELIMSKY, E. 1978. Differing perspectives of evaluation. In *New Directions for Program Evaluations,* no. 2, ed. C. C. Rentz and B. R. Rentz. San Francisco: Jossey-Bass.

Chicago Tribune. 1978. Postal Service may dump billion-dollar parcel plan. June 14, sec. 4, p. 1.

CICARELLI, V. G. 1970. The relevance of the regression artifact problem to the Westinghouse-Ohio University evaluation of Head Start: A reply to Campbell and Erlebacher. In *Compensatory education: A national debate*, ed. J. Hellmuth, pp. 211–16. Vol. 3 of *Disadvantaged child*. New York: Brunner-Mazel.

CICARELLI, V. G.; COOPER, W. H.; and GRANGER, R. L. 1969. *The Impact of Head Start: An evaluation of the effects of Head Start on children's cognitive and affective development.* Westinghouse Learning Corporation, OEO Contract No. B89-4536.

COHEN, R. 1982. To be or not to be: Control and balancing of Type I and Type II errors. *Evaluation and Program Planning* 5: 247–53.

COLEMAN, J. S. 1976. Recent trends in school integration. In *Evaluation studies research annual*, vol. 1, ed. G. V Glass. Beverly Hills, Calif.: Sage.

COLEMAN, J. S.; CAMPBELL, E. Q.; HOBSON, C. J.; McPARTLAND, J.; MOOD, A. M.; WEINFELD, F. D.; and YORK, R. L. 1966. *Equality of educational opportunity.* Washington, D.C.: Government Printing Office.

COLEMAN, J. S.; HOFFER, T.; and KILGORE, S. 1981. *Public and private schools.* Chicago: National Opinion Research Center.

Community Mental Health Plan. 1977. Spoon River, Ill.: Spoon River Community Mental Health Center.

COOK, T. D.; APPLETON, H.; CONNOR, R. F.; SHAFFER, A.; TAMKIN, G.; and WEBER, S. J. 1975. *Sesame Street revisited.* New York: Russell Sage.

COOK, T. D., and CAMPBELL, D. T. 1979. *Quasi-experimentation.* Chicago: Rand-McNally.

COOK, T. D.; COOK, F. L.; and MARK, M. M. 1977. Randomized and quasi-experimental designs in evaluation research: An introduction. In *Evaluation research: A basic guide.* ed. L. Rutman. Beverly Hills, Calif.: Sage.

COOK, T. D., and GRUDER, C. L. 1978. Metaevaluation. *Evaluation Quarterly* 2: 5–51.

COOK, T. D., and REICHARDT, C. S. eds. 1979. *Qualitative and quantitative methods in evaluation research.* Beverly Hills, Calif., Sage.

CRANO, W. D., and BREWER, M. B. 1973. *Principles of research in social psychology.* New York: McGraw-Hill.

CRONBACH, L. J. 1975. Beyond the two disciplines of scientific psychology. *American Psychologist* 30: 116–27.

CRONBACH, L. J. 1977. Remarks to a new society. *Evaluation Research Society Newsletter* 1: 1–3.

CRONBACH, L. J. 1980. *Toward reform of program evaluation: Aims, methods, and institutional arrangements.* San Francisco: Jossey-Bass.

CRONBACH, L. J. 1982. *Designing evaluations of educational and social programs.* San Francisco: Jossey-Bass.

CULLITON, B. J. 1978. Health care economics: The high cost of getting well. *Science* 200: 883–85.

DARLINGTON, R. B.; ROYCE, J. M.; SNIPPER, A. S.; MURRAY, H. W.; and LAZAR, I.1980. Preschool programs and later school competence of children from low-income families. *Science* 208: 202–4.

DATTA, L. 1976a. Does it work when it has been tried? And half full or half empty? *Journal of Career Education* 2: 38–55.

DATTA, L. 1976b. The impact of the Westinghouse/Ohio evaluation on the development of project Head Start. In *The evaluation of social programs*, ed. C. C. Abt. Beverly Hills, Calif.: Sage.

DAVID, E. E. 1975. One-armed scientists? *Science* 189: 679.

DAVIS, D. D. 1982. *Primary prevention through organizational change: Improving program evaluation practices.* Paper presented at the meeting of the American Psychological Association, August, Washington, D.C.

DAVIS, H. R., and SALASIN, S. E. 1975. The utilization of evaluation. In *Handbook of evaluation research*, vol. 2, ed. E. L. Struening and M. Guttentag. Beverly Hills, Calif.: Sage.

DAVIS, J. A. 1971. *Elementary survey analysis*. Englewood Cliffs, N.J.: Prentice-Hall.

DAWES, R. M., and CORRIGAN, B. 1974. Linear models in decision making. *Psychological Bulletin* 81: 95–106.

DAY, C. R., JR. 1981. Solving the mystery of productivity measurement. *Industry Week*, January 26, pp. 61–66.

DEMONE, H. W., JR., and HARSHBARGER, D. 1973. *The planning and administration of human services*. New York: Behavioral Publications.

DENISTON, O. L., and ROSENSTOCK, I. M. 1973. The validity of nonexperimental designs for evaluating health services. *Health Services Reports* 88: 153–64.

DICKEN, A. 1978. Why patients should plan their own recovery. *RN* 41: 52–55.

DIXON, M. G. 1977. Medical records guaranteed to ruin any malpractice defense. *Medical Economics* 54: 79–83.

DIXON, R. H., and LASZLO, J. 1974. Utilization of clinical chemistry services by medical house staff. *Archives of Internal Medicine* 134: 1064–67.

DRUCKER, P. F. 1954. *The practice of management*. New York: Harper.

DRUDE, K. P., and NELSON, R. A. 1982. Quality assurance: A challenge for community mental health centers. *Professional Psychology* 13: 85–90.

EDWARDS, W. 1977. Social utilities. *The Engineering Economist* (Summer Symposium Series) 6: 119–29.

EDWARDS, W.; GUTTENTAG, M.; and SNAPPER, K. 1975. A decision-theoretic approach to evaluation research. In *Handbook of evaluation research*, vol. 1, ed. E. L. Struening and M. Guttentag. Beverly Hills, Calif.: Sage.

EGAN, G., and COWAN, M. A. 1979. *People in systems: A model for development in the human-service professions and education*. Monterey, Calif.: Brooks/Cole.

EGDAHL, R. H., and GERTMAN, P. M. 1976. *Quality assurance in health care*. Germantown, Md.: Aspen Systems.

EGELHOF, J. 1975. Cop layoffs spur slayings. *Chicago Tribune*, July 10, sec. 1, p. 2.

EISENBERG, L. 1977. The social imperatives of medical research. *Science* 198: 1105–10.

ELLSWORTH, R. B. 1975. Consumer feedback in measuring the effectiveness of mental health programs. In *Handbook of evaluation research*, vol. 2, ed. M. Guttentag and E. L. Struening. Beverly Hills, Calif.: Sage.

ELLSWORTH, R. B. 1979. Evaluating treatment outcomes in mental health services. In *Impacts of program evaluation on mental health care*, ed. E. J. Posavac. Boulder, Colo.: Westview Press.

ENDICOTT, J., and SPITZER, R. L. 1975. Designing mental health studies: The case for experimental designs. *Hospital & Community Psychiatry* 26: 737–39.

ENDICOTT, J.; SPITZER, R. L.; FLEISS, J. L.; and COHEN, J. 1976. The Global Assessment Scale: A procedure for measuring overall severity of psychiatric disturbance. *Archives of General Psychiatry* 33: 766–71.

ERS STANDARDS COMMITTEE. 1982. In Standards for practice, ed. P. H. Rossi, pp. 7–20. No. 15 of *New Directions for Program Evaluation*. San Francisco: Jossey-Bass.

Ethical principles of psychologists. 1981. *American Psychologist* 36: 633–38.

EVANS, R. G., and ROBINSON, G. C. 1980. Surgical day care: Measurements of economic payoff. *CMA Journal* 123: 873–880.

EVANS, J. W., and SCHILLER, J. 1970. How preoccupation with possible regression artifacts can lead to a faulty strategy for the evaluation of social action programs: A reply to Campbell and Erlebacher. In *Compensatory education: A na-*

tional debate, ed. J. Hellmuth, pp. 216–20. Vol. 3 of *Disadvantaged child.* New York: Brunner-Mazel.

FIFER, W. R. 1979. Quality assurance: Debate persists on goals, impact, and methods of evaluating care. *Hospitals* 53 (April 1): 163–67.

FILSTEAD, W. J., ed. 1970. *Qualitative methodology: Firsthand involvement with the social world.* Chicago: Rand-McNally.

FITZGERALD, J. M. 1973. *Fundamentals of systems analysis.* New York: Wiley.

FLAY, B. R., and BEST, J. A. 1982. Overcoming design problems in evaluating health behavior programs. *Evaluation and the Health Professions* 5: 43–49.

FLEISS, J. L. 1973. *Statistical methods for rates and proportions.* New York: Wiley.

FOX, B. H. 1976. The psychosocial epidemiology of cancer. In *Cancer: The behavioral dimension,* ed. J. W. Cullen, B. H. Fox, and R. N. Isom. New York: Raven Press.

FOXX, R. M., and AZRIN, N. H. 1973. Dry pants: A rapid method of toilet training children. *Behavior Research and Therapy.* 11: 435–42.

FREEMAN, R., and HOLLOMON, J. H. 1975. The declining value of college going. *Change* 7(7): 24–31, 62.

FRIEDMAN, H. 1982. Simplified determinations of statistical power, magnitude of effect and research sample sizes. *Educational and Psychological Measurement* 42: 521–26.

GARWICK, G. 1973. *Commentaries on Goal Attainment Scaling.* Minneapolis: Program Evaluation Resource Center.

GERSTENFELD, A. 1977. MBO revisited: Focus on health systems. *Health Care Management Review* 4: 51–57.

GILBERT, J. P.; LIGHT, R. J.; and MOSTELLER, F. 1975. Assessing social innovations: An empirical base for policy. In *Evaluation and experiment,* ed. A. R. Lumsdaine and C. A. Bennett. New York: Academic Press.

GLASS, G. V. 1976. Introduction. In *Evaluation studies research annual,* vol. 1, ed. G. V Glass. Beverly Hills, Calif.: Sage.

GOLD, N. 1983. Stakeholders and program evaluation. *New Directions in Program Evaluation,* no. 17, pp. 63–72.

GOLDBERGER, A. S. 1981. Coleman goes private (in public). Cited in D. W. Breneman. 1981. Coleman II and the credibility of social science research. *Change* 13 (6): 13.

"Good news—crime is up!" 1983. *Chicago Tribune,* May 8, sec. 2, p. 2.

GOSFIELD, A. 1975. *PSRO: The law and the health consumer.* Cambridge, Mass.: Ballinger.

GOTTMAN, J. M., and GLASS, G. V. 1978. Analysis of interrupted time-series experiments. In *Single subject research: Strategies for evaluating change,* ed. T. R. Kratochwill. New York: Academic Press.

GRAY, B. H.; COOKE, R. A.; and TANNENBAUM, A. S. 1978. Research involving human subjects. *Science* 201: 1094–1101.

GREELEY, A. 1972. *American priests: A sociological analysis.* Washington, D.C.: National Conference of Catholic Bishops.

GUBA, E. G., and LINCOLN, Y. S. 1981. *Effective evaluation.* San Francisco: Jossey-Bass.

GUTTENTAG, M. 1973. Subjectivity and its uses in evaluation research. *Evaluation* 1 (2): 60–65.

GUTTENTAG, M. 1976. Future trends in evaluation. Paper presented at the Information and Feedback Conference, November 3–5, Toronto.

GUTTENTAG, M. 1977. Evaluation and society. *Personality and Social Psychology Bulletin* 3: 31–40.

GUTTENTAG, M., and SNAPPER, K. 1974. Plans, evaluations and decisions. *Evaluation* 1(1): 58–64, 73, 74.

HAGEDORN, H. J.; BECK, K. J.; NEUBERT, S. F.; and WERLIN, S. H. 1976. *A working manual of simple evaluation techniques for community mental health centers.* Rockville, Md.: U.S. Department of Health, Education, and Welfare.

HAKEL, M. D.; SORCHER, M.; BEER, M.; and MOSES, J. L. 1980. *Making it happen: Designing research with implementation in mind.* Beverly Hills, Calif.: Sage.

HANKE, S. H., and WALKER, R. A. 1974. Benefit-cost analysis reconsidered: An evaluation of the Mid-State project. *Water Resources Research* 10: 898–908.

HANSEN, J. B. 1978. The formative-summative dichotomy and the role of description in program evaluation. *Evaluation News,* no. 6 (August): 14–16.

HARGREAVES, W. A.; ATTKISSON, C. C.; and SORENSON, J. E., eds. 1977. *Resource materials for community mental health program evaluation.* Rockville, Md.: U.S. Department of Health, Education, and Welfare.

HARRIS, M. B., and BRUNER, C. G. 1971. A comparison of a self-control and a contract procedure for weight control. *Behavior Research and Therapy* 9: 347–54.

HASTORF, A. H., and CANTRIL, H. 1954. They saw a game. *Journal of Abnormal and Social Psychology* 49: 129–34.

HAVEMAN, R. H., and WATTS, H. W. 1976. Social experimentation as policy research: A review of negative income tax experiments. In *Evaluation Studies Research Annual,* vol. 1, ed. G. V Glass. Beverly Hills, Calif.: Sage.

HAWKINS, J. D.; ROFFMAN, R. A.; and OSBORNE, P. 1978. Decision makers' judgments: The influence of role, evaluation criteria, and information access. *Evaluation Quarterly* 2: 435–54.

HAYS, W. L. 1963. *Statistics for psychologists.* New York: Holt, Rinehart and Winston.

HELMICK, E.; MILLER, S. I.; NUTTING, P.; SHORR, G.; and BERG, L. 1975. A monitoring and evaluation plan for alcoholism programs. *British Journal of Addiction* 70: 369–73.

HENDRICKS, M. 1981. Service delivery assessment: Qualitative evaluations at the cabinet level. In *New Directions for Program Evalation,* no. 12, ed. N. Smith. San Francisco: Jossey-Bass.

HORST, P., et al. 1974. Program management and the federal evaluator. *Public Administration Review* 34: 300–308.

HOUSE, E. R. 1976. Justice in evaluation. In *Evaluation Studies Review Annual,* vol. 1, ed. G. V Glass. Beverly Hills, Calif.: Sage.

HOUSE, E. R.; GLASS, G. V; McLEAN, L. D.; and WALKER, D. F. 1978. No simple answer: Critique of the follow through evaluation. *Harvard Education Review* 42: 128–60.

INSURANCE INSTITUTE FOR HIGHWAY SAFETY. 1975. Helmet laws reduce fatalities. *Status Report* 10: 1–3.

ISAACSON, W. 1982. A budget that will barely budge. *Time,* March 1, p. 15.

ISAACSON, W. 1983. The winds of reform. *Time,* March 7, pp. 12–16, 23, 26–30.

ISR Newsletter. 1978. Telephone helps solve survey problems. 6: 3.

JACOBS, C. M.; CHRISTOFFEL, T. H.; and DIXON, N. 1976. *Measuring the quality of patient care.* Cambridge, Mass.: Ballinger.

JASON, L. A., and LIOTTA, R. F. 1982. Assessing community responsiveness in a metropolitan area. *Evaluation Review* 6: 703–12.

JOHNSON, R. A. 1967. *The theory and management of systems.* New York: McGraw-Hill.

JOHNSTON, J. 1983. The status of evaluation as an enterprise. *ERS Newsletter* 7 (2): 1, 7.

JUDD, C. M., and KENNY, D. A. 1981. *Estimating the effects of social interventions.* New York: Cambridge University Press.

JOINT COMMITTEE ON STANDARDS FOR EDUCATIONAL EVALUATION. 1981. *Standards for evaluations of educational programs, projects, and materials.* New York: McGraw-Hill.

KAHNEMAN, D., and TVERSKY, A. 1974. Judgment under uncertainty: Heuristics and biases. *Science* 185: 1124–31.

KANE, R. L., and KANE, R. A. 1978. Care of the aged: Old problems in need of new solutions. *Science* 200: 913–19.

KELLING, G. L.; PATE, T.; DIECKMAN, D.; and BROWN, C. E. 1976. The Kansas City preventive patrol experiment: A summary report. In *Evaluative studies review annual,* vol. 1, ed. G. V Glass. Beverly Hills, Calif.: Sage.

KERSHAW, D. N. 1972. A negative income tax experiment. *Scientific American* 227: 19–25.

KIRESUK, T. J. 1973. Goal attainment scaling at a county mental health service. *Evaluation,* Monograph no. 1, p. 15.

KIRESUK, T. J., and SHERMAN, R. E. 1968. Goal Attainment Scaling: A general method for evaluating comprehensive community mental health programs. *Community Mental Health Journal* 4: 443–53.

KIRK, R. E. 1968. *Experimental design: Procedures for the behavioral sciences.* Belmont, Calif.: Brooks/Cole.

KIRSCHT, J. P.; HAEFNER, D. P.; and EVELAND, J. D. 1975. Public response to various written appeals to participate in health screening. *Public Health Reports* 90: 539–43.

KIVENS, L., and BOLIN, D. C. 1977. Profile of a change(d) agent. *Evaluation* 4: 115–19.

KNAPP, M. 1977. Applying time-series research strategies to program evaluation problems. Paper presented at a meeting of the Evaluation Research Society, October, Washington, D.C.

KNAPP, M. S. 1983. To evaluate a block grant: A review of current approaches to studying the new federalism in education. Paper presented at the meeting of the Evaluation Research Society, October, Chicago.

KRAUSE, M. S., and JACKSON, J. C. 1983. The validity of some routine evaluative data: A study. *Evaluation Review* 7: 271–76.

KREITNER, R. 1977. People are systems, too: Filling the feedback vacuum. *Business Horizons* 20 (November): 54–58.

LANDES, H. R. 1973. Treatment of anxiety in the families of children undergoing tonsillectomy. Doctoral dissertation, Northwestern University. In *Dissertation Abstracts International* 34: 2939B. University Microfilms No. 37–30, 640.

LAWLER, E. E., III, and HACKMAN, J. R. 1969. Impact of employee participation in the development of pay incentive plans: A field experiment. *Journal of Applied Psychology* 53: 467–71.

LAZAR, I. 1981. Early intervention is effective. *Educational Leadership,* January, pp. 303–5.

LENIHAN, K. J. 1977. Telephones and raising bail. *Evaluation Quarterly* 1: 569–86.

LEVIN, H. M. 1975. Cost-effectiveness analysis in evaluation research. In *Handbook of evaluation research,* vol. 2, ed. M. Guttentag and E. L. Struening. Beverly Hills, Calif.: Sage.

LEVIN, H. M. 1982. A world without evaluation. Paper given at the meeting of the Evaluation Research Society, October, Baltimore.

LEVINE, M.; BROWN, E.; FITZGERALD, C.; GOPLERUD, E.; GORDON, M. E.; JAYNE-LAZARUS, C.; ROSENBERG, N.; and SLATER, J. 1978. Adapting the jury trial for program evaluation: A report of an experience. *Evaluation and Program Planning* 1: 177–86.

LEVITON, L. C. and BORUCH, R. F. 1983. Contributions of evaluation in education programs and policy. *Evaluation Review* 7: 563–598.

LIGHT, R. J. 1983. Introduction. In *Evaluation studies review annual,* vol. 8, ed. R. J. Light. Beverly Hills, Calif.: Sage.

LIGHT, R. J., and Smith, P. V. 1971. Accumulating evidence: Procedures for resolving contradictions among different research studies. *Harvard Educational Review* 41: 429–71.

LOCKE, E. A. 1968. Toward a theory of task motivations and incentives. *Organizational Behavior and Human Performance* 3: 157–89.

LOHR, K. N.; BROOK, R. H.; and KAUFMAN, M. A. 1980. Quality of care in the New Mexico Medicaid program. *Medical Care Supplement* 18: 1–129.

LUBIN, B. 1967. *Manual for the Depression Adjective Check Lists.* San Diego: Educational and Industrial Testing Service.

LUCAS, H. C., JR. 1975. *Why information systems fail.* New York: Columbia University Press.

LUFT, L. L. 1979. The effects of peer review in a community mental health center. In *Impacts of program evaluation on mental health care,* ed. E. J. Posavac. Boulder, Colo.: Westview Press.

LUND, S., and KIRESUK, T. J. 1979. Individualized Goal Attainment as a method of program evaluation in mental health. In *Impacts of program evaluation on mental health care,* ed. E. J. Posavac. Boulder, Colo.: Westview Press.

MAGER, R. F. 1972. *Goal analysis.* Belmont, Calif.: Fearon Publishers.

MARKSON, E. W., and ALLEN, D. F. 1976. *Trends in mental health evaluation.* Lexington, Mass.: Lexington Books.

MARSHALL, T. O. 1979. Levels of results. *Journal of Constructive Change* 1 (1): 5.

MAZUR-HART, S. F., and BERMAN, J. J. 1977. Changing from fault to no-fault divorce. *Journal of Applied Social Psychology* 7: 300–12.

MCCALL, R. B. 1975. *Fundamental statistics for psychology.* 2nd ed. New York: Harcourt Brace Jovanovich.

MCCAMY, J., and PRESLEY, J. 1975. *Human life styling: Keeping whole in the 20th century.* New York: Harper and Row.

MCCARTHY, M. 1978. Decreasing the incidence of "high bobbins" in a textile spinning department through a group feedback procedure. *Journal of Organizational Behavioral Management* 1: 150–54.

MCCLEARY, R., and HAY, R. A., JR. 1980. *Applied time series analysis for the social sciences.* Beverly Hills, Calif.: Sage.

MCCLINTOCK, C. C. 1983. Internal evaluation: The new challenge. *Evaluation News* 4 (1): 61–62.

MCCONKEY, D. D. 1975. *MBO for nonprofit organizations.* New York: AMACON.

MCGREGOR, D. 1960. *The human side of enterprise.* New York: McGraw-Hill.

MCKAY, H.; SINISTERNIA, L.; MCKAY, A.; GOMEZ, H.; and LLOREDA, P. 1978. Improving cognitive ability in chronically deprived children. *Science* 200: 270–78.

MCKILLIP, J., and KAMENS, L. 1977. Evaluation of a positive health care program. In *Health care research in Illinois,* vol. 2, ed. R. V. Robertson, Southern Illinois School of Medicine.

MCLAUGHLIN, M. W. 1974. *Evaluation and reform: The Elementary and Secondary Education Act of 1965. Title I.* Santa Monica, Calif.: The Rand Corporation.

MEADOWS, D. L., and PERELMAN, L. 1973. Limits to growth. In *The future in the making: Current issues in higher education,* ed. D. W. Vermilye. San Francisco: Jossey-Bass.

MECHANIC, D. 1975. Evaluation in alcohol, drug abuse, and mental health programs: Problems and prospects. In *Program evaluation: Alcohol, drug abuse, and mental health services,* ed. J. Zusman and C. Wurster. Lexington, Mass.: Lexington Books.

Medical World News. May 30, 1977. Hypertension compliance. 18: 20–22; 24–25; 28–29.

MILLENSON, M. L. 1983. New Medicare rules. *Chicago Tribune,* April 7, sec. 4, p. 16.

MILLER, S. I.; HELMICK, E.; BERG, L.; NUTTING, P.; and SCHORR, G. 1975. An evaluation of alcoholism treatment services for Alaskan natives. *Hospital and Community Psychiatry* 23: 829–31.

MIRVIS, P. H., and BERG, D. N., eds. 1977. *Failure in organizational development and change: Cases and essays for learning.* New York: Wiley-Interscience.

MITLYING, J. 1975/76. Managing the use of staff time: A key to cost control. *Alcohol Health and Research World,* Winter, pp. 7–10.

MOELLER, A. D. 1982. Quality assurance—A view from the forest. *Forum,* May/June, pp. 43–45.

MOORE, P. D., and STATON, T. 1981. Management by objectives in American cities. *Public Personnel Management Journal* 10: 223–32.

MORRISSEY, G. L. 1970. *Management by objectives and results.* Reading, Mass.: Addison-Wesley.

MOSTELLER, F., and MOYNIHAN, D. P., eds. 1972. *On equality of educational opportunity.* New York: Vintage.

MUELLER, J. H.; SCHUESSLER, K.; and COSTNER, H. 1970. *Statistical reasoning in sociology.* Boston: Houghton Mifflin.

NAGEL, S. S. 1983a. Nonmonetary variables in benefit-cost evaluation. *Evaluation Review* 7: 37–64.

NAGEL, S. S. 1983b. Factors facilitating the utilization of policy evaluation research. Paper presented at the meeting of the Evaluation Research Society, October, Chicago.

NATIONAL INSTITUTE OF MENTAL HEALTH. 1971. *Planning for creative change in mental health services: A distillation of principles on research utilization.* Washington, D.C.: Department of Health, Education, and Welfare. Publication No. (HSM) 73-9148.

National Standards for Community Mental Health Centers. 1977. Rockville, Md.: Department of Health, Education, and Welfare.

The nation's toughest drug law: Evaluating the New York experience. 1978. Washington, D.C.: U.S. Department of Justice, Law Enforcement Assistance Administration.

NEIGHER, W., et al. 1982. Evaluation in the community mental health centers program: A bold new reproach? *Evaluation and Program Planning* 5: 283–311.

NEWMAN, D. E., and LUFT, L. L. 1974. The peer review process: Education versus control. *American Journal of Psychiatry* 131: 1363–66.

Newsweek. May 9, 1977. Health-cost crisis. 89: 84, 89, 90.

NUNNALLY, J. C. 1975. The study of change in evaluation research: Principles concerning measurement, experimental design, and analysis. In *Handbook of Evaluation, Research,* vol. 1, ed. E. L. Struening and M. Guttentag. Beverly Hills, Calif.: Sage.

OKRENT, D. 1980. Comment on societal risk. *Science* 208: 372–75.

PATTEN, T. H. 1981. *Organizational development through teambuilding.* New York: Wiley.

PATTON, M. Q. 1978. *Utilization-focused evaluation.* Beverly Hills, Calif.: Sage.

PATTON, M. Q. 1980. *Qualitative evaluation methods.* Beverly Hills, Calif.: Sage.

PENDERY, M. L.; MALTZMAN, I. M.; and WEST, L. J. 1982. Controlled drinking by alcoholics? New findings and a reevaluation of a major affirmative study. *Science* 217: 169–75.

PERLOFF, R. 1983. The uses of roles for evaluation research in the private sector. Paper presented at the Eastern Evaluation Research Society Conference, June, New York.

PERLOFF, R., and PERLOFF, E., eds. 1980. *Values, ethics, and standards in evaluation.* San Francisco: Jossey-Bass.

PETTIGREW, T. F.; USEEM, E. L.; NORMAND, C.; and SMITH, M. S. 1973. Busing: A review of the evidence. *The Public Interest* 30: 88–118.

PETTIGREW, T. F., and GREEN, R. L. 1977. The white flight debate. In *Evaluation studies review annual,* vol. 2, ed. M. Guttentag, Beverly Hills, Calif.: Sage.

POISTER, T. H. 1982. Performance monitoring in the evaluation process. *Evaluation Review* 6: 601–23.

POPHAM, W. J. 1975. *Educational evaluation.* Englewood Cliffs, N.J.: Prentice-Hall.

POSAVAC, E. J. 1974. *A study of the coronary classes.* Park Ridge, Ill.: Lutheran General Hospital.

POSAVAC, E. J. 1975. *Survey of past residents in the Clinical Pastoral Education Program.* Park Ridge, Ill.: Lutheran General Hospital.

POSAVAC, E. J., ed. 1979. *Impacts of program evaluation in mental health care.* Boulder, Colo.: Westview Press.

POSAVAC, E. J., and CAREY, R. G. 1978. Trading evaluative specificity for statistical power. *Evaluation and the Health Professions* 1: 89–95.

POSAVAC, E. J.; CAREY, R. G.; and MARIN, B. V. 1980. Use of resident physicians: An evaluation of the effects of a significant increase. *Evaluation and the Health Professions,* 4: 433–52.

POSAVAC, E. J., and HARTUNG, B. M. 1977. An exploration into the reasons people choose a pastoral counselor instead of another type of psychotherapist. *The Journal of Pastoral Care* 31: 23–31.

PRUE, D. M.; KRAPFL, J. E.; NOAH, J. C.; CANNON, S.; and MALEY, R. F. 1980. Managing the treatment activities of state hospital staff. *Journal of Organizational Behavior Management* 2: 165–181.

QUAY, H. C. 1979. The three faces of evaluation: What can be expected to work. *Criminal Justice and Behavior* 4: 341–54.

RAHE, R. H. 1978. Life stress and illness. Presented at the Stress and Behavioral Medicine Symposium, May 20, Chicago, Ill.

RAIFFA, H. 1968. *Decision analysis: Introductory lectures on choices under uncertainty.* Reading, Mass.: Addison-Wesley.

REICHARDT, C. S., and COOK, T. D. 1980. "Paradigms lost": Some thoughts on choosing methods in evaluation research. *Evaluation and Program Planning* 3: 229–36.

REZMOVIC, E. L.; COOK, T. J.; and DOBSON, L. D. 1981. Beyond random assignment: Factors affecting evaluation integrity. *Evaluation Review* 5: 51–67.

RHEINSTEIN, M. 1959. Divorce and the law in Germany: A review. *American Journal of Sociology* 65: 489–98.

RIECKEN, H. W., and BORUCH, R. F., eds. 1974. *Social experimentation: A method for planning and evaluating social intervention.* New York: Academic Press.

RICE, S. A. 1929. Contagious bias in the interview. *American Journal of Sociology* 35: 420–23.

ROBERTSON, L. S.; KELLEY, A. B.; O'NEILL, B.; WIXOM, C. W.; EISWORTH, R. S.; and HADDON, W., JR. 1974. A controlled study of the effect of television messages on safety belt use. *American Journal of Public Health* 64: 1071–80.

ROBINSON, J. P.; ATHANASIOU, R.; and HEAD, K. B. 1969. *Measures of occupational attitudes and occupational characteristics.* Ann Arbor, Mich.: Institute for Social Research.

ROBINSON, J. P.; RUSK, J. G.; and HEAD, K. B. 1968. *Measures of political attitudes.* Ann Arbor, Mich.: Institute for Social Research.

ROBINSON, J. P., and SHAVER, P. R. 1973. *Measures of social psychological attitudes.* Ann Arbor, Mich.: Institute for Social Research.

ROSS, H. L. 1973. Law, science, and accidents: The British Road Safety Act of 1967. *Journal of Legal Studies* 2: 1–78.

ROSS, H. L. 1975. The Scandinavian myth: The effectiveness of drinking-and-driving legislation in Sweden and Norway. *Journal of Legal Studies* 4: 285–310.

ROSSI, P. H. 1972. Testing for success and failure in social action. In *Evaluating social programs: Theory, practice and politics,* ed. P. H. Rossi and W. Williams. New York: Seminar Press.

ROSSI, P. H., and WILLIAMS, W., eds. 1972. *Evaluating social programs.* New York: Seminar Press.

ROSSI, P. H., ed. 1982. *Standards for evaluation practice.* San Francisco: Jossey-Bass.

ROSSI, P. H. 1983. Pussycats, weasels or percherons? Current prospects for social science under the Reagan regime. *Evaluation News* 4 (1): 12–27.

ROTHENBERG, J. 1975. Cost-benefit analysis: A methodological exposition. In *Handbook of evaluation research,* vol. 2, ed. M. Guttentag and E. L. Struening. Beverly Hills, Calif.: Sage.

SALASIN, S. E., and DAVIS, H. R. 1979. Achieving desired policy or practice changes: Findings alone won't do it. In *Impacts of program evaluation on mental health care,* ed. E. J. Posavac. Boulder, Colo.: Westview Press.

SCHMIDT, R. E.; SCANLON, J. W.; and BELL, J. B. 1979. Evaluability assessment: Making public programs work better. *Human Services Monograph Series,* no. 14, November.

SCHNELLE, J. F.; KIRCHNER, R. E., JR.; CASEY, J. E.; USELTON, P. H., JR.; and McNEES, M. P. 1977. Patrol evaluation research: A multiple-baseline analysis of saturation police patrolling during day and night. *Journal of Applied Behavior Analysis* 10: 33–40.

SCHNELLE, J. F.; KIRCHNER, R. E., JR.; MACRAE, J. W.; McNEES, M. P.; ECK, R. H.; SNODGRASS, S.; CASEY, J. D.; and USELTON, P. H., JR. 1978. Police evaluation research: An experimental and cost-benefit analysis of a helicopter patrol in a high crime area. *Journal of Applied Behavior Analysis* 11: 11–21.

SCRIVEN, M. 1967. The methodology of evaluation. In *Perspectives of curriculum evaluation,* ed. R. W. Tyler, R. M. Gagne, and M. Scriven. Chicago: Rand-McNally.

SCRIVEN, M. 1981. *Evaluation thesaurus.* 3rd ed. Inverness, Calif.: Edgepress.

SECHREST, L.; WEST, S. G.; PHILLIPS, M. A.; REDNER, R.; and YEATON, W. 1979. Introduction. In *Evaluation Studies Review Annual,* vol. 4, ed. L. Sechrest et al. Beverly Hills, Calif.: Sage.

SELIGMAN, C., and DARLEY, J. M. 1977. Feedback as a means of decreasing residential energy consumption. *Journal of Applied Psychology* 62: 363–68.

SELIGMAN, C., and HUTTON, R. B. 1981. Evaluating energy conservation programs. *Journal of Social Issues* 37: 51–72.

SELLS, S. B. 1975. Techniques of outcome evaluation in alcohol, drug abuse, and mental health programs. In *Program evaluation: Alcohol, drug abuse, and mental health services,* ed. J. Zusman and C. R. Wurster. Lexington, Mass.: Lexington Books.

SHIPLEY, R. H. 1976. Effects of companion program on college student volunteers and mental patients. *Journal of Consulting and Clinical Psychology* 4: 688–89.

SHRAUGER, J. S., and OSBERG, T. M. 1981. The relative accuracy of self-predictions and judgments by others in psychological assessment. *Psychological Bulletin* 90: 322–51.

SIEGEL, S. 1956. *Nonparametric methods for the behavioral sciences.* New York: McGraw-Hill.

SINGH, B.; GREER, P. R.; and HAMMOND, R. 1977. An evaluation of the use of the Law in a Free Society materials on "responsibility." *Evaluation Quarterly* 1: 621–28.

SJOBERG, G. 1975. Politics, ethics, and evaluation research. In *Handbook of evaluation research,* vol. 2, ed. M. Guttentag and E. L. Struening. Beverly Hills, Calif.: Sage.

SLOAN, S., and SCHRIEBER, D. E. 1971. *Hospital management—An evaluation.* Monograph No. 4. Bureau of Business Research and Service, Graduate School of Business. Madison, Wisc.: The University of Wisconsin Press.

SLOANE, R. B.; STAPLES, F. R.; CRISTOL, A. H.; YORKSTON, N. J.; and WHIPPLE, K.1975. Short-term analytically oriented psychotherapy versus behavior therapy. *American Journal of Psychiatry* 132: 373–77.

SMITH, M. L.; GABRIEL R.; SCHOTT, J.; and PADIA, W. L. 1976. Evaluation of the effects of Outward Bound. In *Evaluation research studies annual,* vol. 1, ed. G. V Glass. Beverly Hills, Calif.: Sage.

SMITH, M. L., and GLASS, G. V. 1977. Meta-analysis of psychotherapy outcome studies. *American Psychologist* 32: 752–60.

SMITH, N. L. 1981. The certainty of judgments in health evaluations. *Evaluation and Program Planning* 4: 273–78.

SMITH, N. L., ed. 1982. *Communication strategies in evaluation.* Beverly Hills, Calif.: Sage.

SMITH, W. G. 1975. Evaluation of the clinical services of a regional mental health center. *Community Mental Health Journal* 11: 47–57.

SOBEL, M. B., and SOBELL, L. C. 1978. *Behavioral treatment of alcohol problems.* New York: Plenum.

SOLOMON, A. 1975. Charges of resigned aide on prisons will be probed. *Madison Capitol Times,* September 12.

SOLOMON, M. A., and SHORTELL, S. M. 1981. Designing health policy research for utilization. *Health Policy Quarterly* 1: 216–37.

SPEER, D. C., and TRAPP, J. C. 1976. Evaluation of mental health service effectiveness. *American Journal of Orthopsychiatry* 46: 217–28.

SPIELBERGER, C. D., ed. 1972. *Anxiety: Current trends in theory and research,* vol. 1 New York: Academic Press.

"Spotlight: Program evaluation and accountability in Minnesota." 1982. *State Evaluation Network,* 2(5), 2.

Staff working papers of the Drug Law Evaluation Project. 1978. Washington, D.C.: U.S. Department of Justice, Law Enforcement Assistance Administration.

STANLEY, J. C. 1982. Education in the fast lane: Methodological problems of evaluating its effects. *Evaluation News* 4 (1): 28–46.

STOKES, T. F., and FAWCETT, S. B. 1977. Evaluating municipal policy: An analysis of a refuse-packing program. *Journal of Applied Behavioral Analysis* 10: 391–98.

STRAW, M. 1978. Informal presentation delivered at Loyola University, May 22, Chicago, Ill.

STRUPP, H. H., and HANDLEY, S. W. 1977. A tripartite model of mental health and therapeutic outcomes: With special reference to negative effects in psychotherapy. *American Psychologist* 32: 187–96.

STUFFLEBEAM, D. 1978. Meta evaluation: An overview. *Evaluation and the Health Professions* 1: 17–43.

STULL, R. J. 1977. Many concepts mold multiinstitutional systems. *Hospitals* 51: 43–45.

SUCHMAN, E. A. 1967. *Evaluative research.* Englewood Cliffs, N.J.: Prentice-Hall.

SUDMAN, S., and BRADBURN, N. M. 1982. *Asking questions.* San Francisco: Jossey-Bass.

SULLIVAN, J. M., and SNOWDEN, L. R. 1981. Monitoring frequency of client problems. *Evaluation Review* 5: 822–33.

SUSSNA, E., and HEINEMANN, H. N. 1972. The education of health manpower in a two-year college: An evaluation model. *Socio-Economic Planning Science* 6: 21–30.

The Potemkin Factory. 1980. *Time,* February 25, p. 36.

THOMPSON, M. S. 1982. *Decision analysis for program evaluation.* Cambridge, Mass.: Ballinger.

THOMPSON, M. S.; COHEN, A. B.; and FORTESS, E. E. 1981. Evaluation of diagnostic procedures: A review of the issues. *Evaluation and Program Planning* 4: 385–96.

Time. August 4, 1975. More guinea pigs, experiments with LSD. 108: 66.

Time. July 18, 1977. Striking back at super snoops. 110: 16–21.

Time. July 24, 1978. Psst! Wanna good job? 112: 18, 19.

TOONG, H. D., and GUPTA, A. 1982. Personal computers. *Scientific American* 247 (6): 86–107.

TRIANDIS, H. C. 1978. Basic research in the context of applied research in personality and social psychology. *Personality and Social Psychology Bulletin* 4: 383–87.

TUKEY, J. W. 1977. *Exploratory data analysis.* Reading, Mass.: Addison-Wesley.

TURNER, A. J. 1977. Program goal setting in an evaluation system. Paper presented at the Conference on the Impact of Program Evaluation in Mental Health Care, January, Loyola University of Chicago.

U.S. News & World Report. April 21, 1975. $301 million a day for HEW—and no end in sight. 79: 45–47.

WALDO, G. P., and CHIRICOS, T. G. 1977. Work release and recidivism: An empirical evaluation of a social policy. *Evaluation Quarterly* 1: 87–108.

WALLIS, C. 1983. Death of a gallant pioneer. *Time,* April 4, pp. 62, 63.

WALSH, J. 1983. Congress questions NBS [National Bureau of Standards] budget cuts. *Science* 220: 176, 177.

WARHEIT, G. J.; BELL, R. A.; and SCHWAB, J. J. 1974. *Planning for change: Needs assessment approaches.* Gainesville, Fla.: University of Florida.

WASKOW, I. E., and PERLOFF, M. B., eds. 1975. *Psychotherapy change measures.* Rockville, Md.: National Institute of Mental Health.

WEBB, E. J.; CAMPBELL, D. T.; SCHWARTZ, R. D.; SECHREST, L.; and GROVE, J. B. 1981. *Nonreactive measures in the social sciences.* 2nd ed. Boston: Houghton-Mifflin.

WEISS, C. H. 1972a. *Evaluation research.* Englewood Cliffs, N. J.: Prentice-Hall.

WEISS, C. H. 1972b. Utilization of evaluation: Toward comparative study. In *Evaluating action programs,* ed. C. H. Weiss. Boston: Allyn & Bacon.

WEISS, C. H. 1973. Between the cup and the lip. . . . *Evaluation* 1: 49–55.

WEISS, R. S., and REIN, M. 1970. The evaluation of broad-aim programs: Experimental design, its difficulties, and an alternative. *Administrative Science Quarterly* 15: 97–113.

WERTHEIMER, M. 1978. Psychology and the future. *American Psychologist* 33: 631–47.

WINCH, R. F., and CAMPBELL, D. T. 1969. Proof? No. Evidence? Yes. The significance of tests of significance. *The American Sociologist* 3: 140–53.

WHOLEY, J. S. 1979. *Evaluation: Promise and performance.* Washington, D.C.: Urban Institute.

WHOLEY, J. S. 1981. Using evaluation to improve program performance. *Evaluation Studies Review Annual,* vol. 6, ed. H. E. Freeman and M. A. Solomon. Beverly Hills, Calif.: Sage.

WORTMAN, P. M. 1983. Evaluation research: A methodological perspective. *Annual Review of Psychology* 34: 223–60.

YUKL, G. A., and LATHAM, G. P. 1978. Interrelationships among employee participation, individual differences, goal difficulty, goal acceptance, goal instrumentality, and performance. *Personnel Psychology* 31: 305–23.

ZALKIND, D.; ZELON, H.; MOORE, M.; and KALUZNY, A. 1977. A practical reporting and evaluation system for intervention programs: Guiding principles and potential uses. *American Journal of Public Health* 67: 370–73.

ZALTMAN, G., and DUNCAN, R. 1977. *Strategies for planned change.* New York: Wiley-Interscience.

ZAMMUTO, R. F. 1982. *Assessing organizational effectiveness.* Albany, N. Y.: SUNY Press.

ZIGLER, E., and TRICKETT, P. K. 1978. IQ, social competence, and evaluation of early childhood intervention programs. *American Psychologist* 33: 789–98.

ZIMRING, F. E. 1975. Firearms and federal law: The Gun Control Act of 1968. *Journal of Legal Studies* 4: 133–98.

ZINOBER, J. W., and DINKEL, N. R., eds. 1981. *A trust of evaluation: A guide for involving citizens in community mental health program evaluation.* Tampa, Fla.: The Florida Consortium for Research and Evaluation.

Name Index

A

Abelson, P. H., 262
Abt, C. C., 243, 272
Adler, N. E., 106
Albright, J., 88
Allen, D. F., 168
Allport, G. W., 237
Anastasi, A., 66, 188
Anderson, J. F., 64
Armor, D. J., 319
Athanasiou, R., 76
Attkisson, C. C., 76, 119, 124, 145
Azrin, N. H., 158, 200, 203

B

Ball, R. M., 21
Ball, S., 92
Barbour, G. P., 57
Beck, K. J., 76, 145, 274
Becker, H., 258
Beer, M., 322
Bell, J. B., 36
Bell, R. A., 119, 120

Benjamin Franklin, 111
Berdie, D. R., 64
Berg, D. N., 303
Berg, L., 145
Berk, R. A., 48, 56
Berman, J. J., 126, 206
Best, J. A., 235
Bigelow, D. A., 315
Binner, P. R., 266, 267
Bogartz, G. A., 92
Bok, S., 81
Bolin, D. C., 142
Boruch, R. F., 6, 49, 51, 217, 233, 242, 245, 251, 285, 312
Bradburn, N. M., 75
Braithwaite, R. L., 311
Brewer, M. B., 242
Brook, R. H., 159
Brotman, B., 89
Brown, F. G., 61
Bruner, C. G., 244
Bryk, A. S., 31
Buhl, J. M., 119
Bunda, M. A., 92
Burns, M. L., 159
Buros, O. K., 75
Burtle, V., 80

Subject Index